ENLARGING THE EUROPEAN UNION

RELATIONS BETWEEN THE EU
AND CENTRAL AND EASTERN EUROPE

ENLARGING THE EUROPEAN UNION

RELATIONS BETWEEN THE EU AND CENTRAL AND EASTERN EUROPE

Edited by

Marc Maresceau
European Institute, University of Ghent

LONGMAN
LONDON AND NEW YORK

Addison Wesley Longman
Edinburgh Gate
Harlow
Essex CM20 2JE
England
and associated Companies throughout the world.

*Published in the United States of America
by Addison Wesley Longman Inc., New York.*

First published 1997

ISBN 0 582 31848.3 CSD

British Library Cataloguing-in-Publication Data

A catalogue record of this book is available
from the British Library

Library of Congress Cataloging-in-Publication Data

A catalog entry for this title is available
from the Library of Congress

Set by 35 in 10/12 pt Plantin

Printed and bound by Bookcraft (Bath) Ltd

CONTENTS

CONTENTS

CONTRIBUTORS

Péter Balázs is currently Ambassador of Hungary in Germany. He is a Professor of the Budapest School of Economics, lecturing on the theories and praxis of European integration. He graduated at the Budapest School of Economics and joined the Hungarian Ministry of Foreign Trade. He was the Representative of Hungary at the EC in Brussels (1982–87) and afterwards he led negotiations with the OECD, EFTA and other international economic organizations. He was a State Secretary at the Hungarian Ministry of Trade and Industry (1992–93) and Ambassador of Hungary to Denmark (1994–96).

Youri Borko is Deputy Director and Professor at the Institute of Europe, Moscow (Russian Academy of Sciences). He is President of the Association of European Studies and the author of many publications on European integration, in particular EU–Russian relations, including *What is the European Union?* (Moscow, 1995) and *Russland und die Europaische Union: Perspektiven der Partnerschaft* (Köln, 1996).

Günter Burghardt is the Director-General of the Directorate-General IA of the European Commission in charge of External Relations with Europe and the Newly Independent States, the Common Foreign and Security Policy and the Commission's External Service. He joined the Commission in 1970, where he started his career in the Legal Service before joining the Commission's External Relations department. After serving as Deputy Head of Cabinet for Commissioner Narjes (1981–84) and Commission President Delors (1985–88), he became the Commission's Political Director in 1988 and was nominated Director-General in 1993. He holds a PhD degree in law from the University of Hamburg and has published extensively in the field of the European Union's External Relations.

Fraser Cameron is a Foreign Policy Adviser in the Directorate-General IA of the European Commission. Since joining the Commission in 1990, he has specialized in the EU's relations with the countries of Central and Eastern Europe. He has also been Visiting Professor at the College of Europe, Bruges, and at the University of Edinburgh. From 1975 to 1990, he was a British diplomat serving *inter alia* in Bonn and East Berlin.

Marise Cremona is a Senior Fellow in the European Commercial Law Unit, the Centre for Commercial Law Studies, Queen Mary and Westfield College, University of London. She is a specialist in European Community law, and in particular the External Relations of the European Union. She has a particular interest in the relationship between the European Union and the countries of Central and Eastern Europe, and has been involved in a number of training schemes for lawyers from this region.

Willy De Clercq studied law at the University of Ghent and social sciences at Syracuse University, USA. He has been a Vice-Prime Minister, Minister of Finance and Minister of Foreign Trade in the Belgian Government. He was a member of the Commission of the European Communities (Delors I) from 1985 until 1989, responsible for Economic External Relations and Foreign Trade. He is currently a member of the European Parliament and the Chairman of the Committee on Legal Affairs and Citizens' Rights of the European Parliament. He was a member of the Belgian Chamber of Representatives for 26 years and Minister of State since 1985.

Françoise de La Serre is Senior Research Fellow at the Fondation Nationale des Sciences Politiques and Professor at the Institut d'Etudes Politiques, Paris. She is a specialist in European Integration. Her research and teaching focus on the European policy of the United Kingdom, the eastward enlargement of the European Union, and the common foreign and security policy. Recent publications include, among others: *L'Union européenne: ouverture à l'Est?* (PUF, Paris, 1994, with C. Lequesne and J. Rupnik) and *Les relations franco-britanniques dans l'Europe de l'après-guerre froide* (CERI studies No. 1, 1995, with H. Wallace).

Erik Derycke studied law at the University of Ghent. He was for many years a member of the Belgian Chamber of Representatives and Flemish Parliament. Currently he is Minister of Foreign Affairs in the Belgian Government.

Pál Dunay was an Associate Professor in the International Law Department of the ELTE University in Budapest until 1996. He was Director of the Department on Security Policy and Disarmament of the Hungarian Ministry for Foreign Affairs in 1991 and became Deputy Director of the Hungarian Institute of International Affairs in 1994. He is currently at the Geneva Center for Security Policy.

Marc-André Gaudissart holds a law degree from the Catholic University of Louvain and a LLM degree in European law from the University of Ghent. As a research fellow of the Belgian Fund for Scientific Research (FWO), he is currently working at the European Institute (University of Ghent) where he is preparing a PhD on the scope and meaning of association agreements. He is the author of several articles concerning key issues of the European integration process.

Inge Govaere is currently a full-time lecturer at the College of Europe, Law Department. She holds a PhD in law from the European University Institute, Florence. She has published many articles on European Community law, in particular on the external relations of the EC and on intellectual property rights. She is the author of *The Use and Abuse of Intellectual Property Rights in EC Law* (Sweet & Maxwell, London, 1996).

Kamil Janáček holds a MSc degree from the Prague School of Economics and PhD degrees from the University of Nancy (France) and the Academy of Sciences (Prague). He was Research Fellow at the Institute of Economics (1964–92) and Deputy Minister in the Ministry of Labour and Social Affairs (1992–93). Since 1994 he is Chief Economist at Komerčni Banka, Prague. His research focuses on the analysis of the Czech economic transformation. He is the author or co-author of 17 books, 80 research studies and more than 90 articles in Czech and international journals.

Tamás Kende is an Associate Professor in the International Law Department of the ELTE University in Budapest and also teaches in the European programmes of the University of California. He is responsible for the approximation of laws in the Prime Minister's Integration Strategy Working Group. Author of several publications on EU law and public policy, he co-authored and edited a legal and political science manual in Hungarian on *European Law and Politics* (1995, Budapest).

Christian Lequesne has a PhD and is Research Fellow at the Fondation Nationale des Sciences Politiques (Centre d'Etudes et de Recherches Internationale), Paris, and Professor at the Institut d'Etudes Politiques, Paris and at the College of Europe, Bruges. Books published include *Paris–Bruxelles. Comment se fait la politique européenne de la France* (Presses de Science Po, Paris, 1993), *L'Union européenne: ouverture à l'Est* (PUF, Paris, 1994, with F. de La Serre and J. Rupnik), and *Les institutions de l'Union européenne* (La Documentation Française, Paris, 1995, with Y. Doutriaux).

Marc Maresceau studied at the University of Ghent, the Johns Hopkins University, Bologna, and the Institut universitaire de hautes études internationales, Geneva. He was Leverhulme Fellow at the University of Edinburgh and Visiting Professor at King's College, University of London. He teaches European law and institutions at the Universities of Ghent and Brussels and is the Director of the European Institute at the University of Ghent. Many of his publications concentrate on the External Relations of the European Union, in particular the relations between the European Union and Central and Eastern Europe.

Elisabetta Montaguti is an official at the European Commission, Directorate-General I, where she is working in the area of trade defence. She graduated from the Universities of Bologna (JD, 1989; PhD, 1994) and Michigan (LLM, 1990), and has been a member of the Bologna Bar since 1993. Her main area of interest is international and EC trade law, with special emphasis on EC relations with Central and Eastern Europe, on which she worked as a research fellow and adviser at the European Institute, University of Ghent (1994–95).

Peter-Christian Müller-Graff is Professor for Commercial and Economic Law, European Law and Comparative Law at the University of Heidelberg. He is Director of the Institute for Economic Law and European Law at the same university and Visiting Professor at Nancy (France) and Cornell University (USA). He is also a member of the teaching staff at the College of Europe in Bruges.

Sven Norberg LLDhc, is Director at the Directorate-General for Competition of the European Commission. Having been Permanent Secretary in the Ministry of Commerce in Stockholm and Justice of Appeal at the Svea Court of Appeal in Stockholm, he was Director for Legal Affairs of the EFTA Secretariat (1982–93). During 1994 and 1995 he was a Judge of the EFTA Court. He has also been a Visiting Professor at the University of Lund and is a member of the Advisory Boards to the European Law Institutes of King's College, London, and of the Universities of Birmingham and Hull.

Kris Pollet has been a researcher at the European Institute, University of Ghent since 1994. He is currently doing research on immigration and asylum policies of the EU in the framework of a FKFO-project financed by the Fund for Scientific Research (FWO).

Jim Rollo is Chief Economic Adviser at the Foreign and Commonwealth Office. He was educated at Glasgow University and the London School of Economics. He worked as a British Government economist in the Ministry of Agriculture, the Overseas Development Administration and the Foreign and Commonwealth Office between 1968 and 1989. In government he focused mainly on EU policies and international trade. He was Director of the International Economics Programme at The Royal Institute of International Affairs (Chatham House), London between 1989 and 1993, where he led a major research effort. He returned to the Foreign and Commonwealth Office in November 1993. He has published on aspects of EU and global trade policy, transition in Central Europe, and EU enlargement to the East.

Jacek Saryusz-Wolski is Vice-Rector of the College of Europe in Natolin, Warsaw. Formerly he was appointed as Under-Secretary of State for European Integration and Foreign Assistance (1991–96). He was Jean Monnet Fellow at the European University Institute in Florence (1989–90) and Associate Professor at the Lodz University (1980–90), where he graduated in 1971 and defended his PhD thesis in 1980.

Adinda Sinnaeve holds a law degree from the University of Ghent. She continued her law studies at the University of Tübingen, Germany, with an LLM, followed by a PhD on the recovery of illegal state aid. She worked at the European Institute of the University of Ghent as a research fellow. Currently she is working as an official at the European Commission's State Aid Directorate.

Piet Jan Slot is Professor of Economic Law at the University of Leiden, the Netherlands. He is Director of the Europa Institute and Chairman of the International Institute for Energy Law in Leiden. He is editor of *Common Market Law Review*. He has, for more than 20 years, been writing, teaching and advising on EC law.

Tamás Szűcs has a PhD in Legal and Political Sciences and a MA in Aesthetics from Eötvös Loránd University, Budapest. After a further two years of postgraduate research at Oxford University, he held various positions in academic institutions, in the private sector and in the state administration in Hungary. Since 1995 he has been Political Secretary of the Mission of the Republic of Hungary to the EU in Brussels.

Anne-Marie Van den Bossche was educated at the Universities of Ghent and Exeter (UK). She joined the European Institute of the University of Ghent in 1988. Initial research concentrated on the relations between the European Community and Central and Eastern Europe, and then gradually shifted to European competition law and policy. She gained her PhD in 1994, and is now Senior Research Assistant of the Fund for Scientific Research (FWO).

Lode Van Den Hende holds a law degree and an LLM from the University of Ghent and is teaching assistant at the European Institute. He has worked in various areas of Community law and practices Community law with Vlaemminck Holmens Goossens. He is currently acting as legal adviser to the Belgian Delegation to the Intergovernmental Conference.

Jiří Zemánek Czech, Dr. iur. et Dipl. oec. (Prague). Associate Professor of European Law and Vice-Dean of the Law Faculty at Charles University (Prague). He is Visiting Associate Professor at the College of Europe-Natolin and Europa-Kolleg, Hamburg, President of the Czech Association for European Studies and Secretary of the Czech Association for International Law.

PREFACE

The basic bilateral framework governing the relations between the European Union and the countries of Central and Eastern Europe (CEECs) is provided by the Europe Agreements. These agreements pave the way for those countries for a return to Europe after 40 years of highly artificial isolation. At its Copenhagen Summit in 1993, the EU had for the first time acknowledged the accession of the Central and Eastern European countries as a common objective and since then has developed a full scale pre-accession strategy to make Central and Eastern Europe 'fit for the Union'. The White Paper for the integration of the Central and Eastern European countries into the Internal Market, as adopted at the 1995 Cannes Summit, is one concrete but important example of this strategy.

A very crucial factor with a highly political dimension in the development of the relations between the EU and CEECs is the 1996 Intergovernmental Conference (IGC). Originally scheduled to revise the Maastricht Treaty, this conference has now obtained the far more ambitious task of preparing the European Union itself for enlargement to the Central and Eastern European countries. We should not forget that it is not only the applicant countries which have to adapt themselves for membership, but that the EU too will have to adapt for further enlargement. The institutional structures which worked with six member states when the European Economic Community was founded will no longer function with 25 member states. Already today the institutional framework of the European Union, even though revised several times since the Rome Treaty was signed, is hardly adequate to keep the Union of fifteen member states functioning well.

But it is not only institutional reforms which are envisaged at the IGC. The European Union must also adapt most of its structural policies, which could not, as they stand today, be financed if extended to all the candidate states. The Common Agricultural Policy is an often cited example but there are many others. For the first time, the Union will have to change its own 'acquis communautaire' in the perspective of a future enlargement, precisely in order to make this enlargement possible. Therefore, one cannot overestimate the importance of the IGC for successful accession negotiations. This time negotiators have to face a huge responsibility *vis-à-vis* the people not only in the EU member states but also in the countries of Central and Eastern Europe as well. We cannot this time afford nationalistic shortsightedness, which dominated the negotiations on the Maastricht Treaty too often and too much.

No doubt the IGC itself has to be seen in the context of a changing public opinion, both in the EU member states and in the Central and Eastern European Countries. The poor economic situation in most of the EU member states, marked by high unemployment and structural crisis in important branches of industry, has led to many of our citizens becoming more sceptical *vis-à-vis* enlargement of the EU to the East. The initial enthusiasm which was felt all over Europe directly after the fall of the Iron Curtain, and especially the Berlin Wall, has disappeared. Calls for more protection against cheap – and, therefore, considered to be 'unfair' – imports from the East, and against huge immigration inflows, are being heard more and more. There are even some who say (and maybe more who think) that the economic problems we are facing today are caused by the opening up of Central and Eastern Europe, and that the former Iron Curtain should be replaced by something less ugly, but equally efficient. Of course, we completely disagree with this interpretation, even though it must be taken seriously. The economic consequences of the integration of the Central and Eastern European countries have to be seen in the context of the wider process of economic globalization. All these questions are addressed in one way or another in this book.

A successful integration of the CEECs into the European Union is a necessary condition for a lasting peace on our continent. Any attempt to preserve the existing inequalities in living standards between the Western and the Eastern part of Europe inevitably jeopardizes the overall stability of Europe. The events in former Yugoslavia have made it clear to everybody how fragile the security situation in Europe has become after the breakdown of the bipolar security system of the post-World War II era. On the other hand, the people living in the East must understand that democracy on its own creates freedom, but not necessarily prosperity at the same time. In order to close the gap in economic wealth, the recently regained freedoms must be fully used to exploit the endogenous potential which exists in the economies of all Central and Eastern European countries.

A last important aspect of the integration process is timing. It is fully understandable that the Central and Eastern European countries are impatient to become full-fledged member states of the European Union. This impatience is mainly caused by concern over the political and economic development of their big neighbour in the East. Therefore, the EU pre-accession strategy must not neglect the situation in Russia, and also in Ukraine, Belarus, just to mention three of the Newly Independent States. Simultaneously with its pre-accession strategy, the Union must develop a stable framework for its relations with Russia, in order to avoid a situation where Russia perceives enlargement of the Union as a threat of its own economic and security interests (the question of future membership of the countries of Central and Eastern Europe in the NATO may be cited as an example for this attitude). It is highly necessary to put into force, and to deepen, the Partnership Agreement signed with Russia two years ago, in order to put bilateral relations on a more solid foundation.

To reply to the impatience of the CEECs, the European Union must eliminate any possible doubt about the seriousness of its engagement to the common objective of enlargement. The question must no longer be 'whether' but 'when'. The people in Central and Eastern Europe will then understand more easily that a well-timed accession to the European Union provides for more benefits and less costs. Technically speaking, the question of timing will be dealt with during the accession negotiations in the context of transitional periods in the process of integration. Here, each candidate country will be dealt with on its own merits. Those who have made more progress in setting up a well functioning market economy and by doing so have closed the gap in economic development may obtain a shorter transitional period than the other countries. What we must avoid is an uncoordinated race for membership between applicant countries. We should not forget that the results of accession negotiations must be submitted for referendum to the population of the applicant countries. Too ambitious timetables may provoke opposition.

This remarkable book which no doubt is one of the most comprehensive ones on the relations EU–Central and Eastern Europe published so far will easily find its way to lawyers, diplomats, politicians, scholars and in general to all those, who are concerned on how integration, cooperation, peace and stability in Europe are or can be organized.

Willy De Clercq
Minister of State
Chairman Committee on Legal Affairs and Citizens' Rights
of the European Parliament

ACKNOWLEDGEMENTS

This book is the result of a number of different initiatives and projects. In the first place it incorporates a series of papers which were presented at the Third Ghent Colloquium of 7–8 March 1996 on *The Relations between the European Union and Central and Eastern Europe: The Political, Economic and Legal Dimension*. However, this volume is not a 'colloquium proceedings'– publication. Colloquium speeches and the discussion they provoke set the atmosphere of a colloquium but are not necessarily fit for a publication like this one. Therefore, only a selection of colloquium-contributions has been retained and all these papers have been thoroughly revised by their authors in the light of this publication. Some specific research papers covering topics which were not discussed at the Colloquium have also been incorporated. Taken together they form a comprehensive and multidisciplinary analysis of the evolving EU policy towards the economic and political reforms taking place in Central and Eastern Europe. This volume which constitutes a mix of contributions based on thorough scientific research and/or on large practical experience in the field should offer an opportunity to acquire, enhance or update knowledge and understanding of one of the main challenges which the EU is facing at the end of this century.

In preparing and editing this book we have been very fortunate to receive the generous assistance from the European Commission (DG lA), the Government of the Flemish Community (Administratie Economie) and the VZW Europees Instituut. Also the University of Ghent and in particular its Research Council have given their support for advanced research in the field covered in this book. Without the continuous support of these institutions neither the Colloquium nor this publication would have been possible. A special word of thanks goes to our Hungarian projectpartners and in particular to Ambassador Dr Péter Balázs with whom for many years we have had the great pleasure to work together. Our thanks go also to the whole team of the European Institute of the University of Ghent who directly or indirectly has been involved in the various projects leading to this book. We owe many debts of gratitude to Dr Adinda Sinnaeve, for her editorial assistance throughout the preparation of this volume and to Dr Elisabetta Montaguti for her help in the first stage of this project. We would also like to express our very sincere thanks to Mrs Alison McDonnell for her invaluable assistance and final review of the manuscript of this book.

Marc Maresceau
Ghent, 1 January 1997

TABLE OF CASES

EUROPEAN COURT OF JUSTICE, ALPHABETICAL LIST

Court of First Instance

EUROPEAN COURT OF JUSTICE, CASE-NUMBER LIST

Court of First Instance

ABBREVIATIONS

AECos	Associated European Correspondents
AMO	Polish (or Slovak) Anti-monopoly Office
Ann.Dr.	Annales de droit de Louvain
APC	Agreement on Parnership and Cooperation
B.I.S.D.	Basic Instruments and Selected Documents
Bull. EC	Bulletin of the European Communities
Bull. EU	Bulletin of the European Union
CMLR	Common Market Law Reports
CMLRev.	Common Market Law Review
CAP	Common Agricultural Policy
CDE	Cahiers de droit européen
CEECs	Countries of Central and Eastern Europe
CEFTA	Central European Free Trade Association
CFSP	Common Foreign and Security Policy
CIREA	Centre for Information, Discussion and Exchange on Asylum
CIREFI	Centre of Information, Discussion and Exchange on the Crossing of Frontiers and Immigration
CIS	Commonwealth of Independent States
CMEA	Council for Mutual Economic Assistance (Comecon)
COCOM	Coordinating Committee for Multilateral Export Controls
COMECON	Council for Mutual Economic Assistance
CPC	Bulgarian Committee on the Protection of Competition
CR	Czech Republic
CSCE	Conference on Security and Co-operation in Europe
CZK	Czech Crown
EIPR	European Intellectual Property Review

ECJ	Court of Justice of the European Communities
EA	Europe Agreement
EBRD	European Bank for Reconstruction and Development
EC	European Community
ECLR	European Competition Law Review
ECos	European Correspondents
ECR	Reports of Cases before the Court of Justice and the Court of First Instance of the European Communities
ECSC	European Coal and Steel Community
EEA	European Economic Area
EEC	European Economic Community
EFTA	European Free Trade Association
ELR	European Law Review
EMU	European Monetary Union
EPC	European Political Cooperation
EU	European Union
EuR	Europarecht
FTA	Free Trade Agreements
GATS	General Agreement on Trade in Services
GATT	General Agreement on Tariffs and Trade
GDP	Gross Domestic Product
GVH	Hungarian Office of Economic Competition
ILM	International Legal Materials
IGC	Intergovernmental Conference
IP	Intellectual property protection
JCMS	Journal of Common Market Studies
JWT(L)	Journal of World Trade (Law)
LIEI	Legal Issues of European Integration
MEC	Czech Ministry of Economic Competition
Med	Mediterranean
MFN	Most favoured nation
NATO	North Atlantic Treaty Organization
NME	Non-market economy
OJ	Official Journal of the European Communities
OECD	Organization for Economic Cooperation and Development
OSCE	Organization for Security and Co-operation in Europe
PfP	Partnership for Peace
RMC	Revue du Marché Commun et de l'union européenne
RMUE	Revue du Marché Unique européen
RTDE	Revue trimestrielle de droit européen
SEW	Sociaal Economische Wetgeving
TEU	Treaty on European Union
TRIPS	Trade-Related Aspects of Intellectual Property Rights
UNGA	United Nations General Assembly
UNTS	United Nations Treaty Series

VAT	Value added tax
VER	Voluntary export restraint
WEU	Western European Union
WP	White Paper
WTO	World Trade Organization
YEL	Yearbook of European Law

Part I

INTRODUCTION

1

ON ASSOCIATION, PARTNERSHIP, PRE-ACCESSION AND ACCESSION

Marc Maresceau

I. INTRODUCTION

There are a number of key concepts which identify and characterize the relations between the European Union and Central and Eastern Europe. They can be summarized by the expressions *association, partnership, pre-accession* and *accession*. A short analysis of these concepts not only serves as an introduction to the relations between the EU and Central and Eastern Europe as a whole but also to this book in particular. All the contributions in this volume in one way or another address one or more of these notions. It should be noted that the manuscript for this book was completed before the Amsterdam Summit of June 1997.[1]

II. THE DISTINCTION BETWEEN 'ASSOCIATION' AND 'PARTNERSHIP'

For the last decade the relations between the EC/EU[2] and Central and Eastern Europe have constituted a particularly important aspect of EC/EU foreign policy. It is not the proper place here to retrace the history of the political and economic changes which have occurred in Central and Eastern Europe and to analyse in detail how the EC has gradually formulated its response to these changes.[3] Nevertheless, it may be useful to recall a few elements of this policy.

---

[1] The results of the Amsterdam Summit were only known after the completion of the proof-reading of this book. The least one can say of these results is that they are not without a large degree of ambiguity. On the one hand it is noted in the conclusions of the Presidency that the Intergovernmental Conference reached a 'successful conclusion' and that 'the way (was) now open for launching the enlargement process in accordance with the conclusions of the Madrid European Council' while on the other no progress was made in Amsterdam on the vital and crucial issue of the institutional reforms before further enlargement. In the coming years both aspects of the 'enlargement and modernisation of the institutional mechanisms' question will necessarily remain inextricably linked. This also explains why no updating of the various contributions in this book was deemed necessary.

[2] In this contribution the expressions *EC, EU, Community* and *Union* are interchangeable. From a strict legal point of view, it is the European Communities which sign association or partnership agreements with third countries (*EEC* before Maastricht and *EC* after Maastricht). Accession refers to the *EU*.

[3] For a survey see F. de La Serre, C. Lequesne, J. Rupnik, *L'Union européenne: ouverture à l'Est?*, Paris, PUF, 1994; M. Maresceau: 'The European Community, Eastern Europe and the USSR', in Redmond (ed.), *The External Relations of the European Community. The International Response*

First, the Community's policy towards Central and Eastern Europe has always been a complex mixture of political, economic and legal considerations. This state of affairs is not necessarily contributive to an easy perception of the various issues involved, but it provides an explanation and at the same time a justification for the somewhat hybrid structure of this book. The three parts in this volume – the legal, economic and political chapters – are closely intertwined and therefore also very much complementary.

Secondly, the expression 'Central and Eastern Europe' is not well defined and it certainly has a geographical and perhaps above all a geopolitical connotation. One of the most fundamental questions in this respect concerns the precise place of the former USSR within the notion 'Central and Eastern Europe'. The EC policy towards Central and Eastern Europe has gradually led towards an increasing differentiation between the former USSR on the one hand and the other Central and Eastern European countries on the other.[4] This differentiation is now clearly established and formalized by the conclusion of different types of agreements and by a set of different unilateral EC measures. No doubt, in the formative years of the new Community's approach towards the Gorbachev phenomenon and changes in Central and Eastern Europe this differentiation was less outspoken. Just to mention one example: in 1989 the EC still signed a Trade and Economic Cooperation Agreement with the USSR[5] largely based on those it had previously signed with Hungary[6] and Poland.[7] It is only in 1990 that a sharper dividing line in the EC's policy becomes more apparent. The launching of the Europe Agreements policy as something special for a number of Central and Eastern European countries constitutes at least implicitly a clear separation of the USSR from these countries.

The geographical and geopolitical definition of Central and Eastern Europe in the EC's policy is further complicated by the fact that parts of the Balkan are incorporated in the notion while others are not. Leaving aside the specific issue of EU–Turkey relations, it was unavoidable that also the dissolution of Yugoslavia would give rise to fundamental questions, namely with which of the newly created States, and to what extent the Europe Agreements policy could be applied. It progressively became clear that only with Slovenia could a Europe Agreement – and thus a pre-accession strategy – be envisaged.[8] For various and different reasons it was obvious that no

---

to 1992, London, Macmillan, 1992, 93–119; also 'Les aménagements des relations de la C.E.E. avec l'Europe de l'Est', in *L'intégration européenne et la révolution de l'Europe de l'Est*, Luxemburg, Institut Universitaire International, 1991, 143–70.

[4] On this 'changing geography of Ost(europa)politik' see B. Lippert, 'EC-Ostpolitik Revisited: Continuity and New Approaches', in Lippert and Schneider (eds), *Monitoring Association and Beyond. The European Union and the Visegrád States*, Bonn, Europa Union Verlag, 1995, 63–7.

[5] Agreement of 19 December 1989, *OJ*, 1990, L 68.

[6] Agreement of 26 September 1988, *OJ*, 1988, L 327.

[7] Agreement of 19 September 1989, *OJ*, 1989, L 339.

[8] On 15 June 1995 a Europe Agreement was initialled with Slovenia, but it was only signed on 10 June 1996. The main reason for this delay was the request of the Italian Government for restitution of or financial compensation for property lost by Italian refugees after the Second

Europe Agreement could be offered to Serbia, Bosnia-Herzegovina and the Former Yugoslav Republic of Macedonia.[9] The type of agreement with Croatia – which had been recognized officially by the EC together with Slovenia – may for some time have been unclear and uncertain. However, after the ethnic cleansing of Krajina in July 1995, it is impossible to contemplate the conclusion of a Europe Agreement with Croatia. With Albania a non-preferential cooperation agreement was signed in 1992,[10] but no evolution to a classic Europe Agreement is envisaged. However, negotiations on the conclusion of an enhanced *sui generis* cooperation framework may be possible incorporating elements of a Europe Agreement, such as 'political dialogue' and a preferential trade regime but not the establishment of a free trade area. Also, it would appear that the possibility of an accession of Albania to the EU in that new bilateral framework is excluded.

Thirdly – and this may at first sight seem paradoxical – differentiation as practised by the EC towards Central and Eastern Europe also necessarily implies a large degree of globalization. By developing 'a policy' towards Central and Eastern Europe, States with considerably different economic and political backgrounds are brought together. No doubt the 'banalization' of the Europe Agreement strategy has taken away the exclusive treatment which the Visegrád countries originally thought they deserved in the light of their political and economic transformation. The most advanced CEECs do not always appreciate being put in the same basket as the other less developed CEECs. Thus, and this is one of the leading issues addressed in the contribution to this volume by Balázs, the main question is whether the *global handling* of the associated CEECs and other countries of Central and East European region undergoing transformation, 'is the adequate treatment and the most convenient approach in view of the political and economic problems to be solved by integration methods' (below, p. 358). At the moment of writing this introduction, this delicate aspect of the question is at the top of the EU agenda, but no official position by the EU has as yet been taken. While the 1995 Madrid European Council declared that in the preparation of its opinions on the applications for membership the European Commission has '(to) ensure that the applicant countries are treated on an equal basis', it may nevertheless be expected that the first enlargement negotiations

---

World War. Another issue concerned the right for foreigners to acquire property in Slovenia. Finally, a compromise was reached in which Slovenia gave assurances that its real estate market would be opened to foreigners in four years following the ratification of the Europe Agreement. It was also agreed that by an exchange of letters preferential access to the real estate market would be granted to foreigners having resided in Slovenia for at least three years, see *Together in Europe*, 1996, No. 90, 7–8 and No. 91, 5.

[9] For an analysis of the possible EU options in the region see Report from the Commission to the Council and European Parliament on 'Common principles for future contractual relations with certain countries in South-Eastern Europe', COM(96) 476 final. At the moment of writing a Cooperation Agreement with the Former Yugoslav Republic of Macedonia based in particular on Arts 113 and 235 EC Treaty is at the point of being signed; for text see COM(96) 533 final of 25 November 1996.

[10] For text, see *OJ* 25 November 1992, L 343.

will start after the Intergovernmental Conference with only a limited number of countries including the Czech Republic, Hungary and Poland. It remains for the moment pure speculation whether other countries will be included in the first enlargement wave. Certainly, each application for membership must be considered on its own merits. In this case-by-case evaluation the EU should not dissociate the economic and legal conditions from the political considerations. All candidates must be capable of providing the necessary economic and legal guarantees for a workable membership. In other words a mere political argument for membership – for example quick accession of the Baltic States as a compensation for a postponed membership of NATO – should not be accepted by the European Union and can as such not suffice to justify early membership. Another aspect very much linked with the globalization policy is that of introducing a 'variable geometry' approach towards the CEECs. De la Serre and Lequesne (below, p. 357) argue that given the importance of the difficulties raised by the enlargement to the CEECs, 'the Community will probably adopt the *variable geometry* approach without calling it as such'.[11] It is likely, according to them, that this will be achieved 'by stretching to the utmost the Community method and by making the borderline between "transition" and "exemption" vague' (below, p. 357).

A.   Europe Agreements as Association Agreements

A network of Europe Agreements between the EC and the CEECs has gradually been established. After a first round of negotiations, Europe Agreements with Hungary, Poland and the Czech and Slovak Federal Republic were signed on 16 December 1991.[12] Due to the dissolution of the Czech and Slovak Federal Republic the agreement with that country was not ratified. It was renegotiated with the two new independent entities – the Czech Republic and Slovakia – and two separate but almost identical agreements were signed on 4 October 1993.[13] It was also in the same year that Europe Agreements with Bulgaria[14] and Romania[15] were signed. Similar agreements were furthermore agreed upon with the Baltic States on 15 June 1995.[16]

---

[11] H.E. Hartnell introduces at this point of the analysis the idea of the 'concentric circles'. The pattern is one whereby the associated CEECs try to progress from the outer circle towards the centre (EU); see paper *Regional Economic Integration from a European Perspective*, presented at the 66th Conference of the International Law Association, Buenos Aires, 1994, 2–3.

[12] See *OJ*, 1993, L 347/2 and 348/2 (Agreements with Hungary and Poland).

[13] See *OJ*, 1994, L 360/2 and 359/2 (Agreements with Czech Republic and Slovak Republic).

[14] See *OJ*, 1994, L 358/3.

[15] See *OJ*, 1994, L 357/2.

[16] See COM(1995) 207 final. Already on 19 July 1994 far-reaching Free Trade Agreements had been signed with the Baltic States, incorporating also 'political dialogue' and recognizing in the preamble that it is the 'ultimate objective' of the Baltic States to accede to the EU. For the text of these Agreements, see *OJ*, 1994, L 373/1 (Estonia); *OJ*, 1994, L 374/1 (Latvia) and *OJ*, 1994, L 375/1 (Lithuania). It should be noted that the conclusion of these agreements made it superfluous to conclude new interim agreements. For a comment on the Free Trade Agreements, see S. Peers, *The queue for accession lengthens*, ELR (1995), 323–9.

Finally, the last in the series of Europe Agreements is that with Slovenia[17] of 10 June 1996. It is very unlikely that in the near future similar agreements will be signed with other countries in Central and Eastern Europe.

All Europe Agreements are based on Article 238 EC Treaty – the Treaty provision on 'association' – and are mixed, that is to say that they are signed by the Community *and* the member states on the one hand and the associated country on the other. This mixed character implies that each of the member states must ratify the agreement before it can enter into force. This also explains why Interim Agreements on trade and trade-related matters were signed separately from the Europe Agreements, since such agreements did not require ratification from member states. These agreements simply incorporate the trade and trade-related chapters of the Europe Agreements. The Interim Agreements on Trade and Trade-related matters fall within the exclusive competence of the Community and this facilitates considerably the ratification procedure. Such agreements can therefore enter into force much more quickly than mixed agreements. Of course, once the ratification procedure for the Europe Agreements is fully completed the latter enter into force and replace the Interim Agreements.

All Europe Agreements with the ten associated countries follow a similar pattern and are almost identical from the point of view of structure and contents. They emphasize in the first place the need for political dialogue and lay down the basic framework for cooperation. Europe Agreements further aim at establishing a free trade area[18] (see Norberg, below, p. 75), incorporating to a large extent the EC competition rules and practices (see Van den Bossche, below, p. 84, Slot, below, p. 116 and Zemanek, below, p. 108). They organize in a specific way the taking of trade policy protection measures (see Montaguti, below, p. 160, and Van Den Hende, below, p. 140) and contain provisions on the trade-related aspects of intellectual property rights. As far as this last point is concerned, Europe Agreements provide that the associated CEECs undertake to improve the protection of intellectual, industrial and commercial property rights up to a level similar to that existing in the EC. How this objective is to be achieved is analysed in detail through a case-study by Govaere (below, p. 179) of the relations EC–Hungary. Furthermore, Europe Agreements also refer to specific provisions on movement of persons and establishment (see Cremona, below, p. 195 and Pollet, below, p. 209).

There are minor differences between the various Europe Agreements but one difference between the Europe Agreements of the first round and the others of subsequent stages is of a substantial nature. The agreements signed in 1993 refer explicitly in the Preamble to the need to respect 'the rights of

---

[17] See COM(1995) 341 final.

[18] For the specific regulation of trade in agricultural goods, see D. Stuyck, 'L'agriculture dans l'Union Européenne et les pays d'Europe centrale et orientale: de l'association à l'élargissement' and L. Mahe, 'L'agriculture et l'élargissement de l'Union européenne aux PECO: l'intégration, un atout pour la transition, une épreuve pour la PAC', in *Quel avenir pour la politique agricole commune?* (ed. Flaesch-Mougin), Rennes, Apogée, 1996, 135–49 and 151–80.

persons belonging to minorities'. In addition these agreements all contain a provision stipulating that 'respect for the democratic principles and human rights established by the Helsinki Final Act and the Charter of Paris for a New Europe, as well as the principles of a market economy, inspire the domestic and external policies of the Parties and constitute essential elements of the present association'.[19] Unilateral suspension of the Agreement without prior consultation is possible 'in cases of special urgency'.[20]

The choice of the 'association' formula to identify 'Europe Agreements' has had considerable political and legal repercussions. As already mentioned it allowed the Europe Agreements to be concluded on the basis of Article 238 EC Treaty. While this Treaty provision does not really define the concept 'association' it nevertheless stipulates that association agreements create reciprocal rights and obligations for the contracting parties, common actions and special procedures. No doubt the choice of the association-label with regard to an agreement clearly indicates that the contracting parties, and in particular the Community, intends to give a special political impetus to the agreement.[21] Association agreements therefore are something different and something more than other agreements. To use the terminology of the Court of Justice of the European Communities: association agreements create 'special privileged links with a non-member country, which must, at least to a certain extent, take part in the Community system'.[22] But 'association agreements' do not form a monolithic bloc. Some association agreements were conceived with a perspective of possible accession such as those with Greece (1961) and Turkey (1963),[23] while others do not offer that perspective (for example, the Lomé Conventions, the Euro-Med Agreements). Also the European Economic Area Agreement with the EFTA States, establishing

---

[19] See Art. 6 in all Europe Agreements signed after those of the first round. Reference to the respect for the protection of human rights follows the Council Declaration of 11 May 1992 which foresees such reference in the Cooperation and Association Agreements between the EC and its partners in the CSCE. On the reference to the protection of human rights in agreements concluded by the Community in general see P.J. Kuyper, 'Trade Sanctions, Security and Human Rights and Commercial Policy', in Maresceau (ed.), *The European Community's Commercial Policy After 1992: The Legal Dimension*, Dordrecht, Nyhoff, 1993, 410–13.

[20] This led to a further explanation of the various positions in the Agreement with the Czech Republic; see on this point M. Maresceau, 'A Legal Analysis of the Community's Association Agreements with Central and Eastern Europe: General Framework, Accession Objectives and Trade Liberalization', in Konstadinidis (ed.), *The Legal Regulation of the European Community's External Relations After the Completion of the Internal Market*, Aldershot, Dartmouth, 1996, 125–40.

[21] See also I. Macleod, I.D. Hendry and S. Hyett, *The External Relations of the European Communities*, Oxford, Clarendon Press, 1996, 368; D. McGoldrick, International Relations Law of the European Union, London, Longman, 1997, 183.

[22] Case 12/86, 1987 ECR 3719.

[23] The Preamble of the Association Agreement with Turkey recognizes 'that the support given by the European Economic Community to the efforts of the Turkish people to improve their standard of living will facilitate the accession of Turkey to the Community at a later date', while Art. 28 of the Agreement stipulates that 'as soon as the operation of this Agreement has advanced far enough to justify envisaging full acceptance by Turkey of the obligations arising out of the Treaty establishing the Community, the Contracting Parties shall examine the possibility of the accession of Turkey to the Community'.

a very special kind of association, was originally conceived as an alternative to accession. However, it is clear that the far-reaching provisions of that agreement soon afterwards paved the way for a smooth accession of Austria, Finland and Sweden.

As noted previously, Europe Agreements were not originally seen, at least not by the Community, as pre-accession agreements (see Müller-Graff, below, p. 34). It is precisely on this very important point of principle that the role of the European Council of the European Union has become so predominant.[24] It was at the 1993 Copenhagen European Council and without formal amendment of the Europe Agreements that a political reorientation of these agreements transformed them into a basis for a pre-accession strategy, while the 1994 Essen European Council further refined the pre-accession frameworks.

The Copenhagen European Council accepted that accession became a *mutual* goal, notwithstanding the fact that the Preamble of Europe Agreements only recognized accession as the associated country's objective, not as an objective of the Community.[25] In the conclusions of the Presidency at the Copenhagen European Council it was stated 'that accession will take place as soon as an associated country is able to assume the obligations of membership by satisfying the economic and political conditions required'. Besides the guarantee of political stability, democracy, the rule of law and respect for human rights and minorities, membership also implies the capacity to cope with competitive pressures and market forces and 'the existence of a functioning market economy'. Moreover, at the 1994 Essen European Council the condition of good neighbourly relations ('bon voisinage') was added to the requirements which the associated countries must satisfy in order to be eligible for membership. This also means that the EU supports intra-regional and bilateral cooperation among CEECs.[26] The European Union, for its part, must have the 'capacity to absorb new members, while maintaining the momentum of European integration'. This condition brings us necessarily to the Intergovernmental Conference and its impact on the next enlargement debate (see Derycke, below, p. 297; Burghardt, below, p. 306 and Cameron,

---

[24] See also P. Van Den Bempt and G. Theelen, *From Europe Agreements to Accession*, Brussels, European Interuniversity Press, 1996, 30–4.

[25] On the 'strategic ambivalence' of the Europe Agreements see B. Lippert and H. Schneider, 'Association and Beyond: The European Union and the Visegrád States', in Lippert and Schneider, *Monitoring Association and Beyond. The European Union and the Visegrád States*, Bonn, Europa Union Verlag, 1995, 26.

[26] See for example the Central European Free Trade Association (CEFTA) which now includes Poland, Hungary, the Czech Republic, Slovakia and Slovenia, and the bilateral agreements on good-neighbourly relations and cooperation between Hungary and Slovakia of 19 March 1995 or between Hungary and Romania of 14 August 1996. Both agreements concern sensitive issues in the region such as, *inter alia*, the protection of minorities. The Agreement Hungary–Slovakia was ratified by Hungary in June 1995, while the Slovak Parliament gave its approval on 26 March 1996. However, the latter adopted at the same time an explanatory resolution 'interpreting' in a restrictive way certain provisions of the Agreement, see *La Slovaquie ratifie le traité avec la Hongrie mais en limite la portée*, Le Monde, 28 March 1996 but

below, p. 241) and also to the cost-benefit analysis of enlargement to the East and, more precisely, the economic effects of enlargement. This is the main focus of Rollo's contribution in this volume (below, p. 252). He argues that trade will increase in both directions, as well as there being an inflow of investment to the East. Only minor risks of trade diversion are to be expected. But the need to reform European policies in the field of agriculture and the structural funds, which are the largest components of the EU budget, are of a particularly compelling nature. Saryusz-Wolski nuances strongly the often-made calculations on the cost side. Budgetary expenditures caused by enlargement must be considered jointly with the political and economic benefits of integration. Also, the costs of a geographical 'half-Europe' should be taken into consideration (below, p. 285; for a Czech approach to the cost/benefit analysis of membership, see Janáček, below, p. 287).

The reorientation by the European Council of the association agreements with the CEECs made it possible to create important ancillary initiatives in the political and legal field and constituted the basis for the development of a comprehensive pre-accession strategy. An important aspect of the pre-accession policy is the 'structured relations'. They allow the associated CEECs to become progressively involved in the various activities of the European Union. In practice this means that at various levels, from the bottom to the top, meetings are organized to which the CEEC counterparts are invited. Of course, from a legal point of view these 'joint' meetings have no legislative capacity – they cannot replace the formal EU institutions in the decision-making process – but they nevertheless have a great symbolic and above all psychological significance – and a 'classic' European Council is almost always followed by a photograph of an 'enlarged' meeting at the end of the proceedings.[27]

From a legal point of view the approximation of laws exercise as expressed in the Commission's White Paper preparing the CEECs for integration into the Internal Market and endorsed at the 1995 Cannes European Council, is probably of more fundamental importance.[28] It is true that as opposed to the European Economic Area Agreement the White Paper remains a voluntary legislative programme of approximation, but the mere fact that it exists is perhaps the best proof that Europe Agreements can be seen in the light of possible accession (see Gaudissart and Sinnaeve, below, p. 41). Clearly, the

---

see also *Information on the Implementation of the Framework Convention of the Council of Europe on the Protection of National Minorities in the Slovak Republic*, Ministry of Foreign Affairs, Bratislava, 1996. In the past a number of problems have arisen linked with the protection of minorities and the consolidation of democratic institutions in Slovakia, see *Agence Europe*, 27 October 1995; a resolution of 16 November 1995 of the European Parliament went so far as to threaten with a suspension of the Europe Agreement, see *Agence Europe*, 18 November 1995 and reaction by Slovak authorities, *Agence Europe*, 23 November 1995. The Joint Parliamentary Committee Meeting of 22–24 November 1995 managed to keep under control a further escalation of the tension, see *Agence Europe*, 29 November 1995.

[27] So far 'joint meetings' of heads of state or government have taken place in Essen, Cannes, Madrid, Florence and Dublin.

[28] COM(95) 163 final.

White Paper programme is not, as such, a legal condition for accession and for this reason it does not prejudge the result of the negotiations on accession of the applicant State. Yet it is obvious that the approximation process contributes in a fundamental way to the creation of an irreversible legal framework for integration. This brings us back to the more general question of the role of law in the relations between the EU and CEECs, examined in Müller-Graff's contribution. For this author 'it is precisely the law which is expected to provide a permanent, peaceful and stable basis for the relations between States, peoples and individuals, just as it does within the European Union itself' (below, p. 29). This also explains why a considerable part of this volume is devoted to the legal dimension and related aspects of the EU–CEEC relations.

B. Partnership and Cooperation Agreements

In the Commission's proposal of August 1990 to conclude association agreements it was observed that such agreements could not be signed with the former USSR because of the uncertainties of domestic reforms and the magnitude of the problems that country was facing.[29] This basic option taken by the Commission would be further worked out and accentuated. The EC's PHARE programme aiming at supporting transformation in Central and Eastern Europe – which now has become the main financial instrument of the pre-accession strategy – was not extended to the (former) USSR, but a specific programme, called TACIS, was applied. However, the most overt expression of this differentiation policy came indirectly at the 1993 Copenhagen European Council with the political reorientation of the Europe Agreements towards pre-accession agreements. Certainly, this new policy had the great advantage of bringing more clarity into the debate, but at the same time it also further isolated the former USSR from the European Community. In other words, the political reorientation of the Europe Agreements is not without danger and it should therefore be handled with great care. It is the gradual awareness of this side-effect of the reorientation policy which explains why the EC has tried to find new ways to accommodate the relations with the former USSR. It is in the light of this context that the Partnership and Cooperation Agreements have to be situated which were signed in 1994 with Russia[30] and Ukraine[31] and later on with other former USSR Republics.

---

[29] See Communication to the Council of Ministers and European Parliament on the possible conclusion of association agreements with countries from Central and Eastern Europe, COM(90) 398 final, 27 August 1990.

[30] Text signed on 24 June 1994, see COM(94) 257 final. For an analysis see J.-C. Van Eeckhaute, 'De overeenkomst inzake Partnerschap en Samenwerking: een nieuw juridisch en politiek kader voor de betrekkingen tussen de Europese Unie en Rusland', *Rechtskundig Weekblad* (1995), 1041–52; also H. Timmerman, 'Die Europaische Union und Rusland – Dimensionen und Perspektiven der Partnerschaft', *Integration* (1996), 195–207.

[31] Text signed 14 June 1994, see COM(94) 226 final.

However, this fact cannot conceal the immense difference between the two kinds of agreements. The distinction is not just a question of semantics: Partnership Agreements – notwithstanding their nice name – establish and consolidate in reality a new dividing line in Europe. It must be noted that the EC has taken away the Baltic States from the 'Partnership' policy and incorporated them in the Europe Agreements strategy. In other words, the pre-accession policy also applies to these countries, and this certainly gives rise to some additional political and geopolitical questions which for the moment have not all been fully or sufficiently addressed by the EC (dependence on Russian energy, the minorities issue, Kaliningrad as a Russian enclave in the EU, etc.).

Partnership Agreements are mixed agreements[32] and based on Articles 113 and 235 EC Treaty: in other words the same provisions which were used as a legal basis for the former Trade and Economic Cooperation Agreements. The Partnership as established in these agreements did not seem to deserve the qualification 'association' as did, for example, the Europe Agreements or Euro-Mediterranean Agreements.[33] Broadly speaking there are two types of Partnership Agreements with the former USSR: the Agreements signed with Russia, Ukraine, Moldova and Belarus and those signed with the non-European former USSR Republics. The Partnership Agreements of the second category are less detailed than those of the first category. However, the agreements with Russia and the three other European former USSR Republics are in many respects disappointing, and they certainly do not meet the targets which, for example, Russia or Ukraine had set for the negotiations. These countries tried as much as possible to come close to an agreement comparable to the type of Europe Agreements. The EC for its part proposed as an alternative a much looser political, economic and legal framework. This explains why the Partnership Agreement does not aim at establishing a free trade area but only proclaims that the Contracting Parties will 'examine together in the year 1998 whether circumstances allow the beginning of negotiations on the establishment of a free trade area'. Notwithstanding these critical comments there is potential for development of relations (see Borko, below, p. 385). Of course, a lot will depend on the domestic political, economic and social environment in the former USSR and particularly in Russia.[34]

---

[32] In addition to the Partnership Agreements, Interim Agreements on Trade and Trade-related matters have also been signed.

[33] In its Communication 'Future Relations and Cooperation between the Community and Middle East' – COM(93) 375 final, 8 September 1993 – the Commission had developed the idea that future relations had to be 'established on the basic concept of partnership'. However, probably in order to avoid any confusion with the agreements negotiated with the countries of the former USSR the expression 'partnership' was not used in the title of the agreements. Thus, for example, the Euro-Mediterranean Agreements establish 'an association' and are based on Art. 238 EC Treaty.

[34] See in this context also the Communication from the Commission 'The European Union and Russia: The Future Relationship', COM(95) 223 final.

III. THE ACCESSION SCENARIO

A. The general principles applied to CEECs

All the associated Central and Eastern European countries have now applied for membership of the European Union.[35] If the results of the Inter-governmental Conference allow the EU to go ahead with enlargement negoti-ations – which implies that the indispensable institutional adaptations can be agreed upon[36] – the accession procedure of Article O TEU will have to be followed. This provision reads as follows:

> Any European State may apply to become a member of the Union. It shall address its application to the Council, which shall act unanimously after consulting the Commission and after receiving the assent of the European Parliament, which shall act by an absolute majority of its component members.
>
> The conditions of admission and the adjustments to the Treaties on which the Union is founded which such admission entails shall be the subject of an agree-ment between the member States and the applicant State. This agreement shall be submitted for ratification by all the contracting States in accordance with their respective constitutional requirements.

Article O itself does not contain conditions for membership except that the candidate should be a 'European State'. The adjective 'European' has never been officially defined but according to the European Commission 'it combines geographical, historical and cultural elements which all contribute to the European identity'.[37] The term 'European' cannot therefore be con-densed into a simple and static formula. Consequently, still according to the Commission, 'it is neither possible nor opportune to establish now the frontiers of the European Union whose contours will be shaped over many years to come'. This aspect of the accession scenario is of course not of great relevance for the currently *associated* Central and Eastern European coun-tries, but it raises fundamental issues with regard to the CEECs with whom Partnership Agreements have been signed. Leaving aside the special dimen-sion of the relations with Russia, a number of 'European' CEECs – Moldova, Belarus and Ukraine – are not offered associationship and are thus excluded from the pre-accession strategy, notwithstanding the fact that government authorities of some of these countries have already expressed their view that they too would like to join the EU.[38]

---

[35] The ten countries and their dates of application are: Hungary (31 March 1994), Poland (5 April 1994), Slovakia (27 June 1995), Romania (22 June 1995), Latvia (13 October 1995), Estonia (24 November 1995), Lithuania (8 December 1995), Bulgaria (14 December 1995), Czech Republic (17 January 1996) and Slovenia (10 June 1996).

[36] For a summary of these adaptations, see Commission Opinion on 'Reinforcing Political Union and Preparing for Enlargement', COM(96) 90 final; see on this matter also Burghardt, below, p. 310 and Cameron, below, p. 249.

[37] See 'Europe and the Challenge of Enlargement', *Bull. EC*, Suppl. 3/92, 11.

[38] So far no formal application for membership has been forwarded by these countries to the EU.

13

Apart from the condition relating to the 'European identity', the accession practice of the EC demonstrates that other requirements also have to be fulfilled. They consist in the first place of the condition that democracy and human rights are respected, including the protection of minorities.[39] The respect of democracy and fundamental rights was already in the Stuttgart Declaration of 19 June 1983, considered to be a leading principle governing Community activities.[40] Since then its importance has been confirmed and further worked out, *inter alia* at the European Councils of Copenhagen[41] and Essen.[42] Clearly, the fact that the new member state has to accept the full *acquis communautaire*[43] necessarily implies respect of fundamental rights 'as guaranteed by the European Convention for the Protection of Human Rights and Fundamental Freedoms signed in Rome on 4 November 1950 and as they result from the constitutional traditions common to the Member States, as general principles of Community law' (Article F TEU).[44] Respect for the protection of minorities is already a formal legal requirement for the associated countries which have signed Europe Agreements since 1993 (see above, p. 9). It was explicitly mentioned as a condition for membership by the Copenhagen European Council.

However, to be a European State and to respect democracy and human rights are not enough to become a member of the EU. Membership indeed means above all full acceptance of the *acquis communautaire*, that is to say acceptance of all the rights and obligations, actual and potential, of the EU system and its institutional framework. An applicant which is unable to satisfy these conditions immediately at the moment of accession may be granted temporary derogations and transitional arrangements[45] but this is subject of the accession negotiations and they cannot imply that candidates could reject the ultimate goals of the Union.[46] Thus membership presupposes full acceptance of the contents, principles and political objectives of the TEU and

---

[39] See also V. Constantinesco, R. Kovar and D. Simon, *Traité sur l'Union Européenne. Commentaire article par article*, Paris, Economica, 1995, 890.

[40] *Bull. EC*, 6-1983, 19–26.

[41] *Bull. EC*, 6-1993, 7–24.

[42] *Bull. EC*, 12-1994, 7–32.

[43] This also results from the formulation of Art. B which stipulates that one of the objectives of the Union is to 'maintain in full the *acquis communautaire* and to build on it'.

[44] This principle is also firmly established in the case-law of the Court of Justice of the European Communities, see e.g. Case C-260/89, *ERT*, [1991] ECR I-2925: the European Convention on Human Rights, according to the Court of Justice, 'has special significance'. The Court 'draws inspiration from the constitutional traditions common to the Member States and from the guidelines supplied by international treaties for the protection of human rights on which the Member States have collaborated or of which they are signatories' (see e.g. Opinion 2/94, *Accession by the Communities to the Convention for the Protection of Human Rights and Fundamental Freedoms*, [1996] ECR I-1759). The Community 'cannot accept measures which are incompatible with observance of human rights thus recognized and guaranteed' (Case C-260/89, *ERT*, [1991] ECR I-2925).

[45] Transitional periods can be very long. For the accession of Spain, for example, the following transitional periods were applied: customs union and free movement of workers: seven years; agricultural policy: ten years; fisheries policy: seventeen years.

[46] See A. Michalski and H. Wallace, *The European Community: The Challenge of Enlargement*, London, Royal Institute of International Relations, 1992, 35–6.

the various Community Treaties, the Community legislation based on these Treaties, the case law of the Court of Justice (and Court of First Instance) as well as the resolutions and declarations adopted in the framework of these Treaties. Furthermore, agreements concluded with third states and agreements between member states within the framework of the Community's activities belong to the *acquis communautaire*.[47]

The accession procedure as organized in Article O consists of two phases, one at the European Union level and one at the level of the member states. In practice, however, the two phases are intertwined and the whole process is dominated by the EU. To put it plainly, one can say that the accession debate is very much a one-way street: it is the third State which adheres to the EU and not vice versa. Although there is no clear legal provision in the Treaties on how accession negotiations are to be conducted, past practice indicates that a prominent role is being played by the Commission and Council,[48] in particular the Presidency. Once these negotiations have been completed, the Treaty of Accession is to be ratified by the member states. Therefore, there must altogether be a very large consensus between the EU institutions, member states and applicant.[49]

B. The different steps analysed

The accession procedure is a particularly complex diplomatic and legal mixture and it is not always easy to perceive clearly its subsequent stages. Grosso modo the following phases can be distinguished. The first step after the application of the third State is the formulation of a *Commission Opinion*. This (positive) opinion paves the way for the next steps of the enlargement procedure and in particular the accession negotiations proper. At their conclusion they are followed by the *Assent by the European Parliament* and the *Decision of the Council of the European Union*. Then follows the formal signature of the *Treaty of Accession*, the *Act of Accession* and the *Final Act*. Before the Treaty of Accession can enter into force it has to be ratified by all the member states of the EU and the applicant State.

a. Commission Opinion and accession negotiations

There are no set deadlines within which the Commission is expected to deliver its opinion[50] and there are no clear preset legal rules as regards its

---

[47] For a global presentation of the formal and substantive conditions for EU membership, see M.-A. Gaudissart, 'De toetreding van nieuwe lidstaten: stimulans of hinderpaal voor de totstandkoming van de Europese Unie?', *Rechtskundig Weekblad* (1994), 729–43.

[48] J.-P. Puissochet, *L'élargissement des Communautés Européennes*, Paris, Editions Techniques et Economiques, 1974, 21–3.

[49] On the relationship between the procedure within the Community and the reaching of an agreement with the member states, see D. Booss and J. Forman, 'Enlargement: Legal and Procedural Aspects', *CMLRev.* (1995), 98–9.

[50] Two or three years seems a 'normal' average, see for example the time needed by the Commission to formulate its (first) Opinion on the application of Sweden, Austria, Turkey, Malta, Cyprus.

formulation or structure. As a matter of fact the 'Commission's Opinion' is composed of several stages.[51] Moreover, in the context of the application for membership by the CEECs a composite paper ('un document d'ensemble') will complement the Opinions on each individual application.[52] A specific impact study will also be carried out which will certainly have an effect on the formulation of the Opinion.[53] It is at the moment of writing difficult to see where the precise borderline between 'the Opinion' and 'the composite paper' has to be drawn. Be that as it may it can be expected that they are both 'the Opinion' of the Commission and that they should be read in conjunction with each other. In the case of the applications from the Central and Eastern European countries, the timing of the (first) Commission Opinion is very much affected by the Intergovernmental Conference and its results. At the Madrid European Council it was decided that the (first) Commission Opinion on the applications for membership should be forwarded to the Council 'as soon as possible *after* the conclusion of the Intergovernmental Conference'.[54] This Opinion itself is in fact a provisional opinion, presenting no formal, legal character but it largely predetermines the next steps of the procedure. Once the (first) positive Commission Opinion has been delivered and endorsed by the Council the formal enlargement negotiations can start. At the 1996 Florence European Council it was stated that the initial phase of negotiations could coincide with the beginning of accession-negotiations with Cyprus and Malta,[55] that is to say six months after the end of the Intergovernmental Conference. The negotiations will be conducted by the Presidency of the Council on behalf of the member states and with the support of the European Commission. It is the Commission which is in charge of drawing up the common positions of the member states for each of the chapters to be negotiated.

From what has already been mentioned, it is clear that what is called 'Commission Opinion' takes different forms. First, the Commission prepares a comprehensive opinion on the application of each candidate incorporating, *inter alia*, a survey of the state of the bilateral relations – political as well as economic – together with a study of the economy of the applicant and the

---

[51] For example for the first enlargement the Commission gave a first Opinion in 1967, an adapted version in 1969 and a final Opinion on 19 January 1972; on the application of Greece the first Opinion was published on 29 January 1976, the final one on 23 May 1979. The first Opinion on the application of Spain and Portugal was on 29 November 1978 and 19 May 1978, the final Opinion for both applications was on 31 May 1985; on the applications of Austria, Sweden, Finland and Norway the first Commission Opinions were given on, respectively, 31 July 1991, 31 July 1992, 4 November 1992 and 24 March 1993. The (global) final Opinion of the Commission is of 19 April 1994.

[52] See Conclusions of the Presidency at the 1995 Madrid European Council. Basically, the composite paper will examine the horizontal effects of enlargement, in other words issues which go beyond the scope of the opinion on individual applications, see *Enlargement: Questions and Answers, Europe Documents, Agence Europe,* 9 August 1996.

[53] The impact study will *inter alia* analyse the effects of enlargement on the EU policies.

[54] Emphasis added.

[55] However, as a result of the elections of 26 October 1996, Malta has decided not to open negotiations on accession on the scheduled date.

European Union. It may be expected, in the light of the Copenhagen criteria, that in this statement the Commission will first address the quality of the democratic institutions in the applicant country, the application of the rule of law, human rights, protection of minorities and the state of relations with the neighbouring countries and will then turn to the functioning of the market economy. It is certain that the main substantive part of the Opinion will be devoted to an analysis of specific sectors such as customs union, taxation, agriculture, transport, social affairs, environment and consumer protection, competition, Second and Third Pillar of the TEU, etc. The Opinion will also include an evaluation of the applicant's capacity to adopt and implement the *acquis communautaire*.

It is precisely for the preparation of the Commission's views that for the first time in the history of the EU enlargement's practice, the Commission has sent an exhaustive global Questionnaire to all the applicant countries. This Questionnaire was sent in April 1996 and is identical for all applicant countries. It first addresses the political conditions for membership but the major substantive part of the Questionnaire is devoted to domains belonging more or less to classic Community activities. A series of questions also relates to foreign and security policy[56] and to justice and home affairs.

A striking feature of the structure and contents of the Questionnaire is its large size and great number of questions (more than 150 pages with well over 1,000 questions). The questions are very detailed and specific. Broadly speaking, two kinds of questions can be distinguished. First, the Commission wants to obtain general background information, often in the form of statistics, such as data on demography, production, trade, employment, health care, economic growth, school population, etc. Secondly, for each sector falling within the activities of the EU, precise information is requested. Questions on the legislative and administrative framework are asked in view of the compatibility with EU policies and rules. A striking characteristic here is the strong emphasis on the legal dimension. The Commission is indeed interested in the state of law in the various sectors concerned and even more so in the application and enforcement of the legislation in practice (see the detailed questions on public procurement, environment, consumer protection, etc.). Much attention is therefore paid to application, management in practice and control of the existing legal rules. In this respect the CEECs are asked to refer to the mandates, staff resources and staff qualifications.

It is interesting to compare the White Paper approach on approximation of laws (see Gaudissart and Sinnaeve, below, p. 41) with that of the Questionnaire. As the White Paper is a guideline for harmonization and preparation for the Internal Market, one could have expected that the Questionnaire would have been mainly based on this document and on how far implementation of the approximation recommendations has been achieved. This, however,

---

[56] For an account as to how the CEECs react towards the EU's policy under the Second Pillar, see Dunay, Kende and Szücs, below, p. 316.

was not the strategy followed by the Commission. References to the White Paper are not made in a systematic way in the Questionnaire but only occasionally, probably depending on the D-G of the Commission which was in charge of the drafting of a particular section of the Questionnaire.

Between the White Paper and the Questionnaire, however, similar approaches can also be discerned. The White Paper already emphasized that harmonization of legislation alone is not sufficient for the functioning of an internal market. A whole infrastructure, with administration, control, sanctions, etc. is needed. Consequently, a number of questions in the Questionnaire specifically deal with the application and enforcement of existing legislation. This may indicate a concern by the Commission which was perhaps less apparent during the previous enlargement negotiations. Are the CEECs able to put into practice the *acquis communautaire* in terms of human resources? The broad scope of the questions, intended to cover all aspects of society, also indicate that, according to the Commission, accession needs to be seen in the context of the society as a whole. In other words it is not sufficient to harmonize and align legislation in the texts but a whole new legal environment, infrastructure, and indeed legal culture, have to be created which makes accession a workable objective.

By July 1996 the Commission had received from the applicant countries the answers to the questionnaires. Some of these answers have been further refined as a result of additional questions by the Commission on various issues. As regards the CEECs' applications, it can be said that the Commission has now sufficient data available to prepare and finalize the drafts of its Opinion. The Opinion which the Commission formulates on the basis of the answers to the Questionnaire must be distinguished from the Commission's Final Opinion addressed to the Council once the negotiations are completed. If the Commission accepts what has been negotiated, it will observe that 'the provisions so agreed are fair and proper'. All Final Opinions in the past enlargement practice drew attention to the specific legal implications of accession: in joining the European Union the applicant accepts without reserve the Treaty on European Union and all the decisions taken within the framework of the Treaties establishing the Communities and the EU. The Commission further reiterates in the Final Opinion the principles of direct applicability and primacy of Community law which are the cornerstones of the legal order of the Community and also recalls the procedures which exist for ensuring uniform interpretation of Community law. The application of these principles and procedures is a *conditio sine qua non* to guarantee the effectiveness and unity of Community law. Clearly, enforcement of Community law through the domestic courts of the new member states presupposes that judges are trained or prepared to be trained in economic law and other related law areas. Most CEECs still have a long way to go in this respect. Finally, the Commission will observe in the Final Opinion, as it did with regard to previous enlargements, that 'the principles of liberty, democracy and respect of human rights and fundamental freedoms and the rule of law . . . constitute

... essential elements of membership of the (European) Union'. Moreover, accession will be seen as a way to deepen the solidarity between the peoples and to help to strengthen peace and freedom in Europe.

b. Assent by the European Parliament

In the original EEC Treaty the European Parliament was totally absent from the accession procedure. It was only with the introduction of the Single European Act (1987) that the procedural rules were changed. From then onwards assent of Parliament has been required. Approval of an application for accession by Parliament is given with an absolute majority of its members. This new rule was for the first time applied on the occasion of the enlargement with the EFTA countries.[57]

Parliament's power to assent to or reject an application for membership is of fundamental political importance. Therefore, Parliament will want to be kept informed of the negotiations. The formal act of giving assent is situated late in the enlargement procedure after the Commission's Final Opinion but before the Council's Decision. From a legal point of view it could be argued that Parliament's assent is in the first place on the principle of accession but in fact, since the formal assent comes late in the accession procedure – that is to say after the negotiation process – Parliament's intervention should not be underestimated.[58] This interpretation also allows Parliament to express its first views early in the procedure. As far as the request for accession by the CEECs is concerned it may be expected that Parliament will follow with particular attention whether the applicants satisfy the political conditions (human rights protection, rule of law, democratic institutions, relations between the applicant and neighbouring countries),[59] although this by no means precludes Parliament from debating more economically-orientated issues or any other issue arising from membership.

c. Decision of the Council of the European Union

In the accession procedure the Decision of the Council constitutes an essential formal step. It must be taken by unanimity. Such a decision stipulates that the Council accepts a) the application(s) for admission; b) the conditions of admission; and c) the adjustments to the Treaties on which the EU is founded. The decision is made conditional on the acceptance of the agreement between the member states and the applicant.

---

[57] An important step was the adoption of the Hänsch-Report on the enlargement strategy, A3-0189/92, see for more details M. Telo, 'Introduction' in Telo (ed.), *L'Union européenne et les défis de l'élargissement*, Brussels, ULB, 1994, 17–18; see also in the same publication: K. Hansch, 'Le Parlement européen et l'élargissement de la Communauté au cours des années quatre-vingt-dix: aspects politiques et institutionnels', 41–54.

[58] See in this sense D. Booss and J. Forman, 'Enlargement: Legal and Procedural Aspects', *CMLRev.* (1995), 99–100.

[59] The European Parliament, for example, has on several occasions expressed its concern about the quality of democratic institutions in Slovakia, see Resolution B4-1389–1419/RC 1 of 12 December 1996.

d. 'Treaty of Accession', 'Act of Accession' and 'Final Act'

The Treaty of Accession is signed between the member states (*not* the Community or Union) and applicant State(s). It establishes the conditions of admission and adjustments to be made to the Treaties.

The Treaty of Accession is composed of two parts. The 'Treaty' proper is very short but in an Act annexed to the Treaty the detailed conditions of accession and the adjustments to be made are set out. In all the previous accessions the Treaties of Accession only contained three similar articles and it may be expected that for the CEECs the same pattern will be followed.

- First it is stipulated that the applicant country has become a member of the EU and that the Act concerning the conditions of accession and the adjustments forms an integral part of the Treaty. A further provision makes the rights and obligations of the member states and the powers and jurisdiction of the institutions of the Union applicable in respect of the Treaty of Accession;
- Article 2 concerns ratification and entry into force of the Treaty;
- The last article deals with the languages in which the Treaty is drafted and the deposit of the Treaty.

From a quantitative as well as from a qualitative point of view the 'Act of Accession' annexed to the Treaty is really the main, substantive document in the accession procedure.

The structure and composition of the Act is largely as follows. It contains a number of principles, provisions on adjustments to the Treaties and formal adaptations to acts adopted by the institutions (as indicated in an annex). An important part of the Act also concerns the 'Transitional measures' allowing temporary derogations to the EC obligations. A last part of the Act relates to provisions on the implementation of the Act (institutional provisions and applicability of acts of the institutions). 'Annexes' and 'Protocols' are added to the Act. In the Acts, Annexes and Protocols, there is an increasing tendency for precision in the formulation of the conditions and adjustments.[60] It may be expected that the documents related to the Accession of the CEECs will confirm this tendency.

The Final Act is a (short) text signed by the plenipotentiaries of the member states and applicant(s) which acknowledges that the Treaty, Act, Annexes and Protocols have been drawn up and adopted. The Final Act takes the form of a 'Table of contents' of what has been agreed upon and is followed by a list of Declarations (joint or unilateral). Moreover, the Final Act also includes an information and consultation procedure for the adoption of decisions and measures to be taken during the period preceding accession.

---

[60] For the first enlargements the 'Annexes' and 'Protocols' cover respectively 99 p and 46 p; for Spain and Portugal this amounts to 347 p.; for Austria, Finland, Sweden (and Norway), notwithstanding the EEA Agreement, 349 p.

e. Ratification and entry into force of the Accession Treaty

Ratification by applicants and member states takes place according to their respective domestic constitutional procedures.[61]

Once all the instruments of ratification have been deposited, confirmation of the date of entry into force of the Treaty of Accession is published in the *Official Journal of the European Union.*[62]

IV. CONCLUSION

It is in many respects an interesting phenomenon to see how the 'association dimension' of the Europe Agreements has gradually, but on the whole remarkably quickly, made it possible to turn these agreements into pre-accession frameworks. Through a rare combination of political, economic, legal and even psychological factors the indispensable pre-accession atmosphere has been created. Many contributions in this book offer an in-depth analysis of the various facets of the evolution of the Europe Agreements towards pre-accession agreements.

Whatever the follow-up of the Amsterdam Summit, it is obvious that the EU enlargement eastwards needs careful preparation. It is probably in nobody's interest – and certainly not in that of the CEECs – to achieve enlargement as part of a strategy to undermine the EU itself (see also de La Serre and Lequesne, below, pp. 356–7). The need for a workable EU after enlargement has added a very crucial dimension to the agenda of the Intergovernmental Conference. The main problem, of course, is that the handling of this issue also implies a clear perception and political vision of the nature of the ongoing integration and cooperation process in Europe. Perhaps this is not the most propitious moment for this type of fundamental consideration. As a matter of fact, it should already have been made at the occasion of the enlargement towards the EFTA–countries. However, the size of the political, economic and legal implications of further eastward enlargement is such that fundamental reflections on the EU objectives and functioning of EU institutions have necessarily to be addressed. One can only express the hope that this is done in a sufficient and adequate way before the particularly complex accession machinery is put in motion.

Finally, and it has already often been said, enlargement will involve a considerable increase in the EU budget expenditure and affect some of the

---

[61] Negotiations for accession have in a number of instances been followed by a referendum in the applicant state (for example Denmark, Ireland, Finland, Sweden and Austria). Failure of the referendum in Norway in November 1994 meant no accession of Norway to the European Union. Thus far member states of the European Union have never organized a referendum on the question of further enlargement.

[62] As far as the accession of Austria, Finland and Sweden is concerned the Treaty of Accession already stipulated that it would enter into force on 1 January 1995 provided that all the instruments of ratification had been deposited before that date. The information concerning the date of entry into force of the Treaty of Accession of Austria, Finland and Sweden was published in *OJ*, 1995, L 1.

fundamental EU policies such as agriculture, structural funds, movement of persons, etc. It is on these very sensitive issues that negotiations may prove to be very difficult and that a large portion of flexibility will be needed. This will almost certainly result in long transitional periods for certain Treaty segments. Finding the right balance without putting in danger the basic EU objectives will no doubt occupy a prominent place in the EU programme for the immediate years to come. Last but not least, certainly in the hypothesis of a massive enlargement eastwards, the EU will have to demonstrate a very considerable degree of creativity to accommodate the legitimate concerns of those which, for one reason or another, are excluded, particularly Russia. Accessions of CEECs which are in the first place contemplated from a geopolitical perspective should be handled with the greatest care by the EU. Accessions which are not well prepared and accessions for mainly strategic reasons should be avoided. Eastward enlargement cannot be addressed *against* a particular country. Such accessions will not necessarily 'extend the zone of stability in Europe, thus contributing to security and peace throughout the continent'.[63]

---

[63] This paraphrases an often made statement in EU official and semi-official documents, see for example, Commission 'Enlargement: Questions and Answers', Europe Documents, *Agence Europe*, 9 August 1996.

Part II

EUROPE AGREEMENTS AND
PRE-ACCESSION STRATEGIES

A

General Framework

2

LEGAL FRAMEWORK FOR RELATIONS BETWEEN THE EUROPEAN UNION AND CENTRAL AND EASTERN EUROPE: GENERAL ASPECTS

Peter-Christian Müller-Graff[1]

I. INTRODUCTION

The legal framework which has been constructed so far in order to structure the relations between the European Union and Central and Eastern Europe is in fact itself an element of those dynamically developing relations.[2] The form and intensity of that framework have developed according to – basically – two different categories, which can be distinguished more and more clearly not only in legal terms, but also along a geopolitical split between East Central Europe and the countries of Eastern Europe beyond this central area.

The division between these two categories corresponds to the basic difference in the ultimate political orientation of relations, at least as presently

[1] Professor, Universität Heidelberg.

[2] See for the dynamic developments, e.g. Institut Universitaire International Luxembourg, *L'Intégration Européenne et la Révolution de l'Europe de l'Est*, 1991; J.-C. Gautron (ed.), *Les Relations Communauté Européenne – Europe de l'Est*, 1991; M. Brunner, 'Das Verhältnis der Europäischen Gemeinschaften zur Reformpolitik in Mittel- und Osteuropa', in FIW (ed.), *Mittel- und Osteuropa im marktwirtschaftlichen Umbruch*, 1991, 1; M. Anderson, J.J. Hesse, J.-C. Gautron, S. Estrin, P.-C. Müller-Graff and M. Moran, *The Legal, Economic and Administrative Adaptation of Central European Countries to the European Community*, 1993; F. Cameron, 'Die Politik der EG gegenüber den Staaten Mittel- und Südosteuropas', in Weidenfeld (ed.), *Demokratie und Marktwirtschaft in Osteuropa*, 1993, 353; R. Hrbek, 'Die Rolle der EG beim Aufbau einer gesamteuropäischen Ordnung', in Jakobeit and Yenal (eds), *Gesamteuropa*, 1993, 581; Müller-Graff (ed.), *East Central European States and the European Communities: Legal Adaptation to the Market Economy*, 1993; W. Weidenfeld and M. Huterer, *Eastern Europe: Challenges – Problems – Strategies*, 1993; M. Maresceau and E. Montaguti, 'The Relations between the European Union and Central and Eastern Europe: A Legal Appraisal', *CMLRev.* (1995), 1327; W. Weidenfeld (ed.), *Mittel- und Osteuropa auf dem Weg in die Europäische Union*, 1995; F. Mádl and P.-C. Müller-Graff (eds), *Hungary – From Europe Agreement to a Member Status in the European Union*, 1996; P.-C. Müller-Graff and A. Stepniak (eds), *Poland and the European Union – Between Association and Membership*, 1996; see also M. Lesage, *Constitutions d'Europe centrale, orientale et balte*, 1995.

viewed by the respective Eastern State or the Union. This orientation is either towards potential Union membership (or, at least, some defined status within the Union) or towards a relationship *without* this perspective. This distinction in the strategic perspective of relations finds a parallel in whether the legal core of the relationship is characterized by the existence of a so-called Europe Agreement, or alternatively by the existence – or even the non-existence – of another kind of agreement, in particular a so-called Partnership and Co-operation Agreement. In this sense, a dividing line[3] is becoming increasingly visible in the establishment of the new international order in Europe as pursued by the European Union. It is a dividing line which seems to evolve as a result of the interests of the individual East European States on one side, and the Union's own perception of its basic political character, in terms of values, current situation and capacities, on the other.

Hence, there are – at present – ten States which are seeking membership or at least a defined status within the Union. They comprise, from North to South, Estonia, Latvia, Lithuania, Poland, Czechia, Slovakia, Hungary, Slovenia, Romania and Bulgaria. It should be noted that – with the exception of Romania – all these States either have a common land border with a Union State, or at least a facing coastline. Romania has common borders with two candidate States, Hungary and Bulgaria. Beyond this line, relations between the Union and East European States have only partially led to a defined legal framework, and this has been in the looser form of a Partnership and Co-operation Agreement, namely in the case of Russia, Ukraine, Belarus and Moldavia.[4] This looser form is revealed both in the substantial provisions and the dispute settlement mechanism. At the moment, not even such a bridge can reasonably be built to link up with the elements of former Yugoslavia.

This chapter on the legal framework will concentrate on the relations between the Union and the ten Agreement States, but certain differences as compared with the legal framework of relations between the Union and other East European States will also be mentioned where appropriate. The following observations are in three parts: first the role of law in these relations will be briefly looked at in general (II), before secondly analysing the different steps in the development of relations since 1989, as far as their legal nature is concerned (III) and, finally examining the relationship between several of those steps (IV).

II. LAW AS THE BASIS OF RELATIONS BETWEEN THE UNION AND EASTERN EUROPE

As mentioned above, law is only one element in the relations between the European Union, East Central Europe and the rest of Eastern Europe, but

---

[3] Expression used by M. Maresceau and E. Montaguti (note 2), 1329.
[4] See previous note at 1338 et seq. For the special situation in Russia and its neighbours in the CIS see S.A. Karaganow, *Russia – The State of Reforms*, 1993; G. Jawlinskij, *Reform von unten – Die neue Zukunft Rußlands*, 1994.

it is by no means an unimportant one. On the contrary, it is precisely the law which is expected to provide a permanent, peaceful and stable basis for the relations between States, peoples and individuals, just as it does within the European Union itself.

A. The role of law in general

Non-lawyers may ask: What is so special about law? This is a rather general and timeless question. A tentative answer in our context might point out that, first, law policy is peace policy; secondly, any legal rule is devised to steer the conduct of the addressees along a certain path until new rules emerge; and thirdly, the fact that a legal rule which is negotiated between independent partners provides a certain guarantee for the reasonableness of such a binding rule.

The drafting of legal provisions involves an intellectual and ethical challenge in terms of defining self-interest; in other words, it requires the best capacities available. Hence, legal rules developed as a result of these efforts constitute at least the opportunity to work towards the best possible idealistic order, as well as the most reasonable path to be followed in a given historical situation. This has as an important consequence a certain reduction in the complexity of possible conduct by the addressees in general,[5] and particularly in the relations between States and international organizations, which are always threatened by changes in political majorities, discretion and whims. Treaties serve as a reminder of the envisaged conduct that has been agreed upon.

On the other hand, it is also clear that the price for the stability offered by legal rules is the restriction of possible options in a given situation. Legal agreements might even stabilize and protract a situation that one partner considered to be only provisional. Hence, in rapidly developing historical periods, the shaping of legal frameworks requires, in addition to the usual care, a prudent combination of stability and flexibility; besides some binding commitments there must be unilateral leeway.

B. Law in the context of relations with Eastern Europe

This general ambivalence of legal rules has also been understood as providing a crucial opportunity, but at the same time involving a certain risk, in relation to the evolution of the relations between the European Communities and their member states on the one side and the CEECs on the other. Parties have been aware of their dual characteristics since the very beginning of the new epoch.

---

[5] For the theory of the reduction of complexity in social conduct see N. Luhmann, *Vertrauen. Ein Mechanismus zur Reduktion sozialer Komplexität*, 1968.

III. THE DIFFERENT STAGES IN THE DEVELOPMENT OF A LEGAL FRAMEWORK FOR RELATIONS BETWEEN THE UNION AND EASTERN EUROPE

When one looks at this extremely dynamic development since 1989, at least five different steps, each with its own legal character, may be distinguished.

A. Autonomous adaptation

The first phase, which began immediately after the epoch-making about-turn was one of autonomous adaptation of the political, economic and legal order of the relevant CEECs to the political, economic and legal order of Western European States in general, and to that of the European Communities in particular.[6]

The legal nature of this conduct on the part of CEECs was that of a unilateral process, with no binding commitments of these States under international law. It is thus not surprising that the legal implications of this political will to transform a dictatorial political system into a democratic society and to transform a command economy into a market economy, were recognized in a highly individual way by the various States. In each case, this depended on the specific national characteristics and the factual points of departure in 1989, the respective firmness of the political will for transition, but also on the different national backgrounds and experience of the Western advisers who were consulted, sometimes chosen rather randomly.

As a result, different methods, speeds and solutions were adopted, in particular when shaping the legal framework for the adaptation to the market economy. A study covering this period conducted by a working group of the European Community Studies Association shows that different national choices were made as to the form and intensity of privatization and the residual role and amount of public enterprise,[7] as well as on the degree of deregulation and the protection of public goods and interests,[8] and different answers were given to the question of the proper relationship between a competition-driven

---

[6] See M. Anderson, J.J. Hesse, J.-C. Gautron, S. Estrin, P.-C. Müller-Graff and M. Moran, *The Legal, Economic and Administrative Adaptations of Central European Countries to the European Community*, 1993; P.-C. Müller-Graff (ed.), *East Central European States and the European Communities. Legal Adaptation to the Market Economy*, 1993; H.-H. Herrnfeld, *Recht europäisch*, 1995; see also M. Lesage, *Constitutions d'Europe centrale, orientale et balte*, 1995; A. Vida, 'Ungarns freiwillige Anpassung an das Europarecht', *Wirtschaft und Recht in Osteuropa* (1994), 4; M. Hoškova, 'Legal Aspects of the Integration of the Czech Republic and Slovakia into European Security and Economic Structures', *German Yearbook of International Law* (1994), 68.

[7] P.-C. Müller-Graff, in Müller-Graff (ed.), *East Central European States and the European Communities. Legal Adaptation to the Market Economy*, 1993, 22 referring to the reports of J. Frackowiak, T. Sarközy (see also T. Sarközy, *The Right of Privatizations in Hungary (1989–1993)*, 1994; A. Petsche, *Recht in Ost und West* (1996), 69), H. Szurgacz, J. Zemanek.

[8] P.-C. Müller-Graff (note 7), 25 with references to the reports of J. Frackowiak, T. Sarközy, H. Szurgacz, J. Zemánek; see also P. Hardi, *Environmental Protection in East-Central Europe*, 1994.

economy and public industrial policy by means of subsidies, tax legislation and other measures.[9]

However, this study also shows that, despite all these differences, the respective Eastern European countries tried to establish legal rules, institutions and methods which were well known within the legal order of the European Communities and compatible with it,[10] such as the concepts of company law and competition law, as well as setting up competition offices – with a parallel to the relevant Directorate General IV of the Commission, or to national institutions like the German *Bundeskartellamt*.

B. The conclusion of Europe Agreements

The second step, which began in 1991, was marked by the gradual preparation or conclusion of so-called Europe Agreements, between the European Communities and their member states on one side and the individual East European States on the other.[11] These Agreements, with the legal character of association agreements,[12] differ from ordinary or qualified trade agreements such as the Partnership and Cooperation Agreements mentioned above. The pioneer Europe Agreements were those concluded with Hungary, Poland and Czechoslovakia, the latter being replaced by separate Agreements with the respective successors of that State after its dissolution in 1993.[13] These Agreements were followed by six Europe Agreements with Romania, Bulgaria, Slovenia and the three Baltic States: which rather eliminated the privileged character of the pioneer Agreements. All of these Agreements were shaped according to the same basic pattern in their objectives, content and legal nature.

This step put the relationship between the Communities and the respective Eastern States on mutually binding ground, that is legally founded in international *law*. From the point of view of the Union, these Agreements are mixed agreements, in the sense that the Communities as well as the member states are contracting parties.[14] This is due to the division of competences within the Union, as the Agreements not only touch the competence of the Communities to conclude an association (e.g. Article 238 EC Treaty) but also include political cooperation, which falls within the competence of the member states. However, in order to avoid a considerable delay to their entry into force as a consequence of the necessity of a burdensome ratification procedure in all member states, the part covered by the exclusive competences of the Communities was put into force earlier in the form of so-called Interim Agreements.[15]

---

[9] P.-C Müller-Graff (note 7), 27 with reference to the above-mentioned reports.
[10] Ibid., 48.
[11] For an analysis see M. Maresceau, in Müller-Graff (ed.) above note 7, 209.
[12] Ibid., 210. The chosen legal basis is Art. 238 EC Treaty.
[13] See M. Maresceau and E. Montaguti, *CMLRev.* (1995), 1329.
[14] See M. Maresceau, above note 11, 212.
[15] See M. Maresceau and E. Montaguti, *CMLRev.* (1995), 1329.

The objectives and the substantial content of a Europe Agreement are essentially different from the subject matters dealt with in the first stage. The obligation on the Agreement State to approximate its legal order to that of the Community does not occupy a dominant position in a Europe Agreement, although a small, rather 'soft' compatibility provision is included, in the sense that the respective State shall act to ensure that its future legislation is as far as possible compatible with Community legislation. Instead, the Europe Agreements aim at the mutually binding establishment of a political dialogue and a developed free trade area between the contracting parties. As will be discussed later, they do not explicitly aim at accession.

C. Declaration of accession criteria

The third step worth noting in the development of the relationship was the declaration of the general criteria for accession by the European Council at the Copenhagen summit in June 1993.[16] This opened a new policy approach on the part of the Communities and their member states towards the Agreement States, with the prospect of a potential membership and the organization of so-called 'structured relationships' in the sense of involving the associated countries progressively in the Union's work in areas of common interest. This declaration reveals a kind of conditional courage in the Union which is comparable to the situation regarding convergence criteria for accession to the Monetary Union:[17] an ambitious perspective is formulated, but a number of demanding criteria serve as a safeguard against imprudent actions.

As far as the legal nature of the declaration of general accession criteria is concerned, it is a purely unilateral act of the European Council, without any contractual commitment to accept an associated State as a member if the criteria – which are open to interpretation in any case – are met. However, if such were to occur, it does not seem very likely that accession could politically be withheld, quite apart from the question of whether an associated State which fulfills the requirements could rely on a rule similar to the doctrine of promissory estoppel.

D. Presentation of the White Paper

In June 1995 came the fourth step, which was the presentation of a White Paper by the Commission on the Preparation of the Associated Countries of Central and Eastern Europe for Integration into the Internal Market of the Union.[18] This Paper sets out in detail, and very thoroughly, the approximation measures that are recommended for adoption by the associated countries in order to improve their chances of fulfilling one of the general criteria for accession to the Union, namely the so-called market criterion.

---

[16] *Bull. EC* 6-1993, 12.
[17] See Art. 109 j EC Treaty.
[18] COM(95) 163 final, 3 May 1995.

Again, the legal nature of the White Paper is that of a purely unilateral act on the side of the Union, without any contractual commitment to accept an associated State as a member if the recommended approximation measures are taken. However, it is once more doubtful whether the conformity of the conduct of an associated State with these recommendations could be disregarded in the case of negotiations on membership.

E.   Negotiations for membership

Finally as a fifth step, not taken as yet, negotiations for membership will start with those States that are considered by the Union to fulfil the general criteria.

IV.   THE RELATIONSHIP BETWEEN THE EUROPE AGREEMENTS, THE GENERAL CRITERIA AND THE WHITE PAPER

Since this last step has not been taken yet, closer attention should now be paid to the relationship between the three elements that represent the present status of the relations between the Union and the CEECs, namely the Europe Agreements (A), the general criteria for accession (B) and the White Paper (C).

A.   The Europe Agreements

Turning to the first of these elements, the mutually binding Europe Agreements, three questions arise. First, what objectives are pursued by these Agreements? Second, what means are devised by the Agreements to realize these objectives? Third, has the implementation of these Agreements worked or has it encountered problems?

As far as the objectives are concerned, they are clear and yet in one essential point they remain open.

It is clear that the core of the Europe Agreements aims at an association,[19] in the sense of the (asymmetrically evolving) establishment of an extended free trade area for industrial goods between the Communities and the respective State, and at the provision of an appropriate framework for the political dialogue between the member states and the respective country. This comprises not a simple, but an extended free trade area, since the pattern of the different Agreements contains more features than merely the tariff-free exchange of goods between the partners.

At the same time, the Preambles to the Agreements point to the interest of the respective State in the prospect of eventual membership of the Communities, but without any commitment by the Communities or their member states to these ends. The carefully-worded formulation in the Agreement with Hungary gives an example: 'Having in mind that the final objective of

[19] The Europe Agreements are based on Art. 238 EC Treaty.

Hungary is to become a member of the Community and that this association, in the view of the Parties, will help to achieve this objective'. This means, when analysed legally, that (1) one partner is aware of the intention of the other, but (2) does not incur any corresponding contractual obligation, and (3) that both partners only assess the agreement as helpful for the achievement of the objective of one partner. Hence, there is a certain ambivalence relating to the strategy underlying the Agreements and thus to their interpretation. Should the provisions of the Agreements be seen as part of a dynamic, pre-accession strategy, or rather be understood as part of a longer-lasting status? The first view was taken more or less by the Agreement States from the very beginning. On the other hand, seen from the Communities, the Agreements were not originally devised as part of an accession or pre-accession strategy.[20] On the contrary, they were conceived rather as an *alternative* to membership of the Communities.

If one takes into account this ambivalence of intention, the means contained in the Agreements are open. At all events, the means are shaped according to the prime objectives: that is, as provisions to establish a political dialogue by setting up common institutions, as well as provisions to realize the free movement of goods. Whereas, in principle, the EC Treaty provisions on free movement of goods are quoted explicitly, the Treaty obligations concerning the free movement of workers, services, payment and capital, as well as the right of establishment for self-employed people and companies, and the approximation of law, are not copied. Although all these elements are alluded to, and partially or embryonically included in the Agreements, both sides were, for many understandable reasons, reluctant to incur EC Treaty-like obligations in these matters. However, far-reaching rules on competition and state aids were inserted as a necessary consequence of the acceptance of the principle of free movement of goods.

As far as the implementation of these Agreements is concerned, it may still be too early to make an overall evaluation. However, studies such as the one presently being conducted within the European Communities Studies Association[21] show that the speed and intensity of implementation seem to be as different as the various situations in the Agreement States and their capacity and willingness to cope with this great challenge. This would not be a surprising observation by any means; it is simply the result of the extension of the Europe Agreement model to so many States at different levels of development.

B. Declaration of the general criteria for accession

While these Agreements form an accepted and legally binding framework, the second element one should examine in the relationship between the

---

[20] See also M. Maresceau and E. Montaguti, *CMLRev.* (1995), 1332.

[21] European Community Studies Association: Study 'From Europe Agreements to a Member Status in the European Union' (to be published).

Union and CEECs is the unilateral declaration of the European Council on the general criteria for accession for Agreement States.[22] What is their relation to the Europe Agreements, and what is their specific content?

As far as the relation to the Europe Agreements is concerned, the declaration made by the European Council in Copenhagen in 1993 and supplemented in Essen in 1994, contains essentially a political reorientation of the strategy of the Union, and hence a reinterpretation of the Agreements from the side of the Union.[23] Once again, however, this is without any contractually binding commitment. The Agreements, originally devised by the Community as an alternative to membership, have been turned into and used politically as a kind of pre-basis for possible future membership. Accession has even become a common political objective, while the Agreements have remained unchanged in their legal substance. Be that as it may, one thing remains clear: only Agreement States are taken into consideration for member status, and not the Eastern European States beyond this line.

Among the substantial general criteria for accession,[24] three deserve particular attention. First, there is the ability of an associated country to assume the obligations of membership by satisfying the economic and political conditions required, including the capacity to take on such obligations of membership as adherence to the aims of a political, economic and monetary union. Secondly, the existence of a functioning market economy as well as the capacity to meet competitive pressure and market forces within the Union are presupposed. Thirdly, there must be stability of institutions guaranteeing democracy, the rule of law, human rights, and respect for and protection of minorities. The two other conditions relate to the necessity of cooperation at the intra-regional level, among Agreement States, and to the capacity of the Union to admit new members while maintaining the momentum of European integration.

As far as the first criterion is concerned, namely the ability of an associated country to assume the obligations of membership this is clearly a matter of course and – at the same time – a very demanding requirement for the States concerned.

It is a matter of course because the capacity fully to take on the obligations of membership has always been a precondition for accession in all cases of enlargement of the Communities and the Union so far.

Nevertheless, this is a very demanding requirement in the present context, both because the current standard of obligations in the Union is higher than in all prior enlargements and, moreover, because all East European States still carry, to different degrees, the burden of their recent history, affecting their economic, political, legal, social, and cultural structures.[25] On the other hand, it is evident that the basic constitutional framework of European integration

---

[22] *Bull. EC* 6-1993, 12–13.
[23] See also M. Maresceau and E. Montaguti, *CMLRev.* (1995), 1332.
[24] *Bull. EC* 6-1993, 13.
[25] For the different starting points see, e.g. P.-C. Müller-Graff, above note 7, 17.

must, in principle, be recognized in the same way by all members. Otherwise, the Union could not exist as a political, economic and legal Community of *equally* entitled and equally committed members. Nevertheless, the question remains whether *all* provisions in the Treaties making up the Union have to be rated as belonging to the basic – constitutional – framework. In principle, this question should be answered affirmatively, since otherwise the construction of the Union would have to provide for distinctions in the quality of membership and in the participation in decisions; it would thus be threatened by the possibility of incoherent policies. Consequently, the idea of a minimal core of membership seems to contain more problems than solutions. That danger has already appeared in the field of social policy, with Britain abstaining from the Agreement on Social Policy between all other member states. However, this is and should remain an exception for the reasons mentioned. A comparable situation is foreseeable with regard to a Monetary Union between only some members of the Union; however, this case is different in so far as, in principle, all member states have agreed to the basic terms, although it is likely that some or even most of them will not fulfil the strict criteria[26] for qualifying to enter the Monetary Union in 1999. Although this model of generally accepted terms which nonetheless leave a legal opening for different speeds seems to be preferable to the option of concentric circles, as in the case of social policy, it could result in a lasting situation of different types of participation; this could turn into a *de facto* situation of concentric circles around an inner core of the most integrated States.[27] In any case, an accession model with clauses for adjustment periods is preferable.

The second important criterion is that of the existence of a functioning market economy and the capacity to cope with competitive pressure within the Union, which is strongly connected to the first criterion. Since the very basis of the Union is the internal market,[28] the fulfilment of the manifold obligations of the member states in order to make the existence of this market possible is inseparably connected, economically and politically, with the existence of a market order and a national economy strong enough to withstand Community-wide competition. The fate of the former East German economy may serve as an illustrative example of what happens to an economy that lacks this ability. While in the case of East Germany the breakdown of non-competitive industry was, and still is, compensated by national solidarity within one people, it hardly seems realistic to expect an equally strong sense of solidarity on the part of all those Union States that are better off towards newly admitted CEECs. Hence, the requirement that the economy as a whole in a candidate State must be able to meet competition is not only a

---

[26] See Art. 109 j EC Treaty.

[27] See P.-C. Müller-Graff, 'Verfassungsziele der EG', in *Handbuch des EG-Wirtschaftsrechts*, 1993, A I 41; P.-C. Müller-Graff, 'Deutsche Einigung und Europäische Integration', in B. Kohler-Koch (ed.), *Die Osterweiterung der EG*, 1991, 54.

[28] See Art. 9 EC Treaty and Art. 7 A EC Treaty; P.-C. Müller-Graff, *Binnenmarktziel und Rechtsordnung – Binnenmarktrecht*, 1989.

reasonable, but also a crucial prerequisite for full accession to the internal market.

The third important general criterion for accession, namely the stability of institutions guaranteeing democracy, the rule of law, human rights and respect for and protection of minorities, is again inseparably connected with the ability to take on the obligations of membership, and again it is both a matter of course as well as a challenging requirement for the States concerned.

It is connected to the first criterion because the Treaties on which the Union is based and which oblige the member states in a number of ways, constitute an economic, social, cultural, legal and political Community which is deeply rooted in the general positive European traditions of democracy, of human rights and of the rule of law. Some examples may illustrate this sufficiently. The Treaties themselves have been ratified by national Parliaments and/or popular referenda, in other words in democratic procedures. The EC Treaty establishes that a directly elected European Parliament is one – and even the first to be listed – of the institutions of the Community that takes part in the political decision-making process;[29] though this role is not given a very firm shape, it may be considered to be self-evident in the Community that it would not be acceptable for political decisions to be taken without any parliamentary involvement. As another example of the foundation of the Union on certain political values, attention may be drawn to the fact that the Treaty on the European Union confirms the obligations of democracy, human rights and the rule of law.[30] The Court of Justice ensures the rule of law[31] and has developed protection of human rights against acts of the Community according to the common constitutional traditions of the member states.[32] It thus nearly goes without saying that any new member of the Union has to comply with these basic principles. One might well add that a Community combining different peoples and States cannot prosper peacefully and efficiently without these rules.

C. The White Paper

The third and last element in the present legal relationship between the European Union and the CEECs to be examined is the White Paper on the Preparation of the Associated Countries of Central and Eastern Europe for Integration into the Internal Market of the Union, mentioned above.[33] This element is not part of a contractually binding framework, but a unilateral declaration on the side of the Union, in this case represented by the

---

[29] See e.g. Art. 137 et seq. EC Treaty; P.-C. Müller-Graff, *Die Direktwahl des europäischen Parlaments*, 2nd ed., 1979.
[30] See Art. F TEU.
[31] See Art. 164 EC Treaty.
[32] See e.g. (1969) ECR 419; (1974) ECR 491; (1976) ECR 1589; (1989) ECR 4285; (1990) ECR I-95.
[33] COM(95) 163 final, 3 May 1995.

Commission. What is its relation to the Europe Agreements, what is its specific content and its effect?

In terms of the relation to the Europe Agreements and the declaration of the general criteria, it is evident that the purpose of the White Paper is not so much connected to the originally undefined strategic perspectives of the Europe Agreements, but rather to the perspectives opened by the formulation of the general criteria for accession which led to the political reorientation[34] of the Agreements. Yet again there is no contractually binding commitment on the part of the Union. The underlying viewpoint of the White Paper is that of a pre-accession strategy for CEECs to help them to become capable of fulfilling, in particular, the general market requirements for accession; now, however, these are put in the much more concrete and highly demanding shape of the White Paper. In this sense, the Paper aims especially at approximating the internal law of those States to the Community legislation on the internal market. While the purpose of the Paper is to provide a guide in order to assist the associated countries in preparing themselves for operating under the requirements of the European Union's Internal Market, the approximation of law alone is not sufficient to create a competitive position for the respective economies and sectors concerned. Moreover, alignment with the Internal Market must be distinguished from accession to the Union, which will involve acceptance of the *acquis communautaire* as a whole, even if it is obvious that Internal Market legislation constitutes the very core of the substantial law of this acquis.

One can even conclude that the White Paper in fact creates a framework for the preparation of and transition to membership, which is comparable to that established earlier by the Agreement on the European Economic Area for the then remaining members of the European Free Trade Association[35] Austria, Sweden and Finland, which are now members of the Union. The question arises why that model of preparation has not been applied in the case of the CEECs. Special treatment may have been justified by reason of the very different previous economic order; however, that system is now gone, even though legislation, judicial enforcement and recognition of law are still under construction. The most convincing explanation refers to the reluctance of the Agreement States themselves: a reluctance born out of fear that the EEA model could turn into a lasting alternative to membership,[36] as in the case of Norway, and hence into the establishment of a permanent outer concentric circle. The White Paper has the further advantage that it leaves a certain leeway to both sides in an extremely dynamic period of development.

The specific content of the White Paper is shaped far more concretely than the general market criterion contained in the declaration of the European Council, and its substance goes further than the framework of obligations undertaken by the East European Agreement States. The White Paper (its

---

[34] See above IVB, p. 34.
[35] This parallel is drawn by M. Maresceau and E. Montaguti, *CMLRev.* (1995), 1336.
[36] Ibid., 1337.

title alludes to the famous White Paper on the Completion of the Internal Market[37]), gives a thorough exposition of the general aspects of the Internal Market and its requirements. It then lists a wide range of very concrete measures in its annex which are recommended to be taken by the candidate States, in order to approximate their legislation to Community internal market law. These recommendations are not individualized, however, according to the different States and their respective situations and needs, but leave the level of 'tailoring' to the country itself.

The outline in the annex comprises, amongst other things, provisions on the free movement of capital, on the free movement and safety of industrial products, on competition, on social policy, on agriculture, on transport, on environmental requirements, on telecommunications and other areas. The annex is extremely detailed, listing in every area concerned the respective directives or regulations as to their objectives, content and implementation problems, and recommending the key measures to be taken. It would not come as a surprise if the efforts to implement these recommendations revealed the different levels of development in the various States, as far as institutions and procedures are concerned.

It is much too early to evaluate the possible effects of the White Paper. The candidate States will most probably take the White Paper as the authoritative position of the Union, and it is likely that their reaction will be to show a strong tendency to comply with the proposals made therein. On the other hand, the White Paper might also serve as a yardstick by which the candidate States can assess much more clearly than by the general criteria whether they are already seriously capable of meeting the obligations of membership, or even of negotiating for the terms of membership. In a positive sense, serious compliance with the recommendations of the White Paper will most probably ease the way to the fifth step: negotiating the terms of membership in the Union. The Paper itself expressly rejects the idea that it is conceived as part of negotiations for accession or that it could prejudice any aspect of such negotiations. As for its relation to the Europe Agreements, it should also be noted that obviously the Paper is not capable of legally changing the contractual relationship set up by the Europe Agreements between the Communities and their member states on one side and the CEECs on the other side.

V. OUTLOOK

Instead of a summary, four remarks concerning the outlook may be sufficient.

A. General objectives

First, accession without stable fulfilment of the criteria of accession is not in the interest of an Agreement State or in the interest of the Union. In theory,

---

[37] Completion of the Internal Market, 1985; see P.-C. Müller-Graff, 'Die Rechtsangleichung zur Verwirklichung des Binnenmarktes', *EuR* (1989), 110.

any future member status of an Agreement State in the Union can be conceived as full member status, or alternatively as some form of limited status in the sense of a 'minimum core membership' or 'junior membership'. In the interest of a legally, economically and politically homogeneous basic composition of the Union, full membership should be the preferred objective. The need for interim solutions should be reserved for extraordinary developments.

B. Differentiation

Secondly, the candidate States are all at different stages of transition, implementation and adaptation. This implies that the fifth step, namely negotiating the terms of membership, had better not be tackled for all East European States at the same time. It would be preferable to tailor the procedure according to the individual level of development of each country in terms of compatibility with the Union; every application should be judged on its own merits.

C. Increasing the capability of the Union

Thirdly, negotiations should not (and will not) be opened before the Union has successfully finished the Intergovernmental Conference, whereby the Union aims to increase its own institutional and procedural capacity to cope with an enlargement to the East. It seems clear, after all, that forging and implementing the future status of CEECs within the Union is not just a challenge for the East European States but also for the stability and the success of the Union itself.

D. Inspiring a climate of new European dynamism

Fourthly and finally, the development of the relations between the Union and the Agreement States should be considered as a great chance to inspire, to create and to win a climate of new self-generating economic and political dynamism and of new self-confidence for all East and West European States involved in this process and for the Union as a whole. The development of Eastern Europe may seem a huge challenge, and it certainly is that, but the even bigger challenge lies in the impressive dynamism in the East of Asia and in the USA. The transformation of Eastern Europe carries with it a great opportunity to stimulate a new impetus for Europe in relation to its global competition and cooperation with Asia and North America. A proper legal framework cannot be a substitute for this impetus, but it can contribute to this prospect.

3

THE ROLE OF THE WHITE PAPER
IN THE PREPARATION OF THE
EASTERN ENLARGEMENT

Marc-André Gaudissart[1] and Adinda Sinnaeve[2]

I. INTRODUCTION

With the formal acceptance of the perspective of an eastward enlargement of the European Union, at the 1993 Copenhagen European Council, a new era has begun in the relations of the Community with the associated countries of Central and Eastern Europe. These countries are now regarded as fully-fledged partners in the definition of the post-cold war architecture of the European continent. This evolution marks a significant shift in the Community's policy towards Central and Eastern Europe. While the Twelve had welcomed the transition process on which most Central and Eastern European countries (CEECs) had embarked after the fall of the Berlin Wall, they were, at the same time, remarkably silent on the implications such a process could have for the further development of European integration. No clear long-term perspective was offered to the CEECs. This attitude was reflected, *inter alia*, in the Preamble of the Europe Agreements which had been signed with Czechoslovakia, Hungary, Poland, Bulgaria and Romania.[3] The Contracting

---

[1] Research fellow, Belgian National Fund for Scientific Research (NFWO), European Institute, University of Ghent.
[2] Research fellow, European Institute, University of Ghent. This contribution has been written in the framework of a project financed by the Ministry of the Flemish Community ('administratie economie') and an IUAP-Project between the University of Liège and Ghent.

[3] For an analysis of the EA, see A. Toledano Laredo, 'L'Union européenne, l'ex-Union soviétique, l'Europe centrale et orientale: un aperçu de leurs accords', *CDE* (1994), 543–62; M. Maresceau, 'Europe Agreements: A New Form of Cooperation Between the European Community and Central and Eastern Europe' in P.-C. Müller-Graff (ed.), *East Central European States and the European Communities: Legal Adaptation to the Market Economy*, Baden-Baden, Nomos, 1993, 209–33; F. Benyon, 'Les "accords européens" avec la Hongrie, la Pologne et la Tchécoslovaquie', *RMUE* (1992), No. 2, 25–50; C. Lucron, 'Contenu et portée des Accords entre la Communauté et la Hongrie, la Pologne et la Tchécoslovaquie', *RMC* (1992), 293–9.

Parties underlined the importance they attach to their 'existing traditional links' and to the 'common values that they share' but they were evasive as to the form these relations could take after the consolidation of the ongoing political and economic reforms. No direct link was made between the full achievement of the agreement's goals and a possible accession of the associated country to the EC, such as had been the case e.g. in the agreements concluded with Greece or Turkey, in the early 1960s.[4] The Community and its member states only admitted that accession was the associated country's final objective. Clearly, such a formula did not imply a firm legal or political commitment from the Twelve. As a consequence, reforms in the CEECs were carried out without a clear sense of direction.

The Copenhagen Summit put an end to these uncertainties. By declaring that 'the associated countries in Central and Eastern Europe that so desire shall become members of the European Union . . . as soon as (they will be) able to assume the obligations of membership',[5] the Twelve unequivocally confirmed the CEECs' eligibility for membership. However, they also specified the conditions under which such an enlargement was to take place. Accession implied not only the continuation of the ongoing reforms; it also required the 'stability of institutions guaranteeing democracy, the rule of law, human rights and respect for and protection of minorities' and 'the existence of a functioning market economy as well as the capacity to cope with competitive pressure and market forces within the Union'.[6] Such conditions clearly went beyond the scope of the Europe Agreements, even after the improvements decided in Copenhagen.[7] Additional steps had to be made towards the associated countries if the enlargement promise was to be realized within a reasonable period of time. At the Corfu Summit, in June 1994, the Council and the Commission were thus asked to draw up reports on 'the progress made (by the CEECs) in the process of alignment . . . and on the strategy to be followed with a view to preparing for accession'.[8] The results of that analysis were forwarded to the Essen European Council which decided to give a further impetus to the enlargement process by defining a comprehensive 'pre-accession strategy'. It was the first time in the Union's history that such a formula was applied. It basically consisted of two elements: the development of 'structured relations' between the EU institutions and the associated

---

[4] See Art. 72 of the Athens Agreement (*OJ*, L 26, 18 February 1963) respectively Art. 28 of the Ankara Agreement (*OJ*, L 217, 29 December 1964).

[5] *Bull. EC*, 6-1993, pt I-13.

[6] Ibid. The Twelve mentioned further, as a fundamental prerequisite for an eastward enlargement, the 'Union's capacity to absorb new members while maintaining the momentum of European integration'.

[7] In order to meet in a more adequate way the expectations of their partners, the Twelve had decided to develop structured relationships with the associated countries, to improve the access to their markets and to make the assistance provided through the PHARE programme more effective (see Annex II to the Conclusions of the Presidency, *Bull. EC*, 6-1993, pt I-26). Nevertheless, however positive they might be, these measures were still marginal in view of the magnitude of the task.

[8] *Bull. EU*, 6-1994, pt I-13.

countries of Central and Eastern Europe and the latter's preparation for their progressive integration into the EU Internal Market. If the first pillar of this strategy was, in fact, the mere continuation of the Copenhagen decisions – be it with new means and more consistency than was previously the case – the pillar relating to the Internal Market was, by contrast, wholly new. It aimed at narrowing the gap between the Community rules and practices and those of their partners in a field which is crucial in the evaluation of a candidate's ability to take on the obligations of membership. In Essen, the Community only set out in broad terms the key elements of this task. They were further worked out in a Commission's White Paper of May 1995 on the *'Preparation of the Associated Countries of Central and Eastern Europe for Integration into the Internal Market of the Union'*.[9] The latter – which was presented at the Cannes European Council in June 1995 – forms the cornerstone of the present phase of pre-accession.

It is impossible, within the scope of this contribution, to analyse in detail all the Commission's recommendations.[10] Moreover, this would not make it possible to illuminate fully the innovative character of the approach followed by the European Commission, which is that of a voluntary approximation programme. Hence the importance which is given, in the following pages, to the analysis of the purpose and nature of the White Paper (II). This is an essential prerequisite for a proper understanding of the proposals which are made in that document. It gives a better insight into their underlying rationale and their implications for the associated countries (III). Further, such an analysis also helps to assess the real impact the White Paper may have in the preparation of the Eastern enlargement. Attention will be paid, in this respect, to the substantive and institutional dimensions of that document and to the numerous differences which exist between the White Paper and the EEA Agreement signed with the EFTA countries (IV).

II. OBJECTIVES AND LEGAL NATURE OF THE WHITE PAPER

A. The objectives of the White Paper

The White Paper aims at 'preparing the associated countries of Central and Eastern Europe for integration into the Internal Market' through the implementation of a detailed programme of law approximation. The emphasis on the latter aspect of the EU–CEECs relationship – notwithstanding the fact that it is already covered by several provisions of the Europe Agreements[11] – is a direct consequence of the political reinterpretation of these agreements in Copenhagen. Law approximation in the field of the Internal Market is not

---

[9] See COM(95) 163 final, 3 May 1995 and its Annex issued one week later, COM(95) 163 final/2, 10 May 1995.

[10] Together, the two parts of the White Paper amount to approximately 500 pages.

[11] See Arts 67–69 of the EA with Hungary, 68–70 of the EA with Poland and Arts 69–71 of the EA with Bulgaria, Romania, Slovakia and the Czech Republic.

a goal in itself but rather an instrument that should contribute to achieving a more fundamental objective: the full integration of the CEECs into the EU.

For several years, law approximation was not a priority in the relationship between the EU and the CEECs. The associated countries were much more interested in obtaining better access to the Community market than in achieving a scrupulous alignment with the Community rules. It is true that the EA provisions on law approximation were – and still are – of a rather programmatic nature. They characterize the approximation exercise as a 'major precondition' for the economic integration of the associated countries into the Community but they give no further indication regarding the modalities and timetable, nor do they specify to what extent the CEECs have to comply with the Community rules in order to qualify for EU accession. As a consequence, each associated country could have its own view on – and practice of – law approximation. Moreover, divergences in legislation did not always work in favour of the Community. In some cases, they clearly turned out to be advantageous to the CEECs for the latter could bring their products on the market at more competitive prices than the Community due to the application of less stringent rules regarding e.g. health and safety, working conditions or environmental protection. Under such circumstances, the associated countries did not always feel the need to realize a strict parallelism between their rules and those of the Community. Of course, the Copenhagen Summit brought a fundamental change in that attitude. Once the Twelve had reached a consensus about a possible enlargement of the EU to the East, it appeared quickly to the CEECs that the existing disparities between their legislation and the Community rules were much more an obstacle to EU accession than a possible advantage. The EC member states, on their side, did not want the cohesion of the Internal Market to be endangered by possible distortions in its regulatory framework. Hence, the decision was taken to improve that framework by taking – albeit only in the form of recommendations[12] – additional measures. This is the aim of the White Paper. It pursues to a certain extent a comparable purpose to that of the Commission White Paper of 1985 on the Completion of the Internal Market,[13] namely the removal of all the remaining barriers to free movement. The underlying intentions are clear: in aligning their internal legislation with the Community's rules in such a crucial field as the Internal Market, the associated countries will not only reinforce the competitiveness of their economies and allow business to expand. They will also be better prepared to meet the Copenhagen criteria regarding accession, especially the requirement of 'the existence of a functioning market economy and the capacity to cope with competitive pressures'.[14]

No doubt the White Paper makes a significant contribution to the achievement of these goals but one must not underestimate the magnitude of the

---

[12] See below, II. B, p. 45.
[13] COM(85) 310 final, 14 June 1985.
[14] On the relation of the White Paper to the Europe Agreements respectively the Copenhagen accession criteria, see the contribution of P.-C. Müller-Graff, above, p. 38.

task assigned to the associated countries. As the Commission rightly observes, the degree of economic integration achieved in a 'frontier-free Internal Market' goes further than any other form of cooperation through the establishment of free-trade areas or customs unions. It implies – and relies on – a high level of mutual confidence and the equivalence of regulatory approaches. Therefore, 'any substantial failure to apply the common rules in any part of the Internal Market puts the rest of the system at risk and undermines its integrity'.[15] Thus, some time may be needed before all the requirements for a properly functioning Internal Market are met. This was true for the Community itself: more than ten years have elapsed since the publication of the 1985 White Paper, and yet some measures still need to be taken by the Community, particularly in the field of free movement of persons, taxation and company law.[16] The same applies, *a fortiori*, to the Central and Eastern European countries, which have been engaged, since the early 1990s, in a difficult process of economic and political transformation. The alignment of the CEECs with the EC Internal Market rules and practices can only be achieved through a gradual process. The pace of approximation with the EC legislation has to be adapted, in each country, to the ongoing process of economic reform. This factor, among others, explains the very nature of the White Paper, which is that of a non-binding document.

B. The legal nature of the White Paper

By definition the White Paper has a non-binding character. In each sector of the Internal Market, key measures are identified and approximation scenarios are put forward but they are merely indicative. No timetables are set for the implementation of the Commission recommendations and no sanctions are attached to their possible non-implementation. The associated countries may establish their own priorities and determine their own timetables in the light of their economic, social and political realities. This factor results from a deliberate choice of the Commission. There were, at the time of the adoption of the White Paper, considerable divergences among the CEECs in the scope and type of legislation that had been enacted. In some countries, the approximation task had begun a long time before the White Paper was issued – even before the signature of the Europe Agreements[17] – while other countries had just started with that process. Under such circumstances, the Commission did not consider it appropriate to set up a uniform harmonization programme with strict deadlines to comply with. The Internal Market legislation is listed regardless of what has already been accomplished by the associated countries.

---

[15] See COM(95) 163 final, at pt 2.4.

[16] See, in that respect, the Commission Report on 'The Single Market in 1995', COM(96) 51 final.

[17] This was notably the case of Hungary where a resolution passed in 1990 – still under communist rule – prescribed that all future legislation should be guided by the EC law principles (see Decree 41/1990 of 15 September 1990).

This approach presents, in itself, the important advantage of flexibility. Being a simple 'guide' or a 'general reference document',[18] the White Paper can be used by all prospective member states of the European Union. This was clearly demonstrated by the successive enlargements in the circle of its beneficiaries. When it was adopted, in May 1995, the White Paper was addressed in the first place to the six countries that had already signed Europe Agreements with the EC: Poland, Hungary, the Czech Republic, Slovakia, Bulgaria and Romania. It was later extended to the Baltic States and Slovenia, after the signature of similar agreements respectively in June 1995 and June 1996. At a later stage, it is not excluded that the White Paper might be a reference for all the countries of Central and Eastern Europe, including Albania and the whole territory of the former Yugoslavia. Such an evolution would be a logical consequence of the open character of the White Paper. Since the latter is not tailored to the specific needs of a particular associated country, nothing prevents the Community from extending the recommendations included therein to other countries than its original addressees. However – and this is the other side of the coin – this flexible approach also implies that there is no guarantee that the recommendations of the White Paper will be followed by the associated countries. They are free to follow or to deviate from the Commission proposals. However, it remains to be seen whether the latter hypothesis is a realistic one. The Commission offers, in the White Paper, a thorough analysis of the Internal Market legislation. In view of the CEECs' desire to join the European Union, it would not be wise for them to pass legislative acts that would significantly contravene the core of the Community obligations. This would not only create significant market distortions but also be counterproductive for their future integration into the European Union (even if the Commission formally acknowledges in the Preamble of the White Paper that, as an element in the pre-accession strategy, it is 'not part of negotiations for accession and does not prejudge any aspect of such negotiations, including possible transitional arrangements'[19]). This remark brings us inevitably to the examination of the structure and contents of the White Paper proposals.

III. STRUCTURE, APPROACH AND CONTENTS OF THE WHITE PAPER

A. Structure and approach of the White Paper

At first sight, the structure of the White Paper is fairly classic. It consists of two parts: a general introductory part and an Annex, which was published

---

[18] See, in that respect, the terms used by the Commission in the executive summary of the White Paper as well as in its various sections, notably at points 1.15, 3.2 and 3.23 of the introductory part of the White Paper.

[19] See pt 1.8 of the introductory part. See also below, section IV, p. 68.

separately, one week later. One could have expected, as it is usually the case, that the first part would be the most important one, the Annex – as the word itself suggests – being only an appendix or a complement to the former. In fact, the reverse is true. The Annex forms the hard core of the White Paper. Whereas the introductory part explains in broad terms the nature, purpose and context of the approximation exercise, it is in the second part that a detailed analysis of the Community's legislation is made. The latter describes the measures to be adopted by the associated countries in not less than 23 sectors related to the Internal Market. The significance of that part of the White Paper results from the fact that, rather than giving a mere enumeration of legislative measures, it also explains their underlying philosophy as well as their implications, both in administrative and organizational terms. This approach may be particularly helpful to countries which switch, in a very short period, from a planned economy system to a market-orientated one.

Basically, each chapter of the Annex is divided in three parts: there is first a general introduction to the relevant area of Community legislation (1); subsequently, the conditions necessary to operate the legislation in question are pointed out (2); finally, concrete approximation scenarios are suggested (3).

(1) The first part of the various sections of the Annex does not call for specific comments. It describes, in a nutshell, the very essence of the Community's legislation. Depending on the section concerned, aspects like the relevance of that legislation for the Internal Market, its final goals, its development over time or the possible relationship between national and Community measures are dealt with. These specifications are intended to give the associated countries a better understanding of the Community rules and mechanisms, the latter being of course an essential precondition for a proper alignment with these rules.

(2) Much more original, from a purely methodological point of view, is the second part of each section of the Annex, which concerns the conditions necessary to operate the legislation referred to in the White Paper. It proceeds from the idea that legislative measures – whatever their nature and importance may be – cannot be isolated from the general framework in which they have to operate. The proper functioning of the Internal Market also depends on the existence of appropriate structures – both on the national and international level – which guarantee a proper implementation of the rules agreed upon. The Commission refers, in that respect, to the importance of an adequate administrative machinery in the associated countries as well as to the significant role public and private bodies can play in the supervision and regulation of the economic activity. Certification bodies, testing laboratories, consumer and trade organizations are only some examples of the structures the Commission bears in mind when it underlines the need of adapting the CEECs' societies 'to the framework conditions necessary to make the legislation work'.[20] Also the judicial systems of the Community partners need to

---

[20] See p. 2 of the Annex to the White Paper (COM(95) 163 final/2, 10 May 1995).

be adjusted to the requirements of the Internal Market. The presence of the necessary enforcing authorities is described as a 'crucial' element in the approximation process. It helps provide the EU members 'certainty that legislation (will be) properly implemented' by their partners.[21] This factor should not be underestimated in view of the CEECs' desire to join the European Union. As a matter of fact, EU accession implies not only a formal alignment with the Community rules; it also requires an effective implementation of these rules under the supervision of the European Commission, which may defer possible cases of infringement to the appreciation of the Court of Justice.

(3) The third part of each section of the Annex is the most concrete one. It proposes, within each area of legislation referred to in the White Paper, a detailed alignment scheme which is characterized by the adoption of the Community legislation in subsequent phases. This approach, introducing de facto a hierarchy in the Community rules, may appear somewhat surprising in view of the complexity of these rules, which are often considered as forming a single – indivisible – block. In fact, it only reflects the Union's desire to avoid too brutal a transition for the associated countries and to maximize the efficiency of the approximation process. As a matter of fact, the Commission acknowledges that the resources available for the approximation exercise are scarce, whether in terms of legal and technical expertise or in terms of financial means. For these reasons, the White Paper provides for a working scheme that should ensure that these resources are focused on areas where they will produce the greatest effect. Within each area of legislation, the Commission identifies 'key measures' which are themselves further subdivided into two categories: the so-called 'stage I' and 'stage II' measures. This division in stages does not necessarily reflect the respective importance of these measures. It is simply based on a coherent approach to the legislation concerned and is intended to help the associated countries organize their approximation work in the most effective way. Measures which provide for the overall framework of a well-specified area of Community legislation or which address fundamental principles of Community law are thus considered as 'stage I measures'. They require the highest priority and have to be tackled by the associated countries before all other measures. Measures requiring 'a particularly long lead-time for effective implementation' or forming an essential 'pre-condition for the effective functioning of the Internal Market' fall also in that first category.[22] Stage II measures, on the contrary, have in the Commission's view a more subordinate or complementary character. They may be adopted at a later stage of the approximation process because they

---

[21] See pt 3.26 of the WP introductory part.

[22] See pt 3.18 of the introductory part. The formulation of the latter criterion is rather vague. Its inclusion in the stage I category seems to be much more guided by the desire to fill in possible gaps than by an objective necessity. As a matter of fact, all the measures that are mentioned in the White Paper may be regarded, in one way or another, as essential to the 'effective functioning of the Internal Market'.

aim at completing a task which will already have started during the first stage of the procedure or simply because they relate to items which can only be adopted after a certain period of time, necessary to put the appropriate legal and administrative structures into place. This is the case e.g. in the field of financial services. A genuine liberalization in that sector depends to a large extent on the prior existence of efficient supervisory bodies able to ensure that credit institutions are taking due account of the laws and regulations within which they operate.[23] In the same perspective, it would make little sense in the Commission's view to adopt the Commission proposal[24] on the legal protection of databases without guaranteeing first – as the Council did in 1991 – the legal protection of computer programs. Such an approach would prove to be both incomplete and inefficient.[25]

If the Commission approach aims precisely at avoiding such inconsistencies (by formulating, for each major area, a logical approximation sequence), the indication of 'key measures' and the division into two subsequent stages are not absolute. In some cases, no distinction is made between the first and the second stage because the legislation concerned represents a single body within which it is impossible to distinguish between 'the most important' measures and the 'less important' ones. All measures are equally important and the isolated adoption of any single part of that compound would not yield any benefit in terms of free movement.[26] In other areas of Community legislation, a third stage has been introduced. This usually reflects the sensitive character of the topic concerned. The Commission prefers to introduce an additional stage in the approximation process rather than to undermine its chances of success by proposing a quick alignment scheme which could cause serious problems in the associated countries and, for that matter, in the EU member states. Such is the case e.g. in the road transport sector. The adoption of the Council Regulations concerning the access to the market of national and international transport operations for goods and passengers is made dependent on the prior adoption of the Community measures regarding the admission to the occupation of road haulage and road passenger transport operator (stage I) and those concerning the obligations inherent in the concept of public service in the transport field (stage II).[27] Such is also the

---

[23] See chapter 13 of the Annex, pp. 281–304.

[24] The 'key measures' identified by the European Commission include measures which were recently adopted by the Community as well as proposals which have not yet been adopted but that are far advanced in the legislative pipeline. The reason for their inclusion in the White Paper is that their importance for the Internal Market evolution does not depend on their date of adoption. It is in the interest of the associated countries to integrate them as soon as possible in their alignment programme because they form part or are likely to form part of the *acquis communautaire* that they will have to take over on the date of their accession to the EU.

[25] See, on that point, the 19th chapter of the Annex, at pp. 352–8.

[26] See e.g. the legislation concerning the radioactive contamination of foodstuffs. In view of the implications of that legislation for public health, it was impossible for the Commission to introduce a hierarchy of importance between the individual measures. Therefore, they are all included in the stage I category (see pp. 218–19 of the Annex).

[27] See chapter 6 of the Annex, 169–207, at p. 176.

case in the field of mutual recognition of professional qualifications. Several Council Directives concerning the exercise of health and legal professions will only be applicable in the third phase of the approximation process.[28]

These few examples clearly demonstrate that the division in two stages has a relative significance. Some flexibility may be needed in order to accommodate the Internal Market requirements and the constraints deriving from the internal situation of the associated countries. In that respect, it may be useful to note that the Commission establishes no global order of priorities between the 23 sectors that are covered by the White Paper. The choice of the sectors to be tackled first and the decision concerning the timetable and modalities of approximation have to be made by the associated countries themselves in the light of their own situation and strategy. No doubt, the cost-benefit analysis of the respective Commission recommendations will play a decisive role in that process.

B. The contents of the White Paper[29]

a. Free movement of goods

Free movement of goods is probably the field where most has been achieved in the EU–CEECs relationship. As a result of the Europe Agreements' provisions and of additional measures adopted by the Community, as a result of the Copenhagen Summit, goods originating from the associated countries circulate nearly freely within the EU. This is not the case for the Eastern European citizens nor for the services they want to provide. A lot of hurdles still have to be taken by the Contracting Parties in order to bring a genuine liberalization in these areas. One could have expected that the White Paper would focus more on such obstacles than on trade liberalization, but this is not the case. Without wholly ignoring the other policy areas,[30] the White Paper still considers the free movement of goods as the first priority in the EU–CEECs relationship. This may be explained by the difference in intensity between the Europe Agreements and the White Paper. As a matter of fact, an Internal Market goes much further than a 'simple' free trade area. It implies not only the abolition of internal border controls; it also requires the removal of all the – direct and indirect – barriers which result from differences between national legislations concerning e.g. the conditions under which

---

[28] See chapter 18 of the Annex, 334–51, at pp. 346–7.

[29] The structure adopted in the present section is the classical structure of the EC-Treaty *and not* that of the White Paper. As a matter of fact, the latter has no (logical) structure! It starts with a chapter on free movement of capital but contains no specific chapters on circulation of goods and services. Direct taxation is listed as chapter 10 whereas indirect taxation only appears in 22nd position, after provisions dealing with civil and company law and personal data (chapters 14 to 17), etc . . . The explanation for such a weird presentation is not to be sought in any rational construction. The order of the 23 chapters of the White Paper is primarily determined by pragmatic reasons: it corresponds, more or less, to the order of the Commission's Directorates-General responsible for the subject matter.

[30] See below, pp. 57–65.

a specific product can be put on the market. This is a much harder nut to crack for the associated countries!

The White Paper deals, basically, with three types of barriers: technical barriers, barriers in the form of veterinary and phytosanitary controls, and tariff and fiscal barriers.[31]

1. Technical barriers

The technical barriers to trade – which usually result from national provisions aiming to achieve public policy goals such as health or environmental protection – are the first to be dealt with in the White Paper. They are mainly concentrated in the second chapter of the Annex concerning the 'free movement and safety of industrial products'.[32] The Commission pursues, in that field, a twofold objective: the prevention of the erection of new trade barriers (1.1) and the removal of the existing ones through a technical harmonization process (1.2).

1.1 On the first aspect – the prevention of new trade barriers – one may be brief. One single measure is referred to in the White Paper: Directive 83/189 EEC of 28 March 1983.[33] This directive organizes a procedure for the exchange of information on national draft technical regulations relating to products.[34] Draft technical regulations and standards have to be notified to the partner countries that are allowed, within well-defined time limits, to comment on such proposals and to request their possible amendment. Such a procedure makes it possible to eliminate – or, at least, reduce as far as possible – any difficulties which these measures could provoke in the exchanges between the EU member states.[35] If this directive thus constitutes a crucial instrument for the management of the Internal Market,[36] its extension to the CEECs, however, could prove to be a much more difficult exercise. It implies

---

[31] This is essentially the same approach which was adopted by the Commission in its 1985 White Paper on the completion of the Community's Internal Market. See, on that point, Schmitt von Sydow, 'The Basic Strategies of the Commission's White Paper', in Bieber, Dehousse, Pinder, Weiler (eds), *1992: One European Market? A Critical Analysis of the Commission's Internal Market Strategy*, Nomos, 1988, 79–106 (at pp. 94–100).

[32] Other examples of similar barriers may be found in the transport and energy sectors as well as in the agricultural field. Many market organization rules are explicitly designed to remove technical barriers to trade through the introduction of common quality standards and labelling requirements. This is notably the case in the following sectors: beef and veal, sheepmeat and goatmeat; fruit and vegetables; wine and derived products; pigmeat, poultrymeat and eggs (see pp. 153–68 of the Annex).

[33] See *OJ*, L 109/8 of 26 April 1983, lastly amended by Directive 94/10/EC of 23 March 1994 (*OJ*, L 100/30, 19 April 1994).

[34] 'Technical regulation' is defined in point (5) of Art. 1 of Directive 83/189 as 'technical specifications . . . the observance of which is compulsory, *de jure* or *de facto*, in the case of marketing or use in a Member State. . . .' Technical regulations should be distinguished from technical standards, which don't have a compulsory nature.

[35] A breach of the rules of this Directive has far-reaching consequences since the court decided that a 'breach of the obligation to notify renders the technical regulations concerned inapplicable, so that they are unenforceable against individuals', Case C-194/94 *CIA Security International*, 1996 ECR I-2201, at p. 2248.

[36] As was confirmed by the recent Commission report on the operation of that directive during the period 1992–94, COM(96) 286 final, 26 June 1996.

not only the political will of each of these countries to disclose all its future technical legislation to its neighbours and to take due account of their observations; it also requires the use of concepts that are similar to the Community ones and presupposes the establishment of suitable structures for the centralization and transmission of the relevant information to the authorities in charge of the preparation of technical regulations. Obviously, such a process cannot be realized overnight. The Commission therefore proposes a gradual approach. The CEECs should not immediately implement Directive 83/189/EEC. In a first phase, they should establish a similar system for the exchange of information between themselves.[37] It is only in the second phase that communication channels and mutual transparency would be achieved between the Community system, on the one hand, and the system of its partner countries, on the other hand.

1.2   The Commission's approach concerning the removal of the existing trade barriers is based on a different technique which reflects the objective difference of situation with the previous hypothesis. Since the regulatory barriers already exist, a simple procedure for the exchange of information between the EU and the CEECs would not be appropriate to achieve fully the goal of a true enlarged Single Market. The Commission therefore recommends a process of technical harmonization with the EU norms and standards. Traditionally, the EU approach to technical harmonization has been divided in two categories: the so-called 'new approach' and the 'sectoral approach'. The sectoral approach is the oldest one. It pursues product regulation on a sectoral basis through the adoption of directives laying down, in a detailed way, both the technical specifications of these products and the conditions necessary to implement them. It usually applies in sectors where health and safety are concerned directly, such as foodstuffs, pharmaceuticals, motor vehicles, chemical products, etc. For a long time, the sectoral approach also applied to industrial products but it has been abandoned, at least in that field, due to its excessive complexity.[38] It has been replaced by the so-called 'new approach'.[39] Unlike the sectoral approach directives, the new approach directives do not follow an *ad hoc* pattern for each sector. They provide for a common model which can be used for large categories of products[40] and/or for horizontal risks.[41] They lay down essential requirements on public policy issues which are then further translated into concrete technical specifications for the producer

---

[37] In the past the Commission always preferred to negotiate with groups of states that already have close relations with each other. This could explain why the Commission strongly encourages cooperation between the CEECs. See Preston, 'Obstacles to EU Enlargement: The Classical Community Method and the Prospects for a Wider Europe', *JCMS* (1995), 451–63, at pp. 455–6. However, the White Paper explicitly requires cooperation only at this place.

[38] It requires, *inter alia*, a continuous up-dating of the technical specifications applying to these products.

[39] See Council Resolution of 7 May 1985 on 'a new approach to technical harmonization and standards', *OJ*, C 136, 4 June 1985.

[40] For example, pressure vessels, medical devices, weighing instruments, construction products, etc . . .

[41] For example, directives on electromagnetic compatibility and the 1973 low voltage directive.

– the 'harmonization standards' – by independent standardization bodies. Such an approach presents, in comparison with the former, the immense advantage of simplicity. Products manufactured in conformity with the essential requirements of the new approach directives may circulate freely within the territory of the EU. However, its proper functioning depends to a large extent on the existence of appropriate implementation and enforcement bodies. This factor explains the importance the White Paper devotes to the necessary 'pre-conditions' for application of the new approach directives. The associated countries are not only requested to organize a standardization system in line with the Community one; they also need to set up transparent conformity assessment procedures and to ensure an adequate market surveillance through the adoption of enforcement programmes and legal penalties against fraud and non-conformity with the legislative requirements.[42] The new approach directives should only be adopted once these conditions are met. The Commission basically adopts the same attitude concerning the sectoral approach directives. Here also, the prior creation (adaptation) of appropriate national regulatory systems is recommended. However, the associated countries enjoy, in that field, far less flexibility than in the previous case. As the sectoral approach directives already contain detailed provisions concerning their operating conditions, the CEECs are often left no other choice than aligning strictly with such provisions without having the possibility to amend them or to take additional or alternative measures.[43] This is the price to pay for participating fully in the Internal Market.

2. Veterinary and phytosanitary controls

After the technical barriers to trade, veterinary and phytosanitary controls are the second kind of obstacles the Commission deals with in the White Paper. They are all situated in the agricultural field[44] and result basically from differences in the level of (animal, plant and public health) protection which is granted respectively by the Community and its Eastern European neighbours. The White Paper aims at achieving, in that field, a similar (high) level of protection throughout the whole area concerned so as to render veterinary and plant health checks at the internal borders superfluous.

In the Commission's view, goods originating in Central and Eastern Europe should circulate freely within the EU because they benefit from an assumption of conformity with the EU norms and standards. This presupposes however two things: first, a considerable approximation task has to be carried out by the associated countries in order to reach a level of protection which

---

[42] See, on that aspect, pp. 13–18 of the Annex.

[43] See the third section of the chapter relating to free movement and safety of industrial products, at pp. 23–48.

[44] This does not mean, of course, that the whole agricultural sector may be reduced to such controls. Many aspects of the common agricultural policy have been excluded from the scope of the White Paper, notably in the field of market support arrangements. These aspects are dealt with in a separate Commission communication that was adopted in November 1995, see COM(95) 607.

mirrors the level prevailing within the Community;[45] secondly, the CEECs have to set up appropriate testing laboratories and inspection services capable of ensuring a proper enforcement of the rules agreed upon. Due to the lack of qualified and experienced staff and to the existence of outdated infrastructure in the associated countries, the latter may prove to be a much more difficult condition to fulfil than the first one which implies a 'simple' alignment on existing Community rules. Nevertheless, it will play a crucial role in the completion of a genuine Internal Market in the EU–CEECs relationship. Internal border controls will only be fully abolished when the EU member states are convinced that the common rules – whatever their nature may be – are applied in the same way by the associated countries. The controversies which arose, within the Community, over the handling of the mad cow disease make clear that this chapter on veterinary and phytosanitary controls is not a theoretical issue.

3. Tariff and fiscal barriers

As a consequence of the hybrid structure of the White Paper, tariff and fiscal barriers are, together with the provisions on consumer protection, the last barriers referred to in this document.[46] They are not, however, the least important ones in the Commission's view. The liberalization of quantitative restrictions and the gradual abolition of customs duties and charges having equivalent effect belong, historically, to the first set of measures which was agreed upon after the changes of 1988–89. The Europe Agreements contain, in that respect, much more detailed provisions than those in the field of technical regulations and standards or veterinary controls.[47] This factor may explain the emphasis in the White Paper on the prior consolidation of the EAs, notably of their provisions concerning mutual assistance. These provisions are described as a crucial element in the fight against fraud and in the protection of the legitimate business and financial interests of the Community and its partners. In the same perspective, the Commission recommends the adoption of the Community's Combined Nomenclature as well as the accession to the fundamental EC/EFTA Conventions on Common Transit and on the Single Administrative Document. These 'stage I' measures are intended to ease the steps towards liberalization and free trade in the relationship between the EU and the CEECs. However, they do not yet result in a full integration of the associated countries into the EU Internal Market. That would also imply the adoption of the Community's Customs Code as well as the full application of the EU tariff and statistical nomenclature and of the Common

---

[45] Out of a total of approximately 1,000 measures, the Commission identifies about 160 'key measures' which are to be adopted by the associated countries. They cover, among others, animal nutrition and welfare, pesticide residues, organic farming, trade and marketing in live animals, semen, ova and embryos, etc. (see chapter 5 of the Annex, at pp. 91–152).

[46] See chapters 21 and 22 of the Annex (at pp. 382–424).

[47] See e.g. Arts 7–17 of the EAs with Hungary and Poland (Arts 8–18 of the EAs with Bulgaria, Romania, Slovakia and the Czech Republic). Most of these provisions appear to meet the basic requirements for being granted 'direct effect'.

Customs Tariff applicable to goods originating from third countries. This is a much more difficult task than the sole adoption of a 'Euro-compatible' customs legislation. It requires from the associated countries the capacity and willingness to assume the responsibilities inherent in the protection and control of the EU external borders, notably in the fields of commercial and agricultural policy. These measures usually correspond to the legislative and regulatory measures which applicant countries are requested to adopt – and to implement[48] – upon their accession to the EU. For such a reason, they are only referred to as 'stage II' measures in the White Paper.

Next to these fundamental provisions on tariff and customs barriers, the White Paper contains provisions in two areas which may significantly affect trade and investment flows: direct and indirect taxation. On the first aspect – direct taxation – the Commission is rather brief. Only four Directives are identified as 'key measures' in the White Paper. They cover the provision of mutual assistance in the field of direct and indirect taxation,[49] capital duty[50] and the elaboration of a common system of taxation applicable (a) to mergers, divisions and transfers of assets and exchanges of shares concerning companies of different member states[51] or (b) in the case of parent companies and subsidiaries of different member states.[52] The picture which is given in the White Paper faithfully reflects the situation prevailing within the Community. The Commission could not have recommended the adoption of additional measures by the CEECs, simply because such measures did not exist at the time of the adoption of the White Paper. So far, no significant progress has been achieved in the harmonization of direct taxation due mainly to the unanimity requirement which still applies for fiscal matters.[53]

The situation is – fortunately – somewhat better in the field of indirect taxation. Harmonization, in that field, is also governed by the unanimity principle[54] but the latter was not an obstacle to the adoption of several directives which form, today, a cornerstone of the EU Internal Market. They cover the Community regime of Value Added Tax and the field of excise duties.[55] As far as the former is concerned, the Commission's task is relatively easy. The *acquis communautaire*, as regards VAT, consists of measures that reflect

---

[48] The Commission underlines once more, in these chapters, the need and the reasons for an effective application of the Community rules. 'A similar level of protection and control at all points on the EU's external frontier is necessary to avoid distortion of competition or deflection of trade in the Internal Market' (p. 389 of the Annex).

[49] See Council Directive 77/799/EEC of 19 December 1977 (*OJ*, L 336/15, 27 December 1977), lastly amended by Directive 94/74/EC of 22 December 1994 (*OJ*, L 365/46, 31 December 1994).

[50] See Council Directive 69/335/EEC of 17 July 1969 (*OJ*, L 249/25, 3 October 1969), lastly amended by Directive 85/303/EEC of 10 June 1985 (*OJ*, L 156/23, 15 June 1985).

[51] Council Directive 90/434/EEC of 23 July 1990 (*OJ*, L 225/1, 20 August 1990).

[52] Council Directive 90/435/EEC of 23 July 1990 (*OJ*, L 225/6, 20 August 1990).

[53] See, in that respect, Art. 100 a, § 2 EC Treaty which formally excludes taxation from the scope of the provisions which may be adopted by qualified majority.

[54] See Art. 99 EC Treaty.

[55] See chapter 22 of the White Paper (at pp. 404–24).

the respective development phases of the EC towards the completion of the Internal Market. The approximation process was initiated in 1967, when the member states decided to replace all the cumulative multi-stage taxes applied on the commercial transactions by a single non-cumulative value added tax, and culminated in 1991 when – as a result of the decision to abolish all fiscal controls at the Community's internal borders on 1 January 1993 – the fundamental Sixth VAT Directive was amended in order to bring an end to the imposition of tax on importations and of the remission of tax on exportations in intra-Community trade. The Commission follows, more or less, the same approach in the present White Paper. The adoption of the complete VAT legislation by the associated countries would only occur at the time of the effective abolition of all border controls in the EU–CEECs relationship. In a first stage, these countries should focus rather on approximation with the basic EC norms regarding VAT, such as the Sixth Directive defining the scope and essential mechanisms of the VAT regime,[56] or the Directives providing for exemption from VAT in certain circumstances.[57] This alignment with the EC legislation should not prove to be too difficult an exercise for the associated countries since their VAT systems are already broadly in line with the Community requirements. The explanation is very simple. The CEECs had to start from scratch in the VAT field and often simply decided to draft their internal legislations after the example of the Community. By contrast, legislative approximation in the field of excise duties could be more difficult to achieve. As a matter of fact, the Community excise system is much more recent than the VAT system – it was only introduced in 1993, as part of the creation of the Internal Market – and consists of a bundle of directives, all adopted in one leap, so that no real logical progressive working scheme can be proposed to the associated countries. Nevertheless, the Commission tries to select, in the White Paper, some parts of the relevant directives which should take precedence under a practical and businesslike approach. They relate to the establishment of a warehousing system of tax collection and to the implementation of taxes on the products subject to Community excise duties.[58] This selection should assist the CEECs better to prepare their integration into the new Community excise system. The most sensitive implication of such an approximation, however, is not referred to in the Annex. It concerns the rates of duties applied on such products by the associated countries. The alignment with the Community system implies, in most cases, a lowering of these rates. This could generate a considerable loss of revenue for the Community's partners.[59]

---

[56] Council Directive 77/388/EEC of 15 May 1977 (*OJ*, L 145/1, 13 June 1977), as lastly amended by Directive 95/7/EC of 10 April 1995 (*OJ*, L 102/18, 5 May 1995).

[57] See e.g. Council Directives 83/181, 83/182 and 83/183/EEC of 28 March 1983 (*OJ*, L 105, 23 April 1983).

[58] These products are mineral oils, cigarettes and tobacco products and alcoholic beverages.

[59] See, on that point, pt 4.15 of the Introductory Part.

b. Free movement of persons

If there was, at the time of the adoption of the White Paper, one field where significant progress had to be made in the EU–CEECs relationship, it was undoubtedly that of free movement of persons. This aspect was almost completely left out in the reports concerning the preparation of the associated countries for accession. It is true that the Europe Agreements already contained some provisions on 'movement of workers'[60] but a close examination of the latter clearly demonstrated that liberalization, in that field, would largely remain a theoretical exercise. The Contracting Parties consolidated – rather than improved – the existing situation. No genuine access was granted to each other's labour market. Moreover, the benefit of the relevant EA provisions was subjected, in several cases,[61] to the conditions and modalities applicable in each member state regarding e.g. residence or working conditions. This may significantly reduce the (already modest) impact of the Europe Agreements.[62] As a consequence, one could have expected that the White Paper would bring some improvements to the position of the Eastern European workers. But this is not the case. The White Paper is, to a certain extent, even more silent on that topic than the Europe Agreements themselves. Ironically, its table of contents announces a chapter on free movement of persons, which . . . does not exist! The 'error' could be symptomatic for the controversial character of the issue. Where free movement of persons should have come (at page 268 of the Annex), a chapter on 'free movement of goods in unharmonized and part-harmonized sectors' has been inserted. It describes, in broad terms, the traditional trade barriers. Undoubtedly, such a description would have fit in better as an introduction to the second chapter of the Annex, relating to the 'free movement and safety of industrial products'.[63]

The absence of a specific chapter on free movement of persons does not mean that this aspect is wholly insignificant in the Commission's view. The latter rightly points to the need for maintaining an appropriate balance between the economic and social dimensions of the European integration process.[64] In practice, however, the balance clearly tilts in favour of the former dimension. Out of a total of 23, only two chapters of the White Paper deal – sometimes very indirectly – with movement of persons: chapter 4 on 'social policy and action' and chapter 18 on 'mutual recognition of professional

---

[60] See Arts 37–43 of the EAs with Hungary and Poland (Arts 38–44 of the EAs with Bulgaria, Romania, Slovakia and the Czech Republic).

[61] See e.g. Arts 37, 38 and 41 of the EAs with Hungary and Poland (Arts 38, 39 and 42 of the subsequent EA).

[62] For a comment on the EA provisions concerning free movement of persons and establishment, see M. Maresceau, op. cit. (note 3), 228–30. See also the contribution of M. Cremona, below, p. 195.

[63] See above, section IIIBa, p. 50.

[64] See e.g. at p. 65 of the Annex.

qualifications'.[65] In the first chapter, the Commission briefly recalls the most important Community initiatives in the social policy field. Five areas are identified for approximation purposes: equal opportunities for men and women, social security schemes, health and safety at work, labour law and tobacco products. If these areas have, a priori, little in common with the freedom of movement – they relate to internal rather than to cross-border issues – some of them, however, can significantly contribute to the improvement of the conditions of access to (and movement within) the European Union. This is clearly the case for the equal pay and equal treatment directives which are intended to confer rights on individuals[66] as well as for the Council Regulations on the coordination of social security schemes.[67] An adequate protection, in that field, is described as a 'precondition to the effective use of the right to move and to stay within the Community'.[68] The Commission thus favours an intensification of the approximation task on the basis of the four principles which usually apply in a Community context: transparency ('only one legislation can be applicable'), equality of treatment, retention of acquired rights and aggregation of periods of insurance or residence. This preparatory work is designed to achieve a convergence between the Eastern and Western social security systems which should facilitate the extension of the above-mentioned regulations to the associated countries upon their accession to the EU. The same reasoning applies, *mutatis mutandis*, to the field of mutual recognition of professional qualifications. The adoption of the (general and sectoral) Community directives on recognition is described, here too, as a 'key element' in the removal of the obstacles to free movement of persons *and* services in the relations with the CEECs. Nevertheless, a closer examination of the White Paper provisions reveals that the approximation, in that field, will be a long-term exercise. The two stages which usually characterize the approximation process in each sector referred to in the White Paper have, in the present case, only a preparatory character. As far as the general recognition system is concerned, the CEECs are thus invited to 'attend, as observers' (during the first stage) or to 'participate actively' in (during the second stage) the meetings of the group of coordinators entrusted with the application of the 1988 and 1992 Directives; but the latter directives are, somewhat paradoxically, not yet

---

[65] See also the last (23rd) chapter of the Annex relating to the 'consumer protection policy'. Several directives which are referred to in its third section, under the title/heading 'protection of economic interests of consumers', may also have an impact on the movement of persons within the Single Market. See e.g. Directive 90/314/EEC of 13 June 1990 on package travel, package holidays and package tours (*OJ*, L 158, 23 June 1990) and Directive 94/47/EEC of 26 October 1994 on time share property (*OJ*, L 280, 29 October 1994).

[66] See Directive 75/117/EEC of 10 February 1975 (*OJ*, L 45/19, 19 February 1975); Directive 76/207/EEC of 9 February 1976 (*OJ*, L 39/40, 14 February 1976); Directive 79/7/EEC of 19 December 1978 (*OJ*, L 6/24, 10 January 1979) and Directive 86/378/EEC of 24 July 1986 (*OJ*, L 225/40, 12/08/1986). The first two directives are referred to as stage I measures while the 1978 and 1986 directives fall into the stage II category.

[67] Council Regulation 1408/71/EEC of 14 June 1971 (*OJ*, L 149/2, 5 July 1971) and Council Regulation 574/72/EEC of 21 March 1972 (*OJ*, L 74/1, 27 March 1972).

[68] See the second section of the fourth chapter of the Annex, pp. 71–3, at p. 71.

applicable to the associated countries. The full application of the 'general systems' directives as well as of the sectoral directives regulating the health-care professions and the exercise of the profession of architect and lawyer is only foreseen in a third stage, after a thorough examination of the progress made during the previous stages. This sequence as well as the exceptional inclusion of a third stage in the approximation process illustrate the paradoxes which sometimes affect the EU policy towards Central and Eastern Europe. While the EU member states are prompt to encourage the deepening of the reforms launched by their partners, they are often far more reluctant when they have to translate their solemn declarations into concrete commitments. This is particularly damaging for the credibility of the European Union, especially in a field like free movement of persons where so little has been achieved in the EU–CEECs relationship. A slight improvement of the conditions of access to the EU labour market would have been one of the most tangible signs of the EU's willingness really to integrate its Eastern European partners.

c. Free movement of services

Fortunately, the balance is better in the services sector. As such, no separate chapter on 'free movement of services' has been included in the White Paper but its provisions reflect *de facto* the EU commitment towards a greater liberalization in that field. Several chapters, covering the main areas of the services sector, have been incorporated in the Annex.[69] They all express the need to guarantee the right to provide cross-border services, without being subject to any discrimination on the grounds of nationality or place of estab-lishment. The White Paper describes, for each area, the measures to be taken in order to achieve this fundamental objective. While several measures are specific to the sector concerned,[70] others have a much more general character and apply, almost systematically, to all the sectors referred to in the White Paper. This is notably the case for the Commission recommendations on quality and pricing of services or concerning the abolition of State mono-polies. The latter apply also in the transport sector[71] and in the field of audio-visual and telecommunications. The Commission strongly underlines that monopoly 'is not the answer to universal service'.[72] Instead, what should be achieved is the effective separation of the regulatory functions (which would still be exercised by public authorities) from the operational responsibilities (that could be in hands of private operators) as well as the development of transparent cost accounting systems. In the light of the own experience of the EU member states – where the liberalization process is still going on in some

---

[69] These chapters are: transport, audiovisual, telecommunications, public procurement and financial services (see, respectively, chapters 6, 7, 9, 12 and 13 of the Annex).

[70] For example the provisions on fiscal and social harmonization in the road transport sector (chapter 6, pp. 185–8).

[71] The Commission mentions in particular the railways sector which suffers in its view from 'excessive government interference' and from 'a heavy debt burden' resulting from the absence of a sound financial structure (see pp. 189–91).

[72] See chapter 9 of the Annex, at p. 260.

sectors[73] – it is obvious that such recommendations will be difficult to implement, especially in countries where the State has played, for more than 40 years, such a dominant role in the regulation of the economic activity. Progress towards efficiency and transparency are however indispensable if the European Union and the CEECs are to create a genuine Internal Market in the field of services. The latter will only be fully achieved when consumers are convinced that they can get the best services – and the best products – under the most attractive conditions. Such an evolution does not mean, of course, that privatization is the sole criterion applying to the services sector. Liberalization is not tantamount to deregulation. The access to (and the exercise of) certain economic activities may be submitted to the respect of specific rules governing e.g. the qualifications required from the economic operators,[74] the protection of the environment[75] or the safety of the passengers carried.[76] These rules do not aim at introducing a disguised form of protectionism in the EU–CEECs relationship. They are only designed to help avoiding possible distortions of competition which could result from the application of different criteria and standards within the Single Market. In the same perspective, the emphasis which is put, in the field of audiovisual and telecommunication services, on the importance of an 'effective regulatory framework'[77] seems to be much more guided by the desire to provide high quality services than by the willingness to restrict the access to the services market. New market players are 'welcome' – the Commission says – but they have to make 'a fair contribution to the cost of universal service'.[78]

If a majority of the White Paper provisions dealing with services reflect the search for an equilibrium between liberalization and harmonization, competition and public service, it is evident, however, that the approximation programme cannot be realized overnight. A gradual approach needs to be

---

[73] For example in the field of postal services or voice telephony where the liberalization is due to happen by 1 January 1998, with transitional periods up to January 2003 for member states with less developed or smaller networks.

[74] See e.g. the road transport sector, where the Commission reaffirms the three requirements which have to be met by every person wishing to exercise as operator in that field: good repute, appropriate financial standing and professional competence (Directives 74/561/EEC and 74/562/EEC of 12 November 1974, as amended by Council Directive 89/438/EEC of 21 June 1989, OJ, L 212/101, 22 July 1989).

[75] This is especially the case in the field of maritime transport. The Commission refers to several directives and regulations that aim at preventing pollution at sea through the elimination of substandard operators, vessels and crews from Community waters, irrespective of the flag of the ships. See e.g. Council Directive 93/75/EEC concerning minimum requirements for vessels carrying dangerous or polluting goods (OJ, L 247, 5 October 1993) or Council Directives 94/57/EC and 94/58/EC on common rules and standards for ship inspection and on the minimum level of training of seafarers (OJ, L 319/28, 12 December 1994) (White Paper, pp. 197–201).

[76] See the directives mentioned in the previous footnote as well as Council Regulation 2407/92 of 23 July 1992 on licensing of air carriers (OJ, L 240, 24 August 1992). The latter provides for common rules for the technical skills of personnel involved in aviation safety and aircraft operations (White Paper, pp. 202–7).

[77] Annex, p. 260.

[78] Ibid.

followed, enabling the CEECs to adjust to EU rules and practices. This is especially true in the field of public procurement. Notwithstanding the fact that the basic legislation, in that sector, already existed at the time of the adoption of the White Paper, the Commission points out that 'firms (in the associated countries) have not yet accepted that they have a genuine chance of winning contracts or, alternatively, old monopolies have not yet accepted that they may lose contracts'.[79] It proposes therefore that the first stage of the approximation phase would be devoted to a simple analysis of the existing or draft legislation of the associated countries in order to check whether the essential features of the Community legislation are present. It is only in a second stage that the CEECs would effectively adopt the six fundamental Community Directives on public procurement.[80] The same technique applies, *mutatis mutandis*, in the financial services sector. The Commission does not recommend the immediate adoption of the Community measures leading to the freedom of establishment throughout the Single Market (the 'home country control' and the 'single licence' principles). It points in the first place to the three basic requirements of a well-functioning financial sector: trained personnel, appropriate legislation and qualified supervisory bodies. These measures are intended to give international and domestic investors a full confidence in the financial system of the associated countries. Only if these preconditions are met can the coordination task be tackled successfully, in the banking as well as in the insurance sector.[81] The latter, of course, also depends on the progress made in the field of capital movements.

d. Free movement of capital

Although the full liberalization of capital movements has only recently been achieved within the Community, it presents another fundamental challenge to the associated countries. Capital movements have become, over time, the fastest growing type of cross-border transactions. They largely determine the international exchange and interest rates which, in turn, play a decisive role in the direction and the structure of international trade. Ignoring them would not only impair the investment flows; it would also affect in a negative way the trade pattern of these countries. These factors explain the importance the White Paper devotes to the alignment with the Community rules. Given 'the relative homogeneity of capital, its high mobility and the substitutability between different forms of capital movements',[82] no distinction is made in that sector between 'key' and 'non key-measures'. All measures are deemed to be essential to the functioning of the Internal Market. However, the

---

[79] See pt 4.34 of the general introductory part.

[80] The latter cover basically three areas: (1) procurement by public contracting authorities; (2) procurement by contracting entities in the water, energy, transport and telecommunications sectors; and (3) the remedies and review procedures which must be available in the event of a breach of the Community legislation (see chapter 12 of the Annex at pp. 274–80).

[81] See chapter 13, pp. 281–304.

[82] See the first chapter of the Annex, at p. 3.

approximation process is still divided in two stages. The liberalization of current payments and of medium- and long-term capital movements would be addressed during the first stage while short-term capital movements and the transfer of assets of a maturity of less than one year would be guaranteed at the end of the second stage.

If that approximation scheme seems, at first sight, rather clear and coherent, its implementation, however, may prove to be a much more difficult exercise. The present liberalization process occurs in a context which radically differs from the context which prevailed ten – or even only five – years ago, when the Community realized the internal liberalization of capital movements. The modalities and the pace of liberalization which were adopted at that time reflected more or less the economic and political reality as well as the development of the financial markets in the sixties and seventies. A distinction could be made between the short- and the long-term capital movements while large similarities existed between the legislative and regulatory frameworks of the EU (then EEC) member states. These factors enabled the Community to anticipate somewhat on the reactions of the markets and to set up a coherent harmonization programme. These conditions are not fulfilled in the present case. Not only do the associated countries present significant differences in terms of investment protection guarantees or tax legislation, but capital markets themselves are also much more sophisticated than some years ago. Capital may be transferred from one country to another nearly instantaneously. New concepts appear in the financial world, that lessen to a certain extent the importance of the traditional schemes such as the distinction between short- and long-term capital movements. The Commission itself acknowledges in the White Paper that 'long-term operations are nowadays partly carried out on a very short-term basis' while 'restrictions on short-term capital movements have increasingly worked as a deterrent for foreign, even long-term, capital inflow'.[83] Consequently, the approximation process could follow a different pattern from that suggested in the White Paper. Moreover, the completion of the liberalization process depends to a large extent on the adoption of several measures relating to the setting up of effective cross-border payment systems, the conclusion of double-taxation agreements, the prudential supervision of institutional investors, etc. These measures are only mentioned incidentally in the White Paper. However, it is obvious that they will play a decisive role in the accession negotiations, especially in the light of the transition to the third stage of the Economic and Monetary Union.

e. *Beyond free movement*

Although the removal of trade barriers and the liberalization of movement of persons, services and capital are essential for the creation of a genuine

[83] Ibid.

Internal Market, they may be insufficient to create a level playing field in the EU–CEECs relationship. Other measures may adversely affect the functioning of the Internal Market. They are to be found in the field of environment, energy, data protection, consumer protection, etc. These areas are included in the White Paper in so far as they '*directly affect*' the operation of the Single Market.[84] Rather than giving here a complete overview of these chapters – some of them have already been referred to in previous sections of this contribution – the present section will focus on three topics which are of crucial importance for the associated countries, not only in the accession perspective, but also for the success of the transition process itself: competition law, intellectual property and company law.

Competition law is, of the three areas, the first to be referred to in the White Paper.[85] It aims at ensuring equal rights – and obligations – for all economic operators whether public or private. Given the obvious links between that issue and the restructuration process of the CEECs' economies, a lot has already been achieved, notably through the adoption and implementation of the Europe Agreements. These agreements contain provisions that refer specifically to the corresponding provisions of the E(E)C Treaty and give precise indications as to the modalities and timetable for the adoption of implementing measures[86] by the Association Councils within three years of their entry into force. These factors explain the 'complementary' character of the White Paper provisions on competition. The main purpose of that chapter is not to lay down the foundations of an effective competition policy in the associated countries. It is 'only' to strengthen and reinforce the existing policy with a view to preparing these countries for their effective integration into the EU Internal Market. The White Paper thus gives a brief picture of the four fundamental branches of EC competition policy[87] and explains, for each of them, both the substantive and procedural key elements to be taken into account by the associated countries. As competition policy is primarily governed by directly effective Treaty provisions, the selected substantive key elements are easy to identify. With the exception of merger control (which is covered by a separate regulation[88]), they consist of the corresponding articles of the EC Treaty. As far as they are not yet covered by the Europe Agreements, they should be adopted by the associated countries during the first stage of the approximation phase. Only one measure is deferred to stage II: the introduction of competition into sectors which are dominated by state

---

[84] On the meaning of these terms, see below, section IV, p. 69.

[85] See chapter 3 of the Annex, pp. 49–64.

[86] See Art. 62 of the Europe Agreement with Hungary, Art. 63 of the EA with Poland and Art. 64 of the subsequent agreements with Bulgaria, Romania, Slovakia and the Czech Republic. For a comparative and critical analysis of these provisions see the contribution of A.-M. Van den Bossche, below, p. 84.

[87] These are (in the following order): (1) state aids; (2) merger control; (3) restrictive agreements and abuse of dominant positions; and (4) state monopolies and public undertakings.

[88] Regulation 4064/89/EEC of 21 December 1989, *OJ*, L 395/1 of 30 December 1989.

monopolies. At the same time, however, the Commission acknowledges the magnitude of the task when it declares that 'the law must not only exist but also be applied and – above all – be expected to be applied'.[89] This process – which implies the establishment of the appropriate monitoring and enforcement bodies – may take much more time than the alignment process itself. It forms nevertheless one of the cornerstones of the Single Market, not only from the perspective of the development of the trade flows between the EC and its Eastern European partners but also with a view to fully achieving the liberalization process in such important sectors as transport, public procurement and telecommunications.[90] Moreover, the effective application of the EC competition rules and principles is a precondition for an adaptation of the EC anti-dumping policy towards Central and Eastern Europe, as the example of the EEA Agreement clearly demonstrated. The EU only decided to give up anti-dumping actions against the EFTA countries on 1 January 1994 (i.e. on the date of entry into force of the EEA Agreement), when it was convinced that the competition rules would be applied in the same way both by the EU and the EFTA countries. A similar attitude can be observed in the relations with the CEECs. It is true that the Europe Agreements and the White Paper go less far than the EEA agreement, notably in the institutional field.[91] No special 'Surveillance Authority' or common court is established in the framework of the Europe Agreements. The latter, however, basically provide for the same substantive rules as the EC Treaty. A more systematic and transparent application of these rules by the associated countries could lead *de facto* to a less systematic application of trade protective measures by the EC.[92]

In the field of intellectual property, the Commission basically adopts the same strategy as in the competition field. It builds further on the provisions of the Europe Agreements. Under these provisions, the associated countries are required to ensure (within five years of the entry into force of the EA) a level of protection of intellectual, industrial and commercial property rights similar to that existing in the Community, notably through the adoption of multilateral conventions which are applied *de jure* or *de facto* by the EU member states.[93] The White Paper proposes a concrete approximation scheme in order to help the associated countries achieve this task.[94] During the first stage, the CEECs could adopt the Community legislation relating to trade mark and copyright while the adoption of Community measures on patents,

---

[89] Chapter 3, at p. 51.
[90] See above, pp. 59–61.
[91] See below, pp. 68–71.
[92] On the EC anti-dumping policy regarding Central and Eastern Europe, see E. Montaguti, below, p. 160.
[93] See Art. 65 of the EA with Hungary, Art. 66 of the EA with Poland and Art. 67 of the EAs with Bulgaria, the Czech Republic, Romania and Slovakia. These provisions are analysed, in more detail, in the contribution of I. Govaere, below, p. 179.
[94] See Chapter 19, pp. 352–8.

designs and counterfeiting can occur in a second stage. This process could take some time since specific measures referred to in the White Paper are not yet adopted at the Community level.[95] Nevertheless, they are already included in the White Paper because of their special impact on the movement of goods and/or services within the EU. A genuine Internal Market will only exist in the EU–CEECs relationship when the protection of intellectual, industrial and commercial property rights will be equivalent in all member states. Here again, a whole organizational structure with competent staff and appropriate means will be needed for implementation of the Commission recommendations.

Finally, a few words on company law and accounting. The White Paper indicates and explains – sometimes in a very detailed manner – the Community measures which have to be complied with by the associated countries. They relate to the conditions for the establishment of companies,[96] the raising, maintenance and alteration of their capital,[97] the running of larger[98] or smaller[99] entities and the publication and verification of their accounts.[100] Although these measures are, at first sight, rather technical, they are as important for the achievement of the Single Market goals as the measures which are referred to in the other chapters of the White Paper. They help create a favourable business environment for undertakings. As a matter of fact, possible creditors and investors will only enter into contact with companies established in the associated countries when they have received the appropriate guarantees concerning the financial situation and the solvency of these companies. This explains the Commission approach in the field of company law and accounting. As in the sector of financial services, the stage I measures do not aim at harmonizing the existing national rules. They will serve as an original framework to build up – or to complete – the sector concerned in the associated countries. It is only once these 'prerequisites' or 'fundamentals' have been laid down, that further refinements are envisaged, drawing on the EU experience.

---

[95] See e.g. the Commission proposal for a Parliament and Council Regulation concerning the creation of a supplementary protection certificate for plant protection products (COM(94) 579 final of 9 December 1994) or the proposal on the legal protection of designs (COM(93) 344, *OJ*, C 345, 23 December 1993).

[96] The so-called 'First company law Directive', i.e. Directive 68/151/EEC of 9 March 1968 (*OJ*, L 65, 14 March 1968).

[97] The 'Second company law Directive', Directive 77/91/EEC of 13 December 1976 (*OJ*, L 26, 31 January 1977).

[98] The 'Third company law Directive', Directive 78/885/EEC of 9 October 1978 (*OJ*, L 295, 20 October 1978).

[99] The 'Eleventh' and 'Twelfth' company law Directives, Directives 89/666/EEC and 89/667/EEC of 21 December 1989 (*OJ*, L 395, 30 December 1989).

[100] See, in particular, Directive 78/660/EEC of 25 July 1978 on the annual accounts of certain types of companies (*OJ*, L 222, 14 August 1978) as well as Directive 84/253/EEC of 10 April 1984 on the approval of persons responsible for carrying out the statutory audits of accounting documents (*OJ*, L 126, 12 May 1984).

IV. THE IMPACT OF THE WHITE PAPER – A COMPARISON WITH THE EEA AGREEMENT

As appears from the analysis of the Commission proposals, the White Paper marks an important step in the relations between the EU and the CEECs. It gives, in one single instrument, a very broad overview of the Community legislation pertaining to the Internal Market. This may be particularly useful for countries whose explicit goal is to become members of the European Union. When looking at the Community practice, one finds only one precedent where such an impressive set of rules has been proposed to third countries: the EEA Agreement. But the nature and the scope of that agreement clearly differ from the White Paper. The EEA Agreement is a legally binding instrument while the White Paper merely *suggests* measures to be taken in the context of pre-accession. Approximation takes place on a voluntary basis. There is more than an academic difference between these two integration models. This appears very clearly when one tries to assess the impact of the White Paper on the preparation of the Eastern enlargement. An analysis of the strengths (A) and weaknesses (B) of that instrument reveals how far these models lie from each other. To a certain extent, one may even suggest that the strengths of the EEA are the weaknesses of the White Paper, and vice versa.

A. The strengths of the White Paper

The mere existence of the White Paper constitutes its first strength. Clearly, with that instrument, the Commission gives more consistency to the pre-accession phase. It is true that, from a strictly legal point of view, nothing has changed. The Europe Agreements remain the sole mutually binding legal framework in the EU–CEECs relationship. However, they are not designed to prepare the latter countries for EU accession. Europe Agreements basically deal with free trade and political dialogue, not with law approximation.[101] If the pattern of the EC Treaty is followed by the EA provisions on free movement of goods, this is not really the case, as far as the free movement of workers, services, payments and capital, or right of establishment for self-employed people and companies and the approximation of law is concerned, as professor Müller-Graff rightly notes (above, p. 34). Moreover, it must be emphasized that the inclusion of EC Treaty-like provisions in the EAs does not mean that these provisions will necessarily be given the same interpretation as in a Community context. The case law of the EC Court of Justice clearly demonstrates that similar provisions may be interpreted differently, according to the purpose and the context of the agreement concerned.[102] As a consequence, the framework of the Union's relations with the CEECs was

---

[101] See above, sections I and IIA.

[102] See *inter alia* Opinion 1/91 of 14 December 1991 (*ECR*, 1991, I-6079, at pp. 6101–4) and the comment by M.-A. Gaudissart, 'Entre autonomie et homogénéité: l'ordre juridique communautaire en péril . . .', *RMUE*, 1992/2, 121–36. See also the contribution by S. Norberg, below, p. 77.

still characterized by important 'loopholes' before the White Paper was issued in May 1995. The White Paper fills in most of these gaps by covering not only chapters that are already dealt with in the EAs (e.g. goods and services) but also areas such as energy, environment, taxation or consumer protection that are not (or hardly). Although the White Paper has no binding character, it may be particularly useful for the associated countries to take due account of the Commission recommendations in these areas, especially in view of the fact that no intermediate stage is foreseen between free trade and full accession to the EU, like the EEA formula.[103] Compliance with the White Paper recommendations is, for the CEECs, probably the best way to prepare for EU accession.

Not only the Community legislation is described in the White Paper, but also the conditions needed in order to make this legislation work. This is the second major contribution of the White Paper. Since that aspect has already been dealt with exhaustively in the previous sections of this study,[104] it will not be further discussed here. Its importance, however, should not be underestimated, especially in a phase of pre-accession.

The process of alignment, of course, will take a lot of time. It implies not only the establishment of the appropriate judicial and administrative structures but also the development of 'a legal and judicial culture which could integrate European Community law and thinking in the legal orders of the potential new Member States'.[105] This could prove to be a much more intransigent problem than the law approximation itself. It depends to a large extent on the improvement of the education and training conditions prevailing in the CEECs. In that respect the Commission provides for specialized technical assistance. This is the third major contribution of the White Paper. The Commission enhances the means put at the disposal of its partners by adjusting the existing assistance programmes to the White Paper recommendations. Assistance provided notably through the PHARE programme includes a direct and rapid access to complete and up-to-date EU legislative texts and case law as well as advice from legal experts on the Union's legal system and on the interpretation of Community texts. This will lead to considerable improvements in the quality of national legislations dealing with Community issues.[106] In the same perspective, the Commission proposal to open the existing Community programmes concerning the Internal Market (such as KAROLUS, MATTHAEUS or MATTHAEUS TAX) to the participation of the CEECs must be warmly welcomed. It helps strengthen the operation of this market in the enlargement prospect while at the same time familiarizing

---

[103] The EEA formula was rejected by the CEECs mainly for political reasons. They feared that such a formula would become an alternative to EU membership. In practice, however, the EEA turned out to be one of the most effective ways for preparing for membership.

[104] See notably section IIB and section III.

[105] M. Maresceau and E. Montaguti, 'The Relations Between the European Union and Central and Eastern Europe: A Legal Appraisal', CMLRev. (1995), 1327–67, 1338.

[106] See, in that respect, chapter 5 of the White Paper introductory part.

the associated countries with the essential principles and mechanisms of the Community legal order. In that perspective, a new body managed by the European Commission, the **T**echnical **A**ssistance **I**nformation **EX**change Office (in short the TAIEX Office) has been established. Its function is twofold. As a focal point the Office provides for advice and expertise on legal and implementing structures, especially through the establishment of a panel of experts from the Commission and the member states. In addition, it also serves as a 'one-stop-shop' or clearing house, to which the CEECs can address requests for assistance with the recruitment of specialist advisors. The Office thus facilitates the provision and coordination of assistance, matching supply and demand. Although the TAIEX Office was only set up in January 1996 and effectively started to work in May 1996 several reports suggest that the associated countries already make an intensive use of its services.[107] This may be particularly stimulating for the strengthening of the approximation process and the deepening of the intra-European cooperation.

B. The weaknesses of the White Paper

Even if the White Paper could significantly contribute to the approximation of the legal systems of the Contracting Parties, its adoption and its implementation are not sufficient to secure an early enlargement. Several areas of the *acquis communautaire* are not included in the White Paper. They cover, among others, the second and third pillars of the Maastricht Treaty as well as important aspects of the common agricultural policy or of the Community regional and environmental policies. Moreover, the White Paper itself has several shortcomings that result mainly from the approach adopted in that document. These shortcomings need to be tackled imperatively if the Union is to proceed to its fifth enlargement within a reasonable period of time.

The first difficulty which could arise, in that respect, results from the non-(or incorrect) implementation of the measures proposed in the White Paper. As has been emphasized earlier,[108] the White Paper is a voluntary approximation programme. The associated countries are free to follow (or to deviate from) the Commission recommendations and to select, among the latter, those they will implement first. If this flexibility forms an important advantage in a pre-accession phase – it allows in particular the CEECs to adjust the White Paper programme to their own economic, social and political realities – it could turn into a handicap at a later stage of the approximation process, notably when accession negotiations start. Priority may *de facto* be given to the countries which are most advanced in the implementation of the White Paper programme. This is logical because the White Paper covers indeed

---

[107] See *inter alia* the monthly newsletters issued by the TAIEX Office.
[108] See above, section IIB, p. 45.

the hard core of the *acquis communautaire*. On the other hand, this attitude may lead to a new form of differentiation in the relations with the CEECs. The associated countries could be treated differently by the European Union according to the progress made in the implementation of the White Paper. This is one of the main differences from the EEA-situation. As the EEA agreement is a legally binding instrument, no distinction was made between the EFTA-countries. Compliance with the *acquis communautaire* in the Internal Market field had to be ensured as from the signature of the agreement. This legal difference should not be overestimated, though. In view of the CEECs' common desire to join the European Union quickly, significant deviations from the White Paper recommendations should not be expected soon.

More worrying is the question of the incomplete scope of the CEECs' obligations under the White Paper. The concept 'Internal Market' which is used in the latter document does not fully correspond to the concept of the Internal Market as it is traditionally understood in a Community (or even in an EEA) context. This divergence may create much more problems than a possible partial implementation of the White Paper recommendations. The difficulty flows essentially from the fact that the White Paper only deals with measures which '*directly* affect the operation of the Single Market'.[109] Measures which have an indirect influence on the free movement of goods, services, persons or capital are not covered by that instrument. Given the volume of secondary legislation involved, such a distinction offers, in the Commission's view, the advantage of 'allow(ing) approximation to be more systematically organized within a coherent work programme and supported by specialized technical assistance'.[110] It remains to be seen, however, whether this approach is correct. In the EU's practice, the distinction between the measures which would *directly* affect the operation of the Internal Market and the measures that would only have *indirect* implications for its functioning is less pronounced than the White Paper suggests. Legislative acts often include both types of measures. Moreover, it must be emphasized that approximation in the fields that are not covered by the White Paper still deserves a lot of attention within the framework of the pre-accession strategy. 'Indirect' measures may be as important for the achievement of the Single Market goals as 'direct' measures. This is the case e.g. in the field of environment. While the White Paper deals with product-related standards, it barely addresses Community legislation which relates to waste management, to pollution from stationary sources and to processes rather than products. This legislation, however, may have a significant impact on the conditions of competition of Eastern European undertakings. This is a second major difference compared to the EEA Agreement. The latter makes no distinction between the types of measures that could affect the functioning of the Internal Market. The

---

[109] These are, in the Commission's view, measures 'without which obstacles to free movement would continue to exist or would reappear' (see pt 3.5. of the Introductory Part of the White Paper).

[110] Ibid., at pt 3.6.

Single Market is – rightly – considered as a whole. As a consequence, the scope of the Internal Market in the EEA Agreement is considerably broader than it is in the EA and/or White Paper context. The field of free movement of persons is, in that respect, particularly illustrative. Workers from the EFTA countries enjoy far more rights than those from CEECs.[111]

Another important difference worth mentioning concerns the attention which is paid to the case law of the European Court of Justice. This can be summarized by one single question: to what extent do the latter's rulings need to be taken into account by the associated countries? In the EEA Agreement, the answer to that question is unequivocal. In so far as they are 'identical in substance' to the rules of the EC or ECSC Treaty (and to acts adopted in application thereof), the provisions of the EEA Agreement are to be interpreted 'in conformity with the relevant rulings of the Court of Justice of the European Communities given prior to the date of signature of that Agreement'.[112] These judgments therefore form an integral part of the *acquis communautaire*. They have to be complied with by the EFTA countries just as much as the interpreted rules themselves. Further, specific mechanisms are introduced in order to ensure a parallel development of the EC and EEA law and case law. They cover, among others, the systematic transmission and classification of the judgments of the respective 'supreme' Courts[113] as well as the possibility, for an EFTA State, to allow its courts or tribunals to ask the ECJ to decide on the interpretation of EEA rules.[114] These rules and mechanisms, which aim at ensuring a uniform interpretation of the rules applying within the EEA, are almost absent from the EU–CEECs relationship. It is true that the White Paper includes references to the case law of the Court of Justice, notably in the field of equal treatment[115] and mutual recognition,[116] but these references are scarce. They do not cover the whole *acquis communautaire* in the Internal Market field, nor do they imply, for the associated countries, a strict obligation to comply with the rulings of the Court of Justice.

These shortcomings could form an additional obstacle on the road to accession, even if the means put at the disposal of the associated countries – notably the PHARE programme and the TAIEX Office – will significantly reduce the possibility of conflicts between the EU law and domestic law of the associated countries.

Finally, one should note the rather static character of the White Paper. Whereas the EEA Agreement provides for a close association of the EFTA

---

[111] Compare, in that respect, Art. 48 EC Treaty, Art. 28 EEA Agreement and Art. 37 (c.q. 38) of the respective Europe Agreements. See also above, section IIIBb, p. 57.

[112] See Art. 6 of the EEA Agreement.

[113] *In casu*, the EFTA Court and the Courts of last instance of the EFTA States, on the one hand, and the Court of First Instance and Court of Justice of the European Communities, on the other hand (see Art. 106 EEA Agreement).

[114] See, in that respect, Art. 107 of the EEA Agreement, as further worked out in Protocol 34.

[115] See the WP Annex at pp. 66–70.

[116] See chapter 18 of the Annex (334–51), at pp. 338 and 340.

countries throughout the whole decision-making process of the Community,[117] the White Paper does not deal with the evolution of the *acquis communautaire* relating to the Internal Market.[118] The Community legislation is described as it stands in May 1995. It is obvious, however, that also this legislation is in permanent evolution. A comprehensive pre-accession strategy will require a continuous vigilance and adaptation on the part of the associated countries.

---

[117] See, in particular, the second chapter of the institutional part of the EEA Agreement (Arts 97–104).

[118] Of course, one could argue that the CEECs may express their views concerning future EU legislation during the meetings of Association Councils or in the framework of the 'structured relations'. However, the impact of these mechanisms is very limited as compared with the possibilities the EEA Agreement offers to the EFTA countries.

B

Trade and Competition

4

THE MOVEMENT OF GOODS IN
EU–CEECs RELATIONS IN THE LIGHT
OF THE EEA EXPERIENCES

Sven Norberg[1]

I. INTRODUCTION

Article XXIV of the GATT sets out the definitions of both a customs union and a free trade area. One characteristic common to both is the abolition of customs duties and quantitative restrictions between the parties involved, thus providing for the free cross-border movement of goods between them. While the customs union also establishes a common customs regime towards third countries, each partner in a free trade area maintains its own trade regime with third countries. The European Community goes beyond a mere customs union, as it is an exceptionally sophisticated and developed one. Through each of the Europe Agreements, concluded between the European Community and one CEEC, a new Free Trade Area is created between them.

In order to examine the movement of goods provided for in EU–CEEC relations, and in particular to see how far access to the EC Internal Market may be achieved thereby, it is necessary to be aware of the differences between the principle of free movement of goods in the Internal Market under EC law and the abolition of barriers to trade required for a free trade area fulfilling the requirements of the GATT.

The experiences of the member states of EFTA provide enlightening illustrations of the importance of these differences under EC law, and will be the main subject of this paper. As may be recalled, the EFTA States created between them a free trade area and each of them also concluded a Free Trade Agreement (FTA) with the European Economic Community (EEC). In 1992, in order to acquire access to the EC Internal Market, they furthermore

---

[1] Director, DG IV, European Commission. Formerly Director Legal Affairs, EFTA Secretariat and Judge of the EFTA Court. All views expressed are purely personal.

concluded with the Community and its member states the European Economic Area (EEA) Agreement.

II. THE FTAS OF 1972 BETWEEN THE EEC AND SEVEN EFTA STATES[2]

EFTA was created in 1960[3] as a reaction to the creation of the EEC and in order to avoid a rift in Western Europe. It had two main objectives:

i) by means of a free trade area to create free trade internally at the same pace as the EEC did; and

ii) to develop close ties and cooperation with the EEC.

The first was an immediate and great success, the second proved, for the first twelve years, to be a most frustrating enterprise.

Upon the accession of Denmark and the UK to the EEC on 1 January 1973, however, it became necessary to avoid a re-establishment of the trade barriers that had been abolished between the remaining EFTA States and the two departing ones. This forced the Community to conclude its first FTAs. The scope and trade coverage were somewhat more limited than the EFTA Convention, in principle covering trade in all industrial goods and a limited number of processed agricultural products.

The FTAs were more or less identical and provided in some 36 Articles for the abolition of import duties and export duties and charges of equivalent effect. Under Article 13 of each FTA, quantitative import restrictions were to be abolished by the entry into force of the FTA, while the same was to apply two years later for measures having an effect equivalent to quantitative import restrictions. The provisions thereon (Articles 13 and 20) were very similar to corresponding provisions of the EEC Treaty (Articles 30 and 36). For almost 20 years the FTAs did not contain any prohibition on quantitative export restrictions. Article 23 contained competition rules, similar to the main principles laid down in Articles 85, 86 and 92 EEC, but instead of prohibiting certain practices it declared them incompatible with the good functioning of the FTA.

For ten years, there was uncertainty as to the legal viability of the FTAs and in particular their validity in the EC compared to that of corresponding provisions of EC law. In 1982, however, two crucial judgments were handed down by the EC Court of Justice (ECJ), which in Article 177 proceedings provided important interpretations of the FTAs. After the *Polydor*[4] and

---

[2] Four of which are now EC members and two EEA members (Iceland and Norway). Only Switzerland still fully applies the FTA.

[3] Founding EFTA States were Austria, Denmark, Norway, Portugal, Sweden, Switzerland and the United Kingdom.

[4] Case 270/80, *Polydor* (1982) ECR 329.

Kupferberg[5] judgments, it became clear that the ECJ had recognized that – contrary to the GATT agreement – the FTAs were capable both of being directly applicable in the Community and of producing direct effect. However, the Court repeatedly emphasized that since the EEC Treaty and the FTAs 'pursued different objectives', provisions which were more or less identically worded in the two instruments would not necessarily have to be given the same interpretation.

Thus in *Polydor*, which concerned the sale in the UK of gramophone records imported from Portugal, the Court did not consider that Articles 13 and 20 FTA, which were worded almost identically to Articles 30 and 36 EEC, could be given the same interpretation as the latter provisions. Thus, in the case before the ECJ, these provisions of the FTAs did not provide for exhaustion of the intellectual property rights regarding 'Spirits Fly High' by the Bee Gees. The imports thereof from Portugal to the UK could thus be prevented by the copyright-holder who had not given his consent.

On the other hand, the ECJ found in *Kupferberg* that the levying of a German alcohol tax on imports of port wine from Portugal was against Article 21 of the Portuguese FTA (Article 18 in other FTAs) which prohibited discriminatory internal taxation.

At the same time as this opened up new avenues and perspectives for the application of the FTAs, e.g. possibilities of invoking them and relying upon them before national courts in EC States, it also made it clear that the actual content of certain provisions in Agreements negotiated with the EC could be difficult to predict and would depend upon interpretation by the Court of Justice.

Today, some fourteen years after *Polydor*, the ECJ has interpreted the FTAs, as well as other agreements with third countries (such as the Association Agreement with Turkey,[6] the FTA with Israel,[7] the Lomé Convention, etc.) in a rather large number of judgments. The case law thus established now makes it possible in the field of movement of goods to distinguish between, on the one hand, a 'hard core' of movement of goods aspects which are essential for the functioning of a free trade area, and, on the other hand, additional elements of a more advanced character which require a more far-reaching objective and level of integration between the parties in order for them also to apply. While certain provisions may be such that they belong exclusively to the first category, the wording of other provisions may be such that they may lend themselves, *depending upon the context in which they appear*, both to the more narrow 'hard core' approach and to an interpretation appropriate to a more advanced level of integration.

To the 'hard core' provisions of a free trade area would thus clearly seem to belong those which are fundamental for the basic functioning of the free

---

[5] Case 104/81, *Kupferberg* (1982) ECR 3641.
[6] Case 12/86, *Demirel* (1987) ECR 3719.
[7] Case 174/84, *Bulk Oil* (1986) ECR 559.

trade area, such as those on abolition of customs duties and charges having equivalent effect. This would mean that provisions thereon in FTAs with the EC in principle should be interpreted in the same way as Articles 12 and 13 of the EC Treaty. In *Legros and others*,[8] which concerned the import of Swedish cars into the French overseas *département* of La Réunion, the ECJ held with regard to the FTA with Sweden that it emerged from the Preamble to the Agreement and the provisions of the GATT relating to the establishment of free trade zones, in the context of the objective of the elimination of obstacles to trade, that the elimination of customs duties played a role of prime importance. The same was true for the elimination of charges having equivalent effect which, according to the case law of the Court, were closely linked to customs charges *strictu sensu*. The Agreement was therefore deprived of an important part of its effectiveness if the concept of a charge having equivalent effect, which was found in Article 6 of the Agreement, was interpreted as having a more limited scope than the same term appearing in the EEC Treaty. In the *Aprile* judgment of 5 October 1995, which also concerned trade with EFTA States covered by the FTAs, the Court added that the member states are not entitled immediately to impose charges having equivalent effect in trade with non-member countries:

> where the prohibition of such charges is contained in bilateral or multilateral agreements concluded by the Community with one or more non-Member countries with a view to eliminating obstacles to trade and in the Council regulations providing for common organization of the markets in various agricultural products regarding trade with non-Member countries, *the scope of that prohibition is the same as in the case of intra-Community trade*.[9]

There is no doubt that certain parts of the ECJ case law regarding the notion of 'measures having equivalent effect' to quantitative restrictions belong to the category of elements which require a more advanced level of integration for their full application. This concept has its origin in the GATT, but is more well known as the main element of Article 30 EC. It is also to be found in all FTAs. Over the years, the ECJ has produced a very rich case law on the interpretation thereof, including such judgments as *Dassonville*,[10] *Cassis de Dijon*[11] and *Keck*.[12] While certain basic parts of this case law might also be relevant for a less ambitious FTA, others, as was made clear by the ECJ in *Polydor*, such as the principle of exhaustion of intellectual property rights as developed by the ECJ case law, cannot be transposed to such FTAs. Nor would it seem likely that the *Cassis de Dijon* principle would follow from those FTAs.

---

[8] Case C-163/90, *Legros and others* (1992) ECR I-4625. See also case C-125/94, *Aprile Srl* (1995) ECR I-2919.
[9] Case C-125/94, *Aprile Srl* (1995) ECR, I-2919 (emphasis added).
[10] Case 8/74, *Dassonville* (1974) ECR 837.
[11] Case 120/78, *Rewe Central* (1979) ECR 649.
[12] Case C-267/91 and C-268/91, *Keck* (1979) ECR I-6097.

III. EXPERIENCES FROM THE WORK ON THE CREATION OF A HOMOGENEOUS AND DYNAMIC EUROPEAN ECONOMIC AREA

The work to create the European Economic Area can be divided in two stages:

i) first, the attempts during the period 1984 to 1989 to establish the EEA through a case-by-case approach; and

ii) secondly, the efforts invested from 1990 to 1992 in negotiating the EEA Agreement.

After the joint decision by EC and EFTA ministers and the Commission, taken in Luxembourg in 1984, to create an EEA, a cumbersome period followed, during which a great number of individual cooperation projects were launched in different fields.[13] It may suffice here to mention just one case, i.e. the attempts, in particular during 1987–88, to negotiate a separate agreement in the field of public procurement, which turned out to be an eye-opener for both sides. After a while, both the Commission and EFTA experts realized that in order to gain access to the EC procurement market, which was being opened up under the Internal Market programme, it was not sufficient simply to reproduce the texts of the Community Directives on public procurement in an agreement. Just as is the case with a national legal system, the Community legal order cannot be applied piecemeal. The full application of the public procurement legislation also requires the possibility to have recourse to other basic provisions of EC law, particularly in primary law, which guide or support the application of acts of secondary legislation. For instance, in the field of procurement the provisions on free movement of goods play an important role, *inter alia*, by preventing the application of discriminatory product specifications. The same goes for the legislation on free movement of workers and services. These aspects would therefore also have to be included in the agreement.

The conclusion drawn from this was that what the experts had been trying to do, i.e. to create an agreement with the limited aim of securing equal access for EFTA traders to an enlarged EC public procurement market, was in fact tantamount to negotiating on access to the internal market in general. A second important element that arose in this context concerned the risks of a 'legal imbalance' in relation to the EC member states, if sufficient instruments to secure uniform interpretation and judicial control were not created for the EFTA States as well.

When the experts had got that far, President Delors in January 1989 presented his initiative regarding the EEA, which now suggested abandoning the sector-by-sector approach, and aiming instead for a global agreement

---

[13] It started in 1984 with work in four identified areas (*inter alia* facilitation of border formalities and technical barriers to trade). By 1989 this had developed to more than 30 specific projects ranging from public procurement to environment.

which would secure access to the Internal Market and establish common institutions.

During the subsequent negotiations on the EEA, five categories of elements were applied, whose general aim was to secure a homogeneous EEA which – in parallel with the EEC Treaty – could achieve the same results as those of the Treaty, and thereby provide for an enlargement of the internal market:

i) the objective of creating a dynamic and homogeneous EEA and to arrive at the equal treatment of individuals and economic operators as regards the four freedoms and the conditions of competition was made absolutely clear, (cf. e.g. the 15th recital of the Preamble and Article 1, EEA);

ii) all relevant primary and secondary EC legislation regarding the internal market was taken over, and a mechanism was created to ensure that all relevant new EC legislation would be taken over (cf. Articles 99–102, EEA);

iii) all ECJ case law relevant for the uniform interpretation for the EC law provisions was taken over (Article 6 EEA);

iv) a special drafting technique was elaborated aimed at making it clear, *inter alia* to the courts, that the objective was to apply the same texts (including possibly obsolete parts, translation errors, etc.) in the EEA as in the EC; i.e. any attempt to update or to codify case law was deliberately avoided;

v) a surveillance mechanism and judicial authority were created, in order to secure uniform interpretation and judicial control in the whole EEA (cf. Articles 105–11 EEA).

The negotiators had learned from the experience of *Polydor*, and went to great lengths to make it clear that the intention of the Contracting Parties really was to achieve equal conditions regarding the four freedoms and competition to those existing in the Internal Market. Thus, for instance, Protocol 28 EEA on intellectual property rights provides *inter alia* for taking over ECJ case law as to exhaustion of rights.

After all those efforts, it is obvious that the first Opinion of the ECJ on the draft EEA Agreement[14] was a disappointment. The Court was indeed very negative as regards the EEA, in particular in questioning the possibility of achieving a homogeneous EEA. In its *Opinion 1/91*, the Court held, in very strong language, that the establishment of a joint EEA Court was a threat to the very foundations of the Community legal order. However, in terms familiar from *Polydor* it also recalled the difference in objectives between the EC and the EEA, the former being a customs union with far-reaching political objectives and the latter 'only' a free trade area.

[14] *Opinion 1/91*, (1991) ECR I-6079.

That criticism forced the negotiators to strengthen considerably the emphasis on uniform interpretation and homogeneity in the renegotiations that followed.[15] In its second opinion, *Opinion 1/92*,[16] the Court approved the new judicial mechanism, the main element of which was the creation of a separate EFTA Court.

Today, some two years after the entry into force of the EEA, the experience is still somewhat unbalanced, since the only judgments interpreting the EEA Agreement are four judgements by the EFTA Court. The first of these, *Restamark*,[17] of December 1994, dealing with the Finnish alcohol monopoly, particularly addressed the homogeneity issue.

IV. THE EUROPE AGEEMENTS

Each of the Europe Agreements aims at creating, within a period of ten years, a free trade area for industrial goods between the EC and the country concerned. To this effect, each one contains the usual type of provisions; these provide for the abolition of customs duties on imports and charges having equivalent effect, as well as for the abolition of quantitative restrictions and measures having equivalent effect, which is to take place gradually in an asymmetric way.

An examination of the declared objectives and the absence of such special provisions and mechanisms as laid down for instance in the EEA Agreement[18] seems to lead to conclusions which are similar to those mentioned above regarding the EEC–EFTA FTAs. This means that provisions regarding the 'hard core' elements of a free trade zone are to be interpreted in the same way as corresponding provisions of the EC Treaty. As to the more sophisticated elements requiring a higher level of integration, such as the *Cassis de Dijon* principle or the exhaustion of intellectual property rights, however, there do not seem to be any indications implying that these would be part of the Europe Agreements.

As the EEA exercise, and in particular Opinion 1/91 showed, the burden of proof is considerable for someone who claims that provisions of a free trade agreement, other than the hard core ones, are to be interpreted in the same way as corresponding provisions of the EC Treaty. Thus, a great deal remains to be done if it is felt desirable for any of the agreements with CEECs to achieve a level of integration which is equal to that of the Internal Market.

---

[15] This led, *inter alia* to the inclusion in the Agreement of the 15th recital in the Preamble and the strengthening of the chapter on surveillance.
[16] *Opinion 1/92*, 1992 ECR I-2821.
[17] EFTA Court Report 1.1.1994–30.6.1995, 15–57 and *CMLR* (1995), 161.
[18] See for instance the five kinds of homogeneity elements referred to in Section III above.

V. THE 1995 WHITE PAPER ON PREPARATION FOR INTEGRATION INTO THE INTERNAL MARKET

In May 1995, the Commission, as a further step towards facilitating the preparation of the CEECs for integration into the Internal Market of the Union, issued a White Paper.[19] This Paper forms part of the pre-accession strategy adopted by the Essen European Council in December 1994. The declared purpose of the White Paper is to provide a guide in order to assist the associated countries to prepare themselves for operating under the requirements of the International Market. It is stressed that this *alignment is to be distinguished* from accession to the Union, which *'will involve acceptance of the* acquis communautaire *as a whole'*.[20]

The Paper identifies measures of secondary legislation in each sector of the Internal Market and suggests a sequence in which the approximation of legislation should be tackled. However, the White Paper emphasizes that such approximation is not sufficient. The establishment of adequate structures for implementation and enforcement is equally important, and may be the more difficult task.

Obviously, this is an extremely heavy programme, which each country must implement at its own pace.

The Paper lists the main EC treaty provisions, constituting primary law, as well as presenting sector-by-sector a great number of acts of secondary legislation; however, it is less explicit as to the stages which are needed in order to realize the adaptation of national legal orders and to ensure the necessary implementing and enforcement mechanisms.

It was certainly very difficult for the EFTA States to understand correctly and to take on board the Community *acquis*, both in the context of the EEA and at the subsequent enlargement. In addition, the fundamental principles of EC law, such as direct applicability and effect as well as primacy of Community law provisions, needed to be understood and accepted: achieving that was an equally difficult task. There is no doubt that it would have been impossible for the EFTA States successfully to accede to the EU without having undergone the experience of the EEA.

The paradox is actually that, when the EEA was signed four years ago, even though it did not cover agriculture and a number of other important common policies, it nevertheless represented a much larger step of integration to be taken in one go than that taken by any previously acceding full member of the EC. It should not be forgotten that the White Paper on the Internal Market only started to be implemented *after* the accession of Portugal and Spain in 1986. And the 'accession threshold' to the EU has certainly not become any lower since the entry into force of the Maastricht Treaty.

---

[19] COM(95) 163 final, May 1995.
[20] p. 37.

VI. SOME CONCLUSIONS

As was emphasized above, the aim of this paper was not primarily to analyse the provisions on free movement of goods in the Europe Agreements or to examine the steps to be taken as part of a pre-accession strategy. It was rather to explain the experiences gained in the ten years it took for the EFTA States and the EC to realize the originally rather vague vision of a European Economic Area. Certainly, as President Delors reminded us, history is accelerating. The challenges faced now by the CEECs, as well as the member states of the Union, were not conceivable just a few years ago. What remains to be done in order to achieve the free movement of goods on equal terms to those applying in the Internal Market is certainly not to be underestimated; however, there is no doubt that it can be done, if there is the necessary political will on all sides.

5

THE COMPETITION PROVISIONS IN THE EUROPE AGREEMENTS. A COMPARATIVE AND CRITICAL ANALYSIS

Anne-Marie Van den Bossche[1]

I. THE COMPETITION PROVISIONS SITUATED

At the moment of writing, the European Community had concluded Europe Agreements with six Central and Eastern European countries,[2] and signed such Agreements with the three Baltic States[3] and Slovenia.[4]

This contribution will concentrate on one aspect of the Europe Agreements; it purports to offer a comparative and critical analysis of the competition provisions applicable to undertakings contained therein.[5]

The inclusion of competition provisions in the Europe Agreements can be seen as contributing to a number of objectives of association: the establishment of new rules, policies and practices as a basis for integration into the Community or, put differently, the provision of an appropriate framework for gradual integration into the Community; support for the efforts to develop

---

[1] PhD, Doctor-Assistant, Europees Insitituut, University of Ghent. This text is an amended version of a paper presented during the Third Ghent Colloquium, March 7–8, 1996, which was first published in the *European Competition Law Review* [1997] 1 ECLR 24.

[2] *OJ* 1993 L 347 (Hungary); *OJ* 1993 L 348 (Poland); *OJ* 1994 L 360 (Czech Republic); *OJ* 1994 L 359 (Slovak Republic); *OJ* 1994 L 357 (Romania); *OJ* 1994 L 358 (Bulgaria).

[3] See for the text of these agreements, COM(95) 207 final.

[4] See for the text of this agreement, COM(95) 341 final. See for information on the signing of the Agreement, *Agence Europe*, June 10–11, 1996, 6.

[5] To date, surprisingly little has been written on the Europe Agreements' competition provisions. See for a general description, T. Jakob, 'EEA and Eastern European Agreements with the European Community', in Hawk (ed.), *1992 Fordham Corp.L.Inst., International antitrust law and policy*, New York, Transnational Juris Publications, 1993, 403–36, and in particular 429–34 and for a first analysis of the Polish provisions, G. Marceau, 'The full potential of the Europe Agreements: trade and competition issues: the case of Poland', *World Competition*, 1995/2, 44–8 and 52–6.

the economy and to complete the conversion into a market economy.[6] This power to support integration which is attributed to competition provisions is not entirely surprising, as it has been one of the characteristic features of EC competition law and policy from the early days of the European Community itself. The idea then was that the realization of a common market (and later on an internal market) would be jeopardized if government barriers to trade within the Community could simply be replaced by private barriers resulting from anti-competitive behaviour by market participants. It is therefore almost logical for the free trade provisions contained in the Europe Agreements to be supplemented by competition provisions, in order to prevent private trade barriers from coming into existence and distorting harmonious economic relations between the Parties.

In all the Europe Agreements, the chapter dealing with competition provisions forms part of Title V on Payments, capital, competition and other economic provisions, approximation of laws. Another common feature which is striking is that all agreements refer to 'rules on competition' as one of the areas to which the approximation of laws shall extend in particular. Such approximation of existing and future legislation is moreover considered as either the major precondition[7] or an important condition[8] for the Parties' economic integration into the Community. Whereas Hungary 'shall act to ensure that future legislation is compatible with Community legislation as far as possible',[9] Poland 'shall use its best endeavours to ensure that future legislation is compatible with Community legislation',[10] and the Czech and Slovak Republic, Romania, Bulgaria, Estonia, Latvia, Lithuania and Slovenia, for their part, 'shall endeavour to ensure that [their] legislation will be gradually made compatible with that of the Community'.[11]

II. THE BASIC STRUCTURE: SIMILAR BUT NOT IDENTICAL

The actual competition provisions in the Europe Agreements all follow a similar pattern, without however being identical.

At the outset, it should be stressed that these provisions do not apply to agricultural and fisheries' products. For these, reference is made to the criteria established by the Community on Articles 42 and 43 of the EC Treaty, and

---

[6] See for the objectives of association: Hungary, Art. 1, 4th resp. 7th indent; Poland, Art. 1, 4th indent; Czech Republic, Art. 1, 4th indent; Slovak Republic, Art. 1, 4th indent; Romania, Art. 1, 4th and 6th indent; Bulgaria, Art. 1, paragraph 2, 5th and 6th indent; Estonia, Art. 1, 2nd indent; Latvia, Art. 1, 2nd indent; Lithuania, Art. 1, 2nd indent; Slovenia, Art. 1, 2nd indent.

[7] Hungary, Art. 67; Poland, Art. 68; Slovenia, Art. 70.

[8] Czech Republic, Art. 69; Slovak Republic, Art. 69; Romania, Art. 69; Bulgaria, Art. 69; Estonia, Art. 68; Latvia, Art. 69; Lithuania, Art. 69.

[9] Hungary, Art. 67.

[10] Poland, Art. 68.

[11] Czech Republic, Art. 69; Slovak Republic, Art. 69; Romania, Art. 69; Bulgaria, Art. 69; Estonia, Art. 68; Latvia, Art. 69; Lithuania, Art. 69; Slovenia, Art. 70.

those established in Regulation 26/62.[12] For ECSC products, a distinction must be made between the formulation of the Europe Agreements with the Central and Eastern European countries, and those with the three Baltic States. In the former, the competition articles do not themselves apply to ECSC products, but these are dealt with in a separate Protocol 2 to the respective Agreements.[13] In the latter, the competition articles directly and explicitly set out an assessment on the basis of the 'corresponding rules of the ECSC Treaty including secondary legislation'.[14]

A. Similarities

The basic structure of the competition Article[15] is the same in all agreements.

A *first paragraph* sets the standard of incompatibility with the proper functioning of the Agreement, to which a clause requiring effects on trade is immediately added. The incompatibility test applies to restrictive agreements, to abuses of a dominant position in the Community or in the other Party as a whole or in a substantial part thereof, and to any public aid which distorts or threatens to distort competition by favouring certain undertakings or the production of certain goods.

According to the *second paragraph*, the assessment will be based on criteria arising from the application of the rules under Articles 85, 86 and 92 EC Treaty.

The *third paragraph* deals with the adoption of implementing rules. In the case of the first series of Europe Agreements with the Central and Eastern European countries,[16] it allows the Association Council three years as from the entry into force of the Agreement to adopt the necessary rules for the implementation of the standard of incompatibility and the criteria for assessment. At first sight, it would therefore seem that this deadline expires for Hungary and Poland on 1 February 1997, and for the Czech Republic, the Slovak Republic, Romania and Bulgaria on 1 February 1998. The time limit is, however, further qualified in the Agreements. Each Agreement explicitly specifies what is to be understood by the term 'date of entry into force of this Agreement' in the event of some provisions being put into effect by means

---

[12] Hungary, Art. 62.5; Poland, Art. 63.5; Czech Republic, Art. 64.5; Slovak Republic, Art. 64.5; Romania, Art. 64.5; Bulgaria, Art. 64.5; Estonia, Art. 63.5; Latvia, Art. 64.5; Lithuania, Art. 64.5; Slovenia, Art. 65.5.

[13] Hungary, Art. 62.8; Poland, Art. 63.8; Czech Republic, Art. 64.8; Slovak Republic, Art. 64.8; Romania, Art. 64.8; Bulgaria, Art. 64.8; Slovenia, Art. 65.8.

[14] Estonia, Art. 63.2; Latvia, Art. 64.2; Lithuania, Art. 64.2.

[15] Hungary, Art. 62; Poland, Art. 63; Czech Republic, Art. 64; Slovak Republic, Art. 64; Romania, Art. 64; Bulgaria, Art. 64; Estonia, Art. 63; Latvia, Art. 64; Lithuania, Art. 64; Slovenia, Art. 65.

[16] Agreements concluded with Hungary, Poland, the Czech and Slovak Republics, Bulgaria and Romania. The Agreement with Slovenia, which is also considered to be a Central European country followed only after the Baltic States' Agreements series, and is therefore dealt with separately.

of an Interim Agreement in 1992[17] or 1993.[18] For obligations taking effect after the date of entry into force by reference to the date of entry into force, such as in this case the implementation of the competition articles, the time limit therefore runs from 1 January 1992 for Hungary, Poland, the Czech Republic and the Slovak Republic, and 1 January 1993 for Romania and Bulgaria. As Interim Agreements with all countries concerned were concluded and have entered into force in the year referred to in the relevant Europe Agreement,[19] the three-year time limit for adoption therefore expired on 31 December 1994 for Hungary,[20] Poland, the Czech Republic and the Slovak Republic.[21] For Romania and Bulgaria, the time limit expired on 31 December 1995.[22]

For the remaining Agreements, the situation differs, not only as regards formulation, but also as to the actual time period allowed for the adoption of implementing rules. The Europe Agreements with the Baltic States are straightforward, in that in these cases, the third paragraph of the competition article explicitly sets the limit at 31 December 1997.[23] The Agreement with Slovenia, even though initialled merely three days after the conclusion of those with the Baltic States, adopts the earlier formula of 'within three years of the entry into force', with this date being qualified should provisions of certain parts of the Agreement be put into effect in 1996 by means of an

---

[17] Hungary, Art. 124; Poland, Art. 122; Czech Republic, Art. 124; Slovak Republic, Art. 124.

[18] Romania, Art. 126; Bulgaria, Art. 125.

[19] See for the Interim Agreement with Poland, Council Decision of 25 February 1992, *OJ* 1992 L 114 (entered into force 1 March 1992); Hungary, Council Decision of February 25, 1992, *OJ* 1992 L 115 (entered into force 1 March 1992); The Czech and Slovak Republics, Council Decision of 25 February 1992, *OJ* 1992 L 116 (entered into force 1 March 1992); Romania, Council Decision 8 March 1993, *OJ* 1993 L 81 (entered into force 1 May 1993) and Bulgaria, Council Decision of 10 December 1993, *OJ* 1993 L 323 (entered into force 31 December 1993).

[20] According to a recent press release (*UE-H 1506/96 (Presse 220)*), it was only during its third meeting (held in Brussels on 16 July 1996) that the Association Council EC-Hungary 'reached an agreement on substance of [the] decision concerning the implementing rules for competition which constitutes an important step forwards in the approximation of legislation process; the decision, which will enter into force on 1 January 1997, will be formally adopted by written procedure'.

[21] This deadline was not respected. In the meantime, implementing rules have been adopted and published in the case of Poland (see Decision 1/96 of 16 July 1996 of the Association Council, *OJ* 1996 L 208/24) and the Czech Republic (see Decision 1/96 of 30 January 1996 of the Association Council, *OJ* 1996 L 31/21).

[22] For Bulgaria, the Commission submitted its proposal for the Council and Commission Decision on 22 November 1995, but the internal proceedings have not been finalized yet. The case of Romania is different again, in that for the time being there is no published proposal.

[23] On 19 December 1994, the Community concluded Free Trade Agreements (FTA) with each of the Baltic States, which entered into force on 1 January 1995. See for the text: Estonia, *OJ* 1994 L 437; Latvia, *OJ* 1994 L 374 and Lithuania, *OJ* 1994 L 375. These Agreements already contain competition provisions very similar to those contained in the Europe Agreements. See FTA Estonia, Art. 32; FTA Latvia, Art. 32 and FTA Lithuania, Art. 33. These provisions also already provide for the adoption of 'the necessary rules for the implementation' of these competition articles, within three years after their entry into force (deadline 31 December 1997). The reference in the Europe Agreements to precisely this date therefore comes as no real surprise.

Interim Agreement.[24] In that case the three-year term will have started on 1 January 1996[25] and therefore only expires on 31 December 1999.

B. Particularities

a. Explicit references to GATT

The Agreements with Poland, Estonia, Latvia and Lithuania have as an addition to paragraph 3 of the Competition Article that, until such implementing rules are adopted, the provisions of the Agreement on interpretation and application of Articles VI, XVI and XXIII of the GATT shall be applied as the rules for the implementation of the provision dealing with incompatible public aid and related parts of paragraph 2. Although not entirely surprising, this specific reference to GATT in the Polish paragraph 3 is rather remarkable. It is not surprising, because Poland was indeed the first European – then – CMEA country to become a full member of GATT in 1967. It is remarkable, however, since Poland was followed by Romania in 1971 and Hungary in 1973. For the Czech Republic and the Slovak Republic, the situation is different again, as Czechoslovakia was a founding member of GATT, and remained so after the changes in its social and economic system. It is therefore somewhat strange to see this reference to GATT only in the Agreement with Poland, and not to find a similar phrase in the respective paragraphs 3 of the Agreements with the other GATT members.

The reference to GATT in the Baltic States' Agreements, on the other hand, is even more striking, as these countries have never been parties to GATT and, pending their application, have so far not become members of the WTO either.

b. Explicit references to national competition legislation

In paragraphs 3 of the Czech, Slovak and Slovenian Agreement, explicit reference is made, not to international law as in the Polish case, but to internal legislation. Until the adoption of implementing rules,[26] the Parties will deal with practices incompatible with paragraph 1 on their respective territories according to their respective legislations. Czech and Slovak competition law is essentially based on the Competition Protection Act of 30 January 1991, which came into force on 1 March 1991. The Act remained valid for some time after the division of the Federation, the only difference being its denomination as the Czech Competition Protection Act, or as the Slovak Act on the Protection of Economic Competition.[27] This reference to internal legislation is, however,

---

[24] To date (August 1996), this has not yet occurred.

[25] Slovenia, Art. 132.

[26] As mentioned before, the Czech implementing rules were adopted on 30 January 1996.

[27] O. Black, 'Competition law in Central and Eastern Europe', *ECLR*, 1993, 133. In 1994, this 1991 Competition Protection Act 1991 was replaced in Slovakia. See for the text of the new Act No. 188 of the National Council of the Slovak Republic of 8 July 1994 on Protection of Economic Competition, *ECLR Supplement 7*, 1995, i–viii and for a comment, M. Banas, 'The new anti-monopoly law in Slovakia', *ECLR*, 1995, 441–5.

not absolute, as the text goes on to state explicitly that this is without prejudice to the safeguard clause of paragraph 6.[28]

This reference to internal competition law in the Czech and Slovak agreements only, is also a strange feature. Czechoslovakia was not the only, and moreover not the first, of the former CMEA countries to introduce competition laws 'as part of their efforts to establish a market economy'.[29] In 1990, Hungary,[30] Romania[31] and Poland[32] passed laws regulating competition, with Bulgaria following in May 1991.[33] However, the Europe Agreements with these countries do not explicitly allow the parties to use their internal criteria for the assessment of practices incompatible with the competition provisions of their Agreement. The question therefore arises whether this amounts to an actual denial for the Parties to do so, or whether this leaves the internal competence of the respective competition authorities intact. Should the latter be the correct answer, then the Czech, Slovak and Slovenian consideration is almost a superfluous one. In that case, the question remains why it was not incorporated in the other Agreements, thus taking away all doubt surrounding the issue. Should, conversely, the former answer be the correct one, then the situation becomes problematic, for this would leave all practices contrary to the competition provisions of the Europe Agreements unassailable as long as the Association Councils do not adopt the necessary implementing rules. This seems so at odds with the objectives of the Europe Agreements, that one can assume that the latter interpretation is to be preferred.

Another matter is whether and how this temporary continued application of domestic competition legislation to practices incompatible with paragraph 1 of the competition article within the territories of the associatied countries, will be influenced by the commitment of these parties to ensuring the compatibility of their domestic legislation with that of the Community, for which no time limit is set.

Discrepancies seem most likely in the field of monitoring dominant positions. According to paragraph 1 (ii) of the Competition Article, abuses by one or more undertakings of a dominant position in the territories of the Community or of the Other Party as a whole or in a substantial part thereof, are incompatible with the proper functioning of the Agreement, in so far as

---

[28] Czech Republic, Art. 64.3; Slovak Republic, Art. 64.3; Slovenia, Art. 64.3. See on this safeguard clause, below.

[29] Black (1993), 129.

[30] Act LXXXVI on the prohibition of unfair market practices. Also relevant are Law LXXXVII of 1990 on pricing and Law IV of 1957 on State Administrative Procedures, Black (1993), 129. As a result of the commitment to align with the European competition rules, this legislation will, however, be modified in the course of 1996.

[31] Chapter V of Law 15, adopted in 1990, on the reorganization of state economic units as autonomous-management units and companies.

[32] 1990 Act on Counteracting Monopolistic Practices. See for an analysis of this Act, A. Fornalczyk, (President of the Polish Antimonopoly Office), 'Competition policy during transformation of a centrally planned economy', in Hawk (ed.), *1992 Fordham Corp.L.Inst.*, *International antitrust law and policy*, New York, Transnational Juris Publications, 1993, 385–402.

[33] Protection of Competition Act, passed in May 1991, Black (1993), 130.

they affect trade between the Community and the Other Party. Following paragraph 2, such practice shall be assessed on the basis of criteria arising from the application of the rules of Article 86 EC. The Central, Eastern European and Baltic countries will therefore have to make their competition provisions dealing with abuses of a dominant position compatible with Article 86 EC law and policy. Until the adoption of implementing rules, the competition authorities can, however, deal with abuses of a dominant position on their territory according to their domestic legislation.[34]

Unlike Article 86 EC, most[35] of these domestic competition rules set thresholds for dominance in terms of market shares ranging from 30[36] to 35 per cent.[37] In Poland, dominance is presumed if the entity has a market share over 40 per cent.[38] Within the Community legal framework, such market shares on their own[39] have seldom been held to amount to a dominant position within the meaning of Article 86 EC. The question therefore arises whether the commitment to bring domestic rules on abuses of a dominant position in line with Article 86 would actually prevent the associated countries' competition authorities from applying their existing legislation to practices which would almost certainly not fall with the ambit of Article 86 EC. Put differently, is the continued application of domestic competition law made dependent upon the fulfilment of the conditions for application of Article 86 EC? If this were the case, it would amount to an immediate acceptance of the *acquis communautaire* in the field of competition law and policy by the Central and Eastern European countries, as their domestic conditions for applicability would be superseded by those of the Community.

In the Czech, Slovak and Slovenian Agreement, the continued application of domestic legislation until the adoption of implementing rules by the Association Council is explicitly said to be 'without prejudice to paragraph 6'.[40] This seems to set a second limit to the autonomy of the Parties' competition authorities during the transitional period. If one of the Parties considers that a particular practice is incompatible with the competition provisions of the Agreement, and causes or threatens to cause serious prejudice to the interest of the Other Party or material injury to its domestic industry, including its services industry, it may take appropriate measures after consultation within the Association Council or after 30 working days following referral for such consultation.[41] This provision will probably have the effect of preventing

---

[34] Due to the adoption of Polish and Czech implementing rules, this possibility no longer exists for the Polish and Czech competition authorities.

[35] Not so in present Romanian legislation, Black (1993), 132.

[36] In Hungary, the Czech Republic and the Slovak Republic. See on this Black (1993), 129 resp. 133.

[37] In Bulgaria, see on this Black (1993), 131.

[38] See on this, Fornalczyk (1993), 388.

[39] Additional elements will then be taken into account, such as the competitive structure of the market concerned, the number of competitors and their market shares. See *inter alia* the Court's decision in *Hoffmann-La Roche*, Case 85/76, (1979) ECR 461, paragraph 40.

[40] Here again, the adoption of the Czech implementing rules made this provision redundant for the Czech agreement.

[41] This paragraph 6 is included in the competition article of all the Association Agreements.

the European Commission from applying its effects doctrine[42] to practices originating in the Other Party's territory and having an adverse effect on competition within the Community, *without* first referring the issue for consultation within the Association Council. At the same time, as a result of the duty to make a preliminary reference for consultation, conflicting decisions on the same practice by the competition authorities are likely to be avoided.

An obvious advantage of the temporary continued application of domestic competition law is that thereby an important gap in the competition articles of the Europe Agreements can be filled. These articles do not provide any sanction for incompatibility with the proper functioning of the Agreements. Such a gap is understandable to a certain extent, as the articles deal with restrictive agreements, abuses of a dominant position and state aid all within one and the same article. In the EC Treaty, no sanction is set for the two last practices either. Article 86 EC Treaty 'merely' prohibits abuses of dominant positions as incompatible with the Common Market. A similar prohibition is laid down in Article 92 EC Treaty with regard to certain state aids. It is only in the field of restrictive practices that the EC Treaty explicitly contains the sanction of rendering such agreements void for incompatibility with the Common Market. In practice, however, the absence of a sanction in Article 86 EC has not posed too many difficulties, largely as a result of the direct effect of this provision.[43] National courts dealing with an alleged abuse of a dominant position have had recourse to their national sanctions for breach of statutory duty, which in most of the member states is precisely the sanction of nullity. The only difference with the nullity expressly provided for in Article 85(2) EC Treaty therefore seems to be that, at least in theory, the sanction attached to abuses of a dominant position is not a Community law concept, so the Court of Justice cannot be called upon to provide an interpretation which is binding for the national courts. This difference is, however, only a theoretical one, as the Court of Justice has systematically held that the actual consequences of the nullity provided for in Article 85(2) are a matter of national law.[44] As this contribution will not examine further the rules on state aids,[45] the somewhat different consequences of illegal state aid will be left aside. The same goes for the specific provisions in the Europe Agreements dealing with public enterprises.

III. A STANDARD OF INCOMPATIBILITY WITHOUT A SANCTION

In paragraph 2 of the Competition Article in the Europe Agreements, explicit reference is made to the 'criteria arising from the application of the rules of

---

[42] See on this doctrine, Case 89, 104, 114, 116, 117, 125–129/85, *Ahlstrom* (1988) ECR 5193.

[43] See on the direct effect of EC competition law, *inter alia*, Case 127/73, *BRT v SABAM* (1974) ECR 51 and 313 and Case 66/86, *Ahmed Saeed* (1989) ECR 803.

[44] See on this position, *inter alia*, Case 319/82, *Société de vente de Ciments v Kerpen* (1983) ECR 4173; Case 10/86, *VAG France* (1986) ECR 4071, paragraph 12.

[45] See elsewhere in this book, the contribution by Prof. Slot, below pp. 116–39.

Articles 85, 86 . . . EC Treaty' for the assessment of practices incompatible with that article. One might therefore have expected that the Association Councils would have complemented the standard of incompatibility with a sanction of nullity, as provided under Article 85(2), and following from the direct effect of both Articles 85 and 86 EC. It could furthermore have been presumed that the actual consequences of this nullity would equally be a matter of national law.[46]

This immediately begs the further question whether this would amount to granting direct effect to the competition provisions of the Europe Agreements. Different positions are taken on this point. Jakob lists a number of reasons for arguing against such an interpretation, of which the reference to the joint declaration relating to Article 63 of the Polish Agreement seems rather convincing.[47] According to this declaration, '[p]arties *may* request the Association Council at a later stage, and after the adopting of the implementing rules . . . , to examine *to what extent* and *under which conditions* certain competition rules *may* be *directly applicable*, taking into account the progress made in the integration process between the Community and Poland'.[48] Such a declaration is, however, absent in *all* other Agreements, so that it is not clear whether the Polish declaration is generally valid. At the same time, it would be strange to deny individuals the possibility of invoking the competition provisions in proceedings before Polish courts only, as this would clearly amount to an unacceptable discrimination *vis-à-vis* individuals in the other associated countries. With Marceau,[49] I would therefore rather conclude in favour of direct effect.

In the eventuality that this concept is unknown in (some of) the associated countries, one may well wonder whether these countries are under an obligation to introduce it, in order to guarantee fully and effectively the proper functioning of the competition provisions of their Agreement. If such a duty is absent, the level of legal protection in these countries against infringements of the provisions in question would be substantially different from that available within the Community, where parties can invoke them in proceedings before a national court.

As the Europe Agreements are acts of the institutions of the Community, and therefore within the terms of Article 177, paragraph 1, sub b) EC Treaty,[50] the courts of the member states can moreover refer questions to the Court of Justice for a preliminary ruling on the interpretation of, for example, the clause requiring effects on trade. On the other hand, if the concept of direct

---

[46] The draft decisions of the Hungarian, Czech, Slovak and Bulgarian Association Councils and the actual – as published – Czech and Polish implementing rules seem, however, to be taking a different view. See on this, below, section VBa, p. 99.

[47] Jakob (1993), 431.

[48] *OJ* 1993 L 438/180, emphasis added.

[49] Marceau (1995), 52–6. It should be recalled that this author only deals with the Polish Agreement.

[50] According to established case law of the ECJ. See e.g. Case 181/73, *Haegemann* (1974) ECR 449.

effect exists or – as the case may be – is introduced, associated countries' national courts have no such access to the Court of Justice, as they are not 'courts or tribunals of a Member State', a condition required under Article 177 EC. The absence of access to the Court might lead to diverging interpretations of the Agreement's competition provisions, since it is unlikely that the binding force, or *quasi erga omnes* effect, of an interpretation given by the Court of Justice upon a reference from a EC national court would be extended to courts which are themselves prevented from asking such questions.

The dispute settlement procedure contained in all Agreements[51] cannot be seen as an alternative for the absence of a genuine judicial guarantee of uniform interpretation of the competition provisions.[52] First of all, the procedure can only be initiated by one of the Parties to the Agreements, thus preventing private parties from doing so. Moreover, disputes relating to the application or interpretation of the Agreement are not submitted to a judicial body, but referred to the Association Council, which may settle the dispute by means of decision. Such a decision is binding, as the parties are obliged to take all the necessary measures to carry it out. If the Association Council is unable to settle the dispute, an arbitration procedure is set in motion, which equally leads to a decision which the Parties to the dispute are obliged to implement.

IV. A STANDARD OF INCOMPATIBILITY WITHOUT AN ARTICLE 85(3) EQUIVALENT

There is a specific possible risk associated with the continued application of domestic competition law for as long as the Association Councils have not adopted implementing rules.[53] It follows from the absence of an Article 85(3) equivalent with regard to practices incompatible with the proper functioning of the Agreement.[54] The central issue here is whether agreements infringing paragraph 1 (i) of the Competition Articles could be exempted on grounds *other* than those referred to in Article 85(3) EC Treaty, but which are part of an associated country's domestic competition legislation. The alternative view would be that the commitment to harmonization would prevent these countries' competition authorities from fully applying their own grounds for

---

[51] See Hungary, Art. 107; Poland, Art. 105; Czech Republic, Art. 107; Slovak Republic, Art. 107; Romania, Art. 109; Bulgaria, Art. 108; Estonia, Art. 112; Latvia, Art. 113; Lithuania, Art. 114; Slovenia, Art. 113; see L. Van Den Hende, below, p. 140.

[52] At the same time it is submitted that this procedure was never intended for dealing with problems arising from the application of the Agreements' competition articles.

[53] Which did occur, as mentioned earlier, only in the case of Poland and the Czech Republic.

[54] Marceau (1995), 45, seems to submit that this comes down to the introduction of a rule of reason in the application of the Europe Agreements' competition provisions. Such an interpretation is, however, not entirely convincing because of the above-mentioned explicit reference in the competition articles to an assessment in accordance with the criteria arising from the application of the rules of Art. 85, in which case recourse is rarely had to a genuine rule of reason.

exemption. In the latter case, these authorities would in effect have to take over and act in accordance with the *acquis communautaire* in the field of competition law immediately.

A somewhat different, but linked, question is whether a domestic exemption could be based on only a part of the grounds mentioned in Article 85(3) EC Treaty, or whether the competition authorities would, as from now, have to examine all four EC conditions for exemption before being able to exempt a given practice.

V. THE IMPORTANCE OF IMPLEMENTING RULES HIGHLIGHTED

It may be clear from the foregoing that the competition article in the Europe Agreements is less unequivocal than appears at first sight. It must be stressed, however, that most of the problems or possible difficulties relate to the transitional period between the entry into force of the Agreement and the enactment of implementing rules by the respective Association Councils. If the Parties really intend to establish a guarantee for workable competition within the Community and the Other Parties' territories, it is therefore of the utmost importance that such implementing rules are enacted as soon as possible. Otherwise, the competition provisions in the new Association Agreements might share the fate of the competition provisions contained in the 'old' Association and Free Trade Agreements with Greece,[55] Turkey[56] and the former EFTA countries[57] and become largely insignificant, even almost entirely irrelevant in practical terms.[58]

With the obvious exception of Slovenia,[59] all agreements with the Central and Eastern European countries have been in force for some time now.[60] Even though all the Association Councils have met at least once and adopted

---

[55] See in particular Arts 51 and 52 of the Association Agreement of 9 July 1961 with Greece, *OJ* nr. 26, 18 February 1963.

[56] See Art. 43 of the Additional Protocol of 23 November 1970 to the Association Agreement with Turkey of 12 September 1963, *OJ* 1972 L 293.

[57] Agreements of 22 July 1972 with resp. Switzerland (Art. 23), *OJ* 1972 L 300; Austria (Art. 23), *OJ* 1972 L 300; Portugal (Art. 26), *OJ* 1972 L 301; Sweden (Art. 23), *OJ* 1972 L 300 and Iceland (Art. 23), *OJ* 1972 L 301. Agreement of 14 May 1973 with Norway (Art. 23), *OJ* 1973 L 171 and with Finland (Art. 23), *OJ* 1973 L 328.

[58] See for an analysis of the shortcomings of these competition provisions, mainly due to the absence of implementing rules, M. Baldi, 'Bemerkungen zum EWR-Wettbewerbsrecht aus Grundsätzlicher Sicht', in Jacot-Guillarmod, (ed.), *Accord EEE. Commentaires et réflexions*, Zurich, Schulthess Polygraphischer Verlag, 1992, 285–92; O. Mach, 'Droit des ententes', in Jacot-Guillarmod (1992), 347–8; J.H.J. Bourgeois, 'L'Espace Economique européen', *Revue du Marché unique européen*, 1992-2, 19–20; and A. Haagsma, 'The competition rules of the EEA and the Europe Agreements: lawyer's paradise or user's safe harbour?', in Slot & McDonnell (eds), *Procedure and enforcement in EC and US competition law*, London, Sweet & Maxwell, 1993, 245–8.

[59] As has been mentioned earlier, the Agreement with Slovenia has been signed but not concluded yet.

[60] See on the actual dates of entry into force, above, Introduction.

their rules of procedure,[61] not all of them have so far adopted implementing rules.[62] It should, however, be kept in mind that the enactment of these rules was already provided for in the Interim Agreements on trade and trade related matters as one of the duties assigned to (and to be carried out by) the Joint Committees until such time as the Association Councils were established.[63] This actually means that preparatory work on implementing rules could have started shortly after the entry into force of the Interim Agreements.[64]

The Hungarian rules of procedure indicate that this has indeed been the case, as they explicitly allow for the continued existence of a working group on the implementation of competition rules, which was set up by the Hungarian Joint Committee provided for in the Hungarian Interim Agreement.[65] It may be assumed that such competition working groups were set up by all the other Joint Committees as well.[66] As was mentioned earlier, this preparatory work should have led to the adoption of implementing rules by 31 December 1994 for Hungary, Poland, the Czech Republic and the Slovak Republic. For Romania and Bulgaria, the time limit expired on 31 December 1995.

At the time of writing, two different types of documents were available.[67] On the one hand, there are the proposals for a Council and Commission decision on the position to be taken by the Community within the Association Council established by the Hungarian, Czech, Slovak and Bulgarian Agreements, with regard to the adoption of the necessary rules for the implementation of the competition provisions of the Europe Agreements. For Hungary, the Commission submitted this proposal a mere fifteen days before the expiry of the deadline,[68] while in the case of the Czech and Slovak

[61] See for the first meetings of the Association Councils during which they also adopted their rules of procedure: Hungary: 7 March 1994, UE-H 1504/94 (press 32); Poland: 7 March 1994, UE-PL 1404/94 (press 33); Czech Republic: 10 April 1995, UE-CZ 1703/95 (press 120); Romania: 10 April 1995, UE-RO 1803/95 (press 119); Slovak Republic: 29 May 1995, Pres/ 95/157; Bulgaria: 29 May 1995, Pres/95/156. At Hungary's explicit request, the Decision pertaining to the rules of procedure has been published in the *Official Journal*. See Decision 1/94 of the Association Council between the European Communities and their member states, on the one part and the Republic of Hungary, on the other of 7 March 1994 on its rules of procedure, *OJ* 1994 L 242/23. This Decision was amended by Decision 1/96 of 16 July 1996, pertaining to the setting up of a Joint Consultative Committee, *OJ* 1996 L 192/17.

[62] For the time being, such rules are absent for Hungary, the Slovak Republic, Romania and Bulgaria.

[63] See for example for Hungary, Art. 32.3 and Art. 36 Interim Agreement. Similar provisions are part of all other Interim Agreements.

[64] See on these dates of entry into force, above, note 19.

[65] See Art. 14 of the Rules of Procedure and Annex II attached thereto. The precise date of its setting up could, however, not be detected.

[66] Due to the absence of other published Rules of Procedure, this assumption can, however, not be verified further.

[67] Distributed as COM document, *or* published in the *Official Journal*. The text will, therefore, be based on the documents available.

[68] COM(94) 639 final, submitted on 15 December 1994. As mentioned earlier, during its third meeting (16 July 1996), the EC–Hungary Association Council reached agreement on the substance of the implementing rules, which are intended to enter into force on 1 January 1997, after they have been formally adopted (by way of written procedure), see *UE-H 1506/ 96 (Presse 220)*.

Republics this deadline had long lapsed.[69] The proposal in the Bulgarian case was submitted on 22 November 1995,[70] whereas for Romania[71] no published proposals could be found. On the other hand, there are the Czech and Polish implementing rules, adopted on 30 January and 16 July 1996 respectively.[72]

A. The obvious appeal of the EEA's two-pillar approach

A general point may be made before actually dealing with the (proposals for) implementing rules. It is submitted that the most clear-cut solution to all the above-mentioned problems would have been for all the Association Councils to introduce, as implementing rules, a system comparable to the competition system of the EEA, which is based on a 'two-pillar' approach and establishes a dynamic and homogeneous, integrated system based on common rules and equal conditions of competition.[73] The Agreement Establishing the EEA was signed in Porto, on 2 May 1992 between the European Community, its – then – twelve member states and the – then – seven States of the European Free Trade Association.[74] Due to the negative outcome of the referendum in Switzerland and the consequences thereof for Liechtenstein, it entered into force on 1 December 1993 as between the Community and the remaining five EFTA-States.[75] More changes were made to take into account the accession of three of them – Austria, Finland and Sweden – to the Community on 1 January 1995. Even though it would not have been advisable simply to copy the EEA layout (in which the competition provisions are dispersed over thirteen Articles, eight protocols, two annexes, three common declarations and two paragraphs in the minutes[76]), there is no doubt that the Association Councils could have gained from a genuine reflection on the EEA approach, and this could have assisted in the elaboration of clear implementing rules for the competition provisions of their own Agreements.

The most important characteristic of the EEA competition rules is their homogeneity with EC competition rules, both for the present and the future. As to the present, this follows not only from the fact that the substantive rules

---

[69] Deadline 31 December 1994. Submission of the already mentioned COM(95) 157 final and COM(95) 156 final: 18 May 1995.

[70] COM(95) 528 final (deadline 31 December 1995).

[71] Deadline 31 December 1995.

[72] See for the text of the Czech rules, *OJ* 1996 L 31/21. And for the Polish rules, *OJ* 1996 L 208/24.

[73] Expressions used to describe the EEA Competition system, by the European Commission in its *Brochure concerning the competition rules applicable to undertakings as contained in the EEA Agreement and their implementation by the EC Commission and the EFTA Surveillance Authority*, Luxembourg, Office for Official Publications of the EC, 1992, 32 p. (further referred to as 'the Brochure').

[74] Austria, Finland, Iceland, Liechtenstein, Norway, Sweden and Switzerland.

[75] See for the changes made to the Agreement after the referendum, Commission Regulation 3666/93 of 15 December 1993, *OJ* 1993 L 336/19.

[76] Which led Haagsma (1993), 251 to remark that the Agreement 'is probably the most complicated international agreement which the Community ever negotiated' and that '[t]his will make the EEA the most user-unfriendly legal text ever to have been agreed to by the Community'.

on competition have an identical wording to those contained in the EEC and ECSC Treaty and the acts adopted in application of these provisions. In addition, they are to be interpreted in their implementation and application in conformity with the relevant rulings of the EC Court of Justice prior to the date of the signature of the EEA Agreement.[77] Due to this acceptance by the EFTA States of the EC *acquis communautaire* in the field of competition, existing domestic legislation has no role to play in the application of the EEA competition rules. It is therefore no surprise that – unlike the Europe Agreements – the EEA Agreement does not contain a harmonization clause according to which the EFTA States would have undertaken to gradually make their competition legislation compatible with that of the Community.[78] Through a clearly elaborated system of cooperation between the EC Commission and the EFTA Surveillance authority (ESA),[79] this initial homogeneity is furthermore guaranteed for the future.[80] The main and only difference between the substantive EC competition rules and those contained in the EEA agreement relate therefore to their geographical scope of application which in the EEA includes, in addition to the EC, the EFTA States.[81]

An important consequence of the two-pillar system is that the actual enforcement of the EEA competition rules is carried out by either the EC Commission or the EFTA Surveillance Authority. The actual attribution of cases is specifically dealt with in Articles 56 and 57 EEA. In this respect it must be stressed, however, that the ESA is entrusted with equivalent powers and similar functions to those of the EC Commission for the application of the EC competition rules, and will apply procedural rules similar to those applied in the EC.[82] From the point of view of undertakings, the only possible

---

[77] According to Art. 6 EEA. See on the EEA competition system *inter alia* Jakob (1993), 411–26.

[78] See on this commitment on the part of the Central and Eastern European Countries and the possible problems flowing from this, above, section I.

[79] See on this, Arts 4 to 21 of the Agreement between the EFTA States on the establishment of a surveillance authority and a Court of Justice (further referred to as 'EFTA States Agreement'), *OJ* 1994 L 344; Protocol 4 on the functions and powers of the EFTA Surveillance Authority in the field of competition, *OJ* 1994 L 344/12; and the Protocol adjusting the Agreement to take the Swiss referendum into account, *OJ* 1994 L 344/82.

[80] See Art. 58 EEA: 'With a view to developing and maintaining a uniform surveillance throughout the European Economic Area in the field of competition and to promoting a homogeneous implementation, application and interpretation of the provisions of this Agreement to this end, the competent authorities shall cooperate in accordance with the provisions set out in Protocols 23 and 24.' For more details on this cooperation, see Bourgeois (1992), 16–19; S. Norberg, 'The Agreement on a European Economic Area', *CMLRev.* (1992), 1175–80 and 1183–91; Russotto (1992), 309–12; Poilvache (1993), 62–3 and 66; C. Reymond, 'Institutions, decision-making procedures and settlement of disputes in the European Economic Area', *CMLRev.* (1993), 449–80, S. Norberg, 'The EEA Agreement: institutional solutions for a dynamic and homogeneous EEA in the area of competition', in Hawk (ed.), *1992 Fordham Corp.L.Inst.*, *International antitrust law and policy*, New York, Transnational Juris Publications, 1993, 437–63 and J. Stragier, 'The competition rules in the EEA Agreement and their implementation', *ECLRev.* (1993), 33–4.

[81] *Brochure*, p. 5.

[82] Explicitly provided for in Art. 108, 1 EEA and Arts 1 and 2 of Protocol 21 to the EEA Agreement on the implementation of competition rules applicable to undertakings. See for the actual creation of procedures similar to those existing in the Community, Protocol 4 on the functions and powers of the EFTA Surveillance Authority in the field of competition,

difference in the actual application of the EEA competition rules is therefore the name of the competent authority.

This contrasts sharply with the approach taken in the implementing rules for the Czech Republic and Poland and the proposals with regard to the adoption of the necessary rules for the implementation of the competition provisions of the Europe Agreements with Hungary, the Slovak Republic and Bulgaria.[83] A common feature of all these texts, which is worth mentioning by way of preliminary remark, is that they only contain implementing rules for the application of the competition provisions applying to undertakings. The absence of provisions on the implementation of the state aid rules contained in the Agreement will, however, not pose too many difficulties and should certainly not be understood as leaving aids uncontrollable in the absence of implementing rules,[84] as the Agreements themselves provide some indications as to the application of the provisions on state aid during the first five years following the entry into force of the Agreements. Moreover, depending on the economic situation of the other party, the Association Council can extend this period by further periods of five years.[85] Should one of the parties wish to take measures with regard to incompatible state aid to which the GATT rules apply, it can only do so in accordance with GATT procedures and conditions.[86]

B. And yet, a different approach prevailed:[87] some critical comments

According to the Explanatory Memoranda, the competition provisions are undoubtedly 'one of the basic points of the Europe Agreement between the European Communities and [the other Party]', so that their actual

---

attached to the EFTA States Agreement (further referred to as 'Protocol 4, EFTA States Agreement'), *OJ* 1994 L 344/12. See for the adaptations on the EC-side, Commission Regulation 3666/93 of 15 December 1993 amending Regulation 27 and Regulations 1629/69, 4260/88, 4261/88 and 2367/90 with a view to implementing the competition provisions laid down in the Agreement on the European Economic Area, *OJ* 1993 L 336.

[83] The already mentioned COM(94) 639 final, COM(95) 157 final, COM(95) 156 final and COM(95) 528 final.

[84] With regard to the elaboration of state aid implementing rules, no proposals have been elaborated yet.

[85] Hungary, Art. 62.4; Poland, Art. 63.3, second paragraph; Czech Republic, Art. 64.4; Slovak Republic, Art. 64.4; Romania, Art. 64.4; Bulgaria, Art. 64.4.

[86] Hungary, Art. 62.6, second paragraph; Poland, Art. 63.6, second paragraph; Czech Republic, Art. 64.6, second paragraph; Slovak Republic, Art. 64.6, second paragraph; Romania, Art. 64.6, second paragraph; Bulgaria, Art. 64.6, second paragraph. This last reference to GATT is strange, as Bulgaria is not a GATT member (yet), see below, Slot, pp. 128–9.

[87] Jakob (1993), 430 points out two possible reasons for this difference in approach. First of all 'the fact that negotiations of the Europe Agreements took place in a bilateral context, unlike the multilateral EEA negotiations. There was thus no room for creating a concept as elaborate as the EEA concept. [Secondly] another reason would appear to be that whereas EFTA members are economically highly developed countries, allowance had to be made for the difficult economic situation of the new democracies.'

implementation is 'a prerequisite for the smooth development of trade relations between the two parties'.[88]

a. On the absence of truly common rules

As in the EEA Agreement, the application of the competition provisions follows a two-pillar approach. Cases relating to restrictive agreements and to abuses of dominant positions will be dealt with by the EC Commission (DG IV). For the other Parties, reference is made to the Hungarian Office of Economic Competition (GVH),[89] the Polish Anti-monopoly Office (AMO),[90] the Czech Ministry for Economic Competition (MEC),[91] the Anti-monopoly Office of the Slovak Republic (AMO)[92] and the Bulgarian Committee on the Protection of competition (CPC).[93]

The EEA analogy ends there, however. According to the [Draft] Articles 1,[94] the competences of these competition authorities 'shall follow from the existing rules of the respective legislations of the EC and [the other Party], including where these rules are applied to undertakings located outside the respective territory.' Moreover, 'both authorities shall settle the cases in accordance with their own substantive rules, and having regard to the provisions set out below.' For the EC Commission, the relevant substantive rules are 'the competition rules of the Treaty establishing the European Community as well as the ECSC Treaty including the competition-related secondary legislation'. For the Other Parties, reference is made to the Hungarian Act LXXXVI of 1990 on the Protection of Unfair Market Practices for the GVH, the Polish Anti-monopoly Law for the AMO, the Czech Competition Protection Act for the MEC, the Slovak Act on the Protection of Economic Competition for the AMO and the Bulgarian Act on the Protection of Economic Competition for the CPC.

Unlike the EEA Agreement, the Europe Agreements will therefore *not* establish a 'homogeneous integrated system based on common rules'.[95] As mentioned earlier, the competition provisions do not actually copy Articles 85 and 86 EC; they 'limit' themselves to establishing the standard of incompatibility with the proper functioning of the Agreement. The fact that the [draft] implementing rules refer to existing internal legislation as the substantive rules for settling cases, clearly invalidates the earlier assumption that the standard

---

[88] Explanatory Memorandum COM(94) 639, COM(95) 157 final, COM(95) 156 final and COM(95) 528 final.

[89] COM(94) 639, Draft Art. 1.

[90] Decision 1/96 of the EC–Poland Association Council, *OJ* 1996 L 208/24 (further referred to as 'Polish Decision 1/96'), Art. 1.

[91] COM(95) 157, Draft Art. 1, and Decision 1/96 of the EC–Czech Republic Association Council, *OJ* 1996 L 31/21 (further referred to as 'Czech Decision 1/96'), Art. 1.

[92] COM(95) 156, Draft Art. 1.

[93] COM(95) 528, Draft Art. 1.

[94] See COM(94) 639, Draft Art. 1; Polish Decision 1/96, Art. 1; COM(95) 157, Draft Art. 1 and Czech Decision 1/96, Art. 1; COM(95) 156, Draft Art. 1; COM(95) 528, Draft Art. 1.

[95] Which is one of the objectives of the EEA Agreement, see *Brochure*, p. 1.

be complemented with a sanction of nullity, as mentioned in Article 85(2) EC and following from the direct effect of both Articles 85 and 86 EC.[96]

What is even more striking is that the implementing rules do not contain an Article 85(3) equivalent either, and yet explicitly 'confirm that the principles embodied in the block exemptions in force in the Community will apply [integrally]'.[97] Whereas this is understandable as far as the EC Commission is concerned,[98] one may wonder whether the mere provision of being informed 'of any procedure related to the adoption, abolition or modification of Block exemptions by the EC' is a sufficient legal basis for the other Party's competition authority to accept this important part of the *acquis communautaire* in the field of competition policy. One could of course play on the words used, and argue that the GVH, the AMO, the MEC, the AMO and the CPC do not have to actually apply the block exemptions – which in practice would most probably amount to *not* taking action against certain practices covered by these regulations – but 'only' the principles contained therein. There is ample room for doubt, however, whether this literal approach would solve the problem of possible conflicts between the other Party's legislation and practice in the field of exemptions[99] and the block exemptions.

b. On judicial protection

A different but linked question relates to judicial protection in the field of competition law. According to Hungarian and Bulgarian legislation, private parties can bring actions for unfair competition in the respective national courts.[100] Although in Hungary, the GVH must be petitioned,[101] such action will always lead to a decision from the court. If the action relates to a practice covered by one of the block exemptions, several elements remain unclear. As the Draft Article 6 does not mention national courts, it is not clear whether Hungarian or Bulgarian courts[102] would be bound to apply the principles embodied in the block exemptions in force in the Community. If not, this would erode much of the protection offered to parties to an agreement covered by these block exemptions, and moreover amount to a serious discrimination

---

[96] See on this, again above section III, pp. 99–3.

[97] COM(94) 639, COM(95) 157, COM(95) 156 and COM(95) 528, Draft Decision, Explanatory Memorandum and Art. 6; Czech Decision 1/96, Art. 6 and Polish Decision 1/96, Art. 6.

[98] This follows clearly from the reference to the 'competition rules of the Treaty establishing the EC as well as the ECSC Treaty including the competition-related secondary legislation' in Art. 1 of the [Draft] Decision.

[99] See on some questions in relation to how to reconcile possible differences between the other Party's exemption grounds and Art. 85, 3 grounds also above, section IV, pp. 93–4.

[100] Black (1993), 130 and 131. Such direct right of private action seems absent in Czech and Slovak legization, where civil courts can only hear appeals against the competition authorities' decisions, ibid., 134. No information could be found on the situation under Polish or Romanian law.

[101] Black (1993), 130.

[102] This question does not need to be examined for EC national courts, as it is established case law that group exemption regulations have direct effect and that the conformity of a given practice with their provisions can be examined by national courts.

vis-à-vis companies with similar agreements within the Community. If, on the other hand, a block exemption-defence were possible before Hungarian or Bulgarian courts, this raises some other difficulties. Within the EC, national courts asked to apply the competition provisions of the Treaty, have several options in case of doubt as to the applicability and/or application of group exemptions or interpretation of certain provisions contained therein. They can stay proceedings and refer the case to the Court of Justice for a preliminary ruling under Article 177 EC, or request the Commission's assistance according to the procedures set out in the 1993 Notice on cooperation between national courts and the Commission in applying Articles 85 and 86 of the EEC Treaty.[103] Neither option is, however, available to Hungarian or Bulgarian courts, so the possibility of diverging interpretations cannot be entirely excluded. It would futhermore be difficult to argue that doubts encountered by these courts with regard to block exemptions could be seen as a situation 'where . . . block exemption regulations encounter serious objections on the [Hungarian or Bulgarian] side', so that the consultation provided for in Article 6 of the Draft Decision is most probably not likely to provide a sufficient and genuine solution for the difficulties of the courts.

c. On De Minimis *thresholds*

A strange feature of the draft implementing rules, at least at first sight, is that they refer to the old turnover threshold for *de minimis* purposes.[104] One might have expected that the actual decisions of the Association Councils would have taken the Commission Notice of 31 December 1994[105] into account, and accordingly raise the turnover threshold under Article 8 from 200 million ECU to 300 million ECU. It is therefore somewhat surprising that the mistake was not corrected in the 1996 Czech implementing rules[106] and that, moreover, this was repeated in the 1996 Polish implementing rules.[107]

d. On the concentration control gap

Another striking difference between the competition provisions contained in the EEA Agreement and those in the Europe Agreements is that the latter only deal with competition provisions applicable to undertakings as contained in the EC Treaty, without making any reference whatsoever to secondary legislation adopted for the implementation or application of the Treaty provisions

---

[103] *OJ* 1993 C 39/6. In the case of group exemptions, this assistance will most probably relate to points of law (see point 38) or to information regarding factual data: statistics, market studies and economic analyses (see point 40). Information of a procedural nature (see on this point 37) will seldom be relevant in these cases.

[104] COM(94) 639, COM(95) 157 and COM(95) 156, Draft Art. 8, and COM(95) 528, Draft Art. 7, where reference is made to the 1986 threshold of 200 million ECU turnover.

[105] Notice of the Commission concerning the updating of the 1986 communication on agreements of minor importance, *OJ* 1994 C 368/20.

[106] See Czech Decision 1/96, Art. 8 still mentioning the 200 million ECU threshold.

[107] See Polish Decision 1/96, Art. 8, also mentioning the old 200 million ECU threshold.

on competition.[108] As a result, the Europe Agreements' competition provisions applying to undertakings are entirely based on the twofold structure laid down in the EC Treaty itself. The third aspect of EC competition law, introduced in 1989 by Regulation 4064/89 on the control of concentrations,[109] is totally absent, and therefore entirely outside the scope of application of the Europe Agreements. The European Commission may therefore continue to apply Regulation 4064/89 to all concentrations with a Community dimension,[110] even if the domestic legislation of the associated country also applies.[111] The one-stop-shop rule, laid down in Regulation 4064/89, according to which member states' national legislation on competition cannot be applied to concentrations with a Community dimension,[112] would therefore not apply in the relations between EC and Associated countries. It is clear that such parallel application of Regulation 4064/89 together with national legislation might entail serious problems and difficulties for the undertakings concerned.

At first sight, this important gap in relation to concentration control can not be filled in the implementing rules, as these can only relate to the necessary rules for the implementation of the competition provisions contained in the Europe Agreements themselves. Nevertheless, in the Czech and Slovak proposals,[113] the Commission introduced a formula which apparently allows it to deal with Regulation 4064 cases, by deducing from Article 2(1) of the Council and Commission Decision on the conclusion of the Europe Agreement[114] that

> Articles 87, 228 and 235 of the EC Treaty as well as Articles 65 and 66 of the ECSC Treaty are appropriate legal basis for the position to be adopted by the Commission in the Association Council with regard to rules for the implementation of the competition provisions applicable to undertakings, *specifically* because of the inclusion of all types of mergers and acquisitions, including those falling outside the scope of Article 86 of the Treaty in the text of the implementing rules.[115]

---

[108] See for such explicit reference in the EEA Agreement, Art. 6 EEA.

[109] Council Regulation 4064/89 of 21 December 1989 on the control of concentrations between undertakings, *OJ* 1989 L 395/1, corrected in *OJ* 1990 L 257/13. The regulation entered into force on 21 September 1990.

[110] According to Art. 1, Reg. 4064/89, a concentration has a Community dimension, if the combined aggregate worldwide turnover of all the undertakings concerned exceeds 5,000 million ECU and the aggregate Community-wide turnover of each of at least two of the undertakings concerned exceeds 250 million ECU. In such cases the Regulation will apply, unless each of the undertakings concerned achieves more than two-thirds of its aggregate Community-wide turnover within one and the same member state.

[111] According to Black (1993), merger control is part of the competition legislation of Hungary, Bulgaria, Romania, and the Czech and Slovak Republic.

[112] See on this basic principle, Regulation 4064/89, Preamble, 27th indent.

[113] Proposals for the Czech and Slovak agreements, COM(95) 157 and COM(95) 156.

[114] This Article reads as follows: 'the position to be adopted by the Community within the Association Council shall be determined by the Council on a proposal from the Commission, or, where appropriate, by the Commission, each in accordance with the corresponding provisions of the Treaties establishing the European Community, the European Coal and Steel Community and the European Atomic Energy Community'. See e.g. the European Agreement with the Czech Republic, *OJ* 1994 L 360/1.

[115] COM(95) 157 and COM(95) 156, Explanatory Memorandum, emphasis added.

This view leads to one of the very few – but quite important – differences as between the proposed implementing rules for the Europe Agreement with Hungary on the one hand and with the Czech and Slovak Republics on the other. Whereas the Hungarian proposed rules have Article 113 and Article 228(2) as their legal basis,[116] the Commission took a different view in the Preamble to the proposed implementing rules for the Czech and Slovak Europe Agreements, by stating that 'resort to Article 235 of the Treaty of the European Community is necessary since Article 7 of the Draft Decision of the Association Council deals with provisions of Council Regulation (EEC) 4064/89, which is mainly based on aforementioned Article 235'.[117]

In the Hungarian, Czech[118] and Slovak Draft Decisions, and in the Polish Decision,[119] (Draft) Article 7 deals with mergers falling within the scope of Regulation 4064/89. According to the proposed Article, the other Party's competition authority shall be entitled to express its view on concentrations with a Community dimension which have significant impact on the other Party's economy. Even though the Commission shall 'give due considera-tion to that view', it will not be bound by it: the Draft Article explicitly states that this view and the consideration given to it cannot prejudice 'any action under the Parties' respective competition laws'. This Draft Article does not, therefore, contain a mechanism to deal with possible conflicts of jurisdiction, neither does it remove the possibility of conflicting decisions with regard to one and the same concentration. This contrasts sharply with the provisions on concentration control in the EEA Agreement, where the EC Commission is solely competent to deal with all concentrations falling under the EC Merger Regulation.[120] A mixed competence only arises for concentrations which meet the thresholds only in the territory of the EFTA States. In such cases, the application of the one-stop-shop rule is not absolute, as the com-petence of the Surveillance Authority is without prejudice to the competences of the EC member states.[121] This means that in such cases, companies will have to check whether they might also have to notify to an EC member state

---

[116] COM(94) 639, Preamble.

[117] COM(95) 157 and COM(95) 156, Preamble. It is somewhat strange that the reference to Art. 87 EC Treaty is not repeated here.

[118] The actual implementing rules did not introduce any changes to the proposal. The following information on the Draft Art. 7 therefore remains valid for the actual Art. 7 of Czech Decision 1/96. Whenever relating to the Czech situation, read 'draft/proposed Article' as 'draft/proposed Article and Article'.

[119] As mentioned before, the implementing rules were adopted and laid down in Decision 1/96 of the EC–Poland Association Council. Therefore, whenever relating to the Polish situation, read 'Draft Article' or 'proposed Article' as 'Article'.

[120] See for the modalities of cooperation between the EC Commission and the EFTA Surveil-lance Authority even in the case of sole competence for the Commission, Protocol 24 to the EEA Agreement, Art. 2. Cooperation will take place in the following situations: 1. if the undertakings achieve at least 25 per cent of their turnover in EFTA territory; 2. if each of at least two undertakings have a turnover of more than 250 million ECU in EFTA territory; and 3. if there is a danger of a dominant position impeding effective competition in EFTA territory or a substantial part thereof.

[121] Art. 57 EEA; *Brochure*, p. 11.

authority.[122] EFTA States' authorities, on the other hand, are precluded from applying their internal merger control rules, as the Surveillance Authority has exclusive jurisdiction with regard to concentrations that have an EFTA dimension.[123]

In the most recent Bulgarian Draft Decision, on the other hand, the situation is different again. Not only do the proposed rules have yet another legal basis,[124] but also, the issue of merger control is simply not dealt with at all. Thus, the Bulgarian competition authority is apparently not even entitled to express its view on concentrations with a Community dimension which would have a significant impact on the Bulgarian economy.

e. On the procedures for cooperation between the Parties' competition authorities

With regard to the implementing rules for the application of the competition provisions dealing with restrictive practices and abuses of a dominant position, the Draft Decisions[125] distinguish between cases coming within the competence of both competition authorities and cases falling under the exclusive competence of one competition authority. It has been mentioned above that the preliminary issue of competence will be dealt with according to the existing rules of each competition authority.

Where, as a result of these rules, both authorities are competent, the draft rules provide for notification by the authority dealing with a given case to the other authority, if it 'appears also to fall' under its competence.[126] In addition, consultation may be requested in all cases where a competition authority considers that 'anticompetitive activities carried out on the territory of the other authority are substantially affecting [its own] important interests'.[127] Another possibility in such circumstances is to request the other Party's competition authority to initiate any appropriate procedures, with a view to taking remedial action under its legislation on anticompetitive activities. Such a request will, however, not prevent the requesting authority from acting according to its own competition law. At the same time, it cannot 'hamper the full freedom of ultimate decision of the competition authority so

---

[122] *Brochure*, p. 17.

[123] Art. 21 of Protocol 4, EFTA States Agreement, *OJ* 1994 L 344/14.

[124] Art. 87 and Art. 228, 2. Cf. Arts 113 and 228, 2 for Hungary and Arts 87, 228 and 235 for the Czech and Slovak Republic.

[125] To take into account the adoption and publication of Decision 1/96 on the Czech implementing rules, replace 'draft/proposed Article' by 'draft/proposed Article *and Article*' whenever relating the text to the Czech situation. The same goes for 'draft/proposed rules', where one should read 'draft/proposed rules *and the rules*'. For Poland, as a result of the adoption and publication of Decision 1/96 of the EC–Poland Association Council, replace 'draft/proposed rules' by 'rules'.

[126] COM(94) 639, COM(95) 157, COM(95) 156 and COM(95) 528: Draft Art. 2.1; Czech Decision 1/96 and Polish Decision 1/96: Art. 2.1.

[127] COM(94) 639, COM(95) 157, COM(95) 156 and COM(95) 528: Draft Art. 2.2. Czech Decision 1/96 and Polish Decision 1/96: Art. 2.2.

addressed'.[128] Nevertheless, the competition authorities involved in such consultations will try to find a mutually acceptable solution in the light of the respective important interests involved. To this end, the requested competition authority 'shall give full and sympathetic consideration to [the] views and factual materials . . . provided by the requesting authority and, in particular, to the nature of the anticompetitive activities in question, the enterprises involved and the alleged harmful effects on the important interests of the requesting Party'.[129] These rules on reaching an understanding can, however, not prejudice any of the rights or obligations of the respective competition authorities.[130]

According to the Draft Articles 3, these rules on notification, consultation and comity and on finding an understanding apply *mutatis mutandis* to cases falling under the exclusive competence of one competition authority. The main difference here is that their application will follow from a conclusion on the part of the competition authority dealing with the case that it also affects 'important interests of the other Party'.

At this stage, it is not possible to predict how workable these rules on notification, consultation and comity and on finding an understanding, will be. First of all, it is not clear at the moment what exactly is needed for a case to qualify as 'affecting important interests'.[131] Apart from this, much, if not all, will depend on the actual use made of the repeated references to the continued application of the respective competition authorities' own legislation. Even if this is the logical result of the absence of truly common competition rules and procedures in the Europe Agreements, it remains to be seen whether the cooperation approach taken in these Draft Articles 2 and 3, or for that matter the exchange of views formula provided for in Draft Article 9,[132] will suffice to make up for this initial weakness.

Even though the 'actual implementation [of the competition provisions, one of the basic points of the Europe Agreements]' is described as 'a prerequisite for the smooth development of trade relations between the two parties',[133] the proposed 'procedures for cooperation between the two parties' competition authorities'[134] in essence go little further than the procedures for

---

[128] Ibid. It has been argued that this obligation of positive comity 'has direct effect and could be enforced by private firms, transforming this obligation into some form of "private positive comity"', Marceau (1995), 56. From an EC point of view, this reference to direct effect is, however, greatly confusing and almost misleading as one would not be dealing with judicial proceedings before the courts, but in essence be inviting a competition authority to take action.

[129] COM(94) 369, COM(95) 157, COM(95) 156 and COM(95) 528: Draft Art. 2.3. Czech Decision 1/96 and Polish Decision 1/96: Art. 2.3.

[130] Ibid.

[131] This is also a precondition for the existence of the right to request information. See on this right, Draft Art. 4.

[132] 'Whenever the procedures provided for in Arts 2 and 3 above do not lead to a mutually acceptable solution . . . , an exchange of views shall take place in the Association Council at the request of one Party within 3 months following the request.'

[133] COM(94) 639, COM(95) 157, COM(95) 156 and COM(95) 528, Explanatory Memorandum.

[134] Ibid.

notification, exchange of information, and consultation provided for in the EC–US administrative competition laws cooperation agreement of 23 September 1991 as reconcluded on 10 April 1995.[135] The approach taken in this Agreement differs from both the EEA's and the Europe Agreements' competition provisions, as its purpose is 'merely' 'to promote cooperation and coordination and lessen the possibility or impact of differences between the Parties in the application of their competition laws'.[136] In other words, the Agreement does not intend to establish 'a dynamic and homogeneous integrated system based on common rules and equal conditions of competition',[137] nor to provide for a common standard for incompatibility, and even less for a gradual harmonization of competition law along European standards.[138]

VI.   CONCLUDING REMARKS

It has been explained above that the Parties to the Europe Agreements have not adopted the EEA approach to competition. It is submitted that the EC–US approach could have offered a suitable alternative.[139] The cooperation between competition authorities dealing with cases according to their own legislation and procedures has the obvious merit of 'simplicity' when compared with the half-way position taken in the Europe Agreements. Their laying down of a common standard of incompatibility without at the same time establishing common procedures and competences for the respective competition authorities is bound to create difficulties, even if these are expected gradually to diminish as a result of the associated countries' commitment to harmonization. But what pleaded against the EC–US approach was, of course, the differences in the level of development of domestic competition law and policy between the EC and the Central, Eastern European and Baltic countries. Notwithstanding their internal differences, US and EC competition law and policy can both be described as mature and more or less equivalent as to the actual protection of the competition process, which at the same time allows for a substantial degree of mutual respect for the other's law and procedures.[140] The economic and legal situation in the Central,

---

[135] An action for annulment was lodged against the original Agreement (concluded by the EC Commission) by France (Case C-327/91), leading to the annulment on 4 August 1994, by the ECJ of the act on which it was based. The actual provisions were, however, left untouched by this judgment. The Commission then received a mandate from the Council to formally negotiate a new agreement on behalf of the Community, which led to the adoption on 10 April 1995 of Decision 95/145/EEC, ECSC of the Council and the Commission concerning the conclusion of the Agreement between the European Communities and the Government of the United States of America regarding the application of their competition laws, *OJ* 1995 L 95. See for later corrections, *OJ* 1995 L 131/38.

[136] Agreement EU–US, Art. I.

[137] As in the EEA Agreement, See *Brochure*, p. 3.

[138] As in the Europe Agreements.

[139] Apparently, the functioning of the agreement has been quite satisfactory. During the first three years e.g. the Commission made 61 notifications under the US–EC Agreement, and received 112. See for the Commission's statement, *Agence Europe*, 13 October 1994, 4.

[140] Along the same lines, Jakob (1993), 435.

Eastern European and Baltic countries has been so different for such a long time, that the albeit recently adopted competition laws do not carry a comparable trust or confidence (yet).

On the basis of the foregoing, my overall conclusion has to be that when elaborating their competition article, the parties to the Europe Agreements did either too little or too much. In the absence of harmonization of substantive rules and procedures, it remains to be seen how the article will be put into practice by the associated countries' competition authorities. Therefore, it would probably have been more appropriate to allow the associated parties a given period of time actually to harmonize their domestic legislation along the lines of EC competition law, before obliging them already to assess practices considered to be incompatible with the proper functioning of their Agreement on the basis of criteria arising from the application of the – possibly very different – rules of Articles 85 and 86 EC.

6

CZECH COMPETITION LAW
FACING THE EU CHALLENGE
(RULES APPLYING TO UNDERTAKINGS)

Jiří Zemánek[1]

I. BACKGROUND

Soon after 1989, Czechoslovakia followed Poland and Hungary and enacted antitrust laws to facilitate the transition to a market-based economy and to safeguard the stability of the market.[2] Before the market economy was launched, Czech centrally-planned industry and trade had been almost totally controlled by state-owned enterprises and monopolized to a high degree, amounting on average to 50 per cent (as measured by the single largest domestic producer's share in aggregate sales). The monopolies had been primarily administrative in nature: most decisions regarding allocation of investment, labour costs, credits etc., were made by the state bureaucracy.

Unlike the case of Poland, where a corporate model was adopted, Czecho-slovakia favoured a model based upon an association of independent enter-prises. However, the lack of direct central administrative power over operational decisions of member enterprises was counterbalanced by state control over target-setting and allocation of resources. Technocratic semi-reforms of the late eighties (the Czech 'perestroika') could not save the insulated non-competitive economy from inevitable decline.

As a consequence, deconcentration was not the only aspect of the large-scale privatization process (with a few sectoral exceptions), started by the Czech government in 1991.[3] The fostering of competition (market surveillance), the

---

[1] Dr.iur. et Dipl.oec., Ass. Professor of European Law at the Charles University Law Faculty, Prague.

[2] Act on Protection of Economic Competition No. 63/1991 Sb., reprinted in 13 *Bulletin of Czechoslovak Law* 73–83 (hereinafter '1991 Act').

[3] A three-phased approach was applied: small units were sold to private investors, then offered to the public; enterprises were transformed ('de-etatized') into joint stock companies and privatized by distributing vouchers, which would later be exchanged for shares, to all Czecho-slovak citizens; for the rest, standard methods of privatization were applied. Foreign investors were treated (notwithstanding a few marginal differences) the same way as domestic ones.

restructuring of natural monopolies, and an emphasis upon import liberalization and merger control, rather than price controls or monopolistic behaviour, were features of the transformation concept aimed at avoidance of a new private monopolization. While western countries have been trying to prevent monopolistic concentration, Czechoslovakia and now the Czech Republic – like other Central European countries – has been undertaking steps for its elimination.

II. THE INITIAL DILEMMA: LOOKING FOR A MODEL

The Czechoslovak government turned to both the United States and the European Community in its search for a model for the formulation of antitrust laws and enforcement policy. In 1990 the American Bar Association established the Central and East European Law Initiative (CEELI), the OECD created the Centre for Cooperation with Eastern European Economies (CCEEE), and some EC member states founded agencies (like *Deutsche Stiftung für internationale rechtliche Zusammenarbeit*), all of whom provided technical and policy advice.

The 1991 Act displayed a stronger leaning towards the Community model, because of the Czech Republic's wish to join the EC Internal Market and in order to benefit from the creation of a familiar legal environment for investors coming from the EC. Another reason for the choice of the EC model was that, in contrast to the US antitrust laws' emphasis upon maximum diffusion of competition, the policy behind Community laws is tempered by cooperation to enhance the worldwide competitiveness of the EC.

With regard to available remedies, US laws are essentially 'structuralist', relying on the dissolution of monopolies and the imposition of damages in private suits, whereas Community law emphasizes regulation of obstructionist behavior, being usually drafted in terms of illegality (*per se*) and moderated in its application by 'the rule of reason' or by case-by-case assessment of the economic benefits and liabilities of the alleged activity. This latter approach is considered to be more consistent with an emerging market economy.

Third, the choice of models was based on the extent to which they fit with the Czech Republic's own legal history and culture. The enforcement structure in the new law may serve as a clear example: a centralized enforcement structure coincides with the practice of state (or quasi-state) monopolies employed in the pre-war era. An Authority (now: Office) was entrusted with powers to annul practices and restructure enterprises operating contrary to competition criteria, or to impose fines without judicial decisions (judicial review was limited to the supervision of administrative decisions).[4] Last, and very important, the centrally directed privatization process prevented chaos, which might otherwise have been the inevitable result of an uncontrolled re-entry into market competition.

[4] Act on Cartels and Private Monopolies No. 141/1933 Sb.

Although the influence of US law was to some extent evident, the dominant model upon which the competition law was based was, as noted, the EC model. Upon dissolution of the Czechoslovak Federation, both the Czech and the Slovak Republics adapted the Act to their respective newly independent economies (hereafter for the Czech Republic: the 1993 Act).[5]

III. EVALUATION OF THE LEGISLATIVE ACTS

In the context of European guidance and assistance, Czechoslovakia quickly promulgated and learned to implement rules governing competition. The transformation of the national economy required going beyond the scheme of classical antitrust policy. As a consequence, provisions prohibiting restrictive practices, defining the abuse of dominant positions and standards for mergers have been introduced.

Some examples can explain the difficulty of the option. The 1991 Act, *inter alia*, adopted the limit of a 30 per cent market concentration as the definition of a market-dominating position. This level of concentration, under some foreign legislations adjusted for different market sectors, has become a determining factor in EC as well as in US law as a consequence of a continuing process of judicial examination, tempered by the 'rule of reason'.[6] The circumstances of the Czech Republic, however, may show later that different criteria and yardsticks for determining concentration may be more adequate and seem to favour analysis of antitrust problems on a case-by-case basis, balancing them through relevant economic considerations.

The 1991 Act does not provide an exhaustive list of restrictive practices (s. 3). Instead, like Article 85, par. 1, EC Treaty, this Act enumerates examples of cartel agreements that are unlawful if they result, or may result, in the elimination or restriction of competition. Horizontal agreements (on price fixing, etc.) are declared *ex lege* illegal (s. 3.2.a/) while vertical agreements are subjected to 'rule of reason' scrutiny. The Act establishes individual exemptions (ss 5 and 6) and authorizes the competition authority (Office for Economic Competition) to grant by decree – subject to additional *ad hoc* approval – block exemptions (s. 6a). In addition, it follows the EC model in the *de minimis* approach of differentiating between how the share of restrictive practices is measured in the largest market – the whole country (up to 5 per cent) as opposed to the share in the market which is regularly supplied (up to 30 per cent). The latter would not be subject to scrutiny by the competition authority (s. 3.3.d/).

---

[5] Amendment Acts Nos. 495/1992 Sb. and 286/1993 Sb. (hereinafter '1992 Act' or '1993 Act') for the Czech Republic; No. 188/1994 Sb. for the Slovak Republic. So-called 'Reception Act', pursuant to which all federal laws automatically became the laws of the CR as of 1 January 1993: No. 4/1993 Sb., Arts 152 and 153 of the Slovak Constitution, respectively.

[6] See *inter alia*, the ECJ's decision in *United Brands Co. v Commission*, Case 27/76 [1978] ECR 207 the share in the market which is regularly supplied (up to 30%). The latter would not be subject to scrutiny by the competition authority (s. 3.3.d/).

Unlike restrictive practices, market dominance (s. 9) is not assessed by a balancing test. Instead, an absolute prohibition of an abuse of any monopolistic position left behind by central planning has been introduced. The 'thrust' of many proceedings is the removal of barriers to access to the market. The definition and regulation of state monopolies in the energy, transportation and communications sectors need to be established, while the 'traditional' monopolies in the tobacco, salt and alcohol industries should be abolished.

Refinement and even redefinition of the merger and acquisition control provisions in the 1993 Act (s. 8) in terms of real market impact (based on joint market share of 30 per cent and balancing test) after privatization had progressed somewhat, was necessary. The Office was granted the authority to break up monopolistic mergers, rather than simply approve them, as was the case earlier.

The 1991 Act includes – apparently following the US paradigm – a provision for private individuals to bring claims against parties engaged in anticompetitive activities (s. 17). No doubt, private suits could substantially reduce suits *ex officio*. However, Czech law-makers have rejected immediately taking over the provision on treble damages, which are an essential incentive for a victorious American claimant, and allow only actual damages. There have been a very limited number of private suits in Czech courts until now. The reason might be a lack of incentive for new competitors to engage in litigation. On the other hand, paying treble damages could overburden many enterprises, operating without any large capital assets above their costs of production, and lead to bankruptcy. Such fall-out could seriously damage the emerging plurality of competitors in the market.

Following the EC competition model, the 1993 Act has extended the range of entities which may be potential violators of the prohibitions: professional organizations, chambers of commerce and other associations have been included in the list (s. 2.2). The concept of restrictive practices has been broadened so that vertical restraints have also become *per se* illegal and are no longer outside the scope of control (s. 3.1). Also American-style criminal sanctions for antitrust violations have been introduced into the Czech Criminal Code.[7]

The extensive transplantation of policies and regulations from EC competition law (with some elements taken from US regulations) into the Czech legal environment seems to be – five years after their introduction – fruitful.[8] But no simple quantitative approach would meet the requirements for assessment. The basic imperfection of the Act is that it was drawn up for a functioning market economy. Despite the primary statutory focus on competition, protection of other public interests and values has become – in the absence

---

[7] Act No. 65/1994 Sb., s. 149.
[8] If in 1991–92 the Czech Office dealt with 181 cases involving abuse of dominant or monopolistic position, 39 cases involving mergers and 29 cases involving cartel agreements (restrictive practices), two years later the first two figures have doubled, the third one even tripled.

of appropriate supervisory bodies – a by-product of competition protection. The Office often serves as a watchdog over prices, analysing changes in the business climate to ensure that consumers do not suffer.

More time is still needed to see whether such standards can work in an effective way under the factual limitations caused by recession, higher inflation and strong pressures from special interest groups, which hinder full and stronger enforcement of the Czech competition law, and to see how well they facilitate the transition to, and maintenance of, a competitive market economy. The Czech Republic – like other Central and Eastern European countries – is encountering a different set of monopolistic practices in very different economic circumstances from those EC countries have been facing. The context in which the Act must operate is thus quite different. At present, the authorities responsible for the implementation of the competition policy are discovering the impact of these differences. The Office may impose penalties (s. 17) and its decisions may be appealed to a regular Czech court (s. 13). However, after economic and social stabilization have been reached, the enforcement of the Act will doubtless be more consistent and efficient.

The drafters of Czech competition law kept in mind the larger market into which the country hopes to become integrated.

IV. APPROXIMATION OF LAWS

In return for the possibility of becoming full EU member states, the Central and Eastern European countries must open up their markets and harmonize their laws with that of the EU. The Europe Agreement EU–CR[9] requires linkage between what was previously domestic policy and decision-making in the area of competition, with that of the EU (Article 64). An adequate framework for fair competition is to be developed through approximation of existing and future relevant Czech legislation, ensuring that it will be *gradually made compatible* with that of the EU (Articles 69 and 70).

The *Agreement on the European Economic Area* stipulates that there be 'equal conditions of competition', 'respect for the same rules' (Article 1.1), interpretation of provisions which are 'identical in substance' to corresponding Community rules 'in conformity with the (prior) relevant rulings of the ECJ' (Article 6) and making the (referred to or enlisted) secondary EC legislation binding as 'part of (their) internal legal orders' (Article 7). This is not the case with the Europe Agreements. The Agreement with the Czech Republic does not include a provision which has the same effect of taking-over the *acquis communautaire*. The Community provisions on competition (Articles 85 and 86 EC Treaty, and EC competition regulations) are not directly applicable

---

[9] Europe Agreement establishing an association between the European Communities and their member states on the one side, and the Czech Republic on the other, *OJ* 1993, L 360 (in CR published: No. 7/1995 Sb.), signed 4 October 1993, entered into force 1 February 1995 (hereinafter 'Europe Agreement').

in the Czech territory. Instead, a half-way approach has been adopted: a) the *general principles* have been agreed and the Association Council has been authorized to adopt necessary rules for their implementation and enforcement (Europe Agreement, Article 64); b) the existing *legislation*, however, of each respective Contracting Party (the EC and the Czech Republic), as well as rules on competence of authorities and procedures on settlement of cases, are to be applied in a subsidiary way.

The *Implementation Rules*,[10] adopted by the Association Council on 30 January 1996 (ten months after the time-limit imposed by Article 64.3 of the Europe Agreement expired!), confirmed the structure governing legal standards. They apply to cases of conflict of powers or cases that may substantially affect important interests of the other Contracting Party, authorizing the latter to take notice and bind the former to give due consideration to the other party's respective interests, or to take action which could lead to a mutually acceptable solution. This is a rule which does not prejudice any ultimate remedial action under the respective laws of the Parties. Rules applicable 'to undertakings located outside the respective territory' are included (Article 1 of the Implementation Rules). The provisions of the 1991 Act, which holds that this Act is applicable to anticompetitive 'activities carried out abroad in so far as their consequences may affect the domestic market' (s. 2.3) and that 'this Act is not applicable to activities which have effects on foreign markets' – unless an international agreement claims something different (s. 2.4), do not conflict with the Implementation Rules.[11] The applicability of EC competition provisions under the 'effects doctrine' articulated in the famous *Woodpulp* case, which provided that the European Commission had competence to apply Articles 85 and 86 of the EC Treaty to an agreement made outside the EU by foreigners, if the agreement was implemented *in* the EU and regardless of whether the foreigners conduct activities within the EU,[12] remains untouched by the adoption of the Impementation Rules.

Czech companies trading with the EU may therefore become subject to appropriate Community rules in proceedings before the European Commission. The basic features of these Community rules including 'criteria arising from (their) application' (Article 64.2 of the Europe Agreement), dominate the legal standards governing EU-based cases to be decided by the Czech authorities (the Office or the Courts). Even though no joint EU–CR

---

[10] Implementation Rules for the application of the Competition provisions applicable to undertakings provided for in Art. 64 of the Europe Agreement between the EC and the Czech Republic, OJ (1996) No. L 31/21 (hereinafter 'Implementation Rules').

[11] Decisions of the Association Council (authorized to 'supervise the implementation' of the Europe Agreement, Art. 104) are treated, in accordance with Czech constitutional procedures, as an integral part of the Europe Agreement: they – as such – do not need to be approved by the Parliament, but they are promulgated in the Collection of Laws (Sb.). They become a component part of the Czech legal system with the legal force of an organic law. Therefore, the Implementation Rules take predominance over provisions of the Act due to the general legal principle recognized by Czech law, *lex posterior derogat legi priori*.

[12] *Ahlström Osakyhtio v Commission (Woodpulp)*, joint cases 89, 104, 114, 116, 117 & 125–9/85, (1988) ECR 5193.

Surveillance Authority for the implementation and enforcement of the competition provisions of the Europe Agreement has been established, it may nevertheless be expected that Czech courts will not disregard Community law standards. But, of course, proper application of EC law also in the Czech Republic is more a matter of information, experience, and technical assistance than true policy motivations.

Potential difficulties in this respect, which cannot be removed by the notification and consultation procedures as referred to above, are nevertheless expected to diminish as a result of the approximation of Czech law to the EC law under Articles 69–70 of the Europe Agreement. Any co-existence of double standards – for EU-based and non-EU-based cases – might cause problems, because the distinction between the two is sometimes thin (in competition issues, unlike sales etc., hardly any 'purely territorial' cases exist). The principles of equal treatment and legal certainty, which are among the main guidelines for the Community legal system, justify the aim of harmonization in all countries applying for membership in the EU.

V. CONCLUSION

The process of approximation – as we have seen above – has started. Although the regulatory level of Czech competition provisions is not yet – for obvious reasons – identical with that of the EC, substantial progress has been made. The 1993 Act, responding to the challenge from the EU, has broadened the scope of Czech statutory regulation by involving new potential competitors and by applying the notion of vertical contracts within the concept of competition. It has, among other things, deepened applicable sanctions, opened the door for block exemptions implemented by governmental decrees and deleted the definition of the relevant market.

The recent amendment to the Competence Act,[13] passed by the Czech Parliament on 11 October 1996, replaced the Ministry for Economic Competition by the Office for Protection of Economic Competition, which has the status of an autonomous body, independent of the Government. A next amendment to the Act (expected for 1997) seeks to initiate a review of compatibility of the following provisions of the Commercial Code[14] with the EC rules: a ban on re-export (s. 739), restraints of sales (s. 742), exclusive sale contracts (s. 745), linked transactions (s. 450) and franchising contracts.

With this contribution we have tried to demonstrate that the Czech Republic gives due consideration to the requirements for EU membership laid down at the 1993 Copenhagen European Council, among them '. . . the capacity to cope with competitive pressure and market forces within the Union . . .'.[15] The respective Czech bodies, following the recommendations

---

[13] Act No. 69/1993 Sb.

[14] Act No. 531/1991 Sb.

[15] 'Presidency Conclusions', in *The European Councils*, Brussels-Luxembourg, European Commission, 1995, 86–7, Annex II.

articulated in the White Paper on approximation,[16] drafted the revised Harmonogram of Approximation,[17] which paves the way for the gradual removal of all remaining incompatibilities with EC competition law. The Czech response to the 'Competition chapter' of the *European Commission Questionnaire for the preparation of the opinion on the application for membership of the European Union*, delivered in April 1996 under the pre-accession strategy, could therefore already meet many of those requirements.

---

[16] Cannes European Council, 'Presidency Conclusions', in *The European Councils*, Part B, Brussels-Luxembourg, 1995, 19, COM/95/163; see above, M.-A. Gaudissart and A. Sinnaeve, p. 41.

[17] Governmental decision No. 151 (1995).

7

THE APPLICATION OF RULES ON STATE AIDS AND RULES RELATING TO PUBLIC UNDERTAKINGS

Piet Jan Slot[1]

I. INTRODUCTION

When discussing the rules on state aids and rules related to public undertakings in the relations between the European Union and the CEECs, it is necessary to note that there are basically two types of agreement governing such relations. The first group comprises the Europe Agreements.[2] These Agreements represent the most comprehensive form of economic integration between the European Union and countries that have expressed a clear wish to become full members of the Union in due time. Europe Agreements have been concluded with Poland, Hungary, The Czech and Slovak Republics, Romania, Bulgaria and signed but not yet ratified with the three Baltic States and Slovenia.

The second category of agreements consists of Partnership and Cooperation Agreements. Such agreements have been signed with the former USSR Republics (except the Baltic States). They are necessary in order to achieve the Community's objectives in the field of external relations, but are not concluded with a view to establishing a relation that in time will lead to full membership of the Union.

Only the first category of agreements contains clear provisions regarding competition and state aids. The other category of agreements does not lay down such provisions nor is there a reference to such provisions in the Preamble. This means that the relations between the EU and the countries

---

[1] Professor of Economic Law at Leiden University. Chairman of the International Institute for Energy Law. The author wishes to thank Olivia Swaak-Goldman, who wrote sections IIIC and IVCb, for her valuable assistance.
[2] Cf. M. Maresceau and E. Montaguti, 'The Relations between the European Union and Central and Eastern Europe: A Legal Appraisal', *CMLRev.* (1995), 1327–67.

that are parties to these agreements will be governed by the relevant and applicable multilateral agreements such as the GATT/WTO Agreement and the Energy Charter Treaty.[3]

The next section will provide an overview of the relevant provisions of one of the Europe Agreements: the Agreement with Poland. Thereafter, I will discuss how the rules on state aids and the rules relating to public undertakings are to be implemented. This will be done with reference to the relevant passages of the Commission's White Paper for the preparation of the Associated countries of Central and Eastern Europe for integration into the internal market of the European Union.[4] Reference is also made to the Agreement on Interpretation and Application of Articles VI, XVI and XXIII of the GATT, since the Europe Agreement provides that as long as there is no decision from the Association Council implementing the rules on state aids, the provisions of the GATT shall be applied; the text of the relevant provisions of this Agreement are given in the annex to this chapter. The next section will discuss the enforcement of the relevant provisions. Subsequently, some substantive issues raised by implementation of the rules are reviewed. In the penultimate section, procedural issues will be looked at. Finally, some concluding remarks will be offered.

II. THE RELEVANT PROVISIONS IN THE EUROPE AGEEMENTS

The Europe Agreements lay down detailed rules for competition. Thus Article 63 of the Agreement with Poland[5] provides as follows:

1. The following are incompatible with the proper functioning of the Agreement, in so far as they may affect trade between the Community and Poland:
    (i)   All agreements between undertakings, decisions by associations of undertakings and concerted practices between undertakings which have as their object or effect the prevention, restriction or distortion of competition;
    (ii) abuse by one or more undertakings of a dominant position in the territories of the Community or of Poland as a whole or in a substantial part thereof;
    (iii) any public aid which distorts or threatens to distort competition by favouring certain undertakings or the production of certain goods.
2. Any practices contrary to this Article shall be assessed on the basis of criteria arising from the application of the rules of Articles 85, 86 and 92 of the Treaty establishing the European Community.
3. The Association Council shall, within three years of the entry into force of this Agreement, adopt by decision the necessary rules for the implementation of paragraphs 1 and 2.

---

[3] The Energy Charter Treaty lays down a general framework for the development of the energy sector. The text has been published in *OJ* 1994, L 380/1.
[4] COM(1995) 163 final, Brussels, 10 May 1995.
[5] *OJ* 1993, L 348/1.

Until these rules are adopted, the provisions of the Agreement on interpretation and application of Articles VI, XVI and XXIII of the General Agreement on Tariffs and Trade shall be applied as the rule for the implementation of paragraphs 1 (iii) and related parts of paragraph 2.

4. (a) For the purposes of applying the provisions of paragraph 1 (iii), the Parties recognize that during the first five years after the entry into force of this Agreement, any public aid granted by Poland shall be assessed taking into account the fact that Poland shall be regarded as an area identical to those areas of the Community described in Article 92(3)(a) of the Treaty establishing the European Community. The Association Council shall, taking into account the economic situation of Poland, decide whether that period should be extended by further periods of five years.

    (b) Each Party shall ensure transparency in the area of public aid, *inter alia* by reporting annually to the other Party on the total amount and the distribution of the aid given and by providing upon request, information on aid schemes. Upon request by one Party, the other Party shall provide information on particular individual cases of public aid.

5. With regard to products referred to in Chapter II and III of Title III:
    - the provisions of paragraph 1 (iii) do not apply,
    - any practices contrary to paragraph 1 (i) should be assessed according to the criteria established by the Community on the basis of Articles 42 and 43 of the Treaty establishing the European Economic Community, and in particular of those established in Council Regulation No. 26/62.

6. If the Community or Poland considers that a particular practice is incompatible with the terms of paragraph 1, and:
    - is not adequately dealt with under the implementing rules referred to in paragraph 3, or
    - in the absence of such rules, and if such practice causes or threatens to cause serious prejudice to the interest of the other Party or material injury to its domestic industry, including its services industry,

    it may take appropriate measures after consultation within the Association Council or after 30 working days following referral for such consultation.

    In the case of practices incompatible with paragraph 1 (iii) or this Article, such appropriate measures may, where the General Agreement on Tariff and Trade applies thereto, only be adopted in accordance with the procedures and under the conditions laid down by the General Agreement on Tariffs and Trade and any other relevant instrument negotiated under its auspices which are applicable between the Parties.

7. Notwithstanding any provisions to the contrary adopted in accordance with paragraph 3, the Parties shall exchange information taking into account the limitations imposed by the requirements of professional and business secrecy.

8. This Article shall not apply to the products covered by the Treaty establishing the European Coal and Steel Community which are the subject of Protocol 2.

Article 65 of the Agreement reads as follows:

With regard to public undertakings, and undertakings to which special or exclusive rights have been granted, the Association Council shall ensure that as from the third year following the date of entry into force of this Agreement, the principle of the Treaty establishing the European Economic Community, in particular Article 90, and the principles of the concluding document of the April 1990 Bonn meeting of the Conference on Security and Cooperation in Europe, in particular entrepreneurs' freedom of decision, are upheld.

Articles 68 and 69 lay down the following rules:

> The Contracting Parties recognize that the major precondition for Poland's economic integration into the Community is the approximation of that country's existing and future legislation to that of the Community. Poland shall use its best endeavour to ensure that future legislation is compatible with Community legislation.
>
> The approximation of laws shall extend to the following areas in particular: customs law, company law, banking law, company accounts and taxes, intellectual property, protection of workers at the workplace, financial services, rules on competition, protection of health and life of humans, animals and plants, consumer protection, indirect taxation, technical rules and standards, transport and the environment.

As one can infer from the provisions quoted above, the rules on competition are indeed very comprehensive. The provisions of Article 63(2), in particular, i.e. the obligation to assess the practices on the basis of the criteria arising from the application of the rules of Articles 85, 86 and 92 EC, are far-reaching.

III.   HOW WILL THE RULES BE IMPLEMENTED?

A.   The EEA mechanism: a possible solution?

According to Article 63(3) and Article 65 of the Europe Agreement, the rules on competition, the equivalent of Articles 85, 86, 90, and 92 EC, are to be implemented by a decision of the Association Council within three years of the entry into force of the Agreement. So far, for all the Agreement States, only one such decision has been taken and published.[6] Several other decisions are presently being prepared.[7] An interesting question in this context is whether or not the EEA mechanism for dealing with competition cases would be an appropriate solution. The EEA mechanism provides for an independent authority with powers similar to the EC Commission for the implementation of the equivalent of the Articles 85, 86, 90, 92 and 93 EC. It has been suggested that the EEA mechanism may be too ambitious, since all of the original EEA members already had extensive competition laws and authorities

---

[6] This is the decision for the implementation of the equivalent of Arts 85 and 86 EC for the Czech Republic, *OJ* 1996, L 31/21.

[7] Cf. S. Depypere, T. Jacob, B. Carton and Y. Scaramozzino, 'International Dimension of Competition Policy: Summary of the most important recent developments', *Competition Policy Newsletter*, (Vol. 2) Number 1, Spring 1996, 38–40.

in place, whereas allegedly this is not so for the CEECs.[8] On the other hand, this author's survey of legal developments in the eleven PHARE Countries shows that, of the countries with Europe Agreements, all but one (Romania) have competition laws.[9] Poland, Hungary and the Czech Republic have also demonstrated that they are actually applying these rules. In other words, the EEA mechanism may be a real possibility. Moreover, it should, of course, not be forgotten that the objective of future membership almost of necessity sets an ambitious target.

B. The Commission's White Paper

The Commission's White Paper for the preparation of the Associated CEECs for integration into the internal market of the Union seems to set similarly ambitious goals in the field of application and enforcement of the competition rules.[10] The most striking feature of these guidelines is their reference to procedure. The guidelines clearly envisage that an independent authority will be established to enforce the competition rules. Reading the White Paper, one gets the impression that the Commission has a similar entity to its own DG IV in mind. The Commission writes that the authority must have sufficient powers to carry out its tasks efficiently, and that viable procedural rules must exist addressing both the powers of the authority as well as the rights of the undertakings concerned. If the gist of Article 93 EC is followed, member states seem to be under an obligation to notify their aid schemes in advance. Nowhere in these guidelines is there any indication of the extent of such an obligation. In this respect, we should be aware of the fact that implementing the equivalent of Articles 92 and 90 EC will be much more difficult than implementing the equivalent of Articles 85 and 86, as was also the case in the EC itself. It will be very hard, both from an institutional and from a psychological point of view, to enforce rules which are principally directed towards the government itself. In the EEA context, of course, the EEA surveillance authority provides the necessary independence from national governments.

The relevant parts of the Commission's White Paper sum the situation up as follows:[11]

1.   Key elements
The Community state aid control system is based on Articles 92, 93 EC. The Commission is responsible for applying the Community state aid policy. The

---

[8] T. Jacob, 'EEA and Eastern European Agreements with the European Community', in B.E. Hawk (ed.), *1992 Fordham Corp. L. Inst.*, *International antitrust law and policy*, New York, Transnational Juris Publications, 1993, 403. The EEA mechanism is described in S. Norberg, *The EEA Agreement: Institutional Solutions for a Dynamic and Homgeneous EEA in the Area of Competition*, Fordham Corporate Law Institute, 1992, 437.

[9] Denton Hall, Internationaal Instituut voor Energierecht & Bossard Consultants, *European Energy Charter Phare Regional Programme Legislation/Regulation Project, Final Report Albania; Bulgaria; Czech Republic; Estonia; Hungary; Latvia; Lithuania; Poland; Romania; Slovakia; and Slovenia.*

[10] Above, note 4.

[11] COM(1995) 163 final, 52 and 61.

system is characterized by a certain number of key elements that are of crucial importance for its set-up and functioning. It comprises both substantive and procedural elements.

Substance

The substance of the Community system is characterized by the principle of prohibition of state aids that distort or threaten to distort competition by favouring certain undertakings or the production of certain goods, in so far as they effect trade between Member States. Nevertheless, Article 92 EC lists a number of instances where aid is considered to be acceptable because it promotes certain general objectives. Other forms of aid that have the effect of distorting competition without accompanying benefits must on the other hand be condemned.

Procedure

Viable rules regarding procedures are indispensable in order to ensure effective enforcement and thus the functioning of a state aid control system. These rules must relate both to the powers of the authority charged with the application of the rules as well as to the rights of the undertakings concerned.

The authority must be endowed with sufficient powers to carry out its tasks efficiently. This comprises in particular the obligation in principle of the Member States to notify their aid schemes or cases in advance to and not to implement them before their approval by the Commission, and their obligation to recover aid that they have granted illegally.

With respect to the rights of undertakings that are directly concerned by Commission decisions, it is essential that they have the possibility of judicial review.

For the legislative alignment stage, the EU experience can only be considered of indirect relevance. A legal obligation for Member States to align their legislation to the Community state aid control system does not exist and would indeed be superfluous because of the Commission's role of the controlling authority under the EC Treaty.

For the CEECs, the situation is obviously different. Taking into account their obligations under the Europe Agreements, it is indispensable that they adopt a system similar to that of the Community with a national authority endowed with monitoring powers. This will also help to create an institutional system which will facilitate the fulfilment of the obligations resulting from later membership.

The following requirements represent the key elements of Articles 37 and 90:

A. Articles 85 and 86 EC apply not only to private-sector firms, but also to public enterprises, except where a restriction of competition is essential in order to ensure the performance of certain public-interest tasks (Article 90(2)).

B. Article 37 requires that national monopolies of a commercial character must be gradually adjusted so as to ensure that, when the transitional period has ended, no discrimination regarding the conditions under which goods are produced and marketed exists between nationals of the Member States of the European Union. This means in particular that, by the end of the transitional period, exclusive rights relating to imports, exports and wholesale distribution must be abolished.

C. Article 90(1) prohibits Member States from enacting or maintaining in force, in the case of public undertakings and undertakings to which they grant special or exclusive rights, any measure contrary to the rules laid down in the EC Treaty.

This means that, as regards more particularly the application of Article 90(1) in conjunction with Articles 85 and 86, Member States may neither encourage nor impose on public undertakings or undertakings that have been granted special or exclusive rights, conduct that constitutes an abuse of a dominant position or the conclusion of agreements that restrict competition.

Article 90(1) in conjunction with Article 86 also prohibits Member States from introducing laws, regulations or administrative provisions that place public undertakings and undertakings to which they grant special or exclusive rights in a situation that such undertakings could not achieve themselves by their own conduct without infringing the provisions of Article 86.

For example, Article 90(1) in conjunction with Article 86 prohibits Member States from extending a monopoly, without objective justification, to include ancillary or separate activities belonging to separate markets that could be exercised by other firms.

These provisions also prohibit Member States from giving public undertakings or undertakings enjoying special or exclusive rights regulatory powers over their competitors.

Article 90(1) in conjunction with Article 59 prohibits Member States from granting or maintaining in force special or exclusive rights that restrict intra-Community trade in services, except where this is necessary in order to ensure that certain essential requirements are met.

Article 90(1) in conjunction with the rules on the free movement of goods, and in particular Articles 30 and 34 of the Treaty, prohibits Member States from granting or maintaining in force, after the end of the transitional period provided for in Article 37, special or exclusive rights that restrict intra-Community trade in goods, except where this is necessary in order to ensure that certain essential requirements are met.

As far as telecommunications are concerned, some of these requirements provided for in the Treaty, were spelt out in Commission Directives 88/301/EEC on terminal equipment, 90/388/EEC on telecommunications services and 90/44/EEC on satellites.

The process of achieving compliance with the above mentioned rules on the part of the Member States has been completed, with a few exceptions.

- Commercial monopolies (oil, tobacco, alcohol, etc.) have been adjusted in accordance with Article 37, and exclusive rights relating to the import, export and wholesale distribution of such products have been abolished. However, problems remain in sectors such as electricity and gas.
- In the case of services, exclusive rights have been abolished in areas such as telecommunications (except those involving voice telephony, where a number of transitional periods apply) and express delivery services. However, monopolies still remain in some sectors such as postal services. Action is being taken to open up such sectors to competition as well.

C. The transitional regime for the application of the rules on state aids in the absence of a decision by the Association Council

As long as no decision has been taken by the Association Council, the rules on state aids are applied on the basis of the Agreement on interpretation and application of Articles VI, XVI and XXIII of GATT (the Code).[12] The Code, concluded during the Tokyo Round of Multilateral Trade Negotiation in 1979, is an additional voluntary agreement open to all parties to GATT 1947 but is distinct from the GATT. Thus, adherence to the GATT does not imply acceptance of the Code, and its provisions are only binding between those parties which explicitly agree to be bound. Despite the non-adherence of the CEECs to the Code, the provisions of the Code apply in the absence of a decision by the Association Council. The relevant provisions of the Code are set out in the Annex to this chapter.

The Code, in accordance with Article XV:1 GATT, requires parties to report all subsidies that work to increase exports or decrease imports, and allows parties to request information about these subsidies from each other. It also creates a regime for using subsidies, the relevant provisions of which depend on the form of the subsidy and the products on which it is granted. The Code principally addresses export subsidies (Article 8) and includes an illustrative list of export subsidies in its Annex.[13] Export subsidies on products other than certain primary products are explicitly banned (Article 9). Export subsidies on certain primary products, defined to include farm, forest and fishery items in their natural form, excluding minerals, are prohibited if they result in the party granting such subsidy 'having more than an equitable share of world export trade in such product' (Article 10). For subsidies other than export subsidies, the Code recognizes that these may have negative effects for other parties, particulary where they adversely affect the conditions of normal competition; it also, however, states that it does not intend to restrict the right of parties to use such subsidies to achieve important policy objectives. Parties are therefore instructed to try and avoid such negative effects, by considering possible negative effects on trade when determining whether or not to use these subsidies (Article 11). The Code also sets up enforcement mechanisms for the rights and obligations it creates. These will be discussed in the next section.

The Code, together with the other agreements concluded during the previous multilateral trade negotiation and GATT 1947, was replaced by the Agreement Establishing the World Trade Organization (WTO Agreement), concluded during the Uruguay Round of multilateral trade negotiations.[14] The WTO Agreement contains in one of its annexes an agreement on subsidies and countervailing measures. This agreement makes certain improvements on the Code.[15] Nevertheless, the Europe Agreement refers to the Code, even though all parties to it are members of the WTO. This implies that in the absence of a decision by the Association Council, the provisions of the Europe

---

[12] *BISD*, 1980, 56–83.

[13] See points (a) to (l) in the Annex to the Code, reprinted in the Annex to this article.

[14] The text of the WTO Agreement and its annexes are reproduced in *ILM* (1994), 13.

[15] See G. Depayre, 'Subsidies and Countervailing Measures after the Uruguay Round, An Overview', in Bourgeois, Berrod and Fournier (eds), *The Uruguay Round Results: A European Lawyers' Perspective*, 1995, 247.

Agreement should be implemented in accordance with the Code, although perhaps the Code is to be interpreted in light of the new Agreement.

IV. ENFORCEMENT OF THE RULES CONTAINED IN THE EUROPE AGREEMENTS

A. Preliminary issues

As noted above, the general opinion with regard to the implementation of the rules on state aids as well as those of Article 90 EC seems to be that an authority will be set up endowed with sufficient powers to enforce the rules. Some additional remarks relating to enforcement should be made here.

Article 63(4) of the Europe Agreement provides that both the Community and Poland may take appropriate measures if they consider that a particular practice is incompatible with the competition rules of the agreement. Such measures may only be taken after consultation with the Association Council and must be in conformity with the GATT rules, including those described above.

The rules must of course also be applied by the Commission. For the application of Article 92 EC, this implies that the Commission must verify whether the proposed aid affects not only trade between the member states, but also between the member states and the Europe Agreement partner. Similarly, the Commission must verify, whenever applying Article 90(2) EC, that the development of trade is not affected to such an extent as would be contrary to interests of the Community *and the Europe Agreement partner*. National courts of the member states of the EC are under a similar duty when applying the exemption contained in Article 90(2) EC.[16]

B. Substantive issues in the enforcement of the Europe Agreement rules

a. Article 92 EC

As far as the substance is concerned, it is interesting to note that according to Article 63(4) of the Europe Agreement, Poland shall, for the first five years after the entry into force of the Agreement, be regarded as an area identical to those areas of the Community which, under Article 92(3)(a) EC, are considered to have an abnormally low standard of living or serious underemployment.[17]

---

[16] It should be recalled that in its judgment in Case C-260/89, *ERT v DEP*, (1991) ECR I-2925, the Court ruled that national courts can apply the exemption of Art. 90(2).

[17] It should be noted that there are precedents for a blanket exemption from the prohibition of Art. 92(1). The whole of Greece is classified as eligible for regional aid under Art. 92(3)(a). Cf. Commission Communication on the method for the application of Art. 92(3)(a) and (c) to regional aid, *OJ* 1988, C 212.

Presumably this implies that the Commission's Communications on regional aid are applicable. It should also be noted that after the expiry of the five-year period, the exemption can either be renewed or recourse may be had to the more limited exemption of Article 92(3)(c) EC.

For the CEECs, the application of the competition rules raises interesting questions concerning the concept of an undertaking. The case law of the Court of Justice on this concept in the *Höfner, Poucet, Eurocontrol* and *Port of Genova* cases, shows that it is not always easy to draw the line between governmental and commercial activities.[18] A similar discussion may arise in the context of the question whether certain financial transactions that may constitute an aid can be attributed to the government. Here the Court's judgment in the *Van der Kooy* case may serve as a clear example.[19] I would expect that such questions will be even more relevant for the application of the competition rules in CEECs, given their history of close interrelation between government and businesses.

The case law of the Court and the Commission on preferential tariffs for government-controlled enterprises will be of particular importance for the CEECs. The judgment of the Court in *Van der Kooy*[20] and *COFAZ*,[21] as well as the Commission's decision in the natural gas case,[22] provide clear illustrations of criteria for the assessment of such tariffs.

Another concept of state aid law that may be difficult to apply in this context is the market economy investor principle. According to this principle, a financial transaction effected by the government or through government resources, e.g. the injection of fresh capital in an ailing company, will be considered to be an aid if it takes places in a situation and under conditions that would not be acceptable to private investors operating under normal market economy conditions.[23] The difficulty arises simply because, in the CEECs, there are still many situations where markets have only recently been developed and consequently no standard yet exists against which to assess a particular financial transaction.

Finally, it should be noted that according to Article 63(8), the competition rules shall not apply to ECSC products. These are the subject of Protocol 2.

b. Article 90 EC

The obligation contained in Article 65, implying that as from the third year following the date of entry into force of the Agreement the principles of

---

[18] Case C-41/90, *Höfner*, (1991) ECR I-1979; Joined Cases C-159 and C-160/91, *Poucet and Pistre*, (1993) ECR I-637; Case C-364/92, *Eurocontrol*, (1994) ECR I-43; and Case C-179/90, *Port of Genova*, (1990) ECR I-5889.

[19] Joined Cases C-67, 68 and 70/85, (1988) ECR 219.

[20] Ibid.

[21] Case 169/84, *Cofaz v Commission*, (1986) ECR 391.

[22] OJ 1994, L 35/6; see also OJ 1992, C 344/4.

[23] Joined Cases 296 and 318/82, *Netherlands and Leeuwarder Papierwarenfabriek v Commission*, (1985) ECR 809; see further Hancher, Ottervanger and Slot, *EC State Aids*, 1993, 161.

Article 90 EC must be *ensured* by the Association Council, seems to be a very tall order. It would seem to me that this can only realistically be achieved in those sectors where the Community itself has clearly defined the rights and obligations of both the industry and the government. At present this only holds for the telecommunications sector. In this sector the Commission has, by means of Article 90(3) EC, given the necessary guidelines. In the postal sector this process has just started, as was recently confirmed by the Commission's decision in the French postal services case.[24] A similar development has taken place in the transport sector, as can be inferred from the recent directive to set out rules for groundhandling services in the air transport sector.[25] The developments in the energy sector do not inspire great confidence that clear concepts and guidelines will emerge in the near future. It therefore seems overly optimistic to expect the governments of the CEECs to achieve goals which have so far eluded the governments of the member states of the Community. It also seems fair to note that the case law of the Court of Justice on Article 90 EC does not provide clear and ready-made criteria. Moreover, here the question of who is going to enforce the rules assumes particular importance. As has been observed by several commentators of judgments such as *Corbeau*[26] and *Almelo*,[27] the Court leaves the job essentially to national courts, which will face considerable difficulties in applying the criteria enunciated in these judgments. Are courts in Central and Eastern Europe up to such a job?[28]

In 1994, in *Banco de Credito*,[29] the Court of Justice ruled that the exemption of Article 90(2) EC can also be applied in the context of Article 92 EC. As the recent Commission decision in the French postal services case shows,[30] this obviates the need to analyse whether the financial transaction constitutes an aid or not.

c. *Articles 3(g), 5 and 85 et seq. EC*

According to Articles 68 and 69 of the Agreement, the Contracting Party shall use its best endeavours to ensure that future legislation is compatible with Community legislation. This includes rules on competition. This means that the governments of CEECs will have a duty to screen national legislation on its compatibility with the Court's case law on Articles 3(g), 5 and 85 *et seq* EC. This duty can be summarized in the formula which the Court laid down in *Van Eyke/ASPA*:[31]

---

[24] *OJ* 1995, C 262/11.
[25] Directive 96/67 of 15 October 1996, *OJ* 1996, L 272/36.
[26] Case C-320/91, (1993) ECR I-2533.
[27] Case C-393/92, (1994) ECR I-1508.
[28] Cf. Editorial comments *CMLRev.* (1996), 395.
[29] Case C-387/92, (1994) ECR I-877.
[30] Above, note 24; *XXVth Report on Competition Policy*, point 98.
[31] Case 267/86, (1988) ECR 4769.

It must be pointed out that in that regard Articles 85 and 86 of the Treaty *per se* are concerned only with the conduct of undertakings and not with national legislation. The Court has consistently held, however, that Articles 85 and 86 of the Treaty, in conjunction with Article 5, require the Member States not to introduce or maintain in force measures, even of a legislative nature, which may render ineffective the competition rules applicable to undertakings. Such would be the case, the Court has held, if a Member State were to require or favour the adoption of agreements, decisions or concerted practice contrary to Article 85 or to reinforce their effects, or to deprive its own legislation of its official character by delegating to private traders responsibility for taking decisions affecting the economic sphere.

The Court's judgments in the *Meng, Ohra* and *Reiff* cases can serve as a guideline here.[32]

C. Procedural issues in the enforcement of the Europe Agreement rules

a. Preliminary issues

As has already been observed, the great majority of the CEECs have enacted competition laws which provide for enforcement procedures. The competition authorities are in close contact with the European Commission and several methods for consultation and cooperation have been set up. Implementation of the procedural rules relating to Articles 85 and 86 EC seems to be well on its way.

b. Article 92 EC

The implementation of the principles of Article 92 in particular, and to a lesser extent also Article 90 EC, raises very interesting questions about the procedures for the supervision and enforcement of the prohibition on giving state aid. Article 63 of the Agreement does not mention Article 93 EC. Instead, in paragraph 4 (b), it requires each party to ensure transparency, *inter alia* by reporting annually to the other party on the total amount and the distribution of the aid given and by providing, upon request, information on aid schemes. Parties may also request information on specific individual cases.

A key question for the enforcement of the prohibition under Article 92(1) EC is whether or not the rules of Article 93 EC, including the directly effective obligation to notify new aid, will be implemented. If so, the impressive case law of the Court of Justice on judicial protection, standing and other procedural rules, would become relevant as well.

It will be difficult to ignore Article 93 EC and its case law if a level playing-field for all concerned enterprises is the objective. At the same time,

---

[32] Case C-2/91, *Meng* (1993) ECR I-5751; Case C-245/91, *Ohra* (1993) ECR I-5851; and Case C-185/91, *Reiff* (1993) ECR I-5801.

it is useful to recall that the Court's case law has only recently and gradually been developed.

Another key question relating to the enforcement of the rules on state aid is whether or not an independent authority will be charged with the task of supervising these rules. It seems obvious that only an independent authority can effectively do such a job. Again the example of the EEA Authority seems to be the appropriate parallel.

As was discussed above with regard to the implementation of the obligations in the absence of a decision by the Association Council implementing the rules on state aid, the provisions of the Agreement on the interpretation and application of Articles VI, XVI and XXIII GATT are to be applied. This GATT Code contains its own enforcement mechanism for the enforcement of these rights and obligations. It creates a Committee on Subsidies and Countervailing Measures (the Committee) to oversee enforcement of the Code. If a dispute arises, the party making a complaint is instructed to request consultations with the other party. If these consultations fail to resolve the dispute, either party may refer the dispute to the Committee for conciliation. If conciliation fails to resolve the dispute, any signatory involved may request that a panel be established. The parties to the dispute must agree to the composition of the panel. The panel considers the issue and submits its findings to the Committee. The Committee then considers the panel's report and may make recommendations to the parties with a view to resolving the dispute. If these recommendations are not followed, the Committee may authorize appropriate countermeasures.[33]

The Code's procedure is based on the dispute settlement procedure contained in Article XXII and XXIII of the GATT. This procedure has been criticized because panel reports only became effective as decisions upon their approval by the GATT Council, acting on the principle of one country one vote and requiring unanimity. Thus it was possible for the losing party before a GATT dispute panel to block the adoption of a panel report. In fact, in some cases a GATT party was able either to block completely, or at least delay, the appointment of a panel in the first place.[34]

Again, later developments in GATT law make the reference to the Code in the Europe Agreements slightly ambiguous. For States that are parties to the Code, its dispute resolution mechanism has been replaced by the unitary dispute settlement mechanism contained in an annex to the WTO Agreement.[35] This mechanism, known as the understanding on dispute settlement, is the only legitimate forum for the resolution of disputes concerning the interpretation and application of the WTO Agreement and all the agreements contained in its annexes, including the Agreement on Subsidies and Countervailing Measures, and is binding on all members of the WTO.

---

[33] The Code, above, note 11, at Arts 15, 18.
[34] For example, the *US v the EC* on Citrus and *South Africa v Canada* on Gold coins.
[35] WTO Agreement, above, note 14, at Annex 2.

The WTO dispute settlement mechanism is greatly altered from the mechanism under GATT 1947, on which the Code's dispute resolution procedure was based. Establishment of a panel can no longer be blocked, and panel decisions take effect automatically within 60 days, unless disapproved by consensus. In response to members' desire for a review process, a standing Appellate Body was created to which losing parties can appeal on points of law. If the Appellate Body upholds the decision of the panel, the decision enters into effect within 30 days, again unless the membership decides by consensus not to adopt the appellate report. Thus, the understanding on dispute settlement provides the losing party in a panel proceeding with an opportunity to challenge the panel's decision, but they have only one chance and this is subject to strict time limits. The losing party can no longer block the effectiveness of a decision, nor even substantially delay it. Nor can the losing party ultimately avoid compliance with a decision, or retaliation by the party which has the decision in its favour.[36] It is not clear whether the developments in the enforcement of state aids which occurred in the Uruguay Round will be applicable to the enforcement of the transitional rules for state aids under the Europe Agreements.

c. Article 90 EC

Similar questions about procedures and enforcement arise in relation to the application of the principles of Article 90 EC. I mention here just a few points. Will an independent body be entrusted with similar powers to those of the Commission pursuant to Article 90(3) EC? Will Article 90 have direct effect in the CEECs, in the same way as it has in the member states of the Community?[37] It should be recalled that the direct effect of Article 90 EC depends on the direct effect of the Article to which it refers, i.e. principally Articles 85 and 86 EC. This raises in turn the question of the direct effect of these provisions.[38]

Must there be an explicit authorization in order to demonstrate that individual undertakings are granted special or exclusive rights? Furthermore I assume that the obligations of Articles 68 and 69 of the Agreement will also include the transposition of the Commission's Directive 80/723,[39] as amended by Directive 85/413,[40] on the transparency of financial relations between member states and public undertakings.

---

[36] For more information on the dispute settlement procedure in the WTO, see A.F. Lowenfeld, 'Remedies along with Rights: Institutional Reform in the new GATT', *American Journal of International Law* (1994), 477. See also E.-U. Petersmann, 'The Dispute Settlement System of the World Trade Organization and the Evolution of the GATT Dispute Settlement System since 1948', *CMLRev.* (1994), 1157.

[37] Case C-260/89, *ERT*, (1991) ECR I-2925.

[38] This topic is further discussed by A.-M. Van den Bossche, above, p. 92.

[39] *OJ* 1980, L 195.

[40] *OJ* 1985, L 229.

V. CONCLUSION

As is shown by the description above, the implementation of the EC rules on state aids and those relating to public enterprises in the CEECs is a daunting task. It is even more challenging than the application of the common competition rules, i.e. the equivalent of Articles 85 and 86 EC, because, after all, the latter are addressed to enterprises. The former set of rules, on the contrary, is addressed to governments.[41] Can these governments really be expected to discipline themselves, even where their counterpart governments of the EC seem to need the supervision and control of an independent body: the Commission. Furthermore, there is serious doubt as to whether the direct effect of Articles 90(2) and 93(3) EC will be recognized by the judiciary of the Europe Agreement partners.[42] Problems in this context may be compounded by the fact that the courts in these countries lack the possibility of seeking the guidance of the Court of Justice under the Article 177 EC procedure.

[41] This is generally true, even though Art. 90 EC is also addressed to enterprises.
[42] The author has been informed by his colleague Raijko Pirnath of Ljubljana University, that the courts in Slovenia may be willing to recognize direct effect.

ANNEX
THE AGREEMENT ON INTERPRETATION AND APPLICATION OF ARTICLES VI, XVI AND XXIII OF GATT
Article 7
Notification of subsidies

1.   Having regard to the provisions of Article XVI:1 of the General Agreement, any signatory may make a written request for information on the nature and extent of any subsidy granted or maintained by another signatory (including any form of income or price support) which operates directly or indirectly to increase exports of any product from or reduce imports of any product into its territory.

2.   Signatories so requested shall provide such information as quickly as possible and in a comprehensive manner, and shall be ready upon request, to provide additional information to the requesting signatory. Any signatory which considers that such information has not been provided may bring the matter to the attention of the Committee.

3.   Any interested signatory which considers that any practice of another signatory having the effect of a subsidy has not been notified in accordance with the provision of Article XVI:1 of the General Agreement may bring the matter to the attention of such other signatory. If the subsidy practice is not thereafter notified promptly, such signatory may itself bring the subsidy practice in question to the notice of the Committee.

Article 8
Subsidies – General provisions

1.   Signatories recognize that subsidies are used by governments to promote important objectives of social and economic policy. Signatories also recognize that subsidies may cause adverse effects to the interest of other signatories.

2.   Signatories agree not to use export subsidies in a manner inconsistent with the provisions of this Agreement.

3.   Signatories further agree that they shall seek to avoid causing, through the use of any subsidy
   (a)   injury to the domestic industry of another signatory
   (b)   nullification or impairment of the benefits accruing directly or indirectly to another signatory under the General Agreement, or
   (c)   serious prejudice to the interests of another signatory.

4.   The adverse effects to the interests of another signatory required to demonstrate nullification or impairment or serious prejudice may arise through
   (a)   the effects of the subsidized imports in the *domestic market* of the importing signatory,
   (b)   the effects of the subsidy in displacing or impeding the imports of like products into the *market of the subsidizing country*, or

(c)   the effects of the subsidized exports in displacing the exports of like products of another signatory from a *third country market.*

Article 9
Export subsidies on products
other than certain primary products

1.   Signatories shall not grant export subsidies on products other than certain primary products.

2.   The practices listed in points (a) to (l) in the Annex are illustrative of exports subsidies.

Article 10
Export subsidies on certain primary products

1.   In accordance with the provisions of Article XVI:3 of the General Agreement, signatories agree not to grant directly or indirectly any export subsidy on certain primary products in a manner which results in the signatory granting such subsidy having more than an equitable share of world export trade in such product, account being taken of the shares of the signatories in trade in the product concerned during a previous representative period, and any special factors which may have affected or may be affecting trade in such product.

2.   For purposes of Article XVI:3 of the General Agreement and paragraph 1 above:

(a)   *'more than an equitable share of world trade'* shall include any case in which the effect of an export subsidy granted by a signatory is to displace the exports of another signatory bearing in mind the developments on world markets;

(b)   with regard to new markets traditional patterns of supply of the product concerned to the world market, region or country, in which the new market is situated shall be taken into account in determining 'equitable share of world export trade';

(c)   'a previous representative period' shall normally be the three most recent calendar years in which normal market conditions existed.

3.   Signatories further agree not to grant export subsidies on exports of certain primary products to a particular market in a manner which results in prices materially below those of other suppliers to the same market.

Article 11
Subsidies other than export subsidies

1.   Signatories recognize that subsidies other than export subsidies are widely used as important instruments for the promotion of social and economic

policy objectives and do not intend to restrict the right of signatories to use such subsidies to achieve these and other important policy objectives which they consider desirable. Signatories note that among such objectives are:

(a) the elimination of industrial, economic and social disadvantages of specific regions,

(b) to facilitate the restructuring, under socially acceptable conditions, of certain sectors, especially where this has become necessary by reason of changes in trade and economic policies, including international agreements resulting in lower barriers to trade,

(c) generally to sustain employment and to encourage re-training and change in employment,

(d) to encourage research and development programmes, especially in the field of high-technology industries,

(e) the implementation of economic programmes and policies to promote the economic and social development of developing countries,

(f) redeployment of industry in order to avoid congestion and environmental problems.

2. Signatories recognize, however, that subsidies other than export subsidies, certain objectives and possible form of which are described, respectively, in paragraphs 1 and 3 of this Article, may cause or threaten to cause injury to a domestic industry of another signatory or serious prejudice to the interests of another signatory or may nullify or impair benefits accruing to another signatory under the General Agreement, in particular where such subsidies would adversely affect the conditions of normal competition. Signatories shall, therefore seek to avoid causing such effects through the use of subsidies. In particular, signatories, when drawing up their policies and practices in this field, in addition to evaluating the essential internal objectives to be achieved, shall also weigh, as far as practicable, taking account of the nature of the particular case, possible adverse effects on trade. They shall also consider the conditions of world trade, production (e.g. price, capacity utilization etc.) and supply in the product concerned.

3. Signatories recognize that the objectives mentioned in paragraph 1 above may be achieved, *inter alia*, by means of subsidies granted with the aim of giving an advantage to certain enterprises. Examples of possible forms of such subsidies are: government financing of commercial enterprises, including grants, loans or guarantees; government provision or government financed provision of utility, supply distribution and other operational or support services or facilities; government financing of research and development programmes; fiscal incentives; and government subscription to, or provision of, equity capital.

Signatories note that the above form of subsidies are normally granted either regionally or by sector. The enumeration of forms of subsidies set out above is illustrative and non-exhaustive, and reflects these currently granted by a number of signatories to this Agreement.

Signatories recognize, nevertheless, that the enumeration of forms of subsidies set out above should be reviewed periodically and that this should be done, through consultations, in conformity with the spirit of Article XVI:5 of the General Agreement.

4. Signatories recognize further that, without prejudice to their rights under this Agreement, nothing in paragraphs 1–3 above and in particular the enumeration of forms of subsidies creates, in itself, any basis for action under the Agreement, as interpreted by this Agreement.

Article 12
Consultations

1. Whenever a signatory has reasons to believe that an export subsidy is being granted or maintained by another signatory in a manner inconsistent with the provisions of this Agreement, such signatory may request consultations with such other signatory.

2. A request for consultations under paragraph 1 above shall include a statement of available evidence with regard to the existence and nature of the subsidy in question.

3. Whenever a signatory has reason to believe that any subsidy is being granted or maintained by another signatory and that such subsidy either causes injury to its domestic industry, nullification or impairment of benefits accruing to it under the General Agreement, or serious prejudice to its interests, such signatory may request consultations with such other signatory.

4. A request for consultations under paragraph 3 above shall include a statement of available evidence with regard to (a) the existence and nature of the subsidy in question and (b) the injury caused to the domestic industry or, in the case of nullification or impairment, or serious prejudice, the adverse effects caused to the interests of the signatory requesting consultations.

5. Upon request for consultations under paragraph 1 or paragraph 3 above, the signatory believed to be granting or maintaining the subsidy practice in question shall enter into such consultations as quickly as possible. The purpose of the consultations shall be to clarify the facts of the situation and to arrive at a mutually acceptable solution.

Article 13
Conciliation, dispute settlement and authorized countermeasures

1. If, in the case of consultations under paragraph 1 of Article 12, a mutually acceptable solution has not been reached within thirty days of the request for consultations, any signatory party to such consultations may refer the matter to the Committee for conciliation in accordance with the provisions of Part VI.

2. If, in the case of consultations under paragraph 3 of Article 12, a mutually acceptable solution has not been reached within sixty days of the request for consultations, any signatory party to such consultations may refer

the matter to the Committee for conciliation in accordance with the provisions of Part VI.

3. If any dispute arising under this Agreement is not resolved as a result of consultations or conciliations, the Committee shall, upon request, review the matter in accordance with the dispute settlement procedures of Part VI.

4. If, as a result of its review, the Committee concludes that an export subsidy is being granted in a manner inconsistent with the provisions of this Agreement or that a subsidy is being granted or maintained in such a manner as to cause injury, nullification or impairment, or serious prejudice, it shall make such recommendations to the parties as may be appropriate to resolve the issue and, in the event the recommendations are not followed, it may authorize such countermeasures as may be appropriate, taking into account the degree and nature of the adverse effects found to exist, in accordance with the provisions of Part VI.

Article 16
Committee on Subsidies and Countervailing Measures

1. There shall be established under this Agreement a Committee on Subsidies and Countervailing Measures composed of representatives from each of the signatories to this Agreement. The Committee shall elect its own Chairman and shall meet not less than twice a year and otherwise as envisaged by relevant provisions of this Agreement at the request of any signatory. The Committee shall carry out responsibilities as assigned to it under this Agreement or by the signatories and it shall afford signatories the opportunity of consulting on any matters relating to the operation of the Agreement or the furtherance of its objective. The GATT secretariat shall act as the secretariat to the Committee.

2. The Committee may set up subsidiary bodies as appropriate.

3. In carrying out their functions, the Committee and any subsidiary bodies may consult with and seek information from any source they deem appropriate. However, before the Committee or a subsidiary body seeks such information from a source within the jurisdiction of a signatory, it shall inform the signatory involved.

Article 17
Conciliation

1. In cases where matters are referred to the Committee for conciliation failing a mutually agreed solution in consultations under any provision of this Agreement, the Committee shall immediately review the facts involved and, through its good offices, shall encourage the signatories involved to develop a mutually acceptable solution.

2.   Signatories shall make their best efforts to reach a mutually satisfactory solution throughout the period of conciliation.

3.   Should the matter remain unresolved, notwithstanding efforts at conciliation made under paragraph 2 above, any signatory involved may, thirty days after the request for conciliation, request that a panel be established by the Committee in accordance with the provisions of Article 18 below.

Article 18
Dispute settlement

1.   The Committee shall establish a panel upon request pursuant to paragraph 3 of Article 17. A panel so established shall review the facts of the matter and, in light of such facts, shall present to the Committee its findings concerning the rights and obligations of the signatories party to the dispute under the relevant provisions of the General Agreement as interpreted and applied by this Agreement.

2.   A panel should be established within thirty days of a request therefor and a panel so established should deliver its findings to the Committee within sixty days after its establishment.

3.   When a panel is to be established, the Chairman of the Committee, after securing the agreement of the signatories concerned, should propose the composition of the panel. Panels shall be composed of three or five members, preferably governmental, and the composition of panels should not give rise to delays in their establishment. It is understood that citizens of countries whose governments are parties to the dispute would not be members of the panel concerned with that dispute.

4.   In order to facilitate the constitution of panels, the Chairman of the Committee should maintain an informal indicative list of governmental and non-governmental persons qualified in the fields of trade relations, economic development, and other matters covered by the General Agreement and this Agreement, who could be available for serving on panels. For this purpose, each signatory would be invited to indicate at the beginning of every year to the Chairman of the Committee the name of one or two persons who would be available for such work.

5.   Panel members would serve in their individual capacities and not as government representatives, nor as representatives of any organization. Governments would therefore not give them instructions with regard to matters before a panel. Panel members should be selected with a view to ensuring the independence of the members, a sufficiently diverse background and a wide spectrum of experience.

6.   To encourage development of mutually satisfactory solutions between the parties to a dispute and with a view to obtaining their comments, each panel should first submit the descriptive part of its report to the parties concerned, and should subsequently submit to the parties to the dispute its

conclusions, or an outline thereof, a reasonable period of time before they are circulated to the Committee.

7. If a mutually satisfactory solution is developed by the parties to a dispute before a panel, any signatory with an interest in the matter has a right to enquire about and be given appropriate information about that solution and a notice outlining the solution that has been reached shall be presented by the panel to the Committee.

8. In cases where the parties to a dispute have failed to come to a satisfactory solution, the panels shall submit a written report to the Committee which should set forth the findings of the panel as to the questions of fact and the application of the relevant provisions of the General Agreement as interpreted, and applied by this Agreement and the reasons and bases therefor.

9. The Committee shall consider the panel report as soon as possible and, taking into account the findings contained therein, may make recommendations to the parties with a view to resolving the dispute. If the Committee's recommendations are not followed within a reasonable period, the Committee may authorize appropriate countermeasures (including withdrawal of GATT concessions or obligations) taking into account the nature and degree of the adverse effect found to exist. Committee recommendations should be presented to the parties within thirty days of the receipt of the panel report.

Article 19
Final provisions

1. No specific action against a subsidy of another signatory can be taken except in accordance with the provisions of the General Agreement, as interpreted by this Agreement.

Annex
ILLUSTRATIVE LIST OF EXPORT SUBSIDIES

(a) The provisions by governments of direct subsidies to a firm or an industry contingent upon export performance.

(b) Currency retention schemes or any similar practices which involve a bonus on exports.

(c) Internal transport and freight charges on export shipments, provided or mandated by governments, on terms more favourable than for domestic shipments.

(d) The delivery by governments or their agencies of imported or domestic products or services for use in the production of exported goods, on terms or conditions more favourable for delivery of like or directly competitive products or services for use in the production of goods for domestic consumption, if (in the case of products) such terms or conditions are more favourable than those commercially available on world markets to their exporters.

(e) The full or partial exemption, remission, or deferral specifically related to exports, of direct taxes or social welfare charges paid or payable by industrial or commercial enterprises.

(f) The allowance of special deductions directly related to exports or export performance, over and above those granted in respect of production for domestic consumption, in the calculation of the base on which direct taxes are charged.

(g) The exemption or remission in respect of the production and distribution of exported products, of indirect taxes in excess of those levied in respect of the production and distribution of like products when sold for domestic consumption.

(h) The exemption, remission or deferral of prior stage cumulative indirect taxes on goods or services used in the production of exported products in excess of the exemption, remission or deferral of like prior stage cumulative indirect taxes on goods or services used in the production of like products when sold for domestic consumption; provided, however, that prior stage cumulative indirect taxes may be exempted, remitted or deferred on exported products even when not exempted, remitted or deferred on like products when sold for domestic consumption, if the prior stage cumulative indirect taxes are levied on goods that are physically incorporated (making normal allowance for waste) in the exported product.

(i) The remission or drawback of imported charges in excess of those levied on imported goods that are physically incorporated (making normal allowance for waste) in the exported product; provided, however, that in particular cases a firm may use a quantity of home market goods equal to, and having the same quality and characteristics as, the imported goods as a substitute for them in order to benefit from this provision if the import and the responding export operations both occur within a reasonable time period, normally not to exceed two years.

(j) The provision by governments (or special institutions controlled by governments) of export credit guarantee or insurance programmes, of insurance or guarantee programmes against increases in the costs of exported products or of exchange risk programmes, at premium rates, which are manifestly inadequate to cover the long-term operating costs and losses of the programmes.

(k) The grant by governments (or special institutions controlled by and/or acting under the authority of governments) of export credits at rates below those which they actually have to pay for the funds so employed (or would have to pay if they borrowed on international capital markets in order to obtain funds of the same maturity and denominated in the same currency as the export credit), or the payment by them of all or part of the costs incurred by exporters or financial institutions in obtaining credits, in so far as they are used to secure a material advantage in the field of export credit terms.

Provided, however, that if a signatory is a party to an international undertaking on official export credits to which at least twelve original signatories to this Agreement are parties as of 1 January 1979 (or a successor undertaking which has been adopted by those original signatories), or if in practice a signatory applies the interest rates provisions of the relevant undertaking, an export credit practice which is in conformity with those provisions shall not be considered an export subsidy prohibited by this Agreement.

(l)   Any other charge on the public account constituting an export subsidy in the sense of Article XVI of the General Agreement.

8

EU SAFEGUARD MEASURES UNDER THE EUROPE AGREEMENTS: THE NON-SETTLEMENT OF TRADE DISPUTES

Lode Van Den Hende[1]

I. INTRODUCTION

In trade agreements, contracting parties generally grant each other better market access through abolition of quantitative import restrictions and import tariffs, the most classical protectionist instruments. Most trade agreements also contain safeguard clauses, which under specified conditions allow a contracting party temporarily to withdraw market access concessions. Such safeguard clauses are essential for upholding a trade agreement. During its functioning, unforeseeable difficulties may arise which objectively justify a contracting party in derogating temporarily from what has been agreed. If such a derogation were not possible under any circumstance whatsoever, the agreement could eventually collapse under too strong domestic pressure. On the other hand, safeguard clauses can be abused by a contracting party in order to undermine its concessions. Generally speaking there are two ways to prevent such 'new protectionism' from emerging. Application of safeguard clauses should be bound to strict conditions, and/or should depend on the consent of (or be subject to review by) a truly independent body.[2]

---

[1] Assistant, Europees Instituut, University of Ghent; Attorney at Law (Vlaemminck, Holmens, Grossens). This study was prepared in the framework of a research programme on the implementation of the Association Agreement EU–Hungary. This programme is financed by the Ministry of the Flemish Community, department of economic affairs. The author wishes to thank P. Eeckhout, M.-A. Gaudissart, M. Maresceau, E. Montaguti and I. Pokorádi for their valuable comments on an earlier draft. Any remaining mistakes are of course the author's responsibility only.
[2] See generally J.H. Jackson, *The World Trading System*, MIT Press, Cambridge, 1989, 149–87; D. Robertson, *GATT Rules for Emergency Protection*, Trade Policy Research Centre, London, 1992, Thames Essay No. 57, Harvester Wheatsheaf.

The Europe Agreements (EAs)[3] contain several safeguard clauses, which vary in nature. Firstly, they contain 'emergency protection' or 'escape' clauses, which enable the contracting parties partially to revoke or suspend import concessions because of 'serious injury' to domestic producers caused by a sudden surge in competitive imports.[4] The more general term 'safeguard measure' is often used to indicate this category only. The Europe Agreements also contain a similar escape clause, allowing the reintroduction of export restrictions in case of 'serious shortage' of an essential product.[5] A second category of safeguard clauses allows a contracting party to retaliate when another party is behaving unfairly, for instance when dumping occurs,[6] or when the other party is in breach of the rules laid down in the agreement.[7] A third category of safeguards comprises those enabling import restrictions for the protection of general national interests: public security, health and life of humans, animals or plants, intellectual property, etc.[8] Each Europe Agreement also contains an infant and restructuring industry clause that allows the associated country to protect such industries by means of increased customs duties.[9] A last category concerns import restrictions introduced to counter balance of payments difficulties.[10]

In the early days of the Europe Agreements, trade restrictive measures of the EC based on several of these safeguard clauses shook the associated

---

[3] Europe Agreement with Hungary: *OJ* 1993, L 347; Europe Agreement with Poland: *OJ* 1993, L 348; Europe Agreement with Romania: *OJ* 1994, L 357; Europe Agreement with Bulgaria: *OJ* 1994, L 358; Europe Agreement with the Slovak Republic: *OJ* 1994, L 359; Europe Agreement with the Czech Republic: *OJ* 1994, L 360. Concerning the safeguard clauses, see M. Maresceau and E. Montaguti, 'The Relations Between the European Union and Central and Eastern Europe: a Legal Appraisal', *CMLRev.* (1995), 1327–67, at pp. 1345–62.

[4] Art. 30 EA Hungary. The corresponding articles in other EAs are the following: Art. 30 EA Poland; Art. 31 EA Romania; Art. 31 EA Bulgaria; Art. 31 EA Czech Republic; Art. 31 EA Slovak Republic.

[5] Art. 31 EA Hungary. The corresponding articles in other EAs are the following: Art. 31 EA Poland, Art. 32 EA Romania; Art. 32 EA Bulgaria; Art. 32 EA Czech Republic; Art. 32 EA Slovak Republic.

[6] Art. 29 EA Hungary. The corresponding articles in other EAs are: Art. 29 EA Poland; Art. 30 EA Romania; Art. 30 EA Bulgaria; Art. 30 EA Czech Republic; Art. 30 EA Slovak Republic.

[7] Art. 62, para. 6 EA Hungary contains a safeguard clause related to non-compliance with competition rules; Art. 117, para. 2 EA Hungary contains a general safeguard clause related to failure 'to fulfil an obligation under this Agreement'. The corresponding articles in the other EAs are: Arts 63 and 115 EA Poland; Arts 64 and 119 EA Romania; Arts 64 and 118 EA Bulgaria; Arts 64 and 117 EA Czech Republic; Arts 64 and 117 EA Slovak Republic.

[8] Art. 35 EA Hungary. The corresponding articles in the other EAs are: Art. 35 EA Poland; Art. 36 EA Romania; Art. 36 EA Bulgaria; Art. 36 EA Czech Republic; Art. 36 EA Slovak Republic.

[9] Art. 28 EA Hungary. The corresponding articles in the other EAs are: Art. 28 EA Poland; Art. 29 EA Romania; Art. 29 EA Bulgaria; Art. 29 EA Czech Republic; Art. 29 EA Slovak Republic.

[10] Art. 63 EA Hungary. The corresponding articles in the other EAs are: Art. 64 EA Poland; Art. 65 EA Romania; Art. 65 EA Bulgaria; Art. 65 EA Czech Republic; Art. 65 EA Slovak Republic.

Central and Eastern European countries' (CEECs) belief in the EC's free trade rhetoric.[11] The EC's partners seemed surprised to discover the Europe Agreements' loopholes, big enough, so it appeared, for the EC to drive through a whole coach and horses of protection. This led commentators to plead for a minimization of escape routes, by way of interpretation and even renegotiation of the Europe Agreements.[12] In the meantime, however, it seems that some of the CEECs have themselves discovered the 'benefits' of these loopholes. Poland, namely has referred to the infant and restructuring industry clause (Article 28 EA Poland) to protect its petrol sector against imports from the EC, and the emergency export restriction clause (Article 31 EA Poland) to protect its leather industry from shortages of raw material in the form of skins and hides.[13]

The aim of this paper is to examine, through a theoretical legal analysis, to what extent the framework of the Europe Agreements provides guarantees against abuse of safeguard clauses, and what means there are for plugging the possible legal loopholes.

In view of the restricted area examined in this contribution, the analysis will be performed on two 'samples' from the Europe Agreements' legal framework. The first is the possibility for the EC to issue safeguard measures of the first type, namely emergency protection. Admittedly, the EC has only made use of this possibility on very limited occasions, but the emergency protection regime is a very illustrative case and thus well suited as a 'sample' for legal analysis. The focus is on application of this kind of measures by the EC, largely leaving aside application by the CEECs, but this is mainly due to the lack of precise legal data on the relevant procedures in these countries' internal legislation. The second 'sample' that will be analysed is the broader issue of dispute settlement, which is relevant to all categories of safeguard measures.

[11] See UN Economic Commission for Europe, 45 *Economic Bulletin for Europe* (1993), 107–11. The EU had used the anti-dumping clause, the emergency protection clause and the general 'national interests' clause.

[12] Z. Drabek, *A Call for Renegotiation of the Europe Agreement*, in *Bulgaria and the European Community*, Centre for European Studies, Sofia, 1993, 87–104, at p. 97: 'Nothing seems to be more disappointing than the one-sided applications of safeguard measures in a situation of threat from one of the parties' . . . 'The problem seems to me to be twofold – absence of satisfactory warning signals and absence of a satisfactory mechanism for mutual dispute settlement'. Professor Winters seems to agree as to the disease but not as to the cure when he writes: 'The issue is not so much that the Agreements are directly restrictive – although they are in certain areas – but that they leave a large number of opportunities for future restrictiveness in their implementation. Such opportunities are potentially harmful if they are exercised and actually harmful in that their existence undermines confidence in the EC's willingness and ability to aid the transition process. The fundamental policy issue, then, is not rewriting the Agreements, but minimizing the resort to the restrictions that they currently permit.' (A. Winters, *The Europe Agreements: with a Little Help from Our Friends*, in *The Association Process: Making it Work*, CEPR Occasional Paper No. 11, 1992, 18.)

[13] Arts 28 and 31 EU Poland respectively (see *Agence Europe*, 17 July 1996, 8 and 6 September 1996, 6 and Decision 3/96 of the EC/Poland Association Council, *OJ*, 1996, L 208/31). For other attempts by Poland and Hungary to use the infant industry clause, see M. Maresceau and E. Montaguti, op. cit. note 3, p. 1358.

As to terminology, unless otherwise indicated, the term 'safeguard measure' will be used in its narrow sense, designating the emergency protection type measures only, thus aligning with the language of the new WTO Agreement on Safeguards, the so-called Safeguards Code.[14] For reasons of convenience references will sometimes be limited to Hungary and the Europe Agreement with Hungary, but since the wording in all the Europe Agreements is to a large extent identical, the same remarks also apply to other associated countries and other Europe Agreements.

II. SAFEGUARD MEASURES BY THE EC AGAINST IMPORTS FROM THE ASSOCIATED CEECS

A. The role of safeguards

As opposed to an anti-dumping clause, a safeguard clause allows a contracting party to a trade agreement to protect its domestic producers from imports that are not 'unfair', but that are simply too voluminous for domestic producers to cope with. Because of this difference emergency protection is subject to more stringent conditions than anti-dumping measures, in particular a more important threat to domestic producers (generally 'serious injury' for emergency protection as opposed to 'material injury' for an anti-dumping measure[15]). In GATT, safeguard measures are dealt with in Article XIX, which is the standard of reference for this kind of clause.[16] Under GATT 1947,[17] trade partners injured by the safeguard measures had to be given trade compensation and, according to the prevailing opinion, measures were to be applied on a non-discriminatory basis, that is against all imports of a certain product irrespective of their country of origin.[18] The WTO Safeguards Code

---

[14] The term 'emergency protection' could be misleading. It seems to suggest immediate and short-term measures. This is not always the case. In fact, as to economic result anti-dumping measures, anti-subsidy measures and safeguard measures *stricto sensu* are substitutes (see D. Robertson, above, note 2, 16–17). The term 'emergency' relates to 'unforeseen circumstances'.

[15] Cf. Arts VI and XIX of GATT.

[16] On GATT safeguards rules see T.P. Stewart and M.A. Brilliant, 'Safeguards' in Stewart (ed.), *The GATT Uruguay Round – A Negotiating History (1986–1992)*, Kluwer, Deventer, 1993, Vol. II, 1711–820; J.H. Jackson, above, note 2, 149–87.

[17] The term 'GATT 1947' is used to refer to the 'pre-Uruguay Round Agreement' GATT rules. GATT still exists as a part of the Agreement Establishing the World Trade Organization, and the new version of GATT will be cited as 'GATT 1994'. When the term 'GATT' is used without any further specification, reference is made to both the old and the new regime.

[18] J.H. Jackson, above, note 2, 169–74; T.P. Stewart and M.A. Brilliant, above, note 16, 1768; M.C.E.J. Bronckers, *Selective Safeguard Measures in Multilateral Trade Relations*, Kluwer, Deventer, 1985, 80–1. The validity of this prevailing interpretation is not undisputed, as is clearly shown by the discussion between Bronckers and Koulen in *Legal Issues of European Integration*: see M. Koulen, 'The Non-Discriminatory Interpretation of GATT Art. XIX(1)', *LIEI* (1983/2), 87–111 (in favour of non-discrimination) and M.C.E.J. Bronckers, 'Reconsidering the Non-Discrimination Principle As Applied to GATT Safeguard Measures. A Rejoinder', *LIEI* (1983/2), 113–37, at p. 114 (in favour of selectivity); see also Broncker's above-mentioned book on this issue. The EC has always been in favour of selective safeguards and has actually introduced its safeguard measures on a selective basis. Most GATT members hold the opposite view: see T.P. Stewart and M.A. Brilliant, above, note 16, 1768–9.

has reinforced GATT discipline by adding further procedural and substantive rules. The answer to the question to what extent these GATT/WTO rules apply to imports from the CEECs is, at the time of writing, unclear and varies according to the CEEC concerned.[19] In the foreseeable future, however, all associated CEECs should come to fall under the general GATT/WTO regime.[20]

Closely related to the issue of emergency action is that of voluntary export restraints (VERs). In the case of a VER, the exporting country agrees to limit exports 'voluntarily', mostly to prevent the importing country from introducing unilateral emergency protection. Such an informal safeguard action can take on many different guises, and can be negotiated on a government-to-government basis as well as on an industry-to-industry or government-to-industry basis. Often designated as 'grey area measures', they are true to their name and not often made public.[21] They are selective and do not conform to the principle of non-discrimination. Their compatibility with GATT 1947 was, to say the least, very doubtful, and under the new Safeguards

---

[19] Hungary was a state-trading country when it became a contracting party to GATT 1947. Therefore, some specific rules were provided for in its Protocol of Accession, including a special safeguard clause which applies in addition to Art. XIX. The main difference is that the specific safeguard clause allows discriminatory action, thus enabling a contracting party to restrict imports from Hungary only, or vice versa. Poland and Romania are in the same situation, but Poland accepted a unilateral selective safeguard clause. See Art. 5 of Hungary's Protocol of Accession (GATT, BISD, 20th Supp., 3); Art. 4 of Poland's Protocol of Accession (GATT, BISD, 15th Supp., 46); Art. 4 of Romania's Protocol of Accession (GATT, BISD, 18th Supp., 5). Protocols of accession are part of GATT 1994 (see para. 1(b)(ii)). As a consequence, renegotiation remains necessary, even after the Uruguay Round Agreements (see UNCTAD Secretariat, *Trade Policies, Structural Adjustment and Economic Reform: Increased Participation in International Trade in Goods and Services by Developing Countries and Economies in Transition: Some Problems and Opportunities*, Report, 10 Feb. 1994, TD/B/40(2)/7, 21). However, the *General interpretative note to Annex 1A* of GATT 1994 seems to prevent an application of these special selective safeguard clauses that does not conform to the provisions of the Safeguards Code, even without renegotiation of accession protocols. Czechoslovakia was a founding member of GATT and no specific rules applied to it, but after switching to a state-trading system, it was *de facto* not treated as a full member. As a consequence there is no need for renegotiation. After the split of Czechoslovakia the Czech Republic and the Slovak Republic became separate Contracting Parties in April 1993, under the same terms applied to former Czechoslovakia, without further negotiations (GATT, Press Release 1573, 16 April 1993; for the protocols of accession, see GATT, BISD, 40th Sup. 10 and 32). Bulgaria is not a member but has filed an application. See also J. Martonyi, 'Eastern European Countries and the GATT' in Maresceau (ed.), *The Political and Legal Framework of Trade Relations Between the European Community and Eastern Europe*, Martinus Nijhoff, Dordrecht, 1989, 269–83; A.-M. van den Bossche, 'GATT: The Indispensable Link Between the EEC and Hungary?', *JWT* (1989/3), 141–55; M.C.E.J. Bronckers, 'Selective Safeguard Measures in Multilateral Trade Relations', above, note 18, 9–10; GATT, *Trade Policy Review – Hungary*, 1991, Volume I, 50–3; GATT, *Trade Policy Review – Poland*, 1992, Volume I, 40–1; V. Breskovski, 'Bulgaria and the GATT', *World Competition* (1993/2), 45–67.

[20] All associated CEECs are (re)negotiating their accession protocols in order to become 'ordinary' GATT/WTO members.

[21] P. Eeckhout, *The European Internal Market and International Trade: A Legal Analysis*, Oxford University Press, Oxford, 1994, 163–5; J.H. Jackson, above, note 2, 178; T.P. Stewart and M.A. Brilliant, above, note 16, 1725–7; D. Robertson, above, note 2, 48 and 66; GATT, *Trade Policy Review – EC*, 1993, Volume I, 71, note 20.

Code they are simply forbidden.[22] This makes good sense, since VERs are too often forced upon trading partners by the major trading powers, under the threat of imposing unilateral measures. Whether import restrictions are really justified remains unclear.[23]

In the past, the EC seemed to have a marked preference for VERs over formal safeguard action.[24] It is expected, however, that safeguard actions under WTO rules will increase as the new Safeguards Code forbids VERs and clearly allows, under certain conditions, the introduction of safeguard measures on a selective basis, directed against the most competitive exporters.[25] The legal problems concerning the adoption of Article XIX measures on a selective basis were one of the reasons the EC has so far made little use of that provision.[26]

B. The provisions of the Europe Agreements and their shortcomings

The GATT Article XIX-type safeguard clause in the Europe Agreement with Hungary is incorporated in Article 30,[27] which holds that:

> Where any product is being imported in such increased quantities and under such conditions as to cause or threaten to cause:
> - serious injury to domestic producers of like or directly competitive products in the territory of one of the Contracting Parties, or
> - serious disturbances in any sector of the economy or difficulties which could bring about serious deterioration in the economic situation of a region,
>
> the Community or Hungary, whichever is concerned, may take appropriate measures under the conditions and in accordance with the procedures laid down in Article 33.[28]

---

[22] Agreement on Safeguards, Art. 11 (Agreement establishing the World Trade Organization, *OJ* 1994, L 336/184). See also J.H. Jackson, 'Consistency of Export-Restraint Arrangements with the GATT', *The World Economy* (1988), 485–500, and W.J. Davey, 'An overview of the General Agreement on Tariffs and Trade', in Pescatore (ed.), *Handbook of GATT Dispute Settlement*, Kluwer, Deventer, 47–8 and note 139.

[23] D. Robertson, above, note 2, 3–4 and 18–19; J.H. Jackson, above, note 2, 178.

[24] This is denied by the EC (GATT, *Trade Policy Review – EC*, 1993, Volume II, 117). But compare in Volume I, Table IV.1 at p. 70 with Table IV.2 at p. 73. See also GATT, *Trade Policy Review – EC*, 1991, Volume I, 100 ff.

[25] See, however, a very sceptical M.C.E.J. Bronckers, 'Voluntary Export Restraints and the GATT 1994 Agreement on Safeguards' in Bourgeois, Berrod and Gippini Fournier (eds), *The Uruguay Round Results – A European Lawyers' Perspective*, European Interuniversity Press, Brussels, 1995, 273–9.

[26] During the Uruguay Round negotiations the EC's negotiating position was to allow grey-area measures to come under the control of a multilateral safeguard system if limited selectivity was allowed (T.P. Stewart and M.A. Brilliant, above, note 16, 1769). As to the new rules, Art. 2(2) of the Safeguards Code states: 'Safeguard measures shall be applied to a product being imported irrespective of its source.' However, Art. 5(b) provides the possibility of allocating an import quota in a way that discriminates against the most aggressive exporters.

[27] See also above, note 4.

[28] Special safeguard clauses exist for agricultural products (Art. 21 EA Hungary and Art. 2 of Annex Xa EA Hungary on imports of live bovine animals) and textiles (see Protocol 1 to the EA Hungary on textile and clothing products and Art. 8 of the Additional Protocol to the Europe Agreement on trade in textile products between the European Economic Community and the Republic of Hungary, *OJ* 1992, L 410/391). These specific safeguard clauses will not be dealt with here, but the overall underlying ideas of the paper apply to these sectors also.

The first requirement for the taking of measures ('serious injury . . .') constitutes a classic safeguard clause formula.[29] The second clause ('serious disturbances . . .') resembles Article 226 EC, a safeguard clause that was applicable within the EC until the end of 1969. A similar, transitional clause can be found in the Acts of Accession.[30] In themselves such provisions are of course very vague, and neither the EC Treaty and the Acts of Accession, nor the EAs provide criteria for the assessment of 'serious injury' or 'serious deterioration'.

However, both Article 226 EC and the safeguard clauses in the Acts of Accession do grant procedural guarantees. If a member state wants to use this clause against another member state it must be authorized to do so by the Commission, which acts as a neutral mediator between EC members.[31] This picture is different under the EAs. When a contracting party wishes to invoke Article 30 EA, then, according to Article 33(2) EA, it 'shall supply the Association Council with all relevant information with a view to seeking a solution acceptable to the two parties'. Subpara. 3(a) is more precise:

> as regards Article 30, the difficulties arising from the situation referred to in that Article shall be referred for examination to the Association Council, which may take any decision needed to put an end to such difficulties.
>
> If the Association Council or the exporting Party has not taken a decision putting an end to the difficulties or no other satisfactory solution has been reached within 30 days of the matter being referred, the importing Party may adopt the appropriate measures to remedy the problem. These measures must not exceed the scope of what is necessary to remedy the difficulties which have arisen.

Subpara. 3(d) provides for a fast-track procedure: 'where exceptional circumstances' require 'immediate action', 'precautionary measures strictly necessary to deal with the situation' can be issued without prior consultation of the Association Council.[32]

Bearing in mind that the Association Council takes decisions by way of consensus between the two Parties,[33] it is clear that when the EC wants to

---

[29] It should be noted, however, that it is wider than the Community's general safeguard clause contained in Art. 16 of Council Regulation No. 3285/94 (*OJ* 1994, L 349/53), which reads 'such *greatly* increased quantities' (emphasis added). See also below, text at notes 35 ff. On the way the EC has applied the first formula in the past see, I. Van Bael and J.-F. Bellis, *Anti-Dumping and Other Trade Protection Laws of the EEC*, CCH Editions, Bicester, 1990, 301–12.

[30] See e.g. Art. 379 of the Acts of Accession of Spain and Portugal (applicable during seven years, and ten years for 'sensitive products'), *OJ* 1985, L 302; Art. 152 of the Act of Accession of Austria, Finland and Sweden (applicable during 1 year only), *OJ* 1994, C 241/9.

[31] See G. Schmidt, *Schutzklausel der Übergangszeit*, in Von Der Groeben, Thiesing and Ehlermann (eds), *Kommentar zum EWG-Vertrag*, Nomos, Baden-Baden, 1991, 5611–26; A. Mattera, *Le Marché unique européen*, Jupiter, Paris, 1990, 627–40; Y. Gautier, *Clauses de sauvegarde*, in *Dictionnaire juridique Communautés européennes*, Presses Universitaires de France, Paris, 1993, 169–77.

[32] The corresponding articles in the other EAs are: Art. 33 EA Poland; Art. 34 EA Romania; Art. 34 EA Bulgaria; Art. 33 EA Czech Republic; Art. 33 EA Slovak Republic.

[33] Art. 106 EA Hungary. The corresponding articles in the other EAs are: Art. 104 EA Poland; Art. 108 EA Romania; Art. 107 EA Bulgaria; Art. 106 EA Czech Republic; Art. 106 EA Slovak Republic.

invoke Article 30 EA at least one of the two Parties will have to give in if unilateral action is to be prevented. In this respect, it cannot go unnoticed that the EC generally holds the stronger bargaining position. If the EC really wants to restrict imports and Hungary is not willing to restrict its exports 'voluntarily', then the Association Council cannot prevent the EC from imposing unilateral safeguard measures.[34] So it is impossible for the Association Council to play a neutral role similar to that of the Commission within the EC when applying Article 226 EC or the equivalent clauses in the Acts of Accession.[35]

A vaguely worded provision and the absence of real decision-making powers on the part of the Association Council add up to a potential loophole of considerable size. This conclusion is reinforced by the procedure that is applicable within the European Union to start up a safeguard procedure against imports from the associated CEECs. This is a *sui generis* procedure because for each Europe Agreement a separate regulation has been adopted 'on certain procedures for applying the Europe Agreement'.[36] While the rules applicable to the Europe Agreements are basically the same, they are remarkably different from the general safeguard procedure provided for by the regulation containing the EC's general import regime, that is, Council Regulation No. 3285/94 which implements the WTO Safeguards Code.[37]

The latter provides criteria to assess 'serious injury' or 'threat of serious injury' and the trend of imports supposedly responsible for that. Furthermore, it provides for an administrative investigation procedure comparable to the anti-dumping one.[38] The Commission must gather information on the trend

---

[34] Z. Drabek, above, note 12, 98 concludes: 'In brief the Association Council has only consultative powers, it has no executive powers'.

[35] Certainly in the relations between the EC and the CEECs the Commission cannot play such a role because it cannot be seen as neutral.

[36] Council Regulation No. 3491/93 on certain procedures for applying the Europe Agreement establishing an association between the European Communities and their member states, of the one part, and the Republic of Hungary, of the other part, *OJ* 1993, L 319/1. For ECSC products basically the same rules are provided for in Commission Decision No. 264/94/ECSC, *OJ* 1994, L 32/3. For Poland see Council Regulation No. 3492/93, *OJ* 1993, L 319/4 and Commission Decision No. 265/94/ECSC, *OJ* 1994, L 32/6. For the Czech Republic see Council Regulation No. 3296/94, *OJ* 1994, L 341/14. For the Slovak Republic see Council Regulation No. 3297/94, *OJ* 1994, L 341/17. For Romania see Council Regulation No. 3382/94, *OJ* 1994, L 368/1. For Bulgaria see Council Regulation No. 3383/94, *OJ* 1994, L 368/5. It is the EC's practice to issue a special regulation for the application of safeguard clauses in its free trade agreements. Their content, however, is not always alike.

[37] *OJ* 1994, L 349/53. Another regulation lays down more or less the same procedure for safeguard measures against some (former) state-trading countries: see Council Regulation No. 519/94 on common rules for imports from certain third countries and repealing Regulations (EEC) No. 1765/82, 1766/82 and 3420/83, *OJ* 1994, L 67/89 (this regulation applies to imports from Republics of the former Soviet Union, except the Baltic States, China, Albania, Mongolia, North Korea and Vietnam; the Baltic States were removed from the country list annexed to this regulation by Council Regulation (EC) No. 839/95, *OJ* 1995, L 85/9). The scope of the regulation was broadened to include ECSC products by Regulation (EC) No. 168/96, *OJ*, 1996, L 25/2.

[38] Regulation 3285/94, Arts 5–6.

of imports and possible economic difficulties of EC producers, and try to find out whether a causal link exists between these two elements. It must verify this information with importers, traders, agents, producers, trade associations and organizations. Interested parties may inspect all this information and may demand to be heard. At the end of such an investigation, the Commission and the Council can introduce safeguard measures or surveillance measures or can terminate the investigation without taking any measure. Either decision will be extensively reasoned by describing the results of the inquiry and will be published in the *Official Journal*.[39] In addition, if immediate intervention is necessary to prevent injury which it would be difficult to remedy, there is a procedure that allows provisional safeguard measures to be taken, in the form of increased customs duties, without prior investigation. The duration of such a provisional measure may not exceed 200 days and if the subsequent investigation shows that the relevant conditions were not fulfilled, the provisional measures must be repealed and the increased customs duties automatically refunded.[40] Such public investigations seem to be the only way to guarantee objective decision-making in the field of unilateral trade policy instruments.[41]

Regulation 3491/93 on certain procedures for applying the Europe Agreement with Hungary does not provide for such an investigation procedure for safeguard measures, nor does it provide clear assessment criteria. Its main concern seems to be speeding up intra-EC decision-making, at least as far as safeguard measures are concerned. As regards anti-dumping measures, Article 4 of the Regulation refers to the EC's basic anti-dumping legislation, which, as a consequence, applies to imports from Hungary. As regards safeguard measures, by contrast, Articles 5 and 6 do not refer to general EC legislation in the field, but provide a special procedure which lacks an 'anti-dumping style' investigation and provides for no procedural guarantee for private parties whatsoever. On the other hand, the Preamble of Regulation 3491/93 does refer to general EC safeguards rules in the same way as anti-dumping rules. One might suggest that this could imply that the 'certain procedures' regulation is additional to and not instead of the general safeguard procedure, so that the latter should be applied anyhow. Unfortunately, this seems not to be the case. An implied application of the general safeguard procedure conflicts with the explicit reference to anti-dumping legislation in Article 4 of the 'certain procedures' regulation, and with the explicit references to general safeguards law in similar regulations relating to other trade agreements.[42] Moreover, the decision-making procedure of Regulation 3491/93 simply does

---

[39] Regulation 3285/94, Art. 7.
[40] Regulation 3285/94, Art. 8.
[41] E.L.M. Völker, *Barriers to External and Internal Community Trade*, Kluwer, Deventer, 1993, 68.
[42] See e.g. Council Regulation No. 1658/77 for safeguard measures against Egypt (*OJ* 1977, L 186/7) and Council Regulation No. 1662/77 for safeguard measures against Morocco (*OJ* 1977, L 186/9).

not offer enough time for an examination as provided for by the general import regulation.[43]

Of course, the Europe Agreement does require prior information and consultation of the Association Council, 'which may take any decision needed' to put an end to the 'difficulties' described by Article 30 EA. Bearing in mind the EC's preference for VERs in the past, and the limited alternatives to import limitations for solving the kind of difficulties described in Article 30, this consultation procedure seems to be an 'institutionalized' VER negotiating procedure.[44] This is confirmed by the way safeguard measures against steel imports from the Czech and Slovak Federal Republic have been dealt with by the EC–Czech Republic and Slovak Republic Joint Committee.[45] In August 1992, the EC adopted safeguard measures against imports of certain steel products from the Czech and Slovak Federal Republic.[46] These were 'fast track' measures, issued without either preceding or subsequent public investigation.[47] In June 1993, the EC–Czech Republic and Slovak Republic Joint Committee issued Decision No. 1/93 introducing limits on imports into the Union of the same steel products that had been subject to the unilateral safeguard measure, and thus replacing it.[48] Again there had been no public investigation. Of course, formally such a decision is not a real VER, because it is not a measure issued by a single party. It is a decision of a joint body, requiring implementation from both sides. However, more important than its formal nature is the fact that imports into the EC are limited and that the partner country has agreed to this limitation.

---

[43] Where a member state requests the Commission to apply safeguard measures the Commission must respond within *five working days* (Regulation 3491/93, Art. 5). The general import regime of Regulation 3285/94 provides for a maximum duration of the investigation of *nine months*. The nine-month term was introduced by Regulation 518/94 (*OJ* 1994, L 67/77), predecessor to Regulation 3285/94, 'with a view to ensuring that such determinations are made *quickly*' (Regulation 518/94, Preamble, Recital 16 – emphasis added).

[44] VERs thus become the counterpart of undertakings accepted by an exporter in an antidumping case (I. Van Bael and J.F. Bellis, above, note 29, 319). Of course undertakings are more acceptable because they remedy 'unfair' behaviour, they are allowed by GATT and they have been preceded by an investigation. None of this is true as regards the VERs which are dealt with here.

[45] Under the Interim Agreements, which, as regards trade, preceded the Europe Agreements, the powers of the Association Council were exercised by a Joint Committee.

[46] Commission Decision No. 92/433/EEC, *OJ* 1992, L 238/24 and Commission Recommendation No. 92/434/ECSC, *OJ* 1992, L 238/26.

[47] At least one element of that safeguard measure seems dubious as it applies to products having a market share as low as 3.2%; 3.3% and 4.6%. Van Bael and Bellis mention that, as a rule, market shares are very substantial when import restrictions are introduced under the normal procedures (I. Van Bael and J.-F. Bellis, above, note 29, 304).

[48] *OJ* 1993, L 157/59 and 67. In answer to Written Question E-2044/93 on market access from the CEECs, Sir Leon Brittan, who at that time was the Commissioner responsible for trade relations with Eastern Europe, made the following statement concerning this arrangement: 'The safeguard clause does, however, allow rapid and effective action to be taken in case of disturbance on the Community market, and it was used to negotiate a tariff quota arrangement in 1993 with the Czech and Slovak Republics for importation into the Community of certain ECSC products' (*OJ* 1994, C 234/32).

One could state that the absence of a thorough public investigation is counterbalanced by the fact that measures are negotiated between the contracting parties, which will ensure their objectiveness. However, this argument cannot be accepted in a situation where one party holds a much stronger bargaining position, and the stronger party is able to act unilaterally anyway when no agreement is reached.[49] In such circumstances, offering an associated country a choice between a unilateral import restriction or an import restriction introduced by means of a bilaterally negotiated decision of a joint body resembles offering a choice between the plague and cholera.

In conclusion, it can be stated that because of substantive and procedural deficiencies, the safeguard provision of the Europe Agreements leaves the EC a virtually unrestricted margin of discretion. As a consequence it is easier for the Community to impose a safeguard measure on imports from the associated CEECs, than on imports from e.g. Hong Kong, to which the general, WTO-inspired, import regime is applied. That conclusion is confirmed by another, institutional, 'safeguards dispreference' towards these countries. Under the general safeguards procedure of Regulation 3285/94, a Commission decision to introduce safeguard measures can be referred to the Council. If the latter has not confirmed, amended or revoked the Commission's decision by qualified majority within three months, the measure is deemed revoked.[50] Exactly the opposite is true under the 'certain procedures regulations' in the EA concerned: if the Council does not react by a qualified majority within two months the Commission's safeguard measure remains valid.[51]

The only possible justification for these dispreferential rules seems to be that these newly associated CEECs enjoy a better market access than countries falling within the scope of the general import regimes, and, as a consequence, imports from these countries are more likely to cause serious injury. The argument would be that the EC must be able to use fast and effective means of protection against these 'dangerous' imports. But even if one recognizes the need for a possibility of fast intervention, there is absolutely no reason why a system of intermediate measures followed by a thorough re-examination should not suffice. The alleged argument certainly does not justify a margin of discretion so wide that it opens up a possibility of arbitrariness.

Of course, when confronted with a unilateral EC safeguard measure which it considers unjustified, an associated CEEC could introduce unilateral countermeasures itself: Article 117(2) EA offers a possibility to take 'appropriate measures' to either party that considers the other party to be in breach of an obligation under the Europe Agreement.[52] However, this kind of unilateralism,

---

[49] C. Lycourgos, *L'association avec union douanière: un mode de relations entre la CEE et des Etats tiers*, Presses Universitaires de France, Paris, 1994, 101.

[50] Regulation 3285/94, Art. 16, para. 8 (this is variant (b) of the procedure provided for in Art. 3 of Decision 87/373 on 'Comitology', *OJ* 1987, L 197/33).

[51] Regulation 3491/93, Art. 5, paras 6 and 8 (variant (b) of the procedure provided for in Art. 3 of the Comitology Decision).

[52] See above, note 7.

resembling a 'trade war', does not improve market access and is certainly not a good solution.

C. Proposed solutions

One way which a legal duty could be constructed for the EC to conduct a thorough public investigation based on clear rules before introducing a unilateral safeguard measure, might be by means of Article 190 EC. This Article requires Community decisions to state the reasons on which they are based. The reasoning of the type of trade policy measures we are dealing with here is usually extensive, and contains the results of the public investigation. Measures introduced without an investigation are less well reasoned.[53] One could argue that a safeguard measure only fulfils the reasoning requirement of Article 190 EC when there has been a real investigation.

The legal route most likely to lead to an obligation for the EC to introduce safeguard measures[54] only after a public investigation has established clearly worded conditions to be fulfilled, seems to be along the lines of GATT/ WTO rules. First of all, for market access rights that are granted by GATT, Hungary could invoke the non-discrimination principle of GATT Articles I and XIII. It would be contrary to this principle to apply to Hungarian products a safeguard procedure that offers less guarantees than the procedure applied to products originating in other GATT contracting parties. Of course Hungary and the EC have concluded an *inter se* agreement (the EA), through which they could be understood to have set aside certain GATT rights and obligations.[55] However, nothing in the Europe Agreement suggests that this might have been the case.[56]

Secondly, resort could be made to the WTO Safeguards Code, which entered into force on 1 January 1995. The general safeguards procedure of Regulation 3285/94 constitutes the implementation of the Safeguards Code into EC law, so both texts provide more or less the same guarantees. Since the EC does not seem inclined to apply its implementing legislation to the associated CEECs, Hungary – for example – could try to invoke the Safeguards Code directly.

Then, however, the question arises whether the Uruguay Round Agreement on Safeguards can have a legal influence on EC–Hungary relations, even though their mutual relations are governed by the Europe Agreement.

---

[53] Compare e.g. Commission Regulation No. 2227/93, introducing safeguard measures on imports of aluminium from the former Soviet Union (*OJ* 1993, L 198/21), and the measures against steel imports from the Czech and Slovak Federal Republic (see above, note 46).

[54] Or ask the Association Council for any other 'solution'.

[55] On this issue see J.H. Jackson, above, note 22, at p. 492; P. Eeckhout, above, note 21, 212–3; N. Blokker, 'GATT en vrijwillige exportbeperkingen; het panelrapport over Japanse halfgeleiders', *SEW* (1989), 90–104.

[56] See also below, text at note 61.

There are two ways to answer that question affirmatively.[57] The first 'route' concerns the whole of the WTO Agreements, and, as a consequence, the entire Safeguards Code. Since the WTO Agreements have been signed later than the Europe Agreements, one could invoke the rule of international law which states that where all parties to an earlier treaty are parties also to a later treaty having the same subject matter, without the earlier treaty being terminated or its operation suspended, the earlier treaty applies only to the extent that its provisions are compatible with those of the later treaty.[58] Accordingly, the legal reasoning would be that for issues dealt with by both the Europe Agreement and the Uruguay Round Agreements, the latter govern the relationship between the EC and Hungary directly, thus 'replacing' the Europe Agreement, for those market access rights that are granted both by the Europe Agreement and the WTO Agreements. A counterargument could be that another rule of general international law, the *lex specialis* rule, provides that a specific (in this case regional) treaty prevails over a general (in this case global) treaty that deals with the same subject matter, even when the specific treaty predates the general treaty.[59] This could be a legal obstacle to applying the Uruguay Round Agreements to the EC–Hungary relationship. The counter-counterargument is provided by the rule of international law stating that when a treaty specifies that it is subject to, or that it is not to be considered as incompatible with, an earlier or a later treaty, the provisions of that other treaty prevail.[60] Combining this latter rule with Article 7(1) EA seems to push the scale towards application of the Uruguay Round Agreements. Article 7(1) EA provides for a free trade area 'in accordance

---

[57] The position of the EC on this issue is not clear, but its attitude seems to suggest a negative answer: see GATT, *Trade Policy Review – EEC*, 1993, Vol. I, 70–1; see also the GATT Working Parties on the trade agreements between the EC and Egypt, Syria, Jordan and Lebanon. Asked by a member of the Working Parties why the parties to the trade agreements concerned had not referred to Art. XIX GATT when dealing with the issue of safeguard measures, the Community spokesman answered that the particular provisions of the bilateral agreement 'referred to safeguard measures that the parties might take with respect to their reciprocal trade. Any measures taken with respect to third countries would be in accordance with the relevant provisions of the General Agreement' (GATT, BISD, 25th Supp., 122, 131, 141 and 150).

[58] Art. 30(3) of the Vienna Convention on the Law of Treaties, 23 May 1969, 8 *ILM* (1969), 679, and Art. 30(3) of the Vienna Convention on the Law of Treaties Between States and International Organisations or Between International Organisations, 21 March 1986, 25 *ILM* (1986), 543. The latter has not yet entered into force, and not all EC member states are contracting parties to the 1969 Convention. In spite thereof, these rules can be considered as applying to the EC because they are part of general international customary law. This view seems to be shared by the Court of Justice, *see* ECJ, Case C-432/92, *Anastasiou*, [1994] ECR I-3087, para. 43, on the interpretation of the Association Agreement between Cyprus and the EC; see also Case C-327/91, *France v Commission*, [1994] ECR I-3641, para. 25; see also I. Macleod, I.D. Hendry and S. Hyett, *The External Relations of the European Communities*, Clarendon Press, Oxford, 1996, 77.

[59] I. Sinclair, *The Vienna Convention on the Law of Treaties*, Manchester University Press, Manchester, 1984, pp. 96 and 98; P. Reuter, *Introduction to the Law of Treaties*, Pinter Publ., London, 1989, 102.

[60] Art. 30(2) of both Vienna Conventions.

with the provisions of this Agreement and in conformity with those of the General Agreement on Tariffs and Trade (GATT).'[61] [62]

The second 'legal route' to invocability of the Safeguards Code is interpretation of the terms of the Europe Agreement in conformity with GATT/WTO. In this way, the Safeguards Code could be seen to cover all safeguard measures against Hungary, including those restricting preferential market access, going beyond WTO requirements. The starting point of the legal argumentation is that the broad wording of Article 30 EA offers opportunity for interpretation. Article 7(1) EA provides for conformity of the Europe Agreement with GATT and it is a rule of international law that treaties should be interpreted, taking into account, among other things, any relevant rules of international law applicable in the relations between parties.[63] It follows that Article 30 EA should be interpreted in conformity with the Safeguards Code to which both Hungary and the EC are contracting parties. As a consequence, the criteria and procedures of the Safeguards Code should be used to assess, for example, the serious injury condition of Article 30 EA. Contrary to the first 'route', this 'interpretation route' can of course only be used as far as the Europe Agreement contains a provision capable of being interpreted in conformity with the Safeguards Code. This will certainly not be possible in case of a clear conflict between provisions.

III. DISPUTE SETTLEMENT

The best way of closing legal loopholes created by unclear provisions and possibilities for unilateral action is an effective dispute settlement procedure.

---

[61] The corresponding articles in the other EAs are: Art. 7 EA Poland; Art. 8 EA Romania; Art. 8 EA Bulgaria; Art. 8 EA Czech Republic; Art. 8 EA Slovak Republic. See also the Preambles of all EAs (except EA Hungary) which read 'CONSIDERING the commitment of the Community and [Poland, Romania, . . .] to free trade, and in particular to compliance with the rights and obligations arising out of the General Agreement on Tariffs and Trade (GATT)' (the reason why the EA Hungary does not contain such a consideration is not clear). A counterargument could be that Art. 7(1) only refers to Art. XXIV GATT, stating the rules to which regional free trade areas have to conform in order to be compatible with GATT rules. The latter relates to rights of third countries.

[62] It should be mentioned that the Agreement on Partnership and Cooperation between the EC and Russia signed in Corfu in June 1994 (COM(94) 257) contains the opposite rule in a 'Joint declaration': 'The Community and Russia declare that the text of the safeguard clause (Art. 17) does not grant GATT safeguard treatment'.

[63] Art. 31, para. 3(c) of both Vienna Conventions. See also ECJ, Case C-163/90, *Legros*, [1992] ECR I-4625, paras 24–26 (interpretation of the EC–Sweden Free Trade Agreement in the light of GATT). An argument against interpretation of Art. 30 EA in conformity with the Safeguards Code could be that Art. 29 EA on anti-dumping and Art. 62(6), para. 3 EA on anti-subsidy explicitly refer to GATT and the GATT Codes, while Art. 30 EA makes no such reference. This can be explained, however, by the fact that there was no Safeguards Code at the moment the EAs were negotiated and signed, while an Anti-Dumping and an Anti-Subsidy Code already existed.

Suppose the EC invokes Article 30 EA, but Hungary disagrees in the Association Council because it sees no link between its exports to the EC and the problems of EC producers. Then the EC can act unilaterally, and the only way for Hungary to remedy this unfavourable situation is to seek for impartial dispute settlement.

A. The provisions of the Europe Agreements and their shortcomings

Article 107 EA provides for a two-level dispute settlement procedure.[64] The first level of the procedure is political, as the dispute is referred to the Association Council, which 'may settle the dispute by means of a decision'.[65] In the case of a dispute concerning safeguard measures, this does not seem very useful, since the Association Council already dealt with the issue before the unilateral measure was introduced. When the problem is not solved within the Association Council, it is possible to move on to the second level of the dispute settlement procedure, namely arbitration. Either party can appoint an arbitrator and notify this to the other party. Then the other party has to appoint an arbitrator within two months and the Association Council appoints a third arbitrator. The arbitrators' decisions are taken by majority vote and are binding. This procedure can provide a solution and is potentially very valuable. However, two remarks have to be made. First, since the Association Council acts by unanimity, there is a possibility for one contracting party to block the appointment of the third arbitrator by the Association Council. There is no provision stating what should happen in that situation, and a contracting party might exploit this to block the establishment of an arbitration committee indefinitely.[66] Secondly, a three-man committee, with neither fixed composition nor an institutional framework to provide backup and support, might not inspire much confidence in policymakers. In addition, it should be mentioned that under the many preferential agreements concluded by the EC the actual use of this kind of arbitration procedures seems to be (almost)[67] nil. This seems to suggest that the EC's partners, especially associated countries, are reluctant to use the unfriendly means of arbitration, because they do not want to disturb their preferential

[64] The corresponding articles in the other EAs are: Art. 105 EA Poland; Art. 109 EA Romania; Art. 108 EA Bulgaria; Art. 107 EA Czech Republic and Art. 107 EA Slovak Republic.

[65] The only practical application of this procedure so far can be found in Decision 3/96 of the EC–Poland Association Council settling the dispute concerning the resctriction of exports of skins and hides from Poland to the EC, *OJ*, 1996, L 208/31.

[66] Compare to the Association Agreement with Greece (*OJ* 1963, L 26) which did provide a remedy for such a situation in Art. 67(4): the President of the International Court of Justice could appoint the third arbitrator.

[67] P. Gilsdorf mentions a case in the framework of Yaoundé I, but without reference (P. Gilsdorf, 'Assoziierungsabkommen – Artikel 238 EWG' in Von Der Groeben, Thiesling and Ehlermann (eds), *Kommentar zum EWG-Vertrag*, Nomos, Baden-Baden, 1991, 5927).

relationship with the EC, from which they receive aid and which they would like to join.[68]

B. Proposed solutions

A first step towards any solution in this context should be that both the EC and the associated CEECs adopt the correct attitude towards dispute settlement. Seeking an impartial judgment in order to solve a dispute on interpretation should not be seen as a hostile act against which retaliation should be taken by a retreat in future relations. It is quite natural for two parties to an agreement to have a difference of opinion on the interpretation of a clause. But in a good relationship the correct interpretation should eventually prevail, not the interpretation of the strongest party. In its bare essence this comes down to respect for the rule of law by the stronger partner, as opposed to what has been called 'power-based resolution of trade disputes'.[69] It would be unacceptable that an associated country, standing up for the rights it has been granted under the Europe Agreements, should be punished for that by not being granted new or other rights. Such action by the EC would disregard the rule of law it urges the CEECs to respect.[70] It would also deny the association framework an element that has proved to be a fundamental building-block of the Community's success.

A first possibility for obtaining an impartial ruling on a dispute is to activate the arbitration procedure of the Europe Agreement. But, as has been said, that procedure has some severe deficiencies. A second one is to bring the case before the European Court of Justice. It is, however, not possible to refer the dispute as such to the European Court. The Association Agreements with Turkey and Greece provide the Association Council with the opportunity to refer a dispute directly to the Court of Justice, in addition to a possibility of referring it to an arbitration panel.[71] In the past, however, the EC's partner countries did not appear to be very keen on such a procedure. From a point of view of sovereignty it is indeed certainly not common for a country to subject its rights emerging from an international agreement to the

---

[68] The procedure concerning the Polish export restrictions mentioned in note 64 was started by the Community (see COM(95) 75). For this and other criticism concerning such arbitration procedures see C. Lycourgos, above, note 49, 105–9 and M. Hilf, 'Europäische Gemeinschaften und internationale Streitbeilegung', in *Festschrift für H. Mosler – Völkerrecht als Rechtsordnung*, Springer, Berlin, 1983, 419; see also M. Maresceau and E. Montaguti, above, note 3, 1358. For similar criticism concerning the arbitration procedure of the EEA Agreement see C. Reymond, *Institutions, Decision-Making Procedure and Settlement of Disputes in the European Economic Area*, CMLRev. (1993), 476–8; J. Steenbergen, *Het EER-Verdrag, een beknopte samenvatting*, SEW (1993), 140–58, at p. 150.

[69] D. Robertson, above, note 2, p. 22; see also J.H. Jackson, *Restructuring the GATT System*, The Royal Institute of International Affairs, Pinter Publishers, London, 1990, 49–54.

[70] EA Hungary and EA Poland, Preamble, para. 4.

[71] Art. 67, para. 2 of the Association Agreement with Greece (*OJ* 1963, L 26); Art. 25, para. 2 of the Association Agreement with Turkey (*OJ* 1964, L 217). This possibility also exists in the EEA Agreement, but only as far as concerns the interpretation of the *acquis communautaire*, not for safeguard issues.

jurisdiction of a court of the other party to the agreement.[72] But in the case of the kind of agreements under examination here, it might make sense to do just that. The European Court of Justice has widely proven its impartiality and has built up considerable experience in dealing with problems of 'integration law'.[73]

Under the current regime there do exist possibilities to refer a dispute to the Court of Justice (or the Court of First Instance) indirectly, for it is possible to challenge the legality of unilateral EC measures.[74] If the Courts find that such a measure infringes an Association Agreement or any other rule of Community law having a higher 'legal ranking', it will be annulled or declared invalid. Such actions are also available for private parties. Anti-dumping measures can without any doubt be challenged by the exporting firms. For safeguard measures there might be some problems of standing,[75] though in many cases some access to the Court of Justice or the Court of First Instance will be available, for private parties, and, under certain conditions, also for governments of the associated countries.[76] However, it should be mentioned that it might be difficult, if not impossible, to invoke GATT/WTO rules directly as a part of the legal basis for the Court's review of legality.[77] Invoking the GATT/WTO indirectly, through interpretation of a

---

[72] During the negotiations of the first Association Agreement (with Greece) the EC proposed to make the Court of Justice competent for all disputes in the framework of the Association Agreement. The EC even proposed adding a special chamber to the Court, including a Greek judge. Greece refused because it did not want to subject itself to the judgment of an institution with a majority of EC judges. (C. Lycourgos, above, note 49, p. 103; D. Vignes, 'Chronique sur le droit européen', *Revue de droit international et de droit comparé* (1964, Nos 1–2) 121–2). During the negotiations of the EEA Agreement it was also proposed to introduce the Court of Justice of the EC as judiciary for the whole EEA. This was reported as unacceptable to Finland and Switzerland, but not to Sweden and Austria (A. Evans, 'Judicial Bodies' in Evans and Falk (eds), *Transformation and Integration – The New Association Agreements*, Centre for European Community Law & International Trade Law, Umeå, 1992, 408, note 41).

[73] During the negotiations for the EC–Sweden Free Trade Agreement in 1971 Sweden pushed for an arbitration body, and showed itself willing to accept that such a body should take into account the case law of the Court of Justice. Evans comments that: 'Apparently, the prospect of judicial pressure from a court in which there was no Swedish judge was preferable to the prospect of the economic pressure which could otherwise be exercised by the Community, particularly pursuant to safeguard clauses.' (A. Evans, above, note 72, p. 405).

[74] An interesting point of reference is Case T-115/94, pending before the Court of First Instance (*OJ* 1994, C 132/17). It concerns an action for annulment introduced by General Motors Austria against a Community anti-subsidy measure (Council Regulation No. 3697/93, *OJ* 1993, L 343/1) issued under the Free Trade Agreement with Austria.

[75] See e.g. ECJ, Joined Cases C-15 and C-108/91, *Buckl* [1992] ECR I-6061.

[76] If a direct Art. 173 action is not available, an Art. 177 reference from a national court of a member state will be possible in most cases. On the issue of *locus standi* before the Court of Justice in trade policy matters, see E. Creally, *Judicial Review of Anti-Dumping and Other Safeguard Measures in the European Community*, Butterworths, London, 1992, 170–210.

[77] According to the current position of the Court of Justice towards GATT this is only possible 'if the Community intended to implement a particular obligation entered into within the framework of GATT, or if the Community act expressly refers to specific provisions of GATT' (ECJ, Case C-280/93, *Germany/Council* [1994] ECR I-4973, para. 111; see also Joined Cases 21 to 24/72, *International Fruit Company* [1972] ECR 1219 and Case C-69/89, *Nakajima* [1991] ECR I-2069). However, the Court might be forced into an even less liberal attitude towards the Uruguay Round Agreements for the Preamble to the Council Decision concerning the conclusion of the Uruguay Round Agreements provides: 'Whereas, by its nature, the

Europe Agreement in conformity with GATT/WTO should not raise such 'invocability problems'.[78]

Nevertheless, the Court of Justice will not be able fully to provide the necessary dispute settlement through actions contesting the legality of EC acts. The reason for that is that in such cases it is not the Court's task to deliver a final ruling on a dispute concerning e.g. the existence of (serious) injury in a particular situation. Its task is to rule on the legality of a EC act and thereby it must respect the discretionary powers enjoyed by the Commission and the Council in trade policy matters. It cannot verify if there really was injury but only if, under the given circumstances, injury could reasonably be supposed to exist.[79] As a consequence it is hard to attack a trade policy measure before the Court of Justice on the merits of the dispute.

A third possibility to obtain efficient dispute settlement could be to invoke the WTO Dispute Settlement Procedure.[80] While under GATT 1947 the dispute settlement procedure originally mainly functioned as a forum to negotiate conciliation (through a working party including the parties to the conflict), it has developed into a real dispute settlement procedure of a legalistic nature (through a panel composed of independent individuals).[81] The Uruguay Round Agreements set the seal to this evolution by abolishing the possibility for the 'losing' party to block the formation of a Panel and the acceptance of a Panel report, and by introducing an Appellate Body. The latter should make it possible to remedy occasional mishandling of a difficult case by a Panel.[82]

Hungary cannot bring a claim before the GATT/WTO forum on grounds only available under the Europe Agreement.[83] It can, however, bring a GATT/WTO claim against the EC to secure its GATT/WTO rights. Although there

---

Agreement establishing the World Trade Organization, including the Annexes thereto, is not susceptible to being directly invoked in Community or member state courts.' (Council Decision No. 94/800, *OJ* 1994, L 336/1).

[78] Cf. ECJ, Case C-216/91, *Rima*, [1993] ECR I-6303, para. 14–15.

[79] ECJ, Case 112/80, *Dürbeck*, [1981] ECR 1095, para. 24; Case 126/81, *Wünsche*, [1982], ECR 1479, para. 17; see also E. Creally, above, note 76, pp. 280–304.

[80] In fact, the GATT dispute settlement procedure seems to be the only procedure for settlement of international economic disputes that has actually been used by Western Europe (see J.H.J. Bourgeois, 'Les relations extérieures de la Communauté européenne et la règle de droit: quelques réflexions', in Capotorti et al. (eds), *Du droit international au droit de l'intégration – Liber Amicorum Pierre Pescatore*, Nomos, Baden-Baden, 1987, 74).

[81] W.J. Davey, above, note 22, 69–73; P. Pescatore, 'Drafting and Analyzing Decisions of Dispute Settlement', in *Handbook of GATT Dispute Settlement*, above, note 22, 7–8; see also E. Canal-Forgues, *L'institution de la conciliation dans le cadre du GATT*, Bruylant, Brussels, 1993.

[82] See P.T.B. Kohona, 'Dispute Resolution under the World Trade Organization – An Overview', *JWT* (1994/2), 23–47.

[83] A 1990 ruling of a GATT arbitrator on a dispute between Canada and the EC concerning a bilateral agreement on wheat, which was negotiated in the context of Art. XXIV: 6 GATT states that: 'In principle a claim based on a bilateral agreement cannot be brought under the multilateral dispute settlement procedures of the GATT. An exception is warranted in this case given the close connection of this particular bilateral agreement with the GATT, the fact that the Agreement is consistent with the objectives of the GATT, and that both parties joined in requesting recourse to the GATT Arbitration procedures.' (GATT, BISD, 37th Supp., 80). Within GATT/WTO 'fast track' arbitration can be an alternative to the general dispute settlement procedure, if both parties to the conflict agree.

has been some legal doubt on this,[84] the associated countries do retain this possibility.[85] As a matter of fact this has been acknowledged by the EC itself.[86] Such a dispute might concern market access rights granted by GATT/WTO, but it might also concern interpretation of the 'side agreements' fixing more stringent rules for the use of trade policy instruments: for instance, the Anti-Dumping Code, the Safeguards Code, the Subsidies Code. As has been explained with regard to the Safeguards Code these 'codes' can be said to apply to the Europe Agreements through interpretation of the latter. The conclusion might be that, as far as concerns disputes on the unilateral use of trade policy instruments, the WTO seems to provide dispute settlement that might be hard to improve by any arbitration procedure proper to the Europe Agreements.

IV. CONCLUSION

The EC has so far made little open use of safeguard measures (including anti-dumping) under the Europe Agreements and recently its attitude seems to evolve towards self-restraint. This, however, does not make redundant a good legal framework for trade. In a report issued in October 1994, the EBRD mentions a substantial negative effect resulting from the mere existence of this kind of legal loophole: they generate uncertainty about market access. Foreign investors that might be attracted by the CEECs' preferential access to EC markets, could be deterred by this uncertainty.[87] For that reason, and simply because it should always be possible to take action against abuse of these kinds of clauses, self-restraint is no alternative to a solid legal framework. One could of course argue that the CEECs will soon all be EC members, which would solve the problem. This might be true for some CEECs, but for others, the EAs will probably remain in force for several years to come. In addition, it is far from unlikely that the same type of legal problem will appear with regard to other agreements, in particular the Partnership and

---

[84] EBRD, *Export Access to Western markets: Recent Issues and Developments*, in *Current Economic Issues – EBRD Economic Review*, July 1993, 18.

[85] The Europe Agreements contain no provision equivalent to Art. 219 EC Treaty which states that member states undertake not to submit a dispute concerning the interpretation or application of the EC Treaty to any method of settlement other than those provided therein. There might, however, be a problem relating to classical international law rule of exhaustion of local remedies (see P.J. Kuyper, 'The New WTO Dispute Settlement System: the Impact on the Community' in Bourgeois, Berrod and Gippini Fournier (eds), *The Uruguay Round Results – A European Lawyers' Perspective*, European Interuniversity Press, Brussels, 1995, 87–114, esp. 106–9; and P. Mengozzi, 'The Marrakesh DSU and its Implications on the International and European Level', ibid., 115–33, esp. 121–4).

[86] GATT, *Trade Policy Review – EEC*, 1993, Vol. II, pp. 5 and 144. An interesting point of reference is NAFTA, which explicitly stipulates that for disputes that can be brought both before NAFTA and GATT, the complaining party can choose either forum (see J.F. Bialos and D.E. Siegel, 'Dispute Resolution Under the NAFTA: The Newer and Improved Model', 27 *The International Lawyer* (1993), 618).

[87] EBRD, *Economic Transition in Eastern Europe and the Former Soviet Union*, Transition Report, Oct. 1994, 119.

Cooperation Agreements with the CIS countries and the Euro-Mediterranean Agreements.

Several suggestions could be made to strengthen the rule of law in the application of agreements of this type. When negotiating such agreements, parties should see to a strict formulation of safeguard clauses and the introduction of a good dispute settlement procedure. It has also been suggested that association agreements be 'multilateralized', which might introduce a better balance between negotiating partners,[88] and a new (permanent) institution competent for dispute settlement be created.[89] However, as far as trade law is concerned, the better solution seems to be to exploit fully the possibilities of the WTO which are already available, rather than to keep on adding new layers of integration, each with their own institutions and rules. In addition, the WTO can provide the legal framework for trade between the different countries that have traditional and preferential trade relations with the EC (the CEECs, the CIS countries and the Mediterranean countries). Of course this is a lawyer's conclusion, and for political reasons these countries probably prefer their relations with the EC to be governed through a specific platform that symbolizes their preferential relationship with the EC. It is also true that even after the Uruguay Round tariff negotiations, they still enjoy preferential access to the EC market (although that is being eroded). If, however, a solid legal framework is the point of reference, the WTO seems to offer, at least, a good starting point for further economic integration within Europe.

---

[88] This would not result in a real multilateralization, but in a bipolar multilateral framework, comparable, from a structural point of view, to the Lomé Conventions.

[89] C. Lycourgos, above, note 49, 70–6. The Yaoundé II Agreement (the predecessor of the Lomé I Convention) provided for a real Arbitration Court for the multilateral association (Art. 53) and contained a 24-article Statute for this Court (see Protocol No. 8, *OJ* 1970, L 282). This construction was considered to be in excess of what was necessary and was abandoned in the Lomé Conventions (M. Hilf, above, note 68, 406).

9

THE EUROPE AGREEMENTS' ANTI-DUMPING PROVISIONS IN EC–CEECS RELATIONS

Elisabetta Montaguti[1]

I. INTRODUCTION

It is clear that the EEA[2] experience, illustrated by Dr Norberg elsewhere in this book (above, . . .), has not been repeated with the countries with which the European Communities[3] have concluded the so-called 'Europe Agreements' (EAs),[4] and that the legal and institutional structure designed for the

[1] European Commission, DGI. Views expressed are strictly personal. This contribution draws extensively on E. Montaguti, *Az EK doempingellenes gyakorlata Kelet-Európával szemben és az Európai Megàllapodàsok*, in *Az Európai Megàllapodàs Végrehajtàsànak Jogi és Elméleti Kérdései*, OMIKK, Budapest, 1995, and on M. Maresceau and E. Montaguti, 'The Relations Between the European Union and Central and Eastern Europe: A Legal Appraisal', *CMLRev.* (1995), 1327–67, of which it constitutes an update. The original texts were drafted within the framework of a project financed by the Ministry of the Flemish Community ('Administratie Economie').

[2] *Agreement establishing the European Economic Area, OJ* 1994, L 1/3.

[3] When discussing relations with Europe Agreement (EA) countries it is difficult to keep to a uniform terminology. The EAs were all signed by the European Communities, along with their member states. Trade policy measures are taken by the *European Community* (EC, formerly European Economic Community, EEC) or the European Coal and Steel Community (ECSC). The Conclusions of the Presidencies of the European Councils refer to relations between the Central and Eastern European Countries and the *European Union* (EU). Of course accession, too, will be to the EU, as provided for by Art. O of the Treaty on European Union.

[4] See *OJ* 1993, L 347/1 (Hungary) and L 348/1 (Poland); *OJ* 1994, L 357/2 (Romania), L 358/3 (Bulgaria), L 359/2 (Slovakia) and L 360/2 (Czech Republic). All these agreements are currently in force. For a clearer understanding of the problems outlined in the text it is, however, appropriate to recall that the entry into force of the Europe Agreements' trade defence provisions was accelerated through the adoption of Interim Agreements (IAs). The Europe Agreements with the Baltic states (Estonia, Latvia and Lithuania) were signed on 12 June 1995 (COM(95) 207 final) but, as far as dumping is concerned, identical provisions are already found in the respective Free Trade Agreements, which entered into force on 1 January 1995 (see *OJ* 1994, L 373/1 (Estonia), L 374/1 (Latvia) and L 375/1 (Lithuania)). Precisely because the typical EA trade provisions are already in force through those agreements, no Interim Agreement is envisaged. The EA with Slovenia (COM(95) 341 final) was signed on 10 June 1996 and is not yet in force. An IA was signed on 11 November 1996 and entered into force 1 January 1997.

latter countries presents significant differences from that currently applying in the EU's relations with most EFTA countries. Whether renouncing a stronger institutional framework to avoid the risk of being caught in a long-lasting 'antechamber' was completely justified[5] is now a rather speculative issue. This paper will therefore try to examine what the EAs' 'system' does include, as far as dumping is concerned. In fact it must be pointed out that, while the EAs have opened the way for a very significant degree of liberalization for trade in goods, particularly industrial goods, trade defence instruments still apply to bilateral trade and this situation has to be accepted for the time being. Because of greater data availability, the analysis will concentrate on the first six EA countries (Hungary, Poland, the Czech Republic, the Slovak Republic, Romania, Bulgaria).

Before reviewing the EAs' anti-dumping regime it is appropriate to recall that any evaluation of the relations between the EU and the Countries of Central and Eastern Europe (CEECs) needs to take into account not only the strictly legal framework, but also the related political developments. Indeed, political initiatives have repeatedly provided the necessary impetus to strengthen those relations beyond what legal rules seemed to allow. While interaction between legal and political factors is a rather general feature of EC external relations, it has particular importance in its relationship with the CEECs in view of the special geopolitical links between those two parties of the European continent. Hence it appears more appropriate to evaluate the EAs not in isolation, rather, as part of a system: not a purely legal system, but one resulting from a combination of different factors. Politics, particularly the post-IGC political climate in the European Union, will also have a primary role in the next step foreseen in EC–CEECs relations, i.e. their accession to the Union.[6]

After illustrating the content and meaning of the Europe Agreements' provisions relating to dumping (paras. 2–3), this paper will review the main changes occurred in EC anti-dumping law and practice *vis-à-vis* EA countries (para. 4). It will then try to give some indication on the prospects in this area of EC-CEECs trade relations (para. 5).

II. THE LEGAL FRAMEWORK LAID DOWN IN THE EAS

Anti-dumping provisions represent a particularly significant feature of the Europe Agreements.[7] Although the inclusion of similar provisions is no

---

[5] For a defence of an EEA-type solution see S. Peers, 'An Ever Closer Waiting Room? The Case for Eastern European Accession to the European Economic Area', *CMLRev.* (1995), 187–213.

[6] All ten of the EA countries have applied for EU membership. The European Commission is preparing its opinions on these applications pursuant to Art O TEU.

[7] For simplicity's sake reference will be made in this paper to the relevant provisions (Arts 29 and 33) of the Europe Agreement with Hungary, bearing in mind that the same dumping provisions can be found in all the ten EAs negotiated so far. Apart from a different numbering in some of the agreements (Arts 30 and 34 in the EAs with the Czech Republic, Slovakia, Bulgaria, Romania and Slovenia; Arts 22 and 26 in the Free Trade Agreement and Arts 28

novelty in European Communities' treaty practice,[8] it will be shown that they have special implications in the context of the post-1989 relations between the European Community and Central and Eastern European Countries. On the other hand, their very existence means that EAs' contracting parties have not immediately renounced the possibility to apply their trade defence rules to each other, unlike what was agreed in the EEA Agreement.[9] In this respect it could be said that to some extent such continuing application represents a counterweight to the Europe Agreements' ultimate objectives, especially as developed in subsequent policy documents: in fact the strengthening of economic links is clearly not only achieved through legal harmonization, but also through abolition of regulatory restrictions.[10] On the other hand, recent policy documents concerning EA countries issued by the European Communities or the European Union envisage the complete elimination of all trade defence measures once the said countries are fully integrated into the Internal Market, including the effective application of competition and state aid rules.[11] As a result, EA anti-dumping rules and related developments may, along with those concerning safeguards, also be revealing of the state and evolution of Central and Eastern Europe's participation in the European integration

---

and 32 in the EA with Estonia; Arts 23 and 27 in the Free Trade Agreements and Arts 29 and 33 in the EAs with Latvia and Lithuania), the only substantive difference concerns the reference either to GATT or to WTO anti-dumping rules made in such provisions, which is discussed below, 3.2.

[8] This is the case not only of agreements based on Art. 238 EC Treaty (i.e. association agreements, like the EAs), but also for those based on Arts 113 and 235, ranging from trade agreements to cooperation agreements and free trade areas (among the latter agreements see e.g. *Agreement establishing a free trade area between the European Economic Community and Switzerland, OJ* 1972, L 300/189; among trade and economic cooperation agreements see e.g. *Trade and economic co-operation Agreement between the European Economic Community and the Republic of Slovenia, OJ* 1993, L 189/1). The *Agreement on Partnership and Cooperation between the European Communities and their Member States, of the one part, and Russia, of the other part*, signed in Corfu on 24–25 June 1994, (COM(94) 257 final) also subjects anti-dumping practices in bilateral trade relations to the GATT system and to domestic legislation, but its provisions (Art. 18) provide fewer guarantees than the EA ones (relevant provisions are in force since 1 February 1996 through the Interim Agreement on trade and trade-related measures between the European Communities, of the one part, and the Russian Federation, of the other part, *OJ* 1995, L 247/2).

[9] See Art. 26 EEA. Accordingly, by Regulation No. 5/94 (EEC) of 22 December 1993 (*OJ* 1994, L 3/1) the EC Council decided the suspension of all anti-dumping measures affecting EFTA countries which are also EEA parties.

[10] For the implications in the area of intellectual property see I. Govaere, below, p. 179.

[11] This position was first expressed in Commission of the European Communities, *Communication from the Commission to the Council, The Europe Agreements and Beyond: A Strategy to Prepare the Countries of Central and Eastern Europe for Accession*, COM(94) 320 final; Id., *Follow up to Commission Communication on 'The Europe Agreements and Beyond: A Strategy to Prepare the Countries of Central and Eastern Europe for Accession'*, COM(94) 361 final, at 7, in which the Commission notes: 'The strengthening of competition, state aids control and other relevant parts of the *acquis communautaire* which are related to the internal market will help to eliminate the need for anti-dumping and safeguard action. Antidumping and antisubsidy duties do not apply either in the Union or the EEA where this situation prevails.' On EA competition rules see A.-M. Van den Bossche, below, p. 84.

process.[12] They may also provide further matter for reflection on the interplay between competition and trade policy, which is increasingly being debated in international fora.[13]

The basic provision concerned with anti-dumping in the Europe Agreements is Article 29 of the EA with Hungary. Pursuant to this Article

> If one of the Parties finds that dumping is taking place in trade with the other Party within the meaning of Article VI of the General Agreement on Tariffs and Trade,[14] it may take appropriate measures against this practice in accordance with the Agreement relating to the application of Article VI of the General Agreement on Tariffs and Trade, with related internal legislation and with the conditions and procedures laid down in Article 33.[15]

[12] On EA safeguards rules see L. Van Den Hende, above, p. 140. Safeguard clauses as such, however, are not likely to disappear completely, due to their safety valve function which is essential to the functioning of any international agreement (see, e.g. Art. 226 EC Treaty, applicable during the transitional period, and Arts 112–13 of the EEA).

[13] This issue, along with the adoption of international competition rules, has been the subject of the work of the OECD and UNCTAD, besides being addressed by a GATT Contracting Parties Decision in 1960, and has regularly been placed on the agenda of the WTO since the end of the Uruguay Round. See OECD, *Trade and Competition Policies, Joint Report by the Committee on Competition Law and Policy and the Trade Committee*, OECD/GD (94)63, Paris, 1994, repr. in 18(1) *World Competition* (1994), 185–91; UNCTAD, *The Set of Multilaterally Agreed Equitable Principles and Rules for the Control of Restrictive Business Practices*, 2 May 1980, TD/RBP/CONF/10; Id., *Competition and Trade*, 16 September 1994, UNCTAD/ITD/9; Commission of the European Communities, *Communication to the Council. Towards an International Framework of Competition rules*, 17 June 1996. There is already extensive literature on these issues. On the European Community side see L. Brittan, *A Framework for International Competition*, World Economic Forum, Davos, 3 February 1992; Ibid., *Competition Policy and International Relations*, CEPS Paper No. 76, Brussels, 17 March 1992; J.H.J. Bourgeois, 'Competition Policy and Commercial Policy', in M. Maresceau (ed.), *The European Community's Commercial Policy After 1992: The Legal Dimension*, Dordrecht, Boston, Lancaster, M. Nijhoff, 1993; Id., *The Antitrust/Trade Policy Interface in the EC: Old Wine in New Bottles?* presented at *Competition Law and Trade Policy: An International Symposium*, Brussels, 1994; P. Vandoren, 'Recent Developments in the Area of the Interface Between Anti-Dumping and Competition in the EC', *LIEI* (1993) 21; G. Marceau, *Anti-Dumping and Anti-Trust Issues in Free Trade Areas*, Oxford, Clarendon Press, 1994; N. Yacheistova, 'The International Competition Regulation. A Short Review of a Long Evolution', 18(1) *World Competition* (1994), 99; P. Messerlin, 'Should Antidumping Rules be Replaced by National or International Competition Rules?', 18(3) *World Competition* (1995), 37; E.-U. Petersmann, 'International Competition Rules for Government and for Private Business', 30(3) *JWT* (1996), 5.

[14] See Contracting Parties to the GATT, *The General Agreement on Tariffs and Trade*, GATT, BISD, Vol. IV, GATT, Geneva, 1969, and *Agreement Relating to the Application of Article VI of the General Agreement on Tariffs and Trade*, GATT, Geneva, 1979. These agreements have now been superseded by the *Marrakesh Agreement Establishing the World Trade Organization*, to which the *General Agreement on Tariffs and Trade 1994* and the *Agreement on Implementation of Article VI of the General Agreement on Tariffs and Trade 1994* are annexed (see *The Results of the Uruguay Round of Multilateral Trade Negotiations. The Legal Texts*, GATT Secretariat, Geneva, 1994, pp. 485–558, 168–96). Art. VI of GATT 1947 (unchanged in GATT 1994) defines dumping as introducing the products of one country 'into the commerce of another country at less than its normal value', which is, as a rule, 'the comparable price, in the ordinary course of trade, for the like products when destined for consumption in the exporting country'.

[15] In the EAs negotiated after the conclusion of the Uruguay Round (Estonia, Latvia, Lithuania and Slovenia) the reference is to Art. VI of GATT 1994 and to the WTO Anti-Dumping Agreement.

Article 33 of the same agreement provides that:

> ... 2. In the cases specified in Article 29, 30 and 31, before taking the measures provided for therein or, in cases to which paragraph 3 (d) applies, as soon as possible, the Community or Hungary, as the case may be, shall supply the Association Council with all relevant information with a view to seeking a solution acceptable to the two Parties.
>
> In the selection of measures, priority must be given to those which least disturb the functioning of this Agreement.
>
> ...
>
> 3. For the implementation of paragraph 2, the following provisions shall apply:
>
> ...
>
> (b) as regards Article 29, the Association Council shall be informed of the dumping case as soon as the authorities of the importing Party have initiated an investigation. When no end has been put to the dumping or no other satisfactory solution has been reached within 30 days of the matter being referred to the Association Council, the importing party may adopt the appropriate measures;
>
> ...
>
> (d) where exceptional circumstances requiring immediate action make prior information or examination, as the case may be, impossible, the Community or Hungary whichever is concerned may, in the situations specified in Articles 29, 30 and 31, apply forthwith the precautionary measures strictly necessary to deal with the situation.

The regime established by the EA as concerns dumping is thus a composite one. Substantive requirements for the adoption of anti-dumping measures are those provided for in Article VI of GATT 1947, as reaffirmed and implemented in the Anti-Dumping Code of 1979 and in domestic legislation, while procedures for assessing the fulfilment of these conditions and calculating the appropriate measures result from the joint operation of multilateral and domestic rules *and* of Article 33 of the EA.

From an EC law perspective the wording of Article 29 calls three sets of rules into play, namely (1) the GATT/WTO system, (2) the Community legal order, and particularly the basic EC regulation and the basic ECSC decision[16] and (3) the additional procedures provided for in the Europe Agreements. Although separated, the first and the third set of rules just mentioned are, of course, closely intertwined with the second one. In fact, the agreements incorporating them 'form an integral part of the Community legal order'[17]

---

[16] See Council Regulation (EC) No. 384/96 of 22 December 1995 on protection against dumped imports from countries not members of the European Community, *OJ* 1996, L 56/1, and Commission Decision (ECSC) No. 2424/88 of 11 July 1988 on protection against dumped and subsidized imports from countries not members of the European Coal and Steel Community, *OJ* 1988, L 209/18.

[17] See Court of Justice of the European Communities (ECJ), judgment of 30 April 1974, *R. & V. Haegemann v Kingdom of Belgium*, case 181/73, (1974) ECR 449, paras 3–5. As to the GATT, the Court of Justice held that since the establishment of the common customs tariff, the Community has replaced member states in the GATT and it is bound by its obligations (judgment of 12 December 1972, *International Fruit Company v Produktschap voor Groenten en Fruit*, joined cases 21/72 and 24/72, (1972) ECR 1219, para. 18).

and take precedence over the acts of the Community institutions, whose interpretation and application must therefore conform to them.[18] As concerns the substantive provisions and requirements for the adoption of anti-dumping measures, the EAs do not add anything to the regime already applicable between the EC and most of the EA countries, since all the latter but one were already contracting parties both to the GATT and to the Anti-Dumping Code.[19] The only (general) addition concerns procedures, namely the information obligation of Article 33(2) and the obligation to refer to the Association Council laid down in Article 32(3)(b), with its exception in Article 32(3)(d). It has rather been through unilateral steps that the EC regime and its enforcement *vis-à-vis* EA countries has evolved. Such an evolution has been reinforced with the entry into force of the WTO Agreement.

Even if their content does not appear particularly innovative, EA dumping provisions raise some interpretative questions, which will be outlined hereafter. After that, the main unilateral changes to the EC domestic anti-dumping regime will briefly be recalled.

III. THE RELATIONS BETWEEN THE EAS AND MULTILATERAL (WTO) PROVISIONS

As already noted, the reference to multilateral dumping provisions is not uniform throughout the ten EAs. Depending on the time when they were negotiated, they refer either to pre-WTO rules (agreements with Hungary, Poland, Czech Republic and Slovak Republic, Romania and Bulgaria)[20] or to WTO rules (agreements with Estonia, Latvia, Lithuania and Slovenia). As a result, four situations can be distinguished for EA partners:

---

[18] In fact, since the first (then) EEC Council Regulation Decision in 1968 the European Communities' anti-dumping rules were adopted not only to implement the Common Commercial Policy envisaged in the founding Treaties, but also to execute the multilateral provisions laid down in the GATT framework (see e.g. Council Regulation No. 459/68 (EEC) of 5 April 1968, OJ 1968, L 93/1, recitals 7 and 9). The objective of implementing EC international obligations has subsequently been interpreted in ECJ case law as authorizing judicial review of EC anti-dumping rules' legality under Art. 173 of the EC Treaty in the light of GATT (*see* judgment of 7 May 1991, *Nakajima All Precision Co., Ltd. v Council*, case C-69/89, (1991) ECR I-2069, para. 31, confirmed in the Court's judgment of 5 October 1994, *Federal Republic of Germany v Council (Bananas)*, case C-280/93, (1994) ECR I-4973, para. 111, and, more recently, in Court of First Instance of the European Communities, judgment of 2 May 1995, *NTN Corporation e Koyo Seiko Co. Ltd v Council of the European Union*, joined cases T-163 and 165/94, (1995) ECR II-1381, para. 65.

[19] On the contrary, for Bulgaria and the three Baltic States the entry into force of the respective IAs and Free Trade Agreements in 1993 and 1995 anticipated the application of multilateral rules. These countries in fact have not yet acceded to the WTO, although Bulgaria's membership is presumably imminent, as the WTO General Council approved the Draft Decision and Protocol of Accession on 2 October 1996.

[20] This led to the peculiar result that the agreements with the Czech Republic, the Slovak Republic and Romania, which took effect on 1 February 1995, i.e. after the entry into force of the WTO for those countries and the EC, refer to the pre-WTO agreements, which the parties no longer applied on that date, except on a transitional basis (see below, note 25).

(1) EA countries which were already parties to the GATT (and to the 1979 Anti-Dumping Code) when the respective EAs' trade defence rules were negotiated, and whose EAs refer to pre-WTO rules (Hungary, Poland, Czech Republic, Slovak Republic and Romania);

(2) countries which were not yet GATT and Code parties at the time of negotiations, and whose EAs refer to pre-WTO rules (Bulgaria);

(3) countries which were already WTO members at the time of negotiations, and whose EAs (IAs) refer to WTO rules (Slovenia);

(4) countries which were not yet WTO members at the time of negotiations, and whose EAs (and Free Trade Agreements) refer to WTO rules (Estonia, Latvia, Lithuania).

The relations between EA and multilateral dumping provisions differ for the four country groups. Theoretically, two interpretative issues arise as to the relations between bilateral and multilateral rules. In the first place, for groups 1 and 2 countries, a question arises as to the current meaning of the reference to pre-WTO rules, notably whether it may be construed as a reference to WTO rules. Secondly, the provision for special consultation procedures in the EAs should be evaluated as to their compatibility with multilateral rules and the possibility for other WTO Members to claim the same treatment from the EC and EA partners which are also WTO Members.

A. Interpretation of Article 29's reference to pre-WTO multilateral rules: identifying the currently applicable multilateral rules

The mention of multilateral rules in the EAs constitutes a case of 'legislative reference',[21] a well-known law-making technique both in international law and in domestic law.[22] Whenever a legislative reference is made, the content of the referring provision is not established directly, but indirectly through incorporation of a rule whose content has, in turn, already been decided in a different context (and possibly by other states).

---

[21] This process is also referred to as 'incorporation par référence' (see Level, 'La clause de la nation la plus favorisée', *Encyclopédie Dalloz*, I, Paris, 1968, quoted in E. Triggiani, *Il Trattamento della nazione più favorita*, Napoli, Jovene, 1984, p. 78).

[22] The same Most favoured nation (MFN) clause represents a very common example of law-making by reference and indeed, all conflicts of laws rules regulate a given case indirectly by referring to a given country's legal order. Other examples may be found in the rules regulating the taking of effect of international rules in domestic legal systems (e.g. constitutional provisions giving automatic domestic effect to certain international rules, or certain acts by which national authorities order that a treaty be executed). For a discussion of legislative reference with respect to incorporation of international treaties and to private international law see the Opinion of Advocate-General Van Gerven in case 70/87, *Fediol v Commission of the European Communities*, (1989) ECR 1781. With respect to MFN see G. Schiavone, *Il principio di non discriminazione nei rapporti commerciali internazionali*, Milano, Giuffrè, 1966; P. Pescatore, *La clause de la nation la plus favorisée dans les conventions multilaterales, Rapport de l'Annuaire de l'Institut de Droit International*, 1969, t. 53, I; E. Sauvignon, *La clause de la nation la plus favorisée*, Grenoble, Presses Universitaire de Grenoble, 1972; E. Triggiani, above, note 21, at p. 77.

In the case of Article 29 of the EA with Hungary, while *specific* multilateral rules (either GATT 1947/1994 and the 1979 Anti-Dumping Code or the WTO Anti-Dumping Agreement) are referred to, their (*variable*) content is incorporated irrespective of what it may be at a certain time. Thus, if they had been amended after the entry into force of the EAs, those multilateral rules, as amended, would still be applicable to EC–EA countries trade. Following the entry into force of the WTO Agreement a question arises as to the continuing effect of the incorporation by reference of pre-WTO rules.

An answer in the negative for all the six countries concerned (Hungary, Poland, Czech Republic, Slovakia, Romania and Bulgaria) seems logical, having regard, in the first place, to the nature of the means through which the pre-WTO rules have been incorporated in the EAs, i.e. the legislative reference. In the case of a legislative reference the rights arising from the referred rules are not autonomous rights, but indirect ones, whose fate depends on that of the referred rules themselves.[23] Accordingly, the same rights are also terminated whenever the rule referred to is terminated or suspended. As a consequence, the right laid down by the EAs to have the pre-WTO regime applied is contingent on the continuing effect of the latter. This is, however, no longer the case, as results not only from customary international rules on conflicting treaties applicable between the same parties,[24] but also from express provisions within the GATT-WTO framework.[25]

The gap created in the EA regime by the termination of pre-WTO rules raises an additional question about their replacement. Filling such a gap with WTO rules seems logical for at least two reasons. First, an obligation to grant full WTO treatment to one another has been undertaken both by the European Communities (and its member states) and by Hungary, Poland,

---

[23] This character and its underlying flexibility rationale is common to all forms of legislative reference and is recognized both in international practice and scholarly works: as regards MFN see e.g. International Court of Justice, judgment of 27 August 1952, in C.J.I., *Recueil*, 1952, pp. 191 ff., at p. 204 and E. Triggiani, above, note 21, at pp. 77–82; as to the domestic effect of international treaties see B. Conforti, *Diritto internazionale*, Napoli, Editoriale Scientifica, 4th ed., 1992, pp. 285–6. The same flexibility rationale is common to all forms of legislative reference.

In the case of the EAs only Bulgaria is in an identical position to a beneficiary of an MFN clause, i.e. is a third party to the agreement referred to, but the same rationale underlying MFN-type references is common to all forms of legislative reference.

[24] See Art. 30(3)–(4) of the Vienna Convention on the Law of Treaties, on which see C. Rousseau, *Droit International Public*, Paris, Sirey, 1970, Tome I, 151–63, 207; I. Sinclair, *The Vienna Convention on the Law of Treaties*, Manchester, Manchester University Press, 1984, 2nd ed., pp. 151–63.

[25] See *Transitional Co-Existence of the GATT 1947 and the WTO Agreement, Decision of 8 December 1994, adopted by the Preparatory Committee for the WTO and the CONTRACTING PARTIES to the GATT 1947*, para. 3 and *Transitional Co-Existence of the Agreement on Implementation of Article VI of the General Agreement on Tariffs and Trade and the Marrakesh Agreement Establishing the World Trade Organization, Decision adopted by the Committee on 8 December 1994 at the Invitation of the Preparatory Committee for the World Trade Organization*, para. 3, repr. in World Trade Organization, *The WTO Dispute Settlement Procedures. A Collection of the Legal Texts*, World Trade Organization, Geneva, 1995. Both decisions provide for the provisional co-existence of pre-WTO and WTO rules and for the termination of GATT 1947 and the 1979 Anti-Dumping Code by 1995.

the Czech and the Slovak Republics, and Romania through acceptance of the WTO Agreement. To the extent that WTO rules conflict with earlier EAs concluded between WTO Members (including their provisions referring to pre-WTO rules), they should prevail (it should, however, be noted that this argument would not apply to Bulgaria until it becomes a WTO Member). Secondly, in more recent EAs the Communities and the member states have accepted a reference to WTO rules even for the benefit of partners which are not yet WTO Members: it would thus be surprising if the same rules could not be applicable as between WTO members by virtue of a reference contained in earlier bilateral agremeents and no longer effective.

A last reason why the gap created in the EA regime by the termination of pre-WTO agreements should be filled with WTO rules is the reference, in Article 29, to domestic legislation of the EA parties. Unlike the *renvoi* to pre-WTO rules, that to domestic legislation is so general that it entails incorporation of the latter whatever its content may be at a given time, i.e. even if it is amended or replaced after EAs are negotiated. Furthermore, since WTO Members have an obligation to bring their domestic rules into conformity with WTO,[26] a new EC basic anti-dumping regulation was adopted after the Uruguay Round which expressly refers to and implements WTO rules, while its compatibility with such rules may be reviewed by the ECJ.[27] Hence, even through the conduit of domestic legislation the EC would appear to have an obligation to apply to *all* the first six EA countries, including Bulgaria, the new multilateral rules.[28]

B. The EA procedural obligations and their relation with multilateral anti-dumping provisions

a. Scope of the procedural obligations

The precise content of the EAs' procedural requirements also deserves some clarification. In fact, Article 33(2) sets out the general principle that, *before* any measures can be taken, the Association Council must be supplied with all relevant information, with a view to seeking a solution acceptable to both parties. However, the general obligation of Article 33(2) is purported to be implemented in Article 33(3)(b), requiring the importing country, on the one hand, to inform the Association Council about the initiation of a dumping procedure, and, on the other hand, 'to refer the whole matter' to such body and only adopt measures where no end has been put to the dumping

---

[26] See Art. XVI:4 of the WTO Agreement. The EC fulfilled this obligation by adopting Council Regulation (EC) No. 3283/94 of 22 December 1994 (*OJ* 1994, L 349/1), now replaced by Regulation No. 384/96. All the five EA countries which are WTO Members are in the process of adjusting their anti-dumping legislation to WTO rules.

[27] See recital 3 of Council Regulations No. 3283/94 and 384/96 and above, note 18.

[28] Thus, while a formal revision of the Agreement is not strictly necessary it might be useful, for the sake of clarity and of legal certainty, to correct the reference to multilateral rules in Art. 29.

or no other satisfactory solution has been reached within 30 days of the referral.

Even if Article 33(3) is said to implement Article 33(2), it is not fully clear whether the 'referral' mentioned in the former must take place simultaneously with information about initiation of a procedure, or rather at the end of an anti-dumping investigation. In the first case the 'referral' clause would imply that the importing party is free to take measures after 30 days following the initiation information (i.e. in practice, little more than 30 days after initiation). If, on the contrary, the information to be referred pursuant to Article 33(3) concerns dumping and injury findings, the 30-day conciliation period only runs after the conclusion of the investigation and only at that (later) stage may the importing party take measures.

In fact, the second solution seems more justified on legal as well as logical grounds. In the first place, Article 33(3) aims to implement the general obligation of para. 2. It would therefore appear more reasonable to relate its 'referral requirement' to that general obligation. In addition to that, if the 30-day deadline for finding an acceptable solution ran from the information about the initiation of a new case, the Association Council could not be provided with all relevant information necessary 'before taking any measures', as required by Article 33(2). It would be difficult to request/offer to stop the dumping practice if there has been no opportunity to establish dumping yet. In turn, dumping can only be established through an investigation in accordance with multilateral and domestic rules of the importing party, which would require much longer than the 30 days afforded for the Association Council's conciliation efforts.

A last remark concerns the possible outcome of the Association Council's activity. Apart from the stopping of the dumping practice, the only lawful alternative seems to be an agreement on the terms of a price undertaking[29] offered on behalf of the exporting industry and on the basis of the information supplied in that context.[30]

b. Compatibility with WTO provisions

Once it is clarified that the references to multilateral rules must currently *all* be read as relating to WTO provisions,[31] the fact that different (additional) procedural rules are set out in the EAs as compared to the WTO Anti-Dumping Agreement calls for an evaluation of their compatibility with the latter treaty.

[29] A price undertaking is a commitment offered by exporters (and accepted by the importing country's authorities) to raise their prices or cease exports at dumped prices so as to eliminate the injury or the dumping margin (see Art. 8 of the WTO Anti-Dumping Agreement and Art. 8 of Regulation No. 384/96).

[30] Since WTO rules only allow the offer of a price undertaking after a preliminary positive determination of both dumping and injury (see Art. 8(2) of the WTO Anti-dumping Agreement), admitting that the conciliation may result in this solution further reinforces the thesis that it should take place after the investigation.

[31] See above, IIIA, p. 166.

While information about new anti-dumping procedures required in Article 33(3)(b) is also a right of all WTO Members even before formal opening,[32] and thus cannot conflict with multilateral rules, the other provisions of the EAs (particularly the activity entrusted with the Association Council) are not expressly paralleled in WTO rules.

Nonetheless, it is submitted that the bilateral regime is fully compatible with multilateral provisions. In fact, nothing in the WTO Anti-Dumping Agreement prevents any WTO Member from adopting more stringent rules on the taking of anti-dumping measures, either in autonomous acts or in international treaties, to the extent that they are not conflicting with, but merely supplementing, multilateral rules. This holds true for substantive and procedural rules alike, and good examples of this approach are provided by the so-called 'lesser duty rule' and the 'public interest clause', which are laid down in the EC basic regulation without implementing any multilateral obligation.[33] On the other hand, the special consultation regime laid down in Article 33 of the EA does not prevent fulfilment of any of the obligations laid down in WTO provisions, and its scope is different.

If, as it seems, the EA regime is not in conflict with WTO rules, it may be wondered whether the EA parties which are also WTO Members – and particularly the European Communities – have an obligation not to discriminate against the other WTO Members, or, in other words, whether they should multilateralize the EAs' special consultation procedure.[34]

Several considerations would however exclude the existence of such an obligation. In the first place, no *general* non-discrimination (Most favoured nation) obligation is embodied in the Anti-Dumping Agreement. Indeed, like its predecessor Anti-Dumping Code, the Agreement prescribes that there should not be discrimination between 'dumpers'.[35] The scope of this non-discrimination obligation is, however, confined to the *collection* of anti-dumping duties once the latter have been imposed on imports from different countries *all* found to be dumped and to cause material injury to the importer's industry. On the contrary, such obligation does not cover the way in which the dumping margin, the injury and the duties are assessed and calculated, which are the subject of other provisions of the Agreement.

Furthermore, if one looks more closely at the EA procedures, and notably at the activities that the Association Council is authorized to perform once

---

[32] See Art. 5(5) of the WTO Anti-Dumping Agreement.

[33] See respectively Arts 7(2), 9(4) and 8(1) (lesser duty rule) and Arts 7(1) and 9(4) (Community interest clause) in Reg. No. 384/96. Art. 9(1) of the WTO Anti-Dumping Agreement, the corresponding multilateral provision, is merely hortatory in nature.

[34] It is clear that if the EA procedures were considered as violating WTO rules, the other WTO Members could not claim their extension based on that Agreement.

[35] Pursuant to Art. 9(2) 'When an anti-dumping duty is imposed in respect of any product, such anti-dumping duty shall be collected in the appropriate amounts in each case, on a non-discriminatory basis on imports of such product from all sources found to be dumped and causing injury, except as to imports from those sources from which price undertakings under the terms of this Agreement have been accepted'.

the matter is referred to it, after the entry into force of the WTO Anti-Dumping Agreement and of the EC implementing regulation, the EA regime can hardly be said to provide additional advantages to those granted to WTO Members at large. In fact the performance of analogous activity can also be requested under the WTO Anti-Dumping Agreement. First, the right of defence, including the possibility to exchange views between interested countries' representatives, is also provided for in very broad terms by the Anti-Dumping Agreement.[36] As to the conciliation activity, nothing prevents any WTO Member from offering either to cease dumping practices or a solution alternative to duties, such as a price undertaking. Since mutual consent is required for the Association Council to decide on alternative solutions, under the EAs, too, an importing party can refuse an undertaking if it does not consider it satisfactory.[37] An additional reason to exclude multilateralization of EA procedures is that the general MFN obligation laid down in GATT 1994's Article I does not seem applicable to the matter at issue either. In fact anti-dumping duties, and more generally GATT Article VI, may be construed precisely as exceptions to the general MFN obligation,[38] for the GATT itself mandates that such duties be imposed *only* on imports found to be dumped, thereby 'discriminating' in favour of non-dumping countries.

Additional confirmation that the GATT MFN obligation is not relevant to the EAs' anti-dumping rules will come once the review of the EAs' trade provisions under GATT Article XXIV is completed.[39]

IV. UNILATERAL CHANGES TO THE EC DOMESTIC ANTI-DUMPING REGIME AND PRACTICE TOWARDS EA COUNTRIES

Despite the fact that anti-dumping continues to be the ECs' most used trade remedy,[40] recent developments evidence a softening in its enforcement

---

[36] See Art. 6(2), reading 'Throughout the anti-dumping investigation all interested parties shall have a full opportunity for the defence of their interests. To this end, the authorities shall, on request, provide opportunities for all interested parties to meet those parties with adverse interests, so that opposing views may be presented and rebuttal arguments offered. . . . Interested parties shall also have the right, on justification, to present other information orally.'

[37] As a consequence, the value of the EAs' 'conciliation' clause seems, at present, mainly political, that is, providing a further opportunity for discussion and for reflection on the impact of the measure envisaged in the light of overall bilateral relations, but certainly not, as such, substantially differentiating the treatment of EA parties.

[38] See e.g. *Swedish Anti-Dumping Duties – Report Adopted on 26 February 1955*, GATT, BISD, 3S/81, at pp. 83–5, paras 8–10; *United States – Countervailing Duties on Fresh, Chilled and Frozen Pork from Canada* adopted on 11 July 1991, GATT, BISD, 38S/30, at p. 44, para. 4.4; Brazil-Measures Affecting Desiccated Coconut – Report of the Panel, 17 October 1996, WT/DSZZ/R, p. 76, para 280; J.H. Jackson, *World Trade and the Law of GATT*, Indianapolis, Bobbs-Merrill, 1969, 407; R.M. Bierwagen, *GATT Article VI and the Protectionist Bias in Anti-Dumping Law*, Deventer, Kluwer, 1991, p. 2.

[39] The WTO Committee on Regional Trade Agreements, established by the General Council in February 1996, is in the process of reviewing the Europe Agreements (see *Focus, WTO Newsletter*, No. 11, June–July 1996, 10).

[40] See European Commission, *Twenty-Ninth General Report on the Activities of the European Union*, 1995, pts 743–9.

towards EA countries.[41] Again, as for other aspects covered by the EAs,[42] adjustments to EC anti-dumping enforcement have also been brought about by supplementing the EAs with autonomous initiatives, both at the legal and the political level.

A.   Changes to EC anti-dumping rules and enforcement

a.   Recognition of EA partners as market economies

From a legal perspective, the most visible unilateral innovation connected with the EAs has been the recognition that the EA countries are no longer to be considered as 'non-market economies' (NMEs) for the purpose of, *inter alia*, calculation of dumping margins, which recognition was simultaneous with the entry into force of the several EAs' trade provisions.[43] Before this change, normal value was calculated on the basis of special rules devised to adjust the anti-dumping instrument to the peculiar features of command economies. It has already been illustrated elsewhere that the transition from the application of the special normal value rules for NMEs to the general ones has not been completely free from difficulties.[44] Nonetheless, since the beginning of 1994 treatment as a market economy in anti-dumping procedures has progressively become established practice in respect of all the EA countries.

Commission Decision (ECSC) No. 67/94 of 12 January 1994 was the first measure against an EA country based on the generally applicable normal value rules.[45] Still, because of the stage of the process of economic transition

---

[41] Since 1991 measures have been imposed in respect of CEECs in only eleven cases, as compared to e.g. twelve measures imposed against Japan, nine against South Korea and seven against Turkey (see Commission of the European Communities, *Fourteenth Annual Report from the Commission to the European Parliament on the Community's Anti-Dumping and Anti-Subsidy Activities*, COM(95) 146 final, 1).

[42] For example, at the Copenhagen Summit the Community recognized accession, which is mentioned in the EAs as an aim of the associated countries only, as a common objective, and simultaneously decided unilateral acceleration of trade liberalization provided for in those agreements.

[43] In the case of imports from NMEs the basic anti-dumping regulation (currently Art. 2(7) of Regulation No. 384/96) provides that normal value be calculated on the basis of the prices charged in a different (market economy) country (the so-called 'analogue'). This special treatment is also authorized at the multilateral level by an interpretative note to GATT Art. VI:1. A series of Council regulations progressively excluded EA countries from the reach of the Community special import rules applying to NME countries, to which the basic anti-dumping regulations always referred for identifying those states: Regulation No. 517/92 (EEC) of 29 February 1992 (*OJ* 1992, L 56/1) for Poland, Hungary and then Czech and Slovak Federative Republic; No. 1013/93 (EC) of 26 April 1993 (*OJ* 1993, L 105/1) for Romania and Bulgaria; No. 839/95 (EC) of 10 April 1995 (*OJ* 1995, L 85/9) for the Baltic States (for the latter countries recognition as market economies took place upon the entry into force of the Free Trade Agreements, which already included the EAs' anti-dumping provisions). An exception is represented by Slovenia, which was never considered a NME, since even Yugoslavia had always been treated as a market economy.

[44] M. Maresceau and E. Montaguti, above, note 1, pp. 1349–50.

[45] Commission Decision No. 67/94 of 12 January 1994 (hematite pig iron), *OJ* 1994, L 12/5, recital 17.

in the country concerned (Poland), the exporting market was considered as not yet fully working like a regular market economy. Thus, in this and several subsequent cases normal value could not be calculated on the basis of the actual selling prices, but had to be reconstructed by referring to costs and profits of the exporting companies.[46] More recently, however, further progress in economic transition was observed and normal value was, accordingly, also calculated on the basis of actual prices verified in the exporting market. In the procedure concluded by Council Regulation (EC) No. 477/95 of 16 January 1995, after a careful review of whether the prices and costs of the domestic (privatized) producers were still influenced by the historical links between state-owned companies, and on the basis of an analysis of accounting records, it could be concluded that domestic sales had been made in the ordinary course of trade.[47] Accordingly, normal value was established on the basis of *actual* prices charged in the exporting country. With the adoption of this measure it can be said that the evolution has been completed and that EA countries are now fully equated with WTO countries as concerns the application of the EC substantive regime.

b. Review applied to economic transition

Notwithstanding the progress brought about by the recognition as market economies, some difficulties related to the previous situation – particularly the continuing enforcement of measures based on the pre-existing state-trading economic structure – may still arise. The Community legislation may nonetheless offer some opportunity to reduce those difficulties through review procedures. In fact under the basic anti-dumping regulation[48] interested parties may request the EC Commission to review existing measures if they can show that the circumstances on which those measures had been based have changed significantly and one year has elapsed since their adoption. The reference to 'changed circumstances' is broad enough to cover a vast array of hypotheses, including a reform of the economic structure of a country, and it is precisely this course of action that was taken by Romanian exporters in respect of certain anti-dumping measures on welded tubes.

After definitive measures (a general duty and the accceptance of a price undertaking by the former import–export monopolist) had been decided in 1990,[49] Romania was recognized as enjoying market economy status for *inter alia* dumping calculations purposes (1 May 1993). A review request was then

---

[46] This method of calculating normal value has been envisaged in the basic regulation (currently Art. 2(3)) precisely for cases when the exporting market is not fully working on the basis of supply and demand.

[47] Council Regulation (EC) No. 477/95 of 16 January 1995, terminating anti-dumping measures on urea from former Czechoslovakia, *OJ* 1995, L 49/1, recitals 21–4. The regulation covered an investigation period (1 January–31 December 1992) which partly preceded formal recognition of such country as a market economy (effective since 1 March 1992). Nevertheless, the country was treated as a market economy for the whole reference period.

[48] Currently Art. 11(3) of Regulation No. 384/96.

[49] Council Regulation (EEC) No. 868/90 of 2 April 1990 (welded tubes), *OJ* 1990, L 91/8.

lodged in 1993 by a Romanian producer based on the economic transition, and offered the Community the first chance to give practical effect to that recognition.[50] Indeed, the exporters' request was upheld by the EC Council, recognizing that (1) Romania had commenced a liberalization process which affected both (2) the pricing of goods and (3) the relations between the different operators on the domestic market,' so that producers . . . 'became progressively independent', and, furthermore, that (4) 'the company's bookkeeping . . . had developed to conform with generally accepted principles of accountancy'. The Council could accordingly conclude that '[c]onsequently . . . the information provided by the Romanian companies could be used for determining the normal value'.[51] While it is a difficult exercise to look beyond the circumstances of the single case, this measure can provide some guidance as to the possibilities offered by the application of the review clause to the issue of economic transition.

c. Preference for price undertakings

Another development which, while taking the form not of a formal amendment but of a guideline for implementation of existing rules, may influence their enforcement, is the clear preference expressed by the Commission for the acceptance of price undertakings as opposed to the imposition of duties in the case where injurious dumping is found.[52] This guideline, presented as one of the 'short-term measures' to prepare CEECs for accession, gives a concrete signal of the EC's readiness to change its practice and can contribute to giving full effect to the EAs' consultation procedures, particularly the search for a 'satisfactory solution' other than the imposition of duties pursuant to Article 33(3).

B. Political initiatives

Political initiatives have also played a specific role in the post-EA evolution of EC anti-dumping practice vis-à-vis the CEECs.

---

[50] For the notice of initiation of the review procedure see *OJ* 1993, C 344/5. More precisely, the Romanian exporter had alleged as 'changed circumstances' (1) the abolition of the centrally planned economy in Romania; (2) the economic reform set in motion in the country; (3) the conclusion of the Interim Agreement based, *inter alia*, on the parties' commitment to market economy principles; and (4) the fact that the price undertaking accepted from the former Romanian monopolist – being more favourable than the duty – had become discriminatory against all new producers and exporters, who were subject to the general country ('residual') duty. As can be seen, all these grounds were directly or indirectly related to the process of economic transition. Although the last one also presents some features of what constitutes a 'newcomer review' under current EC rules, in fact, since the presence of an import-export monopolist was a typical feature of a centrally planned economies it further links the review to economic transition.

[51] Council Regulation (EC) No. 2962/95 of 18 December 1995, *OJ* 1995, L 308/65, recital 24.

[52] See Essen European Council, Conclusions of the Presidency, Annex IV, *Report from the Council to the Essen European Council on a strategy to prepare for the accession of the associated countries of Central and Eastern Europe, Bull. EU* 12-1994, pt I-41(a).

In connection with the acceptance, by the EC, of EA countries' membership as a common objective,[53] the ways by which this aim could be achieved became the subject of increasing attention in the EU. While mainly concentrating on the long and complex path that the EA countries have yet to complete to integrate into the Internal Market, the documents issued by the EC and EU institutions also addressed, albeit in a rather cursory way, the implications of those countries' increased economic integration for trade defence. It was in this context that for the first time in July 1994, with the Commission's Accession Strategy Memoranda, the Community considered the possibility of reducing the application of its trade defence measures once the integration of EA countries into the Internal Market are completed and once competition rules are effectively enforced in their markets.[54]

The orientations expressed in the Commission Memoranda were further elaborated in documents issued in the same year by EU and European Councils in Essen, where a *full waiver* was envisaged for the benefit of those EA countries which would reach that degree of integration. In the Conclusions of the December 1994 European Council, in the framework of the 'medium-term measures' to prepare the CEECs for accession to the EU, an undertaking was made that:

> As satisfactory implementation of competition policy and control of state aids together with the application of those parts of Community law linked to the internal market are achieved, so the Union should be ready to consider refraining from using commercial defence instruments for *industrial* products.[55]

The line taken in Essen appears consistent with the rationale traditionally attributed to trade defence measures (that is, that those measures are necessary because legal and economic disparities in different national markets distort the conditions of competition between companies of different countries). Indeed, dumping practices can only be successful if economic, legal or practical barriers in the exporting country exist, preventing cheaper exports from re-entering the market. Once the segmentation of the several national markets is no longer possible, thanks particularly to legal integration, then the need for protective measures is presumably no longer present. Furthermore, that line builds on obligations already imposed on EA countries by the respective agreements (the approximation obligation – possibly eased by mutual

---

[53] This was the result of the 1993 Copenhagen European Council (*Bull. EC* 6-1993, pt I-13).

[54] See above, note 11. Another change envisaged in these communications is the so-called pre-initiation information, that is, informing the countries concerned about new anti-dumping procedures before their official opening. At the time when the Commission Communications were drafted the entry into force of the WTO Agreement had not yet occurred, thus this development did constitute an additional concession on the part of the EC, whereas, by the time it materialized as a European Council political commitment at the end of 1994, it could no longer be considered so (see above, n. 32).

[55] See Essen European Council, Conclusions of the Presidency, Annex IV, above, note 52, pt I-41.

recognition agreements[56] – affecting legal barriers; the commitment to adopt competition and state aid rules – affecting economic, private barriers), and draws its consequences for trade defence. Therefore, it can rightly be seen as completing and concluding the process of those countries' integration into the Internal Market.

V. PROSPECTS

From a purely legal perspective it is difficult to imagine any major evolution in EC anti-dumping regime *vis-à-vis* EA countries until – regardless of the timing – it is terminated. Observation of other developments may, however, at least help understand the way in which this final change is likely to take place.

As already noted, since the focus of the debate and of Commission activities has now mainly become accession, a considerably bigger effort than originally foreseen in the EAs has been deployed towards legislative approximation that EA countries should undertake,[57] and greater emphasis has been placed on the effects of enlargement on such countries, on the Union and on EC law.

From the point of view of (EC) trade defence, preparation for accession by the EA countries does not require a special law-making activity. Indeed, it can be said that in the extensive pre-accession exercise the role attributed to commercial defence rules is rather marginal, and the non-application of trade measures by the EC rather represents a corollary of this effort. It is true that a general legislative approximation obligation exists in the EAs. Significantly, however, trade defence is not expressly listed among the affected sectors, which suggests that it was not a priority at the time the EAs were drafted.[58] That impression is confirmed by the absence of any reference in the White Paper programme. On the other hand, no harmonization will be needed after accession either, since at that stage all EA countries' own trade defence rules will have been replaced by Community ones[59] (unlike in areas of EC law

---

[56] The harmonization (more accurately, approximation) obligation imposed on EA countries has a general coverage, although some areas of EC law are expressly mentioned in the EAs (see e.g. Art. 68 of the EA with Hungary). The EAs also allow the conclusion of mutual recognition agreements relative to standardization and conformity assessment: see e.g. Art. 73(2) of the EA with Hungary.

[57] This aspect has been the subject of a Commission Communication on the follow-up of the Copenhagen Summit on approximation of laws (COM (94) 361 final) and of a comprehensive reflection within the Commission, which, in June 1995, resulted in the White Paper on the *Preparation of the Associated Countries of Central and Eastern Europe for Integration into the Internal Market of the Union* (on this subject see M.-A. Gaudissart and A. Sinnaeve, above, p. 41).

[58] See above, note 56. This contrasts with the provisions of the Decision on the implementation of the Customs Union with Turkey (Decision No. 1/95 of the EC–Turkey Association Council of 22 December 1995 on implementing the final phase of the Customs Union, *OJ* 1996, L 35/1, Art. 12), where alignment of Turkey's trade defence legislation with EC instruments is expressly required because of the 'move' of the Community customs border.

[59] For some EA countries (e.g. Estonia) benefiting from the application of anti-dumping rules will in fact be a complete novelty. So will be, for all of them, the availability of an instrument designed for opening third country markets, like the Community's 'Trade Barriers Regulation' (Council Regulation (EC) No. 3286/94, *OJ* 1996, L 349/61).

where the competence is shared with member states, for which harmonization will keep its importance even after accession). However, some adjustment may be required to EC measures (in force), which will be extended to the new territories of the EU, to redefine their scope and effects after extension, as already happened for the latest enlargement.[60] Additionally, an alignment to EC rules will, besides facilitating implementation of the WTO Agreement for EA partners, prepare local customs authorities to act as the secular branch of the Community when called to enforce protective measures at the new EU border.

One may reflect on the impact of these developments on the 'Essen commitment' of waiving trade defence enforcement. As a result of the overall pre-accession preparation, especially after the detailed White Paper programme, it is no longer entirely clear whether the political commitment, made at Essen, that the EC will renounce application of its trade defence rules against EA countries once their alignment to internal market rules is completed and effective competition rules are in place and enforced, is still up-to-date, or whether this intermediate stage will be taken over by accession itself.

In fact, once EA countries' legislations are considered to be sufficiently harmonized with EC rules, it may be useless, as well as politically difficult to justify, to delay accession further and merely consider the waiver of trade defence rules on industrial products. Unless the level of harmonization and of competition law enforcement required for the waiver of trade defence measures is lower than that required for accession, an intermediate stage like that designed at Essen could result in a step back to an EEA-type solution, which the EA countries already opposed in the past.[61]

If, however, waiver of trade defence measures required lower standards and was foreseen as an interim stage pending fulfilment of the White Paper programme and of all accession conditions, it could be of some interest to the EA countries should their alignment take longer than expected (which could happen for those lagging somehow behind in the process). In turn, if this scenario materialized, it would imply a clear return to an 'individual' approach to the several EA countries, which had characterized the first years of the Community policy toward these countries. While this differentiation had been blurred by the progressive extension to all the EA partners of concessions originally granted to the most advanced ones, the possibility has carefully been retained in the White Paper (leaving each country free as concerns the timing for its implementation) and in the EU commitment to negotiate accession (for which only a common *initial* date has been envisaged). It therefore may happen that the situation in the trade defence sector is, once again, symptomatic of the general evolution of EC–EA countries relations.

---

[60] The Notice regarding the application of anti-dumping measures in force in the Community following enlargement to include Austria, Finland and Sweden (*OJ* 1995, C 40/5) is the only relevant precedent, but it remains to be seen whether the generalized extension of the territorial scope of EC anti-dumping measures will be repeated in a much broader enlargement as the next one envisaged.

[61] See above, Introduction.

The only aspect of anti-dumping enforcement leaving some scope for development seems to be the actual imposition of measures once the relevant requirements are met, whose 'evolution' has not been linked to the integration process. In this respect, a limited evolution may materialize for measures in force, through review of those measures adopted on the basis of a NME situation. The importance of this limited evolution is, however, bound to decrease as old measures expire.

Another (potentially more promising) avenue is the implementation of the Essen commitment to accord preference to price undertakings where new measures prove justified and necessary in the Community interest. Implementation of this commitment requires, however, a careful evaluation of its implications. For example, the monitoring of the undertakings accepted, traditionally regarded as one of the main drawbacks of such measures, will require increasing resources. Still, in this respect, the new basic regulation seems to afford sufficient guarantees, as it authorizes the immediate imposition of definitive duties on the basis of the original investigation findings where a violation is shown.[62] Caution will also be needed if the commitment inspires a relaxation of the conditions for acceptance of undertakings. Nonetheless, in evaluating the opportunity to take steps in this direction it should be borne in mind that this seems to be the only area of anti-dumping enforcement where the special nature of the relations with the CEECs can for the time being be given further substance.

[62] See Art. 9 of Reg. No. 384/96.

10

TRADE-RELATED ASPECTS OF INTELLECTUAL PROPERTY RIGHTS IN THE EUROPE AGREEMENTS: STIMULUS OR LIMITATION TO PARALLEL IMPORTS?

Inge Govaere[1]

I. ON FREE TRADE AND INTELLECTUAL PROPERTY RIGHTS

One of the main objectives of the Europe Agreements (EA) between the EC and the Central and Eastern European Countries (CEECs) is to establish gradually a free trade area between the Community and the associated country, covering substantially all trade between them.[2] As free trade more and more becomes the rule rather than the exception in the relations between the EC and the CEECs, there is no doubt that the importance of intellectual property rights (hereafter: IP rights) as non-tariff barriers to trade will increasingly be exposed.

The free trade objective essentially relates to tangible or corporeal property, facilitating the movement of products between different states (Article 7 EA). For instance, achieving free trade between Hungary and the EC would imply that after the expiry of the transitional period Hungarian video tapes or garden gnomes could, in principle, freely be imported into the EC. In reality it is not that simple. Most products are subject to intellectual

---

[1] PhD (EUI), Lecturer, Law Department, College of Europe, Bruges.

[2] See for instance Art. 1 of the Europe Agreement establishing an association between the European Communities and their member states, of the one part, and the Republic of Hungary, of the other part, *OJ* L 347/2, 31 December 1993. Europe Agreements with other CEECs contain similar provisions. Throughout this paper reference is made to the Europe Agreement with Hungary. On the Europe Agreements, see M. Maresceau and E. Montaguti, 'The relations between the European Union and Central and Eastern Europe: A legal appraisal', *CMLRev.* (1995), 1327–67; A. Toledano Laredo, 'L'Union Européenne, l'ex-Union Soviétique et les Pays de l'Europe Centrale et Orientale: un aperçu de leurs accords', *CDE* (1994), 543–62; I. Govaere, 'Les Communautés Européennes face au défi de la transition des Pays de l'Europe Centrale et Orientale vers l'économie de marché', *Transitions* (1993), 47–66; M. Maresceau, 'Europe Agreements: A new form of cooperation between the European Community and Central and Eastern Europe', in Müller-Graff (ed.), *East Central European States and the European Communities: Legal adaptation to the market economy*, Nomos Verlagsgesellschaft, 1993, 209–33.

property protection (hereafter: IP protection) in the form of, for instance, trade marks or copyright which are not necessarily subject to the same trade liberalizing rules.

It should be emphasized that intellectual property needs to be distinguished from corporeal property because it exclusively relates to creations of the intellect. It thus basically concerns intangible or incorporeal property, although the result of the creative effort will often be embodied in a tangible product. The intangible property is protected by IP rights, which are inherently temporary exclusive rights granted by law on the basis of the principle of territoriality. This allows the intellectual property owner (hereafter: IP owner) to prohibit certain acts which would be legitimate in the absence of legal protection such as copying, manufacturing, distribution and importation of products incorporating the intellectual property. To take the example of the Hungarian video tape, the video tape might be the carrier of a movie which is subject to copyright in the EC and/or might bear a trade mark which is protected in the EC. Since it is impossible to dissociate the intangible from the tangible property the Hungarian video tape could, thus, be prohibited free access to the EC market in spite of the free trade objective.

In essence this means that, whereas the product itself may in principle be subject to trade liberalization, effective trade in the product may, nevertheless, be prohibited by virtue of the IP rights attached to it. This is a situation which may lead to incomprehension on behalf of certain economic actors, as the following example may show. A Polish national was reported to have said that he no longer understood the meaning of free trade, for '(a)ll I want to do is to sell my garden gnomes. But the Germans will not allow them into the country'.[3] In fact, the Polish gnomes were held to infringe copyright in Germany and were therefore labelled as counterfeit and prohibited access to the EC market. Far from being an isolated case, this is a situation which may potentially arise with regard to virtually all, and in particular manufactured, products not only from Poland but also from the other CEECs. It is therefore necessary to analyse whether, and to what extent, the Europe Agreements have taken the trade-related aspects of IP rights into account when paving the way for free trade between the CEECs and the European Community.

II.   TRADE-RELATED ASPECTS OF INTELLECTUAL PROPERTY RIGHTS: A NEW CONCEPT

It should first of all be pointed out that the Europe Agreements are rather special in that they were among the first agreements concluded by the EC in which the new conceptual perception of the role of IP rights in international trade is expressed.

---

[3] *Financial Times*, 'Germans defend EU against the Polish gnome', 29 September 1994, 1 and 16.

Traditionally, IP rights were merely considered as non-tariff barriers to international trade. The focus was thereby put on the existence of IP rights through pointing out that they are inherently restrictive of trade by virtue of the conferment of an exclusive right based on the principle of territoriality. Nevertheless, IP rights were considered to be indispensable barriers to trade due to their importance for fostering research and development activities and ultimately for their potential of stimulating national economic growth. In international trade relations, national legislation governing the protection of intellectual property was therefore 'permitted', no more no less.[4] This view was reflected in the GATT Agreement which virtually only mentioned intellectual property in the general exceptions to trade provision, namely Article XX(d).[5]

The perception of the role of IP rights in international trade has, however, gradually changed over time. This is illustrated by the Agreement on Trade-Related Aspects of Intellectual Property Rights (TRIPS Agreement) which was recently concluded in the framework of the GATT Uruguay Round and annexed to the Agreement on the World Trade Organization (WTO Agreement).[6] Rather than the existence, it is more and more the absence of, or deficiencies in, IP protection that is considered to be detrimental to international trade.[7] This new perception of the concept of 'trade-related aspects of intellectual property rights' is mainly due to the sometimes considerable investment involved in research and development of technological innovation which, in certain cases, no longer allows for the recoupment of the investment on the basis of the exclusive rights granted in the home country. Furthermore, with the growing awareness of the economic importance of IP rights, estimations have been made as to the amount of economic loss incurred due to the inefficient protection of intellectual property on a worldwide scale. Estimates advancing quite substantial figures such as 10 per cent of world trade or 60–70 billion US$ economic loss due to counterfeiting or piracy are not uncommon in this respect.[8] In international trade relations,

---

[4] On the so-called 'permissive approach' under the GATT Agreement, see for instance A.A. Yusuf and A. Moncayo Von Hase, 'Intellectual property protection and international trade: exhaustion of rights revisited', *World Competition* (1992), 115–31, at p. 115.

[5] Art. XX(d) GATT reads: 'nothing in this Agreement shall be construed to prevent the adoption or enforcement by any contracting party of (intellectual property) measures'. There is only one other reference to intellectual property rights, namely marks of origin, in Art. IX GATT.

[6] Annex 1 C to the Agreement on the establishment of the World Trade Organization (WTO Agreement). For a critical analysis of the TRIPS Agreement, see H. Ullrich, 'TRIPS: Adequate protection, inadequate trade, adequate competition policy', *Pacific Rim Law & Policy Journal* (1995), 153–210. For an overview of the most relevant provisions, see J. Worthy, 'Intellectual property protection after GATT', *EIPR* (1994), 195–8.

[7] On this issue, see U. Joos and R. Moufang, 'Report on the second Ringberg Symposium', in Beier and Schricker (eds), *GATT or WIPO? New Ways in the International Protection of Intellectual Property*, IIC Studies, Vol. 11, VCH, 1989, 31; I. Govaere, 'Trade-related aspects of intellectual property rights: the EC dichotomy uncovered', in *La place de l'Europe dans le commerce mondial*, Institut Universitaire International Luxembourg, Session de juillet 1994, 161–215.

[8] See for instance K. Uchentagen, 'The GATT negotiations concerning copyright and intellectual property protection', *IIC* (1990), 765–82, at p. 770.

nowadays, the emphasis is accordingly put on increasing the level of IP protection offered world-wide so that the traditional permissive approach towards intellectual property legislation has given way to a coercive approach. The adoption of adequate intellectual property legislation by trading partners has become an objective in itself and is now considered to be an indispensable counterpart to trade liberalization.[9]

III. APPROXIMATION AND IMPROVEMENT OF INTELLECTUAL PROPERTY RIGHTS

A. The Europe Agreements

The inclusion of provisions concerning IP rights in an agreement between the EC and CEECs is not new. Already in the Agreement between the EC and Hungary on trade and commercial and economic cooperation of 1988, for instance, IP rights were mentioned, albeit only in an annex.[10] The emphasis was thereby put on the compliance by Hungary with the international intellectual property conventions to which it had already adhered, namely, the Paris Convention for the Protection of Industrial Property and the Universal Copyright Convention.[11]

The innovatory feature of the Europe Agreements therefore lies especially in the content of the intellectual property provisions they contain. The associated country is no longer merely held to comply with international intellectual property conventions it has previously contracted. The Europe Agreements go a step further in that the CEECs have undertaken:

> [to] continue to improve the protection of intellectual, industrial and commercial property rights in order to provide, by the end of the fifth year from the entry into force of (the EA), a level of protection which is similar to that existing in the Community, including comparable means of enforcing such rights (Article 65 (1) EA).[12]

---

[9] On the EC approach concerning this issue, namely from carrot-and-stick over bilateral package deal to multilateral package deal approach, see I. Govaere, 'Intellectual property protection and commercial policy', in Maresceau (ed.), *The European Community's commercial policy after 1992: the legal dimension*, Martinus Nijhoff Publishers, 1993, 197–222.

[10] See the Annex relating to Art. 10 of the 1988 Cooperation Agreement with Hungary, *OJ* L 372/2, 30 November 1988.

[11] The emphasis was specifically put on the protection of both products and processes due to its importance for the sensitive sectors, such as chemicals, pharmaceuticals, fertilizers and pesticides, where R&D investment is considerable, see I. Govaere, 'The impact of intellectual property protection on technology transfer between the EC and the Central and Eastern European Countries', *JWT* (1991), 57–76, esp. at p. 62.

[12] In the Joint Declaration it is specified that the concept 'intellectual, industrial and commercial property' in Art. 65 EA should be given a similar meaning to that in Art. 36 EC, thus including copyright and neighbouring rights, patents, industrial designs, trade marks and service marks, topographies of integrated circuits, software, geographical indications, as well as protection against unfair competition (which is not held to come under Art. 36 EC) and protection of undisclosed information and know-how.

The improvement of IP protection up to a level similar to that existing in the EC should basically be done in two ways. This may be illustrated with reference to the EA with Hungary. First of all, Article 65(2) specifies that Hungary should apply to accede to the Munich Convention on the European Patent, as well as to other intellectual property conventions the EC member states are Parties to or which are *de facto* applied by the member states.[13] Secondly, Article 68 EA, in application of Article 67 EA, stipulates that the approximation of Hungarian intellectual property legislation to the existing and future intellectual property legislation of the EC is a major precondition for Hungary's economic integration into the EC. Hungary therefore undertakes to '. . . act to ensure that future legislation is compatible with Community legislation as far as possible' (Article 67 EA), also in this field.

The main objective therefore seems to be to eliminate distortions to trade due to the different, not to say lower, level of IP protection prevailing in the CEECs as compared to the EC and its member states. It should be noted that no such obligation is put on the EC member states. It is significant to point out in this respect that in the EC, in the absence of harmonization measures, IP rights are granted by national law which may differ, sometimes quite substantially,[14] from one member state to another. Furthermore, as the formulation used in Article 65(2) EA indicates,[15] not all member states have currently adhered to the intellectual property conventions to which the CEECs have agreed to become Party.

B. The White Paper

The approximation of legislation in the CEECs to that of the EC is easier said than done. Considering that it is impossible to change fundamentally the legislation in force overnight, priority areas need to be defined. The European Commission has indicated, in the White Paper on 'The preparation of the associated countries of Central and Eastern Europe for integration into the internal market of the Union',[16] which measures most urgently need to be approximated. Whereas it is acknowledged in the White Paper that the conclusion of the TRIPS Agreement in itself constitutes an important factor of harmonization, it is nonetheless also pointed out that 'although multilateral action is necessary, it is not sufficient to meet the needs of the single market'.[17]

---

[13] Annex XIII lists the main intellectual property conventions envisaged (Madrid and Rome Conventions) and stipulates that the Association Council may extend this obligation to other intellectual property conventions. It also lists the intellectual property conventions the observance of which is considered to be indispensable, such as the Berne and Paris Conventions.

[14] See, for instance, on the difference in the legislation of the member states concerning the protection of industrial designs and models: A. Firth, 'Aspects of design protection in Europe', *EIPR* (1993), 42–7.

[15] Namely, '. . . or (intellectual property conventions) which are *de facto* applied by Member States'.

[16] COM(95) 163 final, 3 May 1995.

[17] COM(95) 163 final/2, 10 May 1995, 352.

The White Paper distinguishes between Stage I measures, which take priority, and Stage II measures which should be approximated subsequently.[18] Specifically in relation to IP rights, the Commission lists secondary legislation in the field of trade marks and copyright and related rights as Stage I measures.[19] It is further pointed out that, according to the Europe Agreements, application for membership of the Munich Convention on the European Patent ought to be submitted to the European Patent Organization (EPO) by the end of 1996. The Commission draws the attention to the possibility for the CEECs to take anticipatory measures in the form of the conclusion of EPO agreements extending to their territory the effects produced by applications for, and conferment of, European patents. It is expressly stated that 'the extension agreements are of value to Community industry in that they enable those applicants for European patents who so wish to secure, by a simple and inexpensive procedure, protection for their patents in countries other than those which are full members of the Convention'.[20]

It was already mentioned that the Europe Agreements provide for the approximation of intellectual property legislation of the CEECs to both existing and future intellectual property legislation of the EC.[21] It is not surprising, therefore, that the Commission not only lists secondary legislation that has already been adopted but, also, pending proposals on the harmonization of intellectual property law, such as the proposal to harmonize design law, as Stage II measures.[22] In essence, the former relates to harmonization measures taken in relation to a specific sector as well as border measures against counterfeit and pirated goods.[23]

---

[18] See COM(95) 163 final/2, 10 May 1995 (Annex) for the reference list of secondary EC legislation.

[19] The following Stage I measures are listed: First Council Directive 89/104/EEC of 21 December 1988 to approximate the laws of the member states relating to trade marks (*OJ* L 40, 11 February 1989); Council Directive 87/54/44C of 16 December 1986 on the legal protection of topographies of semiconductor products (*OJ* L 24, 27 January 1987); Council Directive 91/250/EEC of 14 May 1991 on the legal protection of computer programs (*OJ* L 122, 17 May 1991); Council Directive 92/100/EEC of 19 November 1992 on rental right and lending right and on certain rights related to copyright in the field of intellectual property (*OJ* L 346, 27 November 1992); Council Directive 93/98/EEC of 29 October 1993 harmonizing the term of protection of copyright and certain related rights (*OJ* L 290, 24 November 1993).

[20] COM(95) 163 final/2 of 10 May 1995, 356.

[21] See above, section IIIA, p. 182.

[22] The following proposals are listed as Stage II measures: Proposal for a Parliament and Council Directive on the legal protection of designs (*OJ* C 345, 23 December 1993); Proposal for a Parliament and Council Regulation concerning the creation of a supplementary protection certificate for plant protection products (COM(94) 579); Proposal for a Parliament and Council Directive on the legal protection of data bases (*OJ* C 156, 23 June 1992).

[23] In particular, the following are listed: Council Regulation (EEC) No. 1768/92 of 18 June 1992 concerning the creation of a supplementary protection certificate for medicinal products (*OJ* L 182, 2 July 1992); Council Directive 93/83/EEC of 27 September 1993 on the coordination of certain rules concerning copyright and rights related to copyright applicable to satellite broadcasting and cable retransmission (*OJ* L 248, 6 October 1993); Council Regulation (EC) No. 3295/94 of 22 December 1994 laying down measures to prohibit the release for free circulation, export, re-export or entry for a suspensive procedure of counterfeit and pirated goods (*OJ* L 341, 30 December 1994).

One of the objectives of the White Paper is to facilitate the approximation of CEEC legislation to that of the EC, by identifying key measures and suggesting the sequence for approximation.[24] It should be emphasized, however, that 'the White Paper is a general reference document which does not adjust its recommendations to the requirements of any particular country. Each CEEC will establish its own priorities and determine its own timetable in the light of its economic, social and political realities and of the work it has achieved so far'.[25] In other words, the White Paper merely provides guidance and is in no way binding on the associated countries. The latter have to set their own priorities, thereby taking into account the obligations contracted under the Europe Agreement and which remain unaltered by the White Paper.[26]

IV. FREE TRADE IN INTELLECTUAL PROPERTY PROTECTED PRODUCTS?

The practical implication of the approximation of CEEC intellectual property legislation to that of the EC is, basically, that the status of IP owners in the CEECs will be improved. This should enhance the transfer of both technology and technology-based products from the EC to the CEEC market. EC firms that have invested time and money in research and development will be able to obtain a temporary legal monopoly in the CEECs and, thus, to prohibit counterfeiting and piracy at the source. In this sense, the Europe Agreements potentially give rise to at least partial trade liberalization in IP protected products. The question is whether it suffices to adopt similar levels of IP protection to be able to speak of trade liberalization of IP protected products also in the sense that IP protected products may freely move between the EC and the CEECs. To analyse this issue regard will be had specifically to whether, and to what extent, CEEC intellectual property based products have access to the EC market.

It would seem logical to assume that if an exclusive IP right may be obtained both in the EC and in the associated country, by virtue of the improvement of the latter's intellectual property legislation, then the IP protected product brought on one of those markets should be able to be freely imported into the other market. Nonetheless, the practice is different. All Europe Agreements contain a provision, which is largely modelled on Article 36 EC, explicitly providing for an exception to the free movement of goods between the EC and the associated country based *inter alia* on the protection of IP rights. It reads as follows:

---

[24] COM(95) 163 final, at pt 1.5.
[25] COM(95) 163 final, at pt 1.15.
[26] See COM(95) 163 final, at pt 1.9.

The Agreement shall not preclude prohibitions or restrictions on imports, exports or goods in transit justified on grounds of . . . the protection of intellectual, industrial and commercial property. . . . Such prohibitions or restrictions shall not, however, constitute a means of arbitrary discrimination or a disguised restriction on trade between the Parties. (Article 35 EA).

In essence this means that regardless of the legal protection granted in the export state, be it a member state of the EC or the associated country, an IP owner in the import state may invoke his exclusive right to prohibit the import or transit of IP protected products. It is an implicit reinforcement of the principle of territoriality inherent in all IP rights. The latter implies that the exclusive right both begins and ends at the national border of the state granting the legal protection. What happens outside those borders in principle does not affect the IP owner's exclusive right. He may legitimately prohibit the import of IP protected products which were brought on another market regardless of whether or not he enjoys parallel IP protection in the export state. It is also irrelevant whether or not the product was brought on that market by the IP owner, by a third person with his consent such as a licensee, or by a third person without his consent. Thus, the EA acknowledges that IP rights are, and continue to be, legitimate barriers to trade between the Contracting Parties. To put it differently, this provision clarifies that the free trade objective does not extend to products covered by IP rights. The following two examples of parallel importation from CEECs to the EC may illustrate the importance of this provision.

V.   PARALLEL IMPORTATION

A.   Counterfeit and pirated goods

It is clearly in the interest of any IP owner to invoke his exclusive right to prohibit the import of counterfeit or pirated goods. Those concepts refer to intellectual property based products which were made without the consent of the IP owner. It is interesting to note that it is irrelevant whether or not those products were legitimately marketed in the export state, for instance, in the absence of parallel IP protection. The only relevant criterion is whether or not the IP owner in the import state had consented to marketing those products. As such, the Polish garden gnomes in the example given before were labelled as counterfeit in the EC despite the fact that they might have been legitimately marketed under Polish law.[27]

The right of an IP owner to prevent the import of counterfeit or pirated products is not questioned at all. Any other approach would amount to emptying the exclusive right of its content in the import state. The above mentioned provision (Article 35 EA) will undoubtedly be very useful in this respect, although it will not be the only recourse IP owners in both

---

[27] See above, section I, p. 180.

the associated country and the EC have. It should be pointed out that the TRIPS Agreement specifically provides that specific border measures have to be adopted by the WTO Members against the import of counterfeit goods,[28] thus also by the associated country if it has not done so yet. The adoption by CEECs of border measures to prevent the import of counterfeit and pirated goods is also listed as a Stage II measure in the White Paper.[29] Considering that, at least initially, the EC point of view during the Uruguay Round negotiations on TRIPS was that priority should be given to an agreement on counterfeiting rather than to the elaboration of substantial norms of IP protection,[30] it is somewhat surprising that this was not listed as a Stage I measure in the White Paper.

As far as the EC is concerned, unilateral measures have been enacted to prohibit, at the external Community frontier, the release for free circulation, export or transit of goods which are suspected or established to be counterfeit or pirated. A first Council Regulation was already issued in 1986 specifically with regard to trade mark counterfeiting.[31] Subsequent to the conclusion of the TRIPS Agreement, a new Council Regulation was adopted in 1994 which extends the scope of these unilateral measures to include other types of IP rights.[32] Although at first sight these unilateral measures are aimed at restricting trade, they are nevertheless complementary to, rather than conflicting with, the content of the Europe Agreements and in particular the provision similar to Article 36 EC (Article 35 EA).

B. Parallel importation and parallel protection

The EA should, indirectly, render the unilateral EC border measures on counterfeit and piracy to a great extent redundant in the relations between the EC and the CEECs. The reason for this is that, as was mentioned above, the EA explicitly provide that the associated country will align its intellectual property legislation with that of the EC and its member states.[33] This implies that an IP owner in the EC should eventually also be able to obtain parallel IP protection in the associated country, so that he could then invoke his

[28] See Section 4 of the TRIPS Agreement. It should be noted that protection against counterfeiting was the main objective of the abortive Tokyo Round negotiations on intellectual property rights.
[29] See above, section IIIB, p. 184.
[30] See H. Paemen and A. Bensch, *Du GATT à l'OMC: La Communauté européenne dans l'Uruguay Round*, Leuven University Press, 1995, 88.
[31] Council Regulation No. 3842/86 of 1 December 1986, *OJ* 1986 L 357/1. It entered into force in 1988.
[32] Council Regulation (EC) No. 3295/94 of 22 December 1994, *OJ* 1994 L 341. In respect of this second regulation, a controversy had arisen concerning the competence to deal with this matter, namely, did it belong to the EC alone or was it shared with the member states. The Council agreed in principle with the proposals made by the Commission but objected to the legal basis proposed, i.e. Art. 113 EC. The regulation was eventually adopted on the basis of Art. 113 EC, as the Court held in Opinion 1/94, on the WTO Agreement, that this aspect of intellectual property rights comes within the exclusive commercial policy competence of the EC, see Opinion 1/94 of 15 November 1994, (1994) ECR I-5267.
[33] See above, section IIIA, pp. 182-3.

exclusive right in the associated country to eliminate counterfeiting and piracy at the source. If the IP owner may prohibit the manufacture and marketing of the IP protected product when this is done without his consent under CEEC law, then it is obvious that fewer products, if any at all, will effectively be labelled as counterfeit or pirated in the EC. In other words, the control will largely shift from the EC border to the CEEC territory.

But does this also imply that the provision in the EA, similar to Article 36 EC, (Article 35 EA) will become less important in practice? If an IP owner obtains parallel protection in both the EC and the CEECs, and this will increasingly be so, may IP protected products that have been marketed with his consent in the CEECs be freely imported into the EC?

It should be pointed out that an IP owner may indeed have an interest in preventing intra-brand competition from occurring. The apparent reason for this is that the price at which any given product may be sold is largely dependent on the demand/supply ratio in a given market as well as the need for publicity, manufacturing and transportation costs, etc. If, for instance, a video tape is sold at 10 ECU in the CEECs whereas it may be sold at 20 ECU in the EC, then it is logical that an economic actor will try to prevent price competition from occurring between his own products on the EC market. One way to do this is by invoking exclusive IP rights so as to protect the EC market even against the import of similar, or identical, products that have been brought on the CEEC market by the IP-owner or with his consent. However, such behaviour might not so much be inspired by the need to protect IP rights as by an anti-competitive impulse. Specifically in the case of parallel protection, it is apparent that the IP owner can fully enforce his exclusive right and, thus, get a return for his investment in research and development on both markets. By virtue of IP protection there seems to be no cogent reason why the principle of territoriality should not be put aside in case of parallel protection, in particular in view of the EA objective to create a free trade area. It would therefore seem to be logical that, if an IP owner has parallel exclusive IP rights in the CEECs and the EC, he should no longer be able to invoke his exclusive right in the EC to prohibit the import of an IP protected product which was marketed with his consent in the CEECs.

The problem is that, contrary to the unilateral EC border measures, the EA provision similar to Article 36 EC (Article 35 EA) does not distinguish between goods manufactured or marketed with or without the consent of the IP owner. It merely states by way of a general exception to the rule that IP protection is, and will continue to be, a legitimate barrier to trade. Since it contains no further qualification as to the circumstances in which it applies, this provision may, consequently, be invoked to justify the prohibition of parallel imports by any IP owner in spite of the free trade objective.

In practice, this implies that whereas by virtue of the EA Community industry potentially benefits from increased access to, and exclusivity on, the CEEC market for their intellectual property based products they may, nevertheless, foreclose the EC market to the (re-)importation of those products. This is a situation which is obviously not apt to remedy the CEEC trade deficit *vis-à-vis* the EC but, to the contrary, is likely to enhance the situation whereby the EC exports more manufactured products to CEECs than it imports.[34]

VI. PARALLEL IMPORTATION AND THE PRINCIPLE OF EXHAUSTION

A. Implications of the Europe Agreements

An explicit reference in the EA to the application of the principle of exhaustion in case of parallel IP protection could have remedied this situation.[35] The insertion of the principle of exhaustion would have implied that if the IP protected product was marketed in a Contracting Party with the consent of the IP owner, then he could no longer invoke his exclusive IP right to prevent the importation in the other Contracting Party in which he enjoys parallel IP protection. However, the EA does not mention the issue of exhaustion of IP rights at all.

It should also be emphasized in this respect that the TRIPS Agreement explicitly holds that for the purpose of dispute settlement, subject to the principles of national treatment and most-favoured-nation treatment,[36] nothing in the Agreement shall be used to address the issue of exhaustion of IP rights. Since this is the only provision in the TRIPS Agreement dealing with this issue, the WTO Members will not be obliged to introduce the principle of exhaustion of rights by virtue of the TRIPS Agreement either.[37] However, if they choose to introduce the principle of exhaustion then they will have to comply with the basic principles of national treatment and most-favoured-nation treatment.[38]

This implies on the one hand that there is, and will be, no legal obligation to introduce the principle of exhaustion in the trade relations between the EC and the CEECs. But on the other hand it also implies that nothing in the EA, or the TRIPS Agreement, prevents either party from effectively applying this principle.

---

[34] For instance for figures on the EC–Hungary trade balance, see *European Economy*, Supplement A, No. 7 and No. 8, of July and August 1994 respectively. On p. 11 of No. 8, it is stated that: 'After a temporary reversal in 1993, the share of the European Union in Hungarian trade started to grow again in 1994, reaching 44.1% of imports and 50.1% of exports'.

[35] See in this respect the arguments elaborated in I. Govaere, mentioned note 11.

[36] Arts 3 and 4 TRIPS Agreement respectively. It should be pointed out that, whereas under GATT the basic principles of national treatment and most-favoured-nation treatment normally relate to *products*, in the TRIPS Agreement it is stipulated that those principles refer to *nationals* similarly to the national treatment principle embodied in intellectual property conventions administered by WIPO.

[37] See Art. 6 TRIPS Agreement. On this issue, see also A.A. Yusuf and A. Moncayo Von Hase, op. cit.; I. Govaere, mentioned note 7.

[38] See also H. Ullrich, op. cit., 191.

B. Exhaustion in EC law

As far as the EC is concerned, the EC Court of Justice has, through interpretation of Article 36 EC, introduced the principle of exhaustion specifically in relation to trade between the member states.[39] This principle has, consequently, also been incorporated in EC harmonization measures concerning IP protection. Considering that the EA contain a provision (Article 35 EA) which is largely modelled on Article 36 EC, in theory nothing would seem to prevent the Court of Justice from applying the principle of exhaustion in the relation with the CEECs, through interpretation of that provision in a similar way to Article 36 EC. However, the Court's attempt to bring about trade liberalization in IP protected products is strictly linked to the internal market objective rather than being a goal in itself. This was made clear in *Polydor v Harlequin*, where the Court held that a similar wording to Article 36 EC, in a free trade agreement between the EC and a third country, does not imply that a similar interpretation should also be given to the relation between IP protection and the free movement of goods.[40] The main reason is that the objective of the EC Treaty, which is to establish a single market, is different from the objective of a free trade agreement. The Court thus refused to extend the principle of 'Community' exhaustion to any context other than intra-EC.[41]

The reluctance of the Court to transpose the principle of exhaustion to the extra-EC context by virtue of a similar interpretation to Article 36 EC may, most likely, be explained additionally by the fact that the Court had already ruled in the *Merck* case that the principle of Community exhaustion also applies in the absence of parallel IP protection, inasmuch as the IP owner had consented to putting the IP protected product on the market.[42] It is inconceivable that this far-reaching and much criticized rule would simply be transposed to a context other than intra-EC. It is apparent that otherwise, IP protection granted in the EC would potentially lose most of its meaning.

[39] Case 78/70, *Deutsche Grammophon Gesellschaft* (1971) ECR 487. On the issue of exhaustion of intellectual property rights in EC law, see I. Govaere, *The Use and Abuse of Intellectual Property Rights in E.C. Law*, Sweet & Maxwell, 1996, 72 et seq.

[40] Case 270/80, (1982) ECR 329. This case presented striking resemblances with the *Deutsche Grammophon* case, except for the fact that it concerned the parallel importation into the EC of IP protected products that had been marketed in Portugal, which at that time was not yet an EC member state.

[41] It should be noted that, at least at the moment, only the Agreement on the European Economic Area (EEA) explicitly provides for the extension of the principle of Community exhaustion to third countries, and this under the heading 'regional exhaustion', see *OJ* 1994 L 1. This seems to be consistent with the reasoning of the Court since the aim of the EEA is, precisely, to extend the internal market objective to the signatory EFTA countries.

[42] Case 187/80, *Merck v Stephar* (1981) ECR 2063. This was recently confirmed in the *Merck II* case (Joined Cases C-267/95 and C-268/95, *Merck & Co v Primecrown; Beecham Group v Europharm*, Judgment of 5 December 1996, not yet published). The Court did not follow the Opinion of Advocate-General Fennelly, who proposed to overturn the strongly contested *Merck I* ruling.

C. Exhaustion in CEEC law

The fact that, currently, the EC does not apply the principle of exhaustion in the trade relations with third countries, and it seems highly unlikely that it will do so in the near future, does not, in theory, prevent the CEECs from unilaterally introducing this principle. However, this would have certain far-reaching practical implications.

It should be emphasized that if the CEECs decided to apply the principle of exhaustion to parallel imports from the EC, for instance by simply taking over the relevant provisions in the EC intellectual property harmonization measures, this would not mean that the EC would equally have to do the same as concerns parallel imports from the CEECs. Since there is no formal reciprocity requirement it would, most likely, not be in the CEEC's interest unilaterally to apply the principle of exhaustion in its trade relations with the EC. Otherwise this would imply that, in certain circumstances, IP rights could no longer be invoked as trade barriers in the CEECs, whereas they could still be legitimately invoked as such in the EC. In other words, parallel imports would be permitted in the CEECs whereas they could still be prohibited in the EC. This would clearly not be favourable for the associated country's trade balance with the EC.

Therefore, in the absence of an explicit reference to exhaustion in the EA it does not seem to be in CEEC's best commercial interest to apply the principle of exhaustion unilaterally to IP protected products coming from the EC.

VII. CONCLUSION

By way of conclusion it could be said that the trade-related aspects of IP rights in the Europe Agreements have the potential to act, simultaneously, as a stimulus and as a limitation to parallel imports.

On the one hand, the improvement of the level of CEEC IP protection and its approximation to intellectual property legislation in the EC will undoubtedly incite EC industry to engage more actively in trade, and especially export trade, with the CEECs. It is obvious that the better their commercial interests are safeguarded, the more they will be willing to invest in lasting trade relations. The fact that their intellectual property will not readily fall in the public domain in the associated country, and they can react against copying, counterfeiting and piracy under CEEC law, is increasingly considered to be crucial in this respect.

On the other hand, it is probably even more important to note that this stimulus for EC industry to trade with the CEECs is not counterbalanced by opening up the EC market to IP protected products imported from the CEECs. It is explicitly specified, by way of a general exception to the rule, that IP protection may still be invoked as a legitimate barrier to trade between the EC and the associated country in spite of the free trade objective expressed in the EA. This implies, in practical terms, that according to the EA, an IP

191

owner may invoke his exclusive right to restrict the parallel importation of IP protected products from the CEECs to the EC and vice versa. Since the EA does not mention the issue of exhaustion of rights and the EC has not, at least as yet, extended this principle to an extra-EC context other than the EEA, the EC market may be foreclosed. This is regardless of whether or not the IP protected goods were marketed in the CEECs by the IP owner, with his consent, or by an unrelated third party. However, whether or not the same rule will also apply vice versa will depend on whether the CEECs unilaterally adopt the principle of international exhaustion in its trade relations with third countries, and specifically with the EC. But if it does, this will, most likely, only enhance the asymmetry in the flow of goods between the EC and the CEECs.

As a last point it should be emphasized that the EA merely provides basic rules which may, but do not necessarily have to, be invoked by IP owners. In the absence of the principle of exhaustion which would have limited their rights, it finally remains up to them to consider whether or not parallel importation is in their best commercial interest. It is therefore up to the economic actors in the market in each case to decide whether to invoke their exclusive IP rights in order to restrict trade between the EC and the CEECs. In so far as currently there are more EC IP owners than CEEC ones it is, to a large extent, the former who will decide on the effective application of the free trade objective also to IP protected products. However, to end on a positive note, it should be pointed out that this situation is likely to change in the future. The EA may be helpful in this respect for it contains a section on cooperation in science and technology which stipulates that special attention shall be devoted *inter alia* to:

> The development of an environment conducive to research and the application of new technologies and adequate protection of intellectual property results of research.[43]

This kind of cooperation should allow the CEEC economic actors, in the medium or long term, to obtain their proper share of IP rights not only in CEECs but also in the EC. Concurrently, they would also obtain an equitable part of control on the parallel importation of IP protected products between the EC and CEECs. However, until then it is not unthinkable that the trade-related aspects of IP rights as embodied in the EA will, in a first stage, favour the commercial interests of the EC in particular.

---

[43] Art. 74 EA.

C

Persons and Services

11

MOVEMENT OF PERSONS, ESTABLISHMENT AND SERVICES

Marise Cremona[1]

I. INTRODUCTION

The Europe Agreements with the CEECs contain provisions on movement of goods, workers, services and establishment and capital. Unlike the European Economic Area Agreement, however, these do not seek to mirror the equivalent four freedoms in the EC Treaty. There is no attempt to create a single internal market, or even an economic area, nor is there any unity of approach to the different economic sectors. In this, the Europe Agreements are more pragmatic than earlier Association Agreements; the EC–Turkey Agreement for example, set up an ambitious framework for free movement in 1963 which has yet to be realized. The provisions on persons, establishment and services have to be seen and assessed in the light of the purposes and objectives of the Agreements as a whole, and of subsequent initiatives by the European Council and the Commission.

A major objective of the Europe Agreements is integration: participation of the associated States in the process of European integration, the intention of the associated States to seek 'full integration in the political, economic and security order of a new Europe' (Preamble); and specifically, the integration of those States into the Community through 'new rules, policies and practices' (Article 1).

The Community was not willing to make a firm commitment to accession within the Europe Agreements themselves: accession is mentioned in the Preamble as being an objective specifically of the associated State rather than of all parties. However, the European Council at the Copenhagen Summit in June 1993 made a political commitment (confirmed at the Essen Summit

---

[1] Senior Fellow, Centre for Commercial Law Studies, Queen Mary and Westfield College, University of London.

in December 1994) to accession for those associated States desiring it, when the economic and political conditions are satisfied. These conditions include 'stability of institutions guaranteeing democracy, the rule of law, human rights and respect for protection of minorities, the existence of a functioning market economy as well as the capacity to cope with competitive pressure and market forces within the Union'.[2] Here the Council is following the Commission in its paper of June 1992, 'The Challenge of Enlargement',[3] as well as drawing logical conclusions from the fact that accession is now to the *European Union* and the TEU implicitly lays down a number of political conditions for membership. The Council also refers – for the first time – to the Union's capacity to absorb new members as a relevant factor.

The fulfilment of these conditions – especially the economic ones – is closely linked to the economic integration of the associated States into the Community and is clearly not merely a question of extending access to the Community market. A very striking aspect of the Association Agreements is the number of provisions dealing with the adaptation of the laws of the associated States to those of the EC, and this adaptation is not seen any longer (if it ever was) as merely an objective of the Association relationship, but as part of the necessary pre-accession process for the associated States. This process is taking place within the framework of the structured dialogue, first established at Copenhagen and put on a firmer footing at Essen. The structured dialogue, taking the form of joint ministerial and parliamentary meetings, covers not only the first (EC) pillar of the Union but also the second and third pillars.

The Commission, having produced a number of exploratory documents on the ways in which the Community and its member states may fulfil their obligations under the Association Agreements to assist in this process,[4] published a White Paper which is an attempt to outline (and prioritize) the different fields of Community legislation which need to be addressed by the associated States[5] (above, pp. 41–71). As the Commission points out, formal transposition of legislation is not enough, emphasis must also be placed on full implementation and enforcement. This reflects the emphasis within the Community itself in the context of the internal market programme.

In what follows, I will be considering both the Europe Agreement commitments and the White Paper strategy.

II. MOVEMENT OF PERSONS

A. Immigration and visa policy

No Community agreement grants rights of entry into the Community directly, except the European Economic Area Agreement (EEA Agreement),

---

[2] Conclusions of the Presidency, *Bull. EC*, 6-1993, 12.

[3] Europe and the Challenge of Enlargement, *Bull. EC*, Supplement 3/92.

[4] COM(94) 320 final; COM(94) 361 final.

[5] 'Preparation of the Associated Countries of Central and Eastern Europe for Integration into the Internal Market of the Union', COM(95) 163 final, 3 May 1995.

which extends rights of free movement generally to EEA nationals.[6] The External Frontiers Convention (which provides for common immigration controls at the external frontiers of the Union and which is not yet in force) does not apply to 'persons entitled under Community law' and these persons are defined as including those with rights of entry and residence under Community agreements 'identical with those enjoyed by citizens of the Union'. At present, therefore, this provision is limited to nationals of EEA States (Norway, Iceland, Liechtenstein).

In the Europe Agreements, the provisions on the movement of workers are rather limited. The heading to Title IV is 'Movement of Workers, Establishment, Supply of Services': in contrast with the EC Treaty itself, or the EEA Agreement, there is no mention of freedom of movement or rights of establishment. No rights of entry into the Community are given, the prerogatives of the member states in controlling immigration are maintained, and existing bilateral arrangements preserved.[7] Indeed, some of associated States are included in the list of third countries whose nationals require a visa when crossing the external frontiers of the member states.[8] The powers of the Association Council are limited to making recommendations (not decisions) for improving the movement of workers during the second stage of the Agreement.[9] The Europe Agreements do, however, contain more extensive provisions in relation to equality of treatment for those in legal employment, which will be considered below.

B. Residence rights and access to employment

Under the Europe Agreements, initial access to the labour market within the Community is left firmly within the hands of the member states, and there is no right to a work permit even for those who are legally resident: member states are merely to 'examine the possibility' of granting such permits.[10] There are no Association Council Decisions granting a continuing right to work (and reside) after periods of legal employment, as have been adopted under the Turkish Association Agreement. Nor is it clear that the Association Council is envisaged as being able to grant such rights: although the Agreements state that existing facilities for access to employment ought to be improved 'if possible', this is left in the hands of the member states.[11]

Rights of residence are not extended automatically to members of the family of an associated state worker legally employed within a member state; this will remain a matter for the individual member state (acting in accordance

---

[6] European Economic Area Agreement in force 1 January 1994, *OJ* 1994, L 1/1; in force for Liechtenstein from 1 May 1995, *OJ* 1995, L 86/58; L 140/30. See Arts 28–30 for free movement of persons.
[7] See for example EA Hungary *OJ* 1993, L 347, Art. 40.
[8] Regulation 2317/95, *OJ* 1995, L 234/1. The list in the Annex includes Bulgaria and Romania.
[9] EA Hungary, Art. 42.
[10] See for example EA Poland, Art. 41(3). There is no equivalent in EA Hungary.
[11] See for example EA Hungary, Art. 41.

with the provisions of any bilateral agreements). However, if they are legally resident, and for as long as the worker is legally employed, the worker's spouse and children *are* entitled to access to the labour market of the host member state.[12] An argument, based on *Kus*,[13] that this right to work carries with it a right of residence, is undermined by the qualification 'legally resident' (which will depend on the member state's own national law).

In line with the Association Agreements, the White Paper does not regard matters of immigration and access to the labour market, including rights of entry and residence and residence permits, to be within the scope of the 'progressive alignment' envisaged as part of the pre-accession phase. In this the White Paper programme departs markedly from the EEA model, which extends Article 48 EC and the legislation based on it, including Directive 68/ 360, to the EEA partners (Norway, Iceland and Liechtenstein).

C. Equality of treatment

The Europe Agreements contain a general equal treatment provision applicable to 'working conditions, remuneration or dismissal' for legally employed workers.[14] As a result of *Kziber*, *Yousfi* and *Krid*,[15] equal treatment provisions of Community agreements such as this are potentially highly significant. No cases have yet been decided on this provision, but it appears to satisfy the tests for direct effect, and there is no express provision for its implementation: it is therefore likely to be held to be directly effective, at least in terms of enforcement against state measures. Whether it would be enforceable against a private employer (in the same way as Articles 48 and 119 EC, for example) is perhaps more debatable.

The social security provisions in these Agreements, however, are much weaker. Article 38 of the EA Hungary, for example, contains no general equal treatment clause in relation to social security, only the three specific benefits found in the early Mediterranean Cooperation Agreements:

- provision for the aggregation of periods worked in different member states for the purpose of pensions and annuities in respect of, and for the purpose of medical care for the worker and family members;
- family allowances for members of the family legally resident in the State in which the worker is legally employed;
- transfer of benefits for old age, death, invalidity, industrial accident or occupational disease (excluding non-contributory benefits).

---

[12] See for example EA Hungary, Art. 37(1).

[13] Case C-237/91, *Kus* (1992) ECR I-6781.

[14] Art. 37 of the EA Hungary.

[15] Cases brought under the EC–Morocco and EC–Algeria Cooperation Agreements, giving direct effect to equal treatment provisions in relation to social security. Case C-18/90, *ONEM v Kziber* (1991) ECR 199; Case C-58/93, *Yousfi v Belgium* (1994) ECR I-1353; Case C-103/94 *Krid v CNAVTS* (1995) ECR I-719.

The term 'family members' is not defined but is likely to extend to the same members of the family who are granted access to the labour market where legally resident. These provisions are to be implemented by Association Council decision.[16] There is no doubt that the difference is the result of the Court's case law on the Cooperation Agreements referred to above and as a result these Articles are unlikely to be given direct effect.

For simplicity, I have referred here to the situation in terms of rights within the Community for workers of the associated States; in fact all these provisions are fully reciprocal and thus apply to Community nationals working in an associated State. It must be remembered, however, that the European Court's case law on direct effect is only applicable within the Community legal order.

Equality of treatment in relation to employment conditions and social rights, including acquired social security entitlements, is treated by the White Paper; it also extends to non-employment-related social rights such as access to education and health. The 'legal base' for the employment-related rights and social security provisions can be found in the provisions of the Association Agreements referred to above. In addition, 'protection of workers at the workplace' is listed among the areas of law to which the general approximation of laws provision in the Agreements applies.[17] The reference to education and health goes beyond the Agreements: the provision on education and training is concerned with assistance with the development of education and training in the associated States rather than with rights of access to training courses.[18]

Under the general heading of 'Social Policy and Action' the White Paper groups together legislation dealing with:

- Equal opportunities for men and women;
- Coordination of social security schemes;
- Health and safety at work;
- Labour law and working conditions.

In common with the strategy of the White Paper generally, these sections first set out the basis for and rationale of the legislation, the legal and organizational conditions necessary to operate the legislation, and then summarize very briefly the scope of the applicable Directives, before setting priorities for Stage I and Stage II of the approximation process. There is no space here to go into great detail in analysing the measures identified by the Commission as 'key measures'. A few points of interest only will be noted.

Equal opportunities. Article 119 EC is recognized as the foundation of equal treatment as a fundamental right in Community law, but although the scope of one of the priority directives (86/378/EEC on occupational schemes) is affected by the decision of the ECJ in *Barber*[19] on Article 119, the White

---

[16] Art. 39 EA Hungary; Art. 40 EA Romania.

[17] Arts 67 & 68 EA Hungary; Arts 69 & 70 EA Romania, which also includes an express reference to social security here. See also Art. 88 EA Hungary for a specific provision on social cooperation including health and safety of workers, development of the labour market and adaptation/modernization of social security systems.

[18] Art. 75 EA Hungary.

[19] Case C-262/88, *Barber* (1990) ECR I-1889.

Paper focuses on the Directives, without providing for the enactment of the fundamental principle itself. This illustrates a basic weakness in the White Paper approach: it concentrates on the secondary legislation without taking account of the fact that much of that legislation presupposes the existence of Treaty rules which are absent. There is no equivalent to Article 119 in the Association Agreements themselves.

Coordination of social security schemes. Here the main point to note is the emphasis on coordination rather than approximation or harmonization. The objectives are to ensure:

- that contributions only need to be paid in one State;
- equality of treatment for migrant workers in terms of obligations and benefits;
- retention of acquired rights after movement across frontiers;
- aggregation of periods of insurance and residence.

Extension of the existing social security Regulations to new States does not require substantive changes to the social security legislation in that State, but it does require time to negotiate the necessary technical amendments. This will continue a process already begun under the limited provisions in the Europe Agreements.

Health and safety at work. The protection of workers at the workplace is among the areas of law listed for approximation in the Association Agreements themselves, with cooperation including technical assistance, exchanges of experts and information, and training initiatives.[20] The White Paper highlights the need for an effective enforcement structure, including labour inspectorates and training for workers. As far as legislation is concerned, priority is given to the framework Directive 89/391/EEC.

Labour law and working conditions. Eight Directives are identified as forming the basis for the social dimension of the internal market. They include the transfer of undertakings Directive 77/187/EEC, the insolvency of employers Directive 80/987/EEC, and the Works Council Directive 94/45/EEC. The White Paper recognizes that these directives require a developed system of labour law in which to take effect, including agreed definitions of basic concepts such as 'employment relationship' and 'remuneration'.

III. ESTABLISHMENT

As far as the EC is concerned, the establishment and services provisions of the Association Agreements are particularly significant: EC companies are interested in investing in and selling services to the associated States and EC nationals in establishing or acquiring businesses there. The provisions

---

[20] Arts 69 and 88 EA Hungary.

therefore reflect the EC concern with reciprocity which is found in internal EC legislation on services. Similarly, the approach to company law in the White Paper prioritizes protection for creditors and investors (see below).

Establishment is defined in terms which echo Article 52 EC, to include not only pursuit of economic activity on a self-employed basis but also setting up and managing undertakings.[21] For companies themselves, the right of establishment includes setting up and managing subsidiaries, branches and agencies.[22] The definition of company is close to that found in Article 58 EC, with an interesting proviso designed to avoid the setting up of a shell company in one contracting party in order to gain access to the other: should the company have only its registered office within the Community (or an associated State) its operations must possess a 'real and continuous link' with the economy of one of the member states (or associated State).[23] In addition the parties' rights to apply 'any measure necessary to prevent the circumvention of its measures concerning third country access to its market' are preserved.[24] This provision may be relied on by the Community, for example, in order to enforce action taken under the reciprocity provisions in financial services legislation, such as the second banking Directive.[25]

The boundary between the right of establishment and movement of workers is made clear: 'self-employment and business undertakings by nationals shall not extend to seeking or taking employment in the labour market or confer a right of access to the labour market of another party'.[26] This contrasts with the position within internal EC legislation, under which the distinction between the employed and self-employed is increasingly unimportant, and reflects the restricted rights given to workers under the EAs.

The rights of establishment granted by the EAs are also more limited. In place of the generalized obligation to remove all restrictions found in Article 52 EC, the Agreements are based on the principle of equal – or national – treatment which has also formed the basis for the GATS (General Agreement on Trade in Services). The home country control principle, found in internal EC legislation in regulated sectors, relies on mutual recognition of regulatory systems in order to avoid a multiplicity of regulatory standards and duplication of regulation itself; there is no attempt to achieve the greater degree of economic integration represented by this principle in the EAs, or even to state it as an explicit goal. As far as the Community is concerned, this is signalled by the fact that the equal treatment principle is to be applied by 'each Member State', the comparison being with its own nationals.[27] There is no provision for – for example – the recognition of a licence granted by

---

[21] Art. 44(5) EA Hungary.
[22] Art. 44(5)(a)(ii) EA Hungary; c.f. Art. 52(i) EC.
[23] Art. 48(1) EA Hungary.
[24] Art. 48(4) EA Hungary.
[25] Directive 89/646, *OJ* 1989, L 386/1, Arts 8 and 9. See also Investment Services Directive 93/22, *OJ* 1993, L 141/27, Art. 7.
[26] Art. 44(5)(a)(i) EA Hungary.
[27] Art. 44(3) EA Hungary.

another member state to a national of an associated State. On the contrary, the EAs state that each Party may regulate those companies and persons on its territory, subject to the principle of non-discrimination.[28] In respect of financial services, the Parties may adopt non-discriminatory measures necessary for the conduct of monetary policy, on prudential grounds (to protect investors, policy holders or depositors) or to ensure the 'integrity and stability of the financial system'.[29] Even the non-discrimination obligation may give way if necessary for prudential reasons, in the case of financial services, or where justified by legal or technical differences between the Parties, in the case of branches or agencies of companies not incorporated in the State of establishment.[30]

Ultimately, the national treatment obligation will be fully reciprocal, but whereas the Community member states are to apply the principle straight away,[31] the associated States are given time to phase it in, with the details varying from Agreement to Agreement. Under the Hungary Agreement, for example, Community companies and nationals *already established* in the associated State are entitled to national treatment in respect of laws and regulations governing their operation.[32] The right to set up a new establishment on a national treatment basis will be introduced according to a timetable for different sectors, which varies under the different Agreements. Under the Hungary Agreement, there is a prohibition on new restrictions and an obligation to amend existing legislation within five years of the entry into force of the Agreement where it fails to grant equal treatment;[33] however, for financial services equal treatment need not be achieved until the end of the transitional period (ten years).[34] The process may be accelerated, or hitherto excluded sectors included, by decision of the Association Council; likewise the adaptation period may be extended.[35] In the White Paper the Commission comments in relation to financial services, that although the establishment of companies in the financial sector need not be achieved until the end of the transitional period, 'the Community strongly recommends to the CEECs to make such establishments possible as soon as possible because it would be very much to the benefit of the countries in question to benefit from the know how of such companies.'[36]

The derogations from the right of establishment are of two sorts. First, there are those which are equivalent to those found in the EC Treaty: the exclusion of activities connected with the exercise of official authority and

[28] Art. 45(1) EA Hungary.
[29] Art. 45(2) EA Hungary.
[30] Art. 47 EA Hungary.
[31] Art. 44(3) EA Hungary.
[32] Art. 44(1)(ii) EA Hungary.
[33] Art. 44(2) EA Hungary.
[34] Art. 44(1)(b) EA Hungary.
[35] Art. 44(6) EA Hungary, for example.
[36] White Paper, Annex, 287.

the limitations justified on grounds of public policy, public security or public health.[37] Second are those specific to the Agreements, notably the exclusion of certain sectors: air, maritime and inland waterways transport are excluded altogether.[38] The national treatment rules do not apply to certain sensitive activities: agriculture, forestry and fishing (not including processing products from these sectors or connected services); purchase and ownership of land and natural resources; the organization of gambling, lotteries and similar activities; and legal services (excluding legal advice).[39] In addition, the CEECs are given power to apply temporary, necessary and reasonable protective measures in the case of industries which are newly emerging, undergoing restructuring, or which face a drastic reduction in national market share; a 'grandfather clause' protects EC companies already established in the associated State concerned.[40] This provision is similar in intent and scope to the 'infant industry' clause in relation to trade in goods.

The general provision in the EAs on approximation of laws expressly identifies company law as one of the areas where approximation is required for economic integration. The White Paper expands on this rationale by expressly linking approximation of company law with freedom of establishment:

> with the constant growth in cross border dealings between companies, the existing disparities between national legislations are the main barriers to companies' freedom of establishment in the Community. . . . The objective of the approximation or harmonization of company law at Community level is to ensure an equivalent degree of protection of the interests of shareholders, employees, creditors and third parties throughout the Community.

However, the White Paper largely assumes – here as elsewhere – that the objective of approximation 'at Community level' is an adequate basis for approximation within the framework of pre-accession integration. The closest we get to an attempt to identify the specific aims of the CEECs in this area is the justification offered for inclusion of the First and Second company law Directives in Stage I, on the ground that they guarantee essential protection for creditors and investors wishing to contract with companies incorporated in the associated States. Company law approximation is thus helping to provide the legal infrastructure necessary in order to attract inward investment and indeed business into these States. For the CEECs, this is more important than (as well as a pre-condition of achieving) the goal of 'freedom of establishment'.

---

[37] Art. 53 EA Hungary.
[38] Art. 51 EA Hungary. The Association Council may make recommendations for improving the position in these sectors.
[39] Art. 44(7) and Annex XIIc EA Hungary.
[40] Art. 50 EA Hungary. The Association Council must be consulted; after the end of the transitional period, it will be required to authorize such measures.

IV. SERVICES

A. The principles

At the time when the EAs were negotiated, the GATS Agreement had not yet been finalized and the Community in particular was not prepared to enter into specific time-tabled commitments outside the GATS. As a result, the provisions on services in the Agreements are non-specific: a generalized undertaking on both sides 'to allow progressively the supply of services' where the service-provider is established in a different Party from the recipient (again there is no commitment to remove *all* restrictions on the supply of services).[41] In so far as services are liberalized, the Parties will allow temporary movement of service-providers and their representatives.

There is no timetable or deadline for the liberalization, there is not even any express reference to national treatment as the basis for liberalization; all is dependent on implementation measures to be taken by the Association Council. The existing provisions on both services and establishment are subject to the possibility of amendment by Association Council decision in order to ensure that the Parties receive treatment which matches GATS commitments.[42]

As a consequence of this rather limited, but flexible, treatment, the White Paper programme in relation to services is very important. It concentrates on certain sectors, notably financial services, on the grounds that a well-developed financial sector is one of the cornerstones in the transition to a market economy.[43] Again, there is no space here to undertake a detailed analysis. What follows are a number of comments on specific points.

The key theme is the importance not only of setting up a functioning financial system, but also of creating confidence and trust via prudential legislation and efficient supervision and control of those operating in the market. This theme is of course familiar as the pre-requisite for the principles of the single licence and home country control.

The White Paper observes that 'EU directives dealing with financial institutions have not been tailored to serve as a model for creating a financial sector'.[44] Whereas the Community was essentially co-ordinating already functioning financial sectors, the associated States are engaged in establishing their financial systems virtually *de novo*. This has practical implications. For example, the order of priorities may be different: some decisions which were left until relatively late within the Community (such as the minimum

---

[41] Art. 55(1) EA Hungary. A separate provision deals with transport services, containing specific commitments on maritime transport and providing for the negotiation of separate bilateral agreements on air and inland transport as well as further action by the Association Council in the light of progress made by the associated States in adapting their legislation to Community legislation in those sectors: Art. 56 EA Hungary.

[42] Art. 58(2) EA Hungary.

[43] See White Paper, Annex, 281.

[44] See White Paper, Annex, 284.

capital requirement for credit institutions, or the creation of deposit guarantee schemes) need to be adopted as a priority by the associated States. More importantly, the level of complexity of the Community rules may not be appropriate for the needs of (some of) the associated States at this stage. The White Paper recognizes this but only to some extent: for example, credit risk for banks (the solvency ratio directive) is put into Stage I, whereas market risk (the capital adequacy directive) is left to Stage II.

In the EC Treaty, the liberalization of banking and insurance services is made conditional on the liberalization of capital movements, now achieved (Article 61(2) EC). The EAs envisage that by the end of the fifth year from their entry into force – the same time scale envisaged for the rights of establishment for Community companies in the financial services sector – the Association Council should examine ways to ensure the full application of Community rules on movement of capital. However no explicit link or condition is imposed either in the Agreements or in the White Paper.

B. Seconded workers

In spite of the general absence of provisions on rights of entry and residence for natural persons in the EAs, one category of national is granted such rights, albeit in a dependent capacity as employees. Companies and nationals of the Parties exercising their rights of establishment or providing services, are entitled to employ 'key personnel', including senior management and those with specialized knowledge, qualifications and skills.[45] This provision, appearing for the first time in the Europe Agreements, recalls the decisions of the European Court of Justice in *Rush Portuguesa Lda v Office Nationale d'Immigration*[46] and *Vander Elst*.[47]

What should be the applicable law governing the terms and conditions of employment for such seconded employees? This may be as important as the right to residence and work permits, and exercised Community legislators in an internal context with the directive on seconded (or 'posted') workers.[48] In *Rush Portuguesa*, the Court reassured the French Government that 'Community law does not preclude member states from extending their legislation or collective labour agreements . . . to any person who is employed, even

---

[45] Arts 52 and 55(2) EA Hungary.
[46] Case C-113/89 (1990) ECR I-1417; *CMLR* (1991), 818.
[47] Case C-43/93 (1994) ECR I-3803.
[48] Directive 96/71 *OJ* 1997 L 18/1 on 'the posting of workers in the framework of the provision of services' (COM(93) 225, *OJ* 1993, C 187/5). Employers of seconded workers are to ensure that 'a nucleus of mandatory rules for minimum protection', including maximum working hours, minimum pay, health, safety and equal treatment, conform to mandatory standards applicable to workers in the host State. The Preamble expressly states that 'national laws relating to the entry, residence and access to employment of third-country workers' are not prejudiced: the Directive is solely concerned with terms and conditions of employment. Nevertheless, as long as the employer undertaking to provide the services is established in a member state, the nationality of the workers thus protected is immaterial.

temporarily, within their territory, no matter in which country the employer is established'.[49] This point is reiterated in the EAs:

> nothing in this Agreement shall prevent the Parties from applying their laws and regulations regarding entry and stay, work, labour conditions and establishment of natural persons, and supply or services. . . .'[50]

However, this does not leave the member states (for example) free to exempt seconded workers from these national conditions, which may for example include minimum wages; it is subject to the general obligation of equality of treatment. The employment must be 'in accordance with the legislation in force in the host country of establishment'.[51] In the absence of such a Community-based obligation, the member states are currently free to maintain their own rules as to the applicable law governing such employment relationships (*Sloman Neptun*[52]), acting within the context of the Rome Convention 1980 which is now in force. Although the Rome Convention is only open to ratification by member states, the White Paper points out that other States may, by adopting equivalent rules, bring their private international law relating to contractual obligations *de facto* within the Convention.

V. MUTUAL RECOGNITION OF QUALIFICATIONS

The EAs provide for the Association Council to take measures for the mutual recognition of qualifications in relation to regulated professions.[53] The White Paper picks up this objective and analyses existing Community law in this area in some detail. The measures covered include not only the recognition of qualifications themselves, but also recognition of proof of good repute, sound financial standing, professional liability insurance, membership of professional organizations and compliance with codes of conduct. The essential elements of the role of a professional organization are outlined.

The White Paper stresses that the Community system is based on mutual trust and therefore requires adequate structures to ensure and enforce compliance with training requirements and professional and ethical obligations within regulated professions. The approach adopted is highly incremental and rather cautious; the objective of extending mutual recognition to the associated States is not to take place until Stage III, being preceded by a process of trust-building, technical assistance and coordination of training requirements in some sectors.

Stage I is based on the two general system Directives, 89/48/EEC and 92/51/EEC, since they do not require coordination of training, and the White Paper stresses the need for technical assistance to enable the associated States

---

[49] Case C-113/89, at para. 18.
[50] Art. 58(1) EA Hungary.
[51] Art. 52(1) EA Hungary. Non-discrimination would also be required by Art. 37.
[52] Joined Cases C-72/91 and C-73/91, *Sloman Neptun* (1993) ECR I-887.
[53] For example Art. 46 EA Hungary.

to set up the necessary structures to ensure compliance and enforcement. Attendance as observers at meetings of the coordination groups will help to build up mutual trust and knowledge between different national authorities.

Stage II will focus on the sectoral directives (concerning doctors, nurses, dentists, veterinary surgeons, architects etc.), and in particular on compliance with the minimum training requirements set out in the directives. During Stage II, mutual recognition in specific sectors would be introduced, the general system directives would apply, and the lawyers services Directive 77/249/EEC would also be included.

VI. CONCLUSIONS

It is misleading to regard the White Paper either as having somehow replaced the obligations and agenda set by the Europe Agreements, or as simply a detailed methodology for achieving the objectives of the Agreements. First, because the Agreements are binding bilateral contracts, whereas the White Paper is a unilateral policy document which does not alter this contractual relationship.[54] Secondly, because the White Paper only covers certain ('Internal Market') aspects of the Europe Agreements and even in those areas it is – intentionally – schematic in its approach. And thirdly, because the Europe Agreements are concerned with two connected aspects of integration: market access and approximation; the White Paper deals expressly only with the second of these, although it is recognized that in some cases approximation is a condition of effective market access.

As the Commission acknowledges, the selection and prioritization of measures in the White Paper has been based not on the economic costs or benefits of their adoption, but in terms of the logical structure or organization of the sector. Priority is given to measures which provide for an overall framework, which address fundamental principles or provide basic procedures, or which are in other ways a precondition for the effective operation of the internal market in that sector.

The prioritization exercise however only operates *within* the subdivisions made in the Paper itself; no attempt is made to set priorities *between* these – between technical standards and recognition of qualifications, for example. These choices are left to the associated States, who presumably will here be guided by cost/benefit considerations.

Perhaps understandably in view of the precedents – including not only the Internal Market programme itself but also the EEA model – as well as the nature of the exercise, the emphasis of the White Paper is on 'Community law' as represented by secondary legislation. A few references are made to crucial decisions of the European Court of Justice and to key Articles of the EC Treaty such as Articles 30 and 119 but some key issues are not addressed.

---

[54] White Paper of 3 May 1995, COM(95) 163 final, at para. 1.9.

First, unlike the EEA Agreement, the Europe Agreements do not contain an equivalent to every substantive 'internal market' EC Treaty provision. Some are there in principle, even if the wording differs (such as equality of treatment in working conditions, or the basic principles of competition policy); others are not (such as Article 119). An approach to approximation that relies merely on secondary legislation is likely to result in an oddly incomplete picture, especially when one considers that in many cases, secondary legislation has not been necessary in the internal Community context precisely because of the rights created by the Treaty provisions themselves.

Secondly, there is no discussion of the role to be played by the decisions of the European Court of Justice within the legal systems of the Associated States during this pre-accession phase. Again unlike the EEA (or the more recent EC–Turkey Customs Union Agreement) there is no provision in the Europe Agreements providing for the decisions of the ECJ to be taken into account. Any effect will therefore have to be informal. However, judges (and legislatures) in the Associated States will need at least to address themselves to the question of the extent to which they should take account of judicial interpretation of the secondary legislation to which they are approximating.

Both these points are in fact illustrations of a more fundamental issue. Running through the White Paper is an often very lucid exposition of the rationale for the Community's internal market legislation. But the rationale is – nearly always – defined in terms of the 'internal logic' of the Internal Market itself. One result of this is that – again – the secondary legislation presents an incomplete picture, being inevitably designed to deal with specific barriers to market integration and pre-supposing the existence of complex systems within which to operate. In participating in this pre-accession integration process, the associated States are not of course driven by precisely the same objectives. The financial services sector provides a good example of this, and some attention is paid to the question in the section dealing with banks and investment services; in contrast, the section on insurance analyses insurance services purely in terms of the internal market. 'Integration into the internal market' is the title of the White Paper: however the perspective is very much that of *within* the internal market.

12

FREE MOVEMENT OF PERSONS AND THE ISSUE OF MIGRATION IN EU–CEECS RELATIONS: SCHENGEN AS AN EXAMPLE?

Kris Pollet[1]

I. INTRODUCTION

The Europe Agreements (EAs) concluded with the Central and Eastern European Countries (CEECs) are characterized by limited regulation concerning free movement of persons. As is widely known, provisions on movement of workers are essentially confined to the application of the principle of non-discrimination on grounds of nationality as regards working conditions, remuneration or dismissal of legally employed workers in the territories of the contracting parties.[2] Nevertheless, the EAs state that the final objective of the associated countries is membership of the European Union (EU) and since the 1993 Copenhagen Summit the EU officially shares this ambition.[3] Hence it is obvious that sooner or later this issue should be dealt with in the relations between the EU and the associated countries. After all, free movement of persons is one of the four freedoms to be ensured within the Internal Market, according to Article 7A of the Treaty on European Union (TEU). If the CEECs are to prepare for accession there is no reason why this subject should be excluded. However, even within the EU itself free movement of persons has not yet been fully achieved.

An important initiative in this regard is the Schengen process. The Agreement between the Governments of the States of the Benelux Economic Union, the Federal Republic of Germany and the French Republic on the

---

[1] Research Assistant, Europees Instituut, Universiteit Gent. This contribution was prepared within the framework of a 'FKFO-project'.

[2] See, for instance, Art. 37(1) of the EA with Hungary. See generally the contribution by M. Cremona in this volume, above, p. 195.

[3] The Council stated in Copenhagen that 'the associated countries that wish to become full members of the Union will be admitted as soon as they satisfy the requisite political and economic conditions'. See *Bull. EC*, 6-1993, point I.1.

gradual abolition of controls at the common frontiers of 1985 (hereinafter the 1985 Schengen Agreement) and the Schengen Convention of 19 June 1990 applying the 1985 Schengen Agreement (hereinafter the Implementing Convention)[4] aim precisely at achieving the objective of free movement of persons. Both Agreements will be analysed here in view of the exemplary function they could have for the Central and Eastern European region regarding free movement of persons and migration. A pivotal question to be answered in this respect is whether these countries can participate in the Schengen cooperation and how this participation can be realized.

Therefore, it is first necessary to examine the provisions in the Implementing Convention which could be of particular importance for their participation.[5] It should be stressed that the Schengen Agreements also contain provisions on a wide range of issues other than, although closely related to, movement of persons, such as police and security, the Schengen Information System (SIS), the fight against narcotic drugs and drug-trafficking, etc. It would go far beyond the scope of the present contribution to examine these provisions in detail.

Subsequently, the position of the Central and Eastern European region will be taken into consideration.[6] Here, the feasibility of the CEECs' participation in the Schengen cooperation will be analysed in the light of their, albeit limited, involvement in the Schengen process so far, notably the agreement on readmission of persons in an irregular position between the Schengen contracting parties and Poland.[7] Finally, some remarks will be made on cooperation in the field of justice and home affairs with the associated countries of Central and Eastern Europe.[8]

II. THE SCHENGEN FRAMEWORK: AN INTRODUCTION

A. General remarks

The very start of what has become known as the Schengen process was on 14 June 1985, when five member states of the European Community, namely the Benelux countries, France and Germany, signed the Schengen Agreement. This Agreement in turn grew out of the earlier 1984 Saarbrücken Agreement

---

[4] To date there is no official English version of the two texts. An unofficial translation in English is published in H.G. Schermers (ed.), *Free Movement of Persons in Europe. Legal Problems and Experiences*, The Hague, T.M.C. Asser Instituut, 1993, 547–604. For an official French version of the Implementing Convention, see *Convention d'application de l'Accord de Schengen du 14 juin 1985 entre les Gouvernements des Etats de l'Union économique Benelux, de la République fédérale d'Allemagne et de la République française, relatif à la suppression graduelle des contrôles aux frontières communes, Moniteur Belge*, 15 Oct. 1993, 22648.
[5] See below, section II.
[6] See below, sections III and IV, p. 224 and p. 230.
[7] *Accord relatif à la réadmission des personnes en situation irrégulière, signé à Bruxelles le 29 mars 1991, Tractatenblad* (1991), Nr. 65. See below, section III.
[8] See below, section V, p. 231.

between France and Germany, which aimed at abolishing controls at their common borders. The purpose of this agreement was twofold: to make substantial progress towards the achievement of the so-called 'citizens' Europe' on a limited scale and, at the same time, to set an example for the European integration process. Soon the Benelux countries showed interest in joining France and Germany. The exploratory talks finally resulted in the signing of the Schengen Agreement. Since then, the other member states of the European Union, except the UK, Ireland, Denmark, Sweden and Finland joined the Schengen contracting parties.[9] One of the reasons why the latter States preferred not to become Schengen member states is that they hold different views on how far free movement of persons should go. It is well known that the UK, for instance, has a certain distrust of the way some Schengen contracting parties carry out immigration controls. The difference in policies on narcotic drugs forms another impediment for these States to join the Schengen process.[10]

The 1985 Agreement could be described as a framework for cooperation. Indeed, the five originating countries agreed on a number of short-term and long-term measures which had to be implemented, as the Agreement expressly states, before 1 January 1990.[11] The deadline turned out to be unrealistic because of the scope of the measures to be taken. The measures which aimed at relaxing police and customs controls on persons and goods at the internal borders caused few problems and could be dealt with in the short term. The long-term and compensatory measures were, on the other hand, not so easy to implement.[12] Compensatory measures were deemed necessary because of the ambitious goals of the contracting parties. Indeed, the abolition of internal border controls does not mean that all controls are necessarily eliminated. Rather, it results in the transfer of controls from the internal borders to the external borders. The compensatory measures envisaged concern *inter alia* particularly sensitive areas such as the prevention of illegal immigration into the Schengen territory, the improvement of international cooperation at the level of the police and the judiciary, the harmonization of visa and immigration policies and of legislation on the control of illicit traffic in narcotic drugs and firearms, the transfer of controls on the transport of goods from the borders to the interior of the Schengen territory.

It is important to stress that, although only member states of the Community participate, the whole Schengen process was from the beginning, and

---

[9] Italy became a Schengen Contracting Party in 1990, Spain and Portugal signed in 1991 and Greece in 1992. Finally, Austria signed the Schengen Implementing Convention on 28 April 1995, see *Benelux Newsletter*, May 1995, 3.

[10] For an analysis of the reasons for non-accession of the UK to the Schengen Convention see D. O'Keeffe, 'Non-Accession to the Schengen Convention: The Cases of the United Kingdom and Ireland', in Pauly (ed.), *Schengen en panne*, Maastricht, European Institute of Public Administration, 1994, 145–54.

[11] Art. 30 of the 1985 Schengen Agreement.

[12] H. Blanc, 'Schengen: Le Chemin de la libre circulation en Europe', *RMC* (1991), 722–6, at p. 722.

is still now, developing outside the Community framework. 'Schengen' is a purely intergovernmental initiative, without any significant participation of the Community institutions. It was only after a while that an EC Commission representative was invited to attend the meetings of the Schengen Central Negotiating Group and of the Ministers and Under-Secretaries of State.[13] Moreover, the Commission representative joined these meetings only as an observer, without having the possibility of participating in the discussions or influencing the orientation of the debates. The Commission nonetheless never raised any objections against its observer status.[14] This is a remarkable fact considering that the Schengen contracting parties' aim is also one of the main objectives of the 1985 Commission White Paper on the Completion of the Internal Market, namely the free movement of persons.[15]

The negotiations directed at implementing the objectives of the 1985 Schengen Agreement resulted in the conclusion of a comprehensive Implementing Convention signed, again in Schengen, on 19 June 1990. The name 'Implementing Convention' accurately reflects its content, i.e. provisions implementing the objectives and measures mentioned in the 1985 Agreement. The main part of this study will deal with Title II of the Implementing Convention which addresses the abolition of checks at internal borders and the movement of persons.

B. Entry of aliens into the Schengen territory

a. General remarks

Chapter I of Title II of the Implementing Convention distinguishes between crossing internal frontiers and crossing external borders. The ultimate aim is to do away with the last impediments for achieving the free crossing of *internal frontiers*. According to Article 2, internal borders may be crossed at any point without any checks on persons being carried out. However, an exception can be made when public policy or national security so require. In that case, a contracting party may decide that for a limited period of time national border checks will be reinstalled (Article 2(2)) and the other contracting parties should be informed about the measures taken.

---

[13] The Central Negotiating Group is composed of representatives of the Ministries of Foreign affairs of the Schengen States. This Group prepares the decisions to be taken by the ministers, see Ch. Elsen, 'Les strucures administratives de Schengen', in Pauly (ed.), *Les accords de Schengen: Abolition des frontières intérieures ou menace pour les libertés publiques?*, Maastricht, European Institute of Public Administration, 1993, 19–26, at p. 21.

[14] The Commission considers the political will to speed up the removal of controls throughout the Community, demonstrated by some members of the Community in the Schengen Agreement, to be a wholly positive development, see COM(88) 640 final, 13.

[15] According to the European Parliament the Schengen Implementing Convention 'has primarily been used to hide the total lack of political will on the part of the Council and the Commission to institute full freedom of movements for persons'. See European Parliament, *Resolution on the Schengen Agreement and Political Asylum, OJ* 1995, C 109/169.

As regards the crossing of external borders, attention should be drawn first to the definition of 'alien' in the Implementing Convention, as this is an important concept throughout the entire Convention and especially in the section discussed here. The Implementing Convention defines in its first title the concepts used in the following provisions. An alien is defined as 'any person other than a national of a member state of the European Communities', while the term 'third State', however, 'shall mean any State other than the Contracting parties'. As a consequence, the term 'third country national' could theoretically refer to nationals of one of the member states that do not yet belong to the Schengen group. Thus, while a distinction is made between Schengen contracting parties and other member states of the European Union, no similar distinction is made between Schengen contracting party nationals and nationals of a EU member state which has not signed the Schengen Convention. The reason is to be found in the already mentioned parallel between the Schengen initiative and the free movement of persons objective within the Community. The simple fact that all the Schengen contracting parties are EU member states and the fact that the Schengen initiative partly pursues the same goals as the EC Internal Market programme could possibly create problems of compatibility with relevant Community rules. The definition of alien was inserted in order to avoid those conflicts. In particular, the principle of non-discrimination between EU nationals was at stake. By inserting the alien definition in the Implementing Convention, non-discriminatory treatment of all EU-nationals, whether they are Schengen State nationals or not, is assured.

b. Short visits

According to Article 5, contracting parties may grant entry into their territories for visits not exceeding three months to aliens who fulfil the following conditions: being in the possession of a valid document or documents and a valid visa if so required, having sufficient means of support, not being reported as a person not to be permitted entry and not being considered as a person to be a threat to public order, national security or the international relations of any of the contracting parties.[16] The expression 'may be granted', is of particular importance here. The contracting parties have indeed the possibility of granting entry to the alien who fulfils all the conditions of Article 5, but are by no means obliged to do so. Moreover, the conditions mentioned in Article 5 are in fact minimum standards, so contracting parties can always decide to impose other or stricter conditions for entry into their territories. In the words of Steenbergen 'contracting parties will have the competence to still adopt an admission policy with regard to aliens who fulfil all the treaty conditions'.[17]

[16] Long visits (exceeding three months) remain within the competence of the member states.
[17] J. Steenbergen, 'Schengen and the Movement of Persons', in Meijers et al., *Schengen. Internationalization of Central Chapters of the Law on Aliens, Refugees, Security and the Police*, W.E.J. Tjeenk Willink-Kluwer Law and Taxation Publishers, 1991, 57–73, at p. 64.

On the other hand, the contracting parties have the obligation to refuse entry to any alien who does not fulfil all the conditions mentioned above.[18] Moreover, the conditions must be fulfilled regarding each Schengen contracting party. As a consequence, the controlling State becomes the watchdog for all the Schengen States, because it is obliged to examine, for instance, the threat to public order, national security or international relations in each Schengen State individually.[19] If the alien at the Schengen border is considered a threat in one of the Schengen contracting parties, he no longer fulfils the conditions of Article 5. Therefore, the examining State must refuse entry. Thus, in practice the most restrictive standard applied by one of the contracting parties becomes the common standard. However, an exception to this obligation to refuse entry can be made according to Article 5(2). In case a Contracting Party considers it necessary to derogate from Article 5(1) on humanitarian grounds or in the national interest or because of international obligations, entry may be granted. But in this case permission to enter the territory will be restricted to the territory of the contracting party concerned.

It is striking that the common approach of the Schengen States towards admitting or refusing an alien is only formulated in a negative way. In fact, if one of the contracting parties raises an objection to the entry of an alien, the refusal must be taken into account by all the other contracting parties. Should, on the contrary, a State decide to derogate from the obligation to refuse entry on humanitarian grounds, the others are not obliged to share that opinion. The derogation is restricted to the territory of the member state concerned.

c. Visa policy

Before analysing the relevant provisions in the Implementing Convention, it should be noted that the entry into force of the Treaty on European Union, subsequent to the signature of the Implementing Convention, created new perspectives for developing a visa policy at EU level. Moreover, the first steps in this direction have already been taken by the Commission and the Council. As it is obvious that these efforts interfere with the Schengen initiative, they will be examined briefly in section IIBc(2).

1. Visa policy in the Implementing Convention

Visas are dealt with in Chapter 3 of Title II of the Implementing Convention. This chapter contains provisions on visas for long visits and visas for short visits. As regards the latter, the contracting parties will try to harmonize their individual policies by common agreement.[20] Some aspects have already been harmonized; a uniform Schengen visa has been introduced which is

---

[18] Art. 5(2) of the Implementing Convention.

[19] H. Verschueren, 'Het vrije verkeer van personen in de Schengen-Verdragen', in C. Fijnaut, J. Stuyck, P. Wytinck (eds), *Schengen: Proeftuin van de Europese Gemeenschap?*, Antwerpen, Kluwer Rechtswetenschappen, 1992, 13–54, at p. 23.

[20] Art. 9 of the Implementing Convention.

valid for the entire territory of the contracting parties.[21] Consequently, only one visa is needed for the alien wishing to travel throughout the Schengen territory, and this uniform visa is sufficient to cross the internal borders of the Schengen territory, once the external border is crossed.[22] Nevertheless, a visa will be issued only if the alien fulfils the rather severe conditions of Article 5.[23] This means that the entry conditions of Article 5(1) will be controlled when issuing the visa *and* when entering the Schengen territory.

Furthermore, some gaps remain in the visa arrangements. The Schengen system sets out three lists of countries regarding the issuing of visas. First, the Schengen contracting parties agreed on a list of third countries, whose nationals are subject to visa requirements common to all the contracting parties (the so-called negative list).[24] Secondly, there is a list of countries whose nationals do not need a visa to enter the Schengen territory (the so-called positive list). A third list contains those countries on which the Schengen contracting parties could not reach an agreement as to visa requirements (the so-called grey list).[25] Some Schengen States do require a visa from nationals of those countries, others have abolished visa requirements for them. This system clearly has consequences for the principle of free movement within the Schengen territory.

A contracting party still has the possibility to derogate from these provisions and issue a territorially restricted visa. This derogation applies where a contracting party would like to issue a visa to an alien who does not fulfil all the conditions of entry laid down in Article 5. In that case the derogation possibilities of Article 5(2) can be applied.

An important role in visa issues is also reserved for the Schengen Executive Committee, an intergovernmental body which was set up by the Convention in order to guarantee its correct implementation. Each of the contracting parties is represented in the Committee by the Minister responsible for the execution of the Implementing Convention. As regards visas, this Committee is responsible for adopting common rules for the examination of applications for visa, ensuring their correct implementation and adapting them to new situations and circumstances.[26] It also specifies the cases in which the issue of a visa shall be subject to consultation with the central authority of the contracting party to which application is made and, where appropriate, the central authorities of other contracting parties. However, it is the State of destination which issues the visa, except when the State of destination

---

[21] This has been done in execution of Art. 10(1) of the Implementing Convention.

[22] W. De Lobkowicz and X. Denoel, 'Vers une politique commune vis-à-vis des ressortissants d'Etats tiers?', *Revue de la Faculté De Droit De Liège/Actualités Du Droit*, (1994), 393–428, at p. 413.

[23] Art. 15 of the Implementing Convention.

[24] J.-Y. Carlier, 'L'Europe et les ressortissants des Etats tiers: de la coopération intergouvernementale vers le droit communautaire', *Ann. Dr.* (1993), 207–19, at p. 214.

[25] J. Benyon, L. Turnbull, A. Willis, R. Woodward and A. Beck, *Police Cooperation in Europe: An Investigation*, Leicester, Centre for the Study of Public Order, 1994, 121–85, at p. 142.

[26] A so-called Common Visa instruction was adopted by the Schengen Executive Committee at its meeting in Paris on 14 December 1993, see *Tractatenblad* (1993), Nr. 39.

cannot be determined.[27] In that case, the contracting party of first entry is the competent authority.[28]

No common arrangement is provided for visas for visits exceeding three months; such visas continue to be national visas. The holder of such a visa is not granted full freedom of circulation, as the validity is restricted to the territory of the Contracting Party of destination.

2. Initiatives at EU level

As mentioned above, efforts on this issue have recently been made at EU level. It is beyond the scope of the present contribution to examine these thoroughly, but a short overview seems useful here. Since the beginning of EC integration, visa issues and even the entire immigration question were deemed to belong to the exclusive competence of the member states. However, when the Commission presented its White Paper on the Completion of the Internal Market in 1985, it became clear that sooner or later an initiative would have to be taken at Community level. Free movement of persons in an Internal Market without internal frontiers could not exclusively be reserved to EC citizens, simply because otherwise frontier controls would have to be maintained after all. If not how could one differentiate between EC nationals and non-EC nationals?[29] It was equally beyond doubt that the Community would take the Schengen philosophy as a guideline for the completion of the Internal Market: the transfer of controls from the internal borders to the external borders seemed to be the best solution. This necessitated *inter alia* a common visa policy. It took some time, in fact until the Maastricht Treaty, before substantial progress was made concerning visa policy. According to the new Article 100C of the EC Treaty, '[t]he Council, acting unanimously on a proposal from the Commission and after consulting the European Parliament, shall determine the third countries whose nationals must be in possession of a visa when crossing the external borders of the Member States' (Article 100C(1)). The Council shall also 'adopt measures relating to a uniform format for visas' (Article 100C(3)).

Shortly after the entry into force of the TEU, the Commission presented an important communication in which two proposals were made. One concerned a proposal for a regulation determining the third countries whose nationals must be in the possession of a visa when crossing the external borders of the member states. The second proposal, complementary to the first one, concerns a decision establishing the Convention on the crossing of the external frontiers of the member states.[30] While the regulation has already

---

[27] P. Stangos, 'Les ressortissants d'Etats tiers au sein de l'ordre juridique communautaire', *CDE* (1992), 306–47, at p. 334.

[28] A similar arrangement governs the chapter on the examination of asylum applications. For more details see below, p. 218.

[29] C.D. De Jong, 'Cooperation in the Field of Aliens Law. The Granting of Visas, Passports and Asylum and Refugee Status' in Schermers (ed.), above, note 4, 183–98, at p. 194.

[30] Both proposals are published in *OJ* 1994, C 11. The explanatory memorandum of the proposals is laid down in COM(93) 684 final.

been adopted by the Council,[31] the decision establishing the external borders Convention is still pending. Based on the draft External Borders Convention agreed upon by the EC Immigration Ministers in the Ad Hoc Group on Immigration[32] in 1990, a Council decision remains blocked by the dispute between the UK and Spain on the status of Gibraltar.[33]

Council regulation 2317/95 of 25 September 1995 establishes a list of countries whose nationals require a visa when crossing the external borders of the member states. The objective of this regulation is very limited. Only a negative list of countries has been established. Although the Commission had stated in its proposal that Article 100C also implied a competence for drawing up a positive list,[34] the Council rejected this point of view and simply deleted the reference to a positive list. Moreover, only visas issued for a three-month period or for transit through a member state's territory are covered by the regulation. On the other hand, transit through the international zones of airports and transfer between airports in a member state are not within the scope of the regulation.[35] According to the Preamble of the regulation, these and other aspects of the harmonization of visa policy, including the conditions for the issue of visas, are matters to be determined under Title VI of the TEU. As a result, visa policy is now being dealt with at three different levels: the national level (visas valid for more than three months); the intergovernmental level (Schengen); and the EU level (both the first and the third pillar). This dispersion of competences makes a harmonized visa policy within the EU illusory.

It is striking in this respect that Article 2 of the Commission proposal was not included in the final Council text. This provision stated that 'A Member State shall not be entitled to require a visa of a person who seeks to cross its external frontiers and who holds a visa issued by another Member State where that visa is valid throughout the Community'. The Commission considered this provision as the cornerstone of the proposal. It would not only have linked the visa regulation with accompanying measures such as the External Borders Convention,[36] but also with the concept of the Internal Market itself. By inserting this Article in the proposal, the Commission made

---

[31] *OJ* 1995, L 234/1.

[32] The Ad Hoc Group on Immigration was set up, at the UK's initiative, in October 1986. It comprises the Interior Ministers of the member states and concentrates in particular on immigration, asylum and related issues. The Group operates outside the Community framework and produces draft conventions and resolutions at intergovernmental level. Nevertheless it has a permanent secretariat based at the Council of Ministers and the Commission participates in its meetings as a full member.

[33] K. Hailbronner, 'Visa Regulations and Third-Country Nationals in EC Law', *CMLRev.* (1994), 969–95, at p. 970.

[34] The Commission stated that 'prior to 30 June 1996 the Council shall decide with respect to each third country whether its nationals are to be subject to a visa requirement or are to be exempted from that requirement', see footnote 30.

[35] These aspects are dealt with by the Joint Action of 4 March on airport transit arrangements, see *OJ* 1996, L 63/8.

[36] Art. 18 External Borders Convention provides for the application of a uniform visa valid throughout the territory of the member states, see footnote 30.

clear that it considered Article 100C as an internal market provision, and thus contributing to the realization of the objective set in Article 7A EC, which is *inter alia* the end of controls on persons at the internal borders of the Community. The non-inclusion of this provision in the final text means that the Council considers the application of the principle of mutual recognition in visa issues a matter to be dealt with under Title VI of the TEU.

A third country national holding a valid visa issued by one member state still does not enjoy the right of access to the other States. This clearly runs counter to the Commission's philosophy laid down in several documents.[37] In its recent proposal for a Council directive on the right of third country nationals to travel in the Community, based on Article 100 EC, the Commission reiterates that the completion of the internal market presupposes the abolition of all controls at internal frontiers, and that this objective must be attained in relation to all persons, whatever their nationality. This proposal would grant third country nationals who are lawfully in a member state the right to travel in the territories of the other member states. The right to travel would thus be granted to third country nationals who hold a valid residence permit issued by another member state (Article 3) or who hold a visa which is valid throughout the Community and which is mutually recognized for the purpose of crossing the external frontiers of the member states (Article 4).[38] It is obvious that the diverging approaches of the Commission and the Council on mutual recognition prevent any progress towards a harmonized visa policy in the short run.

Finally, it should be mentioned that the Council adopted Regulation (EC) No. 1683/95 of 29 May 1995 laying down a uniform format for visas.[39] The EU format is different from the one introduced by the Schengen contracting parties. This is because the list of countries whose nationals need visas used by the Schengen States, is not identical to that used at EU level.

d. Asylum seekers

The Implementing Convention also addresses the handling of asylum applications within the Schengen territory. The whole Chapter VII of Title II deals with this subject, even though the objectives in this area are rather limited, as will be shown below. The European continent has a long tradition of receiving refugees and asylum seekers. In recent years, however, numbers of asylum seekers reaching the territory of the EU member states have increased considerably. During the period 1985–94, over 3,400,000 asylum applications

---

[37] See for example SEC(92) 877 final.

[38] See COM(95) 346 final. Together with this proposal two other proposals were made. A proposal for a directive on the practical application of the principle of the elimination of controls on persons, COM(95) 347 final and a proposal for a directive adapting the secondary legislation on the free movement of citizens of the Union (and their families), COM(95) 348 final.

[39] *OJ* 1995, L 164/1. However, the visa is to be introduced six months after the additional technical specifications have been adopted by the Commission, see Art. 8.

were registered in the fifteen EU member states. The number of applications was more or less stable between 1985 and 1987. As from 1988, however, the number of asylum applications rose steadily, reaching its peak in 1992 with a total number of 675,000. After 1993 the total number dropped considerably, to 30,000 in 1994.[40] It is interesting to note that from 1985 to 1989, most asylum seekers in the member states came from the Middle East and Central European countries, while after 1989 the former Soviet Union and Romania became the major sending countries. Since 1990, the EU member states received more asylum applications from the European continent than from any other. The major sending country was the former Yugoslavia.

The significant decrease in the total number of asylum applications after 1992 can be explained by various factors. Confronted with these high numbers, member states implemented legislation to curb abuses of asylum procedures.[41] The introduction of accelerated procedures, computerization of determination procedures and fingerprinting has led to a reduction in the length of the procedures.

At the same time, more and more countries draw a distinction between 'genuine' or 'real' asylum seekers and 'economic' refugees: as a consequence it has become very difficult to fulfil the conditions for being recognized as a refugee in terms of the Geneva Refugee Convention of 1951.[42] This is, of course, a consequence of the migratory pressures which the Community has been facing since 1985, mentioned above.[43] In order to be able to cope with these challenges, it was clear that twelve individual approaches were doomed to fail. The Schengen contracting parties were in fact the first to recognize the need for coordination of their asylum policies.

As was stated above, the aim of the asylum chapter in the Implementing Convention is rather limited. The Contracting Parties set up a system of rules determining which State should process an application for asylum in such a way that one and only one Contracting Party will be responsible.[44] This system should, on the one hand, prevent the phenomenon known as 'asylum shopping'[45] and, on the other, guarantee that every application for asylum is examined by one of the Contracting Parties.

The most important criteria used for determining the responsible State are the following: 1) once a Contracting Party has issued a visa or residence

---

[40] See EUROSTAT, *Statistics in Focus. Population and Social Conditions*, 1996–1.

[41] As the asylum procedures are the only immigration channels left in the EU member states, it is not surprising that there are abuses.

[42] The Convention relating to the Status of Refugees, 1951, *189 UNTS 150*, as modified by the Protocol relating to the Status of Refugees, 1967, *606 UNTS 267*, is the common point of reference for all European States as regards refugee matters. It contains *inter alia* the definition of a refugee and the principle of non-repression.

[43] See also EUROSTAT, *Statistics in Focus. Population and Social Conditions*, 1995–3.

[44] Art. 30 of the Implementing Convention.

[45] A practice consisting in multiple applications by the same asylum seeker to various countries in the hope that at least one country will recognize the applicant as a refugee. See also H.U.J. D'Oliveira, 'Fortress Europe and (Extra-Communitarian) Refugees: Cooperation in Sealing off the External Borders', in Schermers (ed.), above, note 4, 166–82, at p. 173.

permit, this State becomes reponsible for processing the asylum application if the holder of the visa or residence permit applies for asylum afterwards; 2) if two or more parties issued a visa or residence permit, the responsible State shall be the one which issued the visa or residence permit which expires last; 3) if no visa or residence permit was issued, the State across the external borders of which the applicant has entered the territory is responsible; 4) if an asylum seeker submits a new application while another contracting party is still processing an earlier application by the same person, the State examining the first application is responsible; 5) if the State responsible cannot be determined by means of these criteria, the contracting party to which the application was submitted is responsible.[46][47] Furthermore, provisions are laid down concerning the taking back of applicants from each other, the expulsion of refused applicants, the exchange of information about applicants for asylum, etc.

A final, though important, remark is appropriate. Article 32 states that 'the Contracting Party responsible for the processing of an application for asylum shall process it in accordance with its national law'. Indeed, the Convention remains silent as regards harmonization of substantive asylum laws in the Schengen countries. No attempt is made to develop a common interpretation of the definitions in the Geneva Refugee Convention. These definitions, especially the definition of refugee status (Article 1) and of non-refoulement (Article 33) are central concepts in the asylum laws of all the Schengen countries and should, as such, form the basis for any initiative in the matter.[48] The lack of such common interpretation is one of the

---

[46] A. Barav and C. Philip, *Dictionnaire juridique des Communautés européennes*, Paris, Presses Universitaires de France, 1993, 981–92, at p. 987.

[47] The State through the external border of which the asylum seeker reached the Schengen territory is thus of crucial importance in this mechanism. In most cases this will be the reponsible State. Consequently, in order to determine the State reponsible, much depends on whether or not there is a direct connection between the country of origin of the asylum seeker and a Schengen State. De Bruycker and Lew rightly observed that it would be impossible for a refugee departing from former Yugoslavia to apply for asylum in France, since he or she will in most cases have to leave former Yugoslavia via Germany, see P. de Bruycker and S. Lew, 'Les politiques d'harmonization du statut administratif des ressortissants d'Etats tiers en Europe', in Jadoul and Mignon (eds), *Le droit des étrangers. Statuts, évolution européenne, droits économiques et sociaux*, Bruxelles, Facultés universitaires Saint-Louis, 1993, 211–59, at p. 253. Even if an asylum seeker managed to travel by aeroplane, it would be very difficult to pass the rather severe controls carried out by carriers in the country of origin. This negative effect of the Schengen Implementing Convention for the position of asylum seekers is made clear in the next subsection.

[48] A first step has recently been made at EU level. The Council adopted on the basis of Art. K.3 TEU a Joint Position on the harmonized application of the definition of the term 'refugee' in Art. 1 of the Geneva Convention of 28 July 1951 relating to the status of refugees, see *OJ* 1996, L 63/2. As the title suggests, the joint position gives indications on how to interpret the concepts used in the Geneva Convention, which is the basic document in refugee law. Although such an initiative was needed, given the diverging practices in the EU member states, it is doubtful whether this joint position will be useful. The Preamble states that 'this joint position is adopted within the limits of the constitutional powers of the Governments of the Member States; it shall not bind the legislative authorities or affect decisions of the judicial authorities of the Member States'.

main reasons why there are important differences in state practices towards refugees in the EC.

Finally, it must also be noted that four days before the signature of the Implementing Convention (15 June 1990) all the EC member states signed the Dublin 'Convention determining the State reponsible for examining applications for asylum lodged in one of the Member States of the European Communities'.[49] The Dublin Convention is an almost exact copy of the asylum chapter in the Schengen Implementing Convention. It defines the responsible State according to the same principles and criteria as those used by the Implementing Convention.[50] Recently a Protocol was adopted by the Schengen contracting parties stating that the asylum chapter in the Implementing Convention will be replaced by the provisions of the Dublin Convention, once the latter has entered into force.[51] This Protocol is perfectly in line with Article 142 of the Implementing Convention, dealing with possible conflicts of the Implementing Convention rules with agreements concluded between all EC member states. Pursuant to this provision

> if the Member States of the European Communities conclude agreements with a view to the creation of an area without internal frontiers, the contracting parties shall agree on the conditions of replacing or amending the provisions of the present Agreement in the light of the corresponding provisions of the agreements in question. . . . The provisions that are inconsistent with the provisions agreed upon between the Member States of the European Communities shall be amended in any case.

As long as the Dublin Convention has not entered into force, Article 142 of the Implementing Convention retains its importance as regards conflicts of provisions on the asylum issue, according to the Protocol of the Schengen States. The last clause indicates that the Agreement between the EC member states (the Dublin Convention) prevails over the Implementing Convention in the case of a conflict of norms.[52]

e. Carrier sanctions

Following the example set by certain EC member states, the Schengen Convention obliges the contracting parties to impose sanctions on carriers bringing inadmissible persons into the Schengen territory. Inadmissable persons are

---

[49] For an introduction see P. Stefanini and F. Doublet, 'Le droit d'asile en Europe: La Convention relative à la détermination de l'état responsable de l'examen d'une demande d'asile présentée auprès d'un état membre des Communautés européennes', *RMC* (1991), 391–9.

[50] Apparently the asylum issue is a crucial one for the EU member states, as this is the only issue dealt with in the Schengen Implementing Convention on which agreement could be reached between the then Twelve. In this context it is striking that the UK, not being a Schengen Contracting Party, was one of the first States to ratify the Dublin Convention. See F. Webber, 'European conventions on immigration and asylum', in Bunyan (ed.), *Statewatching the new Europe. A handbook on the European State*, Nottingham, Russel Press, 1993, 142–53, at p. 148.

[51] See L. Lenaerts, 'Réunion du Comité Exécutif de Schengen tenue à Berlin le 26 avril 1994', *Benelux Newsletter*, May 1994, 2–4.

[52] J.J. Bolten, 'From Schengen to Dublin: The new frontiers of refugee law', in Meijers et al., above, note 17, 8–36, at p. 13.

described in the Convention as 'aliens who do not possess the necessary documents' and are transported 'by air or sea from a third State to the territories of the Schengen contracting parties'.[53] Moreover, the carrier should take all the necessary measures to ensure that the alien is in possession of the documents required for entry into the territory of the contracting parties.[54] In other words, carrier personnel is charged with the tasks of border authorities and immigration officers. If an alien is refused entry into the territory of one of the contracting parties, the carrier which brought the alien to the external border is obliged to assume reponsibility for the alien again without delay. The contracting parties must incorporate this guiding principle into their national legislation. The carrier must even return the alien to the third State from which he or she was transported, to the third State which issued the travel document, or to any other third State to which the alien is guaranteed entry.

These provisions have been much criticized. The Dutch Council of State, for instance, makes reference to the Chicago Convention on International Civil Aviation.[55] This Convention permits a distinction to be made between a situation in which there is evidence of a particular negligence by the carrier in taking precautions to ensure that the passenger concerned complied with document requirements for entry, and the situation where the passenger possesses falsified documents. In the latter situation, no reponsibility should be put on the carrier, while in the former the carrier can be held reponsible.[56] No such distinction is made in the Implementing Convention, which will lead to a restrictive attitude towards aliens and refugees in case there is any doubt about them possessing the required (and legitimate) documents. Rather than taking the risk of being imposed severe sanctions, travel operators will most likely refuse to bring such persons to the external borders of the Schengen territory. This practice is already observed in those Schengen contracting parties which had implemented legislation on carrier sanctions before the Implementing Convention was signed.[57]

The system of carrier sanctions is in fact another way of blocking the entry of third country nationals into the Schengen territory. A first elimination of

---

[53] Art. 26(2) of the Implementing Convention.

[54] Art. 26(1)(b) of the Implementing Convention.

[55] More precisely Annex 9 of the 1944 Chicago Convention. This Annex sets out a number of international standards and recommended practices. Carrier sanctions were previously dealt with in Standard 3.36 which stipulated that carriers should not be fined because passengers are in the possession of documents found inadequate by a contracting party. Operators were asked to take precautions on the matter, but there was no question of a binding obligation on individuals. Moreover, by replacing Standard 3.36 by Standard 3.37.1 a possibility of imposing sanctions is thus created, although with the nuances noted by the Dutch Council of State. However, the burden of proof is placed on the contracting State and not on the carrier, according to Standard 3.37.1.

[56] R. Dedecker, 'L'asile et la libre circulation des personnes dans l'accord de Schengen', *Courrier Hebdomadaire du CRISP* (1993) (No. 1393–4), 4–58, at p. 55.

[57] Belgium and the Federal Republic of Germany, for instance. For a thorough analysis see A. Cruz, 'Compatibility of Carrier Sanctions in Four Community States with International Civil Aviation and Human Rights Obligations', in Meijers et al., above, note 17, 37–56.

immigrants (including refugees) is made in the country of origin by the carrier personnel. The United Nations High Commissioner for Refugees (UNHCR) is concerned about the imposition of carrier sanctions and strict visa requirements which do not distinguish asylum seekers from other aliens. By those provisions, a very important reponsibility is placed in the hands of those who are unauthorized to make asylum determinations on behalf of States, are untrained in asylum procedures and are motivated by economic rather than humanitarian principles.[58]

f. Entry into force of the Schengen Implementing Convention

Ten years after the signing of the 1985 Schengen Agreement, the Implementing Convention eventually entered into force on 26 March 1995.[59] Due to political and technical problems, this had been postponed several times. Two important remarks should be made in this regard. First, not all Schengen Contracting parties have applied the Schengen Implementing Convention provisions as of 26 March 1995. Thus far, only the Benelux countries, Germany, Spain and Portugal fully apply the Convention. According to the joint statement concerning Article 139 of the latter 'the Convention shall not enter into force until the prior conditions for its implementation are fulfilled in the signatory States and checks at external borders are effective'. As regards Italy and Greece, both being signatory States, the Schengen Executive Committee will take a decision as soon as both countries fulfil these prior conditions.[60] In other words, as long as Italy and Greece cannot guarantee effective checks at their external Schengen borders, they will both be excluded from participation in the Schengen framework. Secondly, although the Implementing Convention contains no provision on the possibility for the signatory States to denounce it, States can suspend the Convention whenever they judge the Schengen cooperation to be unsatisfactory or to jeopardize their national interest or public security.[61] [62] France is at the moment still applying Article 2(2) with regard to the Benelux countries as a consequence of problems concerning drugs traffic. On the other hand, the application of that Article with regard to Spain and Germany has recently been lifted by France.

---

[58] L. Druke, 'Refugee Protection in the Post Cold War Europe: Asylum in the Schengen and EC Harmonization Process', in Pauly (ed.), above, note 13, 105–69, at p. 121. See also UNHCR, *Press Release*, 31 October 1994. *In most cases it is very hard, if not impossible for asylum seekers to obtain the necessary travel documents.* Imposing carriers sanctions without distinguishing between asylum seekers and other aliens may therefore run counter to the right to seek asylum.

[59] See *Agence Europe*, 28 April 1995.

[60] L. Lenaerts, 'Réunion du Comité Exécutif de Schengen tenue à Bonn le 22 décembre 1994', *Benelux Newsletter*, January–February 1995, 2–5.

[61] The legal basis for such a suspension is Art. 2(2) of the Implementing Convention.

[62] The French Government expressly stated that France has reserved the right to withdraw from the Schengen Implementing Convention if the evaluation of the Schengen system after the transitional period should prove to be negative, see *Le Monde*, 8 April 1995, 4.

III. PERSPECTIVES OF PARTICIPATION OF CENTRAL AND EASTERN EUROPE IN THE SCHENGEN FRAMEWORK

A. General remarks

It was stated above that the Europe Agreements contain very few provisions on free movement of persons. Nevertheless, they all make explicit reference to future EU membership for the associated countries of Central and Eastern Europe. As a consequence, the free movement of persons is an issue to be dealt with in the relations between the EU and the region concerned. The following sections will analyse whether EU–CEECs cooperation within the Schengen structure could be complementary to that already established through the Europe Agreements. The Readmission Agreement concluded between Poland and the Schengen States is the only example so far of such a cooperation.

B. Membership of the Schengen Implementing Convention

It has already been mentioned that from the very start the Schengen initiative has been a purely intergovernmental one, set up by five member states of the Community. The five 'initiators' wanted Schengen to be the 'laboratory' of the Community as regards the abolition of internal border controls. The Schengen process must, therefore, be seen in a Community context. The Schengen initiative does not claim to create a 'Community within the Community'.[63] The purpose was and is merely to set a good example for the other EU member states. The above-mentioned definition of the term alien must be seen in that perspective, and the Preamble to the 1985 Agreement expresses the same approach declaring that the completion of the Internal Market is of prior concern to the Schengen contracting parties: 'aware that the increasingly closer union of the peoples of the Member States of the European Communities should be manifested through freedom to cross internal frontiers for all nationals of the Member States and in the free movement of goods and services.'[64]

Clearly, the idea was to prove that a real internal market, especially as regards the free movement of persons, could be achieved between a limited number of countries. The results of the Schengen process should be transposed to Community level once the initiative proves to be successful. That is apparently one of the reasons why no provision was inserted in the 1985 Schengen Agreement on accession by other States, whether they were members of the EC or not. Of course, this 1985 Agreement was no more than a 'solemn declaration of intent', the real challenge being the effective application

---

[63] Although the Schengen initiative resulted in practice in a two-speed Europe with regard to the abolition of border controls, see *Agence Europe*, 30 March 1995.
[64] Preamble to the 1985 Schengen Agreement, recital No. 2, see above, note 4.

of those intentions.[65] The only reference made to cooperation with other States is to be found in Article 28 of the 1985 Schengen Agreement pursuant to which 'any conclusion on a bilateral or multilateral basis of arrangements similar to this Agreement with the States that are not Parties thereto shall be preceded by consultation between the Parties'. As can be noted, no reference is made to full membership of the 1985 Agreement. Cooperation is restricted to concluding similar arrangements with other States and is subject to preliminary consultation with the other Schengen contracting parties.

The Implementing Convention of 1990 shows a different approach. Firstly, the Convention contains an explicit provision on membership to the effect that '[a]ny Member State of the European Communities may become a Party to this Convention'.[66] The provision is very clear: a preliminary condition for becoming a party to the Convention is membership of the European Communities. Austria can serve here as an example. As soon as it became clear that Austria would become a EU member state, the country was granted observer status to the Schengen negotiations during the meeting of the Schengen Executive Committee on 27 June 1994 in Berlin. The Schengen contracting parties also expressed their wish that Austria would become full member of the Schengen Group very soon.[67] It follows that participation in Schengen, in terms of becoming a party to the Schengen Agreements, is impossible for the CEECs, at least in the near future. As long as these countries have not become member states of the EU, other forms of participation will have to be found.

Furthermore, the Implementing Convention comprises a provision similar to Article 28 of the 1985 Agreement. According to Article 36 'each contracting party has the duty of informing the other parties when deciding to conduct negotiations on border checks with a third State'. However, according to its second paragraph 'no contracting party shall conclude with one or more third States agreements simplifying or abolishing border checks without the prior agreement of the other contracting parties'. Whereas the 1985 Agreement only demanded 'prior consultation', prior agreement of the other contracting parties is needed according to the Implementing Convention. Consequently, contracting parties no longer have any right to conclude such agreements autonomously. Each agreement tending to simplify or abolish border checks with third States will be subject to a common 'Schengen' approach. All contracting parties have to agree should one contracting party want to conclude such an agreement. Thus, objections raised by one of the contracting parties in this respect can block the conclusion of such an agreement.

This does not mean that EU–CEECs cooperation in areas covered by the Implementing Convention is completely foreclosed. On the contrary, the

---

[65] See L. Lenaerts, 'Schengen: de stand van zaken op het einde van 1991', in Fijnaut/Stuyck/ Wytinck, (eds), above, note 19, 1–12, at p. 1.

[66] Art. 140 of the Implementing Convention.

[67] See L. Lenaerts, 'Réunion du Comité exécutif de Schengen tenue à Berlin le 27 juin 1994', *Benelux Newsletter*, June–July 1994, 8–12. As mentioned before, Austria became a Schengen contracting party on 28 April 1995.

1991 Readmission Agreement between the Schengen contracting parties and Poland is a good example of such a cooperation.

C. Agreements on readmission of persons in an irregular position

Readmission agreements are not an innovation in international practice. In fact, the Benelux countries have a long experience in the matter. Benelux, as a single Contracting Party, already concluded agreements on readmission with France (1964), Austria (1965) and Germany (1966).[68] These agreements will be briefly examined, by way of example, before analysing the readmission agreement between the Schengen States and Poland in more detail.

a.   Agreements on readmission in the Benelux framework

Generally speaking, readmission agreements tend to establish a mechanism whereby each contracting party engages to take back every person who, departing from its territory, enters the territory of another contracting party in an irregular way or takes up residence on that territory illegally. Readmitting persons is one of the ways in which States cooperate in order to deal with the negative effects and burdens of illegal immigration. In view of the rather heavy financial implications, readmission agreements are in most cases rigorously applied by States.

The readmission agreements between the Benelux and France, Austria and Germany are nearly identical. Therefore, it may suffice to examine briefly the Readmission Agreement between France and the Benelux. According to this Agreement, there are two situations in which a requesting State can obtain readmittance of a third country national by another State. First, the third country national, legally residing on the territory of the requested State, enters the territory of the requesting State in a legal way but prolongs his or her stay in the requesting State beyond the permitted period. On the sole presentation of the residence permit, the requested State shall be obliged to take the individual back. Secondly, the third country national concerned was in transit on the territory of the requested State to reach the territory of the requesting State illegally. Procedural requirements are reduced to a minimum. If the third country national is found in the requesting State within fifteen days of the irregular entry, an official request is unnecessary. Without any further formalities the person concerned must be readmitted by the requested State on 'indication' of the requesting State. After this fifteen-day period, a formal procedure must be followed at ministerial level. A similar arrangement on readmission applies between the Benelux countries themselves.[69] Obviously, flexibility and lack of formalities are the distinguishing features of these readmission agreements.

---

[68] X. Denoel, 'Les accords de réadmission du Benelux à Schengen et au-delà', *RTDE* (1993), 635–53, at p. 640.

[69] Décision du Groupe de travail ministériel pour la circulation des personnes de L'Union économique Benelux du 28 juin 1967 Relative à l'éloignement et à la reprise de personnes, *Textes de Base, 96e suppl.*, 34–40.

b. The agreement on readmission of persons in an irregular position between the Schengen contracting parties and Poland

The agreement on readmission of persons in an irregular position concluded between the Schengen contracting parties and Poland on 29 March 1991 is broadly similar to those concluded by the Benelux countries. In fact, the Readmission Agreement with Poland is complementary to the Schengen Implementing Convention, in particular the provisions on expulsion of persons who do not (any longer) fulfil the conditions for entry to the territory of one of the Schengen contracting parties. According to the Implementing Convention, expulsion may be effected from the territory of a State to the alien's country of origin or to any other State to which he or she may be permitted entry. Most significant is that the Convention permits expulsion 'under the relevant provisions of the re-entry agreements concluded by the contracting parties'.[70]

It should be noted that at the time of signing the Readmission Agreement, the Schengen States – upon the insistence of Germany – had agreed to abolish all visa requirements in respect of Polish citizens.[71] Only a few days later, as of 8 April 1991, the abolition of visa requirements was a fact.[72] It was suggested by some commentators that Poland accepted this Readmission Agreement as a compensation.[73]

1. Structure of the Readmission Agreement
The Readmission Agreement with Poland consists of no more than ten Articles, preceded by a short Preamble. A Joint Declaration and a Protocol are annexed to the Agreement itself. It is interesting to note that while the Readmission Agreement and the Joint Decalaration have been signed by *all* the contracting parties (i.e. the Schengen contracting parties *and* Poland), the Protocol has been signed by the Schengen contracting parties only. This Protocol contains four declarations concerning certain provisions in the Readmission Agreement. Through these declarations the Schengen States set up mutual arrangements concerning their own obligations under the Readmission Agreement. The Joint Declaration states that the procedures of the agreement will not be applicable to third country nationals who entered the requesting State before the date of provisional application of the Agreement. No joint institutions are established by the Readmission Agreement with Poland. The ministers responsible for border controls of the contracting parties, appoint the local authorities competent for the handling of requests for readmission.[74]

---

[70] Art. 23(4) of the Implementing Convention.
[71] X. Denoel, above, note 68, at p. 646. According to D'Oliveira, the abolition of visas is part of the bilateral German–Polish agreements settling the after-effects of World War II, see H.U.J. D'Oliveira, above, note 45, at p. 172.
[72] See 'Poles ready for easier travel', *Financial Times*, 8 April 1991; *Agence Europe*, 25 et 26 mars 1991, 7 and *Agence Europe*, 3 avril 1991, 8.
[73] X. Denoel, above, note 68, at p. 646.; H.U.J. D'Oliveira, above, note 44, at p. 172. See also recital No. 2 of the Preamble to the Readmission Agreement: 'aux fins de compenser, notamment la charge qu'une circulation des voyageurs en exemption du visa, ressortissants des Parties Contractantes du présent Accord, est susceptible de créer'.
[74] Art. 4 of the Readmission Agreement.

2. Content of the Readmission Agreement

According to this Agreement, each State will readmit to its territory on the request of any other State and without formalities, any person who does not fulfil (or no longer fulfils) the conditions for entry or residence prevailing on the territory of the requesting State, in so far as it can be established that the person concerned possesses the nationality of the requested State.[75] If, after an inquiry, the person concerned turns out not to possess the nationality of the requested State, the requesting State is obliged to readmit him or her to its territory (Article 1(2)). So far, this agreement greatly resembles the Agreement between Benelux and France, except that in the Agreement with Poland proof of nationality is crucial. However, the nationality criterion is already dropped in the second provision of the Agreement. According to Article 2(1), the same readmission obligation applies to the contracting party through the external borders of which a person, who does not fulfil (or who no longer fulfils) the conditions for entry or residence on the territory of the requesting State, entered.

Strictly speaking, Article 2 applies to the Schengen States as well as Poland. In practice, however, migration flows, in the relation Poland–Schengen States, are in the direction of the Schengen territory, not vice versa. The Readmission Agreement must be observed in that context. Apparently, the Agreement seems to be applicable not only to nationals of the contracting parties, but also to any irregular immigrant, whatever his or her nationality, who entered through the external borders of the requested State.[76]

At the time of signature, Poland was becoming more and more a transit country for clandestine migration towards the Schengen territory and it was of major concern to the Schengen contracting parties to stop this evolution. By concluding the Agreement, the Schengen States made a first step in this direction. However, one of the consequences of this is that the burden of migration is shifted towards the Eastern borders of the Schengen territory. It is obvious that the Readmission Agreement places the heaviest burden on the Polish border authorities as the readmission obligation will in most cases be imposed on Poland. It has been pointed out above that the Contracting Party which admitted a person through its external border is obliged to readmit the person concerned if he or she does not fulfil (or no longer fulfils) the conditions for entry or residence. An additional problem for the Polish border authorities is that the Schengen conditions for entry or residence, as well as the national conditions applicable in each Schengen Contracting Party, individually have to be fulfilled.[77] As a consequence, border authorities, *in casu* Polish border authorities, are obliged to check carefully whether the person who wishes to cross the external border complies with all of these

[75] Art. 1(1) of the Readmission Agreement.
[76] D. O'Keeffe, 'The Schengen Convention: A Suitable Model for European Integration?', *YEL* (1991), 185–219, at p. 195.
[77] H. Verschueren, 'Het vrije verkeer van personen in de Schengen-Verdragen', in Fijnaut/Stuyck/Wytinck (eds), above, note 19, at p. 36.

conditions. A slack visa and entry policy will under these circumstances raise the 'readmission costs'. Therefore, at the time of signing the Readmission Agreement, Poland also tightened visa requirements for nationals originating from a number of developing countries, and in specific cases imposed non-visa restrictions (for instance for visitors from Romania).[78] This is the reason why some commentators call Poland the frontier guard of the Schengen territory.[79] If other CEECs decide to join the agreement on readmission of persons in an irregular position with the Schengen States, which is made possible by Article 7 of the Agreement,[80] an effective 'cordon sanitaire' will be established around the Schengen territory.[81] Those countries will then be held responsible for the entry into the Schengen territory through its Eastern borders of persons who do not fulfil the cumulative Schengen-State conditions.[82]

In the Protocol to the Readmission Agreement, a declaration concerning Articles 2 and 5(3) was inserted whereby the Schengen States agree that the readmission obligation applying between them in pursuance of the Readmission Agreement will be restricted for the moment to Polish nationals. Furthermore, a simple decision of the Executive Committee, set up by the Schengen Implementing Convention can extend the readmission obligation to nationals of other States. As Poland is not involved in the Protocol, the Readmission Agreement itself fully applies to Poland.[83] While between the Schengen States only a mutual readmission obligation for Polish nationals is applicable, Poland is obliged to readmit to its territory any person, whatever his or her nationality, who entered the territory of a Schengen State irregularly through the Polish borders.[84]

Finally, a few remarks should be made as regards the possible effects of the Readmission Agreement on the position of asylum seekers in the Schengen territory. The Agreement expressly stipulates that its provisions do not apply to asylum seekers (Article 2(5)). Reference is made to the relevant provisions in both the Schengen Implementing Convention and the Dublin Convention (determining the State responsible for examining applications for asylum lodged in one of the member states of the European Community).

---

[78] M. Okolski, 'Poland' in Ardittis (ed.), *The Politics of East-West Migration*, London, The Macmillan Press Ltd, 1994, 51–67, at p. 56. The author reports also that 'during the first eight months of 1992 more than 25,000 foreigners (mostly Romanians) were prevented from unauthorized crossing of the Polish-German border'.

[79] Ibid.

[80] According to which 'Les Parties Contractantes peuvent décider, d'un commun accord, d'inviter d'autres Etats à adhérer au présent Accord. Cette décision est prise à l'unanimité'.

[81] Or, in the words of D'Oliveira, this may 'represent a rebuilt Iron Curtain', see H.U.J. D'Oliveira, above, note 45, at p. 172.

[82] It was mentioned that visa requirements were abolished for Polish nationals at the time of concluding the Readmission Agreement with Poland. At this moment, however, visa requirements have already been abolished for nationals of most other associated countries of Central and Eastern Europe.

[83] H. Verschueren, above, note 19, at p. 35.

[84] Nederlands Juristen Comité voor de Mensenrechten, *Commentaar op de overeenkomst tussen de Schengenstaten en de Republiek Polen met bijbehorend Protocol tussen de Schengenstaten*, Leiden, 1991, 1–4, at p. 3.

Nevertheless, Poland must take up its readmission responsibility towards any person who fails to meet the conditions for entry to the Schengen territory. An asylum seeker whose application for asylum has been rejected in the Schengen territory is after this rejection no longer an asylum seeker but a person who does not fulfil the entry conditions. As a consequence, Poland will be obliged to take this person (formerly an asylum seeker) back if he or she entered the Schengen territory through the Polish borders. In order to avoid this eventuality, Poland will most likely only let those persons cross the border who fulfil all the entry conditions. This means being in the possession of a visa, having sufficient means of support and not being a threat to public order, national security or external relations of one of the Schengen States. But applying visa requirements to asylum seekers makes asylum in practice impossible.[85] Most asylum seekers are forced by circumstances to travel illegally and it is very unlikely that they obtain the necessary documents from the competent authorities in their countries of origin.

In fact, a clear parallel can be drawn with the provisions in the Implementing Convention on carrier sanctions. Both arrangements are serious impediments for asylum seekers to reach the Schengen territory and receive the protection they need.[86] From a Polish point of view, however, the Readmission Agreement can also be seen as an opportunity to align its own visa policy with the policies of the EU member states.

IV. PERSPECTIVES OF A GENERALIZED APPLICATION OF THE READMISSION TECHNIQUE TO CENTRAL AND EASTERN EUROPE?

As already recalled, the only Readmission Agreement concluded between the Schengen contracting parties and a third State so far is the agreement on readmission of persons in an irregular position with Poland. However, this Agreement could be extended towards other countries in the near future. Switzerland would like to become a contracting party to the Agreement and certain Eastern European States have already showed interest. Bulgaria, for instance, has repeatedly requested to become a party to the Readmission Agreement with Poland. The perspective of the relaxation of visa requirements in exchange for acceptance of the Readmission Agreement is apparently a decisive factor for Bulgaria.[87] The Schengen States, on the other hand, do not seem too keen to abolish visa requirements for certain States in Eastern Europe.[88]

---

[85] On the imposition of strict visa requirements which do not distinguish between asylum seekers and illegal immigrants, see above, section IIBe!!!

[86] D. O'Keeffe, above, note 76, at p. 195.

[87] See L. Lenaerts, 'Le bout du tunnel Schengen', *Benelux Newsletter*, September–October 1994, 2–3.

[88] X. Denoel, above, note 68, at p. 651. Nor do the EU member states. The associated CEECs Bulgaria and Romania remain on the list of countries whose nationals need a visa to enter the EU, recently adopted by the Council, see above, note 31. Bulgaria demanded to be withdrawn from this negative list immediately, see *Agence Europe*, 27 September 1995.

A number of readmission agreements have been concluded between individual Schengen States and certain CEECs, for example, between Belgium and the Slovak Republic or between Germany and the Czech Republic.[89] At this moment, the Schengen partners seem unable or unwilling to tackle this issue within the Schengen framework. Most States still prefer to conclude readmission agreements on a bilateral basis. The same applies for the other EU member states and this evolution seems to be encouraged by the Council. The Council *Recommendation concerning a specimen bilateral readmission agreement between a Member State of the European Union and a third country* is indicative.[90] As opposed to the Schengen Readmission Agreement with Poland, the Recommendation does not suggest concluding readmission agreements on a multilateral basis. It does not impinge upon the member states' competences in the area of immigration. Its objective is to offer a model which can be used as a basis for negotiations with third countries on the conclusion of readmission agreements, not to develop a common policy. Each member state individually remains competent to conclude readmission agreements. The Council Recommendation only contains a modest attempt to develop a loose coordination of member state practice with regard to readmission.

It should be noted that recent mixed agreements concluded by the Community also refer to readmission. In the Euro-Mediterranean association agreement with Morocco, for instance, the parties agree in a joint declaration to 'adopt bilaterally the appropriate provisions and measures to cover readmission of their nationals in cases in which the latter have left their countries'.[91] Here too, it seems that a common approach is not envisaged, but member states are encouraged to take initiatives as regards readmission. However, it must be stressed again that a proliferation of readmission agreements with CEECs will result in shifting the burden of migration of the EU towards this region of Europe.

V. FEASIBLE COOPERATION IN THE FIELD OF JUSTICE AND HOME AFFAIRS

According to Article 140 of the Implementing Convention, only member states of the EU can become a contracting party to the Schengen Agreements, as was mentioned above. At the moment none of the CEECs is yet a member of the EU, so new forms of cooperation will need to be developed if the participation of these countries in the Schengen process is accepted. The conclusion of a readmission agreement similar to the one with Poland could be considered; however, negotiations on participation in the Schengen process could also concentrate on a number of other areas, dealt with in the Implementing Convention. The Berlin Declaration on cooperation between

[89] ECRE, *Safe Third Countries. Myths and Realities*, London, ECRE, February 1995, Appendix D.
[90] *Bull. EU*, 11-1994, point 1.4.8. For the text of the Council Recommendation, see *OJ* 1996, C 274/20.
[91] The agreement was signed on 26 February 1996, see *Bull. EU*, 1/2-1996. For text, see COM(95) 740 final.

the Ministers of Justice and Home affairs of the member states of the EU and the Associated countries of Eastern Europe, shows that there is an interest in this issue on both sides, and it could serve as an example.

Through this Declaration, the countries concerned express their wish to cooperate in combating organized international crime.[92] The latter is recognized as a common challenge, a threat to all European countries, so that a common strategy by the countries involved is needed. The list of areas in which cooperation seems necessary is interesting, as it strongly resembles the title on police and security in the Schengen Implementing Convention.

The first area mentioned is illicit drug-trafficking. Reference is made to the United Nations Convention of 20 December 1988 on Illicit Traffic in Narcotic Drugs and Psychotropic Substances. In the Berlin Declaration, it is stated that the participating countries will try to make progress with the immediate ratification of this Convention. A similar reference to this Convention is to be found in the Implementing Convention as well.[93] The associated countries and the EU member states also agreed to cooperate as regards the organized networks of clandestine immigration. Areas for closer cooperation include visa policies, more efficient controls at the borders of those countries that serve as transit territories for illegal immigration,[94] the consistent imposition of sanctions on carriers transporting foreigners who are not in the possession of valid travel documents and readmission, as soon as possible, of these persons to their countries of origin. Needless to say, these objectives are nearly literally copied from the corresponding Implementing Convention provisions. On the other hand, new areas of cooperation concern radioactive and nuclear products, and trafficking in stolen cars.

Finally, the signatories to the Declaration will examine the possibility of intensified multilateral or bilateral cooperation. Therefore, 'the proposal of the UK and Italy to install a political dialogue in the areas of justice and home affairs must be elaborated and further developed'. This could mean that the EU member states and the associated countries consider this Declaration as a starting point for further cooperation in other areas related to justice and home affairs. A wider cooperation going beyond the limits of a common approach towards international crime is thus envisaged and appears to be necessary. More and more interrelated issues must be dealt with through an integrated approach as, for instance, one can hardly imagine taking measures on illegal immigration by imposing carrier sanctions without elaborating at the same time the highly related issues of visa policy and asylum policy, or even taking into account the problem of family reunification. The Commission came to the same conclusion in its recent Communications on the Europe

---

[92] Conseil de L'Union européenne-Sécretariat général, *Déclaration de Berlin sur une coopération renforcée dans la lutte contre la criminalité en matière de drogue et le crime organisé en Europe, Berlin, le 8 septembre 1994, Communication à la Presse*, Bruxelles, le 14 septembre 1994, 9345/94 (Presse 182).

[93] Art. 71 of the Implementing Convention.

[94] Clearly, the associated countries are referred to.

Agreements.[95] A wider cooperation between the EU member states and the associated countries is necessary in various areas in order to prepare their future membership. In fact, the Commission is convinced that cooperation should take place in all the three pillars of the TEU: areas covered by Community policies, as well as common foreign and security policy and justice and home affairs.

The third pillar areas in particular are closely related to the Schengen initiative. Article K.1 regards as matters of common interest a number of issues dealt with in the Schengen Implementing Convention; asylum policy, rules governing the crossing of external borders, immigration policy, combating drug addiction and international fraud, judicial cooperation in civil and criminal matters, customs cooperation and police cooperation should all be subject to a joint approach by the EU member states. Apparently, the time has come, according to the Commission, to involve the countries of Eastern and Central Europe in this cooperation: 'cooperation between the Union and the associated countries is indispensable if action at the European level in the fields of justice and home affairs is to be fully effective'. The objective is to develop a structured relationship with the institutions of the Union and in this respect the experience already gained by the EU member states in the area can serve as a useful guide. Clearly, the Schengen framework is aimed at by the reference to 'the experience already gained' in the Declaration.

The above-mentioned Berlin Declaration is an immediate outcome of the Commission's appeal for closer cooperation in these matters with the associated countries. Once again, the Schengen process can serve as an example. Although Schengen membership is out of question for the associated countries of Central and Eastern Europe in the short run, it seems appropriate to develop some form of cooperation with these countries in certain areas. Police cooperation, for instance, is an outstanding example of a possible and perhaps necessary participation of the associated countries in the Schengen process. Notwithstanding the many critical remarks that can be made on the elaboration of this topic in the Schengen Agreements, it is too obvious that organized crime does not operate exclusively within the borders of one country.[96] Therefore, international police cooperation seems to be a necessity and should not be limited to cooperation between the Schengen contracting parties or even all the EU member states. Other areas related to justice and home affairs may also be part of this wider cooperation with the CEECs.[97]

---

[95] COM(94) 320 final and the follow up document COM(94) 361 final.

[96] For an overview see A.H.J. Swart, 'Police and security in the Schengen Agreement and Schengen Convention', in Meijers et al., above, note 17, 96–109.

[97] The 'fight against drugs' for instance. Clauses on the combating of drugs are already included in the Europe Agreements, so the example is set. There is, however, need for a structured cooperation, be it in the framework of the second and third pillar of the TEU or other intergovernmental fora. The Commission seems to prefer keeping cooperation with the CEECs in these matters within the TEU structure, although as a first step it will be necessary to examine the possibilities of expanding action and cooperation means in the framework of the PHARE and TACIS programmes, see COM(94) 234 final.

The Berlin Declaration can be regarded as a first step in the right direction, while the Schengen process can serve as a useful reservoir of experiences for both the EU member states and the CEECs.

The Essen Summit of December 1994 also stressed the importance of cooperation with the CEECs in the field of justice and home affairs. This part of the Essen conclusions fits into the strategy introduced by the two communications of the Commission on the strategy for preparing the CEECs for accession and the Berlin Declaration.[98] The latter is explicitly referred to, as it is stated that the EU envisages cooperation with the associated countries in such areas as illicit drug trade, theft of and illegal trade in radioactive and nuclear material, illegal immigration networks and illegal transfer of motor vehicles. The Essen conclusions only seem to repeat the Berlin Declaration at EU level. However, a perspective of enhanced cooperation is offered:

> a comprehensive package of measures with proposals for how cooperation in the individual areas named in the Berlin Declaration should proceed, should be submitted to the European Council under the French Presidency. Cooperation should also be taken forward in the areas of asylum and immigration in particular by establishing links between the associated countries and CIREA and CIREFI.[99]

Both centres are so-called 'clearing-houses'.[100] CIREA was set up in 1992, its main objective is to gather and exchange information on all questions relating to asylum matters. One of the most important acitivities of the Centre is the examination of the situation in certain third countries of origin. Thanks to this information, the EU was able in 1993–94 to approach certain third countries in order to discuss the significant increase in the number of applications for asylum. It should also be noted that in the period during which Finland, Sweden and Austria were negotiating their accession to the EU, informal consultations were already taking place regarding their participation in CIREA. Inevitably, the countries of Central and Eastern Europe must become part of the cooperation within the framework of CIREA. The policy of the EU is directed towards the complete integration of Central and Eastern Europe, whereby the issue of migration is of particular importance and must not be overlooked.

It is striking that the Commission's attitude in this matter is far from clear. In its earlier communications it was stated that 'sight should not be lost of other "Third Pillar" related areas, such as immigration and asylum policies in particular, where closer co-operation between these countries and the Union

---

[98] See above, note 92.

[99] *Bull. EU*, 12-1994, point I.45.

[100] CIREA stands for The Centre for Information, Discussion and Exchange on Asylum. It was set up by the Ministers responsible for immigration during their meeting in June 1992, see *Bull. EC*, 6-1992, point 2.2.1. CIREFI stands for The Centre for Information, Discussion and Exchange on the Crossing of Frontiers and Immigration. Its establishment was approved by the Immigration Ministers during their meeting in London six months later, see *Bull. EC*, 12-1992, point 1.5.12. Both centres function within the General Secretariat of the Council.

is also important'.[101] Nevertheless, at present the Commission seems not convinced of the necessity to include migration and migration-related matters in the global preparation strategy for accession of the Central and Eastern European Countries. The White Paper on preparation of the associated countries of Central and Eastern Europe for integration into the Internal Market of the Union, for instance, remains silent on this subject.[102] It is striking that in a vast document analysing all aspects of the Internal Market not a word has been devoted to issues related to the free movement of persons, such as immigration, right of entry and residence of third country nationals or asylum policy. This is even more surprising as free movement of persons belongs to the core of the Internal Market concept. This may be an illustration of the fact that the issue has never enjoyed top priority for the Commission.[103] Nevertheless, since the very idea of an Internal Market without internal border controls calls for a common policy towards migratory flows, a Commission initiative seems inevitable. In addition to that, recent developments may indicate a change in the Union's policy. Two proposals by the Commission may illustrate this change. First, mention should be made of the (draft) Partnership and Cooperation Agreement with Russia.[104] This text contains a title on the prevention of illegal activities such as illegal transactions of various goods, the illicit traffic of narcotic drugs and psychotropic substances and also illegal immigration. Furthermore, it is stated that cooperation in these matters will be based on mutual consultations and close interaction.[105] Secondly, almost exactly the same title is inserted in the EA with Slovenia.[106] In both cases, it is explicitly stated that the principle and practice of readmission will be taken into account.[107] None of the EAs previously concluded contained an explicit provision on illegal immigration. Although the wording is vague, the inclusion of this provision in the EA with Slovenia certainly constitutes a new element in the policy of the Commission.

VI. CONCLUSION

It is clear that membership of the Schengen arrangements cannot be envisaged by the associated countries of Central and Eastern Europe in the short

---

[101] COM(94) 361 final, at p. 3.

[102] COM(95) 163 final. For an analysis see the contribution by M.-A. Gaudissart and A. Sinnaeve above, p. 57.

[103] It also seems to reproduce the delay with which the free movement of persons was (and is) actually pursued within the EC itself, see above, pp. 209–10.

[104] For text see COM(94) 257 final. The Interim Agreement on trade and trade related matters between the European Communities and Russia entered into force on 1 February 1996, see *Bull. EU*, 1/2-1996, point 1.4.129.

[105] See Art. 84 of the Partnership and Cooperation Agreement with Russia.

[106] COM(95) 341 final. Although the Europe Agreement has been signed, it has not entered into force yet. The Commission was given a negotiating mandate to conclude an Interim Agreement on trade and trade related matters with Slovenia in July 1996. See, *Agence Europe*, 1 August 1996, at p. 5.

[107] See Art. 98 of the Draft EA with Slovenia.

run. On the other hand, cooperation in the areas dealt with by the Schengen framework has become a pressing need. First because, by their very nature, these issues call for an international approach. In particular, migration controls and police cooperation in combating organized crime are areas where such cooperation seems inevitable. Efforts to establish this cooperation, however, have so far not been sufficient. Initiatives such as the Berlin Declaration indicate a political will on both sides, but do not represent adequate answers to the real challenges. The framework offered by the current Europe Agreements is not sufficient in this respect either. The provisions on free movement of persons are very limited, while little or no attention is paid to organized international crime. Secondly, the associated countries all aim at becoming EU member states. The EU subscribes to this ambition and is willing to help these countries. A comprehensive strategy to prepare these countries for accession has been set up by the Commission. Cooperation in justice and home affairs is considered in this strategy as an important issue, although the cooperation announced is described rather vaguely and seems to be far from having top priority. The White Paper on the integration of the CEECs into the Internal Market confirms this impression, as justice and home affairs are not addressed by this important document. Part of the explanation for the EU's hesitant attitude may lie in the doubts on the operation of the three-pillar structure even in intra-EU relations. From the beginning, the pillar structure introduced by the Maastricht Treaty has been criticized as an impediment to efficient action and progress. Two years after the entry into force of the TEU there are very few concrete results of the third pillar. At first sight, this evolution seems to prove above all that the purely intergovernmental option is to be preferred. On the other hand, it could be an indication that the ambiguous nature of the third pillar – combining purely intergovernmental and Community methods – prevents the member states from achieving results in this field. This conclusion has its consequences for the relations between the EU and the CEECs in justice and home affairs. As long as the free movement and migration issue is not adequately dealt with at EU level, the chances are small that progress will be made on cooperation in these matters with the Central and Eastern European region. The conclusion must be that more explicit links should be established between the internal and external aspects of the third pillar issues. Measures concerning illegal immigration taken by the EU member states in the framework of Title VI of the TEU obviously generate effects in the EU's neighbouring countries. Not only the Readmission Agreement between the Schengen contracting parties and Poland, but also the carriers sanctions analysed above, illustrate this interaction.

Part III

THE ISSUE OF ENLARGEMENT

A

Cost/Benefit Analysis of Enlargement

13

THE EUROPEAN UNION AND
THE CHALLENGE OF ENLARGEMENT

Fraser Cameron[1]

I. INTRODUCTION

Enlargement of the Union is a political imperative and a major opportunity. Never before has Europe had such an opportunity to unite under democratic conditions. Never before have so many countries wished to join the Union. The Treaty on European Union makes clear that all European countries who share our values are eligible for membership. Until the end of the Cold War the eastern half of Europe had no opportunity to participate in the process of European integration. Since 1989 the transformation process in Central and Eastern Europe has brought these countries to the stage where they have all applied for EU membership. The EU has an unavoidable duty to respond positively to these developments and contribute to the development of a stable political and economic order for all of Europe.

But never before has the Union envisaged an enlargement of such dimensions – it could add more than a 100 million to its population of 370 million – and in terms of the different economic and social situations involved. The combined GDP of the ten potential new members in Central and Eastern Europe is less than 4 per cent of that of the Union (roughly equivalent to that of the Netherlands) and their average national income per head is still only 30 per cent of the EU average. The percentage of GDP arising from, and percentage of working population engaged in, agriculture (7.8 per cent and 26.7 per cent) is far above the EU average (2.5 per cent and 5.7 per cent). But these problems should not obscure the potential economic benefits that will flow from an enlarged EU with an extra 100 million consumers.[2]

---

[1] Foreign Policy Adviser, European Commission, DG IA. This contribution is written in a personal capacity and does not commit the European Commission in any way.
[2] Report of the European Commission to the European Council in Madrid, December 1995.

II. THE WIDER AGENDA

The next enlargement, therefore, is an unprecedented historic challenge, requiring imagination and political will of the same order as inspired the foundation of the original European Communities. But unless the EU makes thorough preparations for enlargement, including the functioning and decision-making procedures of the institutions, enlargement could lead to paralysis and even disintegration.

Enlargement is of course part of a wider European agenda which has internal and external aspects. *Internally*, the Union will need:

– to reform the Union in a more open, relevant and democratic manner, and in particular, to adjust its institutions which were designed for six member states, to the requirements of a much larger Union with more than 20 member states;
– to introduce the single currency (the Euro) in 1999 according to the criteria in the Maastricht Treaty;
– to agree new financial guidelines for the Union after expiry of the present budget agreement in 1999;
– to reform the structural funds;
– to continue reform of the CAP.

Externally, the EU has a number of major priorities, including:

– reconstruction in the Balkans;
– strengthening transatlantic relations by building on the EU–US Action Plan, as agreed at the Madrid Summit;
– developing a new Euro-Med partnership following the 1995 Barcelona Conference, and the Cannes decision on a new and substantial financial package for the Mediterranean;
– developing a strategic partnership with Russia and Ukraine, and deepening relations with the members of the CIS;
– strengthening ties with Turkey following the conclusion of the Customs Agreement in 1995;
– building a new relationship with Asia following the Bangkok Summit.

Taken together, these internal and external issues make up a challenging 'Agenda for Europe' over the next few years. The by no means exhaustive list of external priorities also gives an indication of the EU's increasing global role.

But if the EU is to punch its true weight in the world, it is essential that agreement is reached on measures to strengthen the common foreign and security policy (CFSP). Our citizens, and indeed our partners in the world, are keen for Europe to speak and act with one voice in dealing with major issues such as, for example, the crisis in Bosnia. So far the CFSP has been rather a disappointment. There is now an opportunity to achieve reforms in the IGC – reforms which will become increasingly urgent with enlargement.

After all, the need for greater security is one of the considerations leading the countries of central and eastern Europe to seek membership in the Union.[3]

III. DEEPENING *V* WIDENING

There are some who argue that there is an inevitable contradiction between widening and deepening. I believe that both are essential for the future of Europe. In this context it is instructive to look briefly at the lessons of previous enlargements, as they have often been accompanied by measures which have led to a deepening of the Community.

Following the first enlargement involving the UK, Ireland and Denmark, the Community agreed common policies in new areas (e.g. regional, environmental, technology) as well as closer cooperation in foreign affairs (EPC). Institutional arrangements were also strengthened with the introduction of the European Council and direct elections to the European Parliament.

Following the accession of Greece, and then Spain and Portugal, the Community further developed the Structural Funds as a mechanism for transfer of resources to the less-favoured regions of member states. This second enlargement wave was also accompanied by the Single European Act, increased involvement of the European Parliament and a new financial resources package for the Community. The Single European Act significantly extended the use of majority voting, without which it would have been impossible to complete the Internal Market.

The latest enlargement involving Austria, Sweden and Finland followed the Treaty on European Union which again involved considerable deepening such as the commitment to Economic and Monetary Union, the establishment of a Common Foreign and Security Policy, and yet further powers for the European Parliament.

It is clear from these examples that enlargement can actually speed up the process of integration and, incidentally, the process of convergence in new member states.[4]

IV. THE BENEFITS OF ENLARGEMENT

Too often, however, enlargement is discussed in negative terms – the cost of taking in poorer members, the difficulty of reforming Union policies, etc. But the problems associated with enlargement pale into insignificance when compared to the potential benefits of enlargement, provided it is well prepared. Successful enlargement of the European Union will be a major factor

---

[3] See Reports by the Commission to the Reflection Group (Intergovernmental Conference 1996 – Commission report for the Reflection Group, Luxembourg, Office for Official Publications of the European Communities, 1995) and to the IGC (Commission Opinion, Reinforcing political union and preparing for enlargement, Luxembourg, Office for Official Publications of the European Communities, 1996).

[4] See H. Wallace, *Widening and Deepening*, RIIA Discussion Paper, London, 1990.

in spreading peace and prosperity throughout the European continent because it will:

- support the newly liberalized market economies by further opening up markets in goods and services between East and West, North and South, stimulating economic growth in Europe and offering new trading opportunities for all;
- *bind the countries* of Central and Eastern Europe into Western European political and economic structures and thus enhance security and stability; both the US (and Russia) support enlargement for this reason;
- *increase effective cooperation* in the fields of Justice and Home Affairs, helping to fight crime and the menace of drugs, the effects of which are felt throughout our continent;
- *bring higher environmental standards* to Central and Eastern Europe, benefiting all of Europe by reducing cross-border and global pollution.

V. EU POLICY TOWARDS CENTRAL AND EASTERN EUROPE

Since 1989, the European Union has been in the forefront of international efforts to support the reform process and thus to increase stability in Central and Eastern Europe. The Union's involvement includes substantial economic assistance, closer political links, wide-ranging association or Europe Agreements, rapidly growing trade relations and now a pre-accession strategy, the centre-piece of which is the White Paper on the adjustments which the Central and East European countries will have to make to meet the requirements of the Internal Market. Thus the Union has a range of policies tailored to the situation and needs of each country and which is constantly evolving to meet changing circumstances.[5]

Following the European Council in Madrid in December 1995, a new phase in the enlargement process has begun with the request from the Council to the Commission to start preparing the opinions on the applicant countries with a view to their being forwarded to the Council *'as soon as possible after the conclusion of the IGC'*. The Council also reiterated its view that all candidates should be treated equally and expressed the hope that the first stage of accession negotiations could begin at the same time as those already agreed for Malta and Cyprus, namely six months after the conclusion of the IGC.[6]

At the 1993 Copenhagen European Council, it had been agreed that 'the associated countries of central and eastern Europe that so desire shall become members of the European Union' and that 'accession will take place as soon as an associated country is able to assume the obligations of membership by satisfying the economic and political conditions required'. These

---

[5] There is now a considerable literature on the EU's relations with the associated countries of Central and Eastern Europe. For a critical assessment, on the trade side, see *inter alia* A. Winters, *Europe's Trade Policy with the East*, London, 1994.

[6] Conclusions of the European Council, Madrid, December 1995, *Bull. EC*, 12-1995, 9.

requirements include stability of political institutions, respect for human rights and the protection of minorities, a functioning market economy, the capacity to cope with competitive pressures and acceptance of the Union's objectives as regards political, economic and monetary union. The Council also drew attention to the Union's capacity to absorb new members. This institutional aspect was 'an important consideration' affecting the interests of both the Union and the candidate countries.[7]

The Union has thus made an unequivocal commitment to the goal of membership for the associated countries who now number ten – Estonia, Latvia, Lithuania, Poland, Czech Republic, Slovakia, Hungary, Romania, Bulgaria and Slovenia. At the same time, however, the Union must seek to ensure that further enlargement lives up to the expectations which it has aroused. Candidate countries must be in a position to accept and implement all the rights and obligations which this involves. It is equally important that the Union be in a position to absorb new members, while maintaining its sense of purpose, its integration, and, above all, its capacity to act in the interests of its citizens.

VI. THE PRE-ACCESSION STRATEGY

Accordingly, the Union has put into place an unprecedented pre-accession strategy to prepare for the next enlargement. The principal elements of this strategy are as follows:

a) Wide-ranging association or Europe Agreements which provide for comprehensive cooperation in political, economic, trade, cultural and other areas. Association Councils meet regularly to discuss issues of common concern, as do parliamentarians from the associated countries with their European Parliament counterparts.

This dialogue is not taking place in a vacuum. Rather it is part of a process of political and economic rapprochement which is, also, without precedent. The Europe Agreements, whose very name conveys a sense of their ambition, provide the framework for rapid progress towards free trade. The Union has already eliminated tariffs and quotas in all but the most sensitive sectors, and remaining restrictions applying to steel and textiles will be phased out by the end of 1997. Improvements in market access are being made in agriculture, and the Commission is examining ways in which integration can be pursued in this complex area. In a report to the European Council in Madrid the Commission proposed a number of alternative strategies for improving the position of agriculture in the Central and East European countries.[8]

Overall, a massive reorientation has taken place in trade flows, with the Union today accounting for 60 per cent of the associated countries' trade. This compares, incidently, with less than 5 per cent for trade with the United

---

[7] Conclusions of the European Council, Copenhagen, June 1993, *Bull. EC*, 6-1993, 12.
[8] See note 6.

States, and less than 2 per cent for trade with Japan. At present the EU runs a trade surplus with the associated countries but this is quite normal given their current stage of development.

There would be little point in the Union opening up its markets if barriers remain in trade among the associated countries themselves. For this reason the Union strongly supports the Central European Free Trade Area (CEFTA) and its extension to all associated countries. As trade barriers fall, direct investment should increase, with further gains to productivity and competitiveness.

b) *The PHARE technical assistance programme*, amounting to over one billion ECU annually, which promotes economic reform in fields ranging from energy and transport to agriculture and privatization. The programme is demand driven and changes to meet the requirements of recipients. For example, in 1995 PHARE has focused increasingly on investment, especially in infrastructure, and on cross-border projects.

c) A *regular structured dialogue* with ministers and senior officials of the Union on an increasing range of Union policies. Never before have candidates, or potential candidates, been invited, well in advance of accession, to participate on a regular basis in joint meetings with the institutions of the Union. Today it has become normal for the associated countries to hold joint ministerial meetings with the member states, prepared in advance by officials. A permanent dialogue among 25 states on issues such as the trans-European networks or international crime prevention can be of immense practical value.

d) *The White Paper*, approved at the Cannes European Council in June 1995, on the steps which the associated countries must take in order to prepare themselves to operate in the Internal Market. The White Paper provides a guide to the complexities of the Internal Market and suggests a logical sequence in which the associated countries should go about bringing their legislation into line with that in the Union. Legislation, to be effective, must be properly implemented and enforced, and so the White Paper also provides guidance on the necessary regulatory and administrative structures.

The principal responsibility for implementing the White Paper's recommendations lies with the associated countries themselves. The sooner their laws, conformity tests, standards institutes, and judicial procedures are adapted to those in the Union, the sooner their businesses will feel the benefit. However, the Union recognizes that advice and support are needed and so the Commission is establishing a new technical assistance office for the purpose. It will draw on the experience of the member states in transposing Union legislation into national law in order to advise partners in central and eastern Europe. The Commission will be working with each associated country to devise its own strategy for alignment with the Internal Market, taking into account its economic situation and reform priorities.

VII. THE NEED FOR CONTINUING REFORMS

This brief, and by no means comprehensive, outline of the pre-accession strategy is sufficient to indicate the Union's deep commitment to the preparations for future enlargement. Equally important, however, are the preparations being made by the associated countries themselves. The Copenhagen European Council set out the broad conditions of eligibility for Union membership, which relate primarily to the rule of law, the respect for human rights and fundamental freedoms, multiparty democracy and a functioning market economy. In addition, candidates are expected to accept the *acquis communautaire*, that is all EU legislation and common policies, as well as the Union's future aims, including economic and monetary union.

The first priority in preparing for Union membership is the consolidation of political and economic reform. This will enable the Commission to confirm, when it issues its opinions on applications for membership, that the Copenhagen principles are fully respected. The free flow of information, and the independence of the media and the judiciary, are essential elements in the consolidation of democracy. On the whole, the record is good, but there are worrying developments in some candidate countries.[9]

Good relations with neighbouring states and the, often related, question of respect for minority rights are also important in preparing for membership. Here, too, a great deal of progress has been made thanks largely to the efforts of the countries concerned, partly within the framework of the Stability Pact.[10] But again a number of sensitive issues remain to be resolved.

Just as important as the consolidation of democracy and stability is the pursuit of sound macro-economic policy and economic reform. The adoption of internal market legislation, as provided for by the White Paper, will only produce the expected benefits if accompanied by the right economic policies. The Treaty on European Union sets out clear criteria for macro-economic policy, with a view to achieving the degree of convergence needed for participation in economic and monetary union. Several associated countries consider that they are already in a position to satisfy these criteria. In others, however, further progress is needed in bringing inflation, debt and government deficits under control.

Privatization is another key feature of economic reform in all associated countries. In general, it is proceeding well. But mere changes in ownership are not sufficient to improve competitiveness: restructuring is also essential. In addition, privatization must take place in transparent and objective conditions, without discrimination or favour if it is to create a climate of confidence which will attract new investment. Foreign investment is a source of growth, development and innovation in all market economies and it should be welcomed as an opportunity and not regarded as a threat.

---

[9] The EU has made a number of démarches concerning Slovakia.

[10] See paper on the Stability Pact presented by Fraser Cameron at the US Defence Agency Conference in Philadelphia, June 1993.

Competition policy and state aids controls also need to be brought into line with the Union in order to create equitable conditions for trade and investment. This will bring distinct benefits both for the Union and for the associated countries. For once satisfactory implementation of competition law and state aids control, as well as other White Paper measures, is achieved, the Union could decide to phase down the use of commercial defence instruments, since there would then be a guarantee of fair competition comparable to that inside the Union itself.

Potential investors will also want to be sure that host countries provide adequate protection for intellectual and industrial property rights, before they supply sophisticated new goods and services. Here, too, adequate mechanisms for implementation and enforcement are as important as the legal framework itself.

VIII. A TIMETABLE FOR ENLARGEMENT

The impatience of the associated countries to speed up their accession to the Union is understandable. After years of hardship under communism, they want to be accepted fully into the institutions, which have, for so long, sustained our own freedom and prosperity. The prospect of accession is especially important for those who are living with the short-term costs of economic transition. But on the question of a timetable for enlargement, at present no clearer answer can be given than the already mentioned statement made in the Madrid European Council, because it depends on a successful outcome of the IGC, and the progress of the applicant countries in continuing the political and economic reforms necessary to prepare for membership.

Meanwhile the Commission has started work on the preparation of the opinions on the candidate countries as well as a composite document on the impact of enlargement on the Union. In the preparation of the opinions the Commission is seeking information from the applicant countries through a number of questionnaires on different policy areas. The aim of the opinions is to evaluate each applicant's readiness and preparations for membership. A key issue is obviously to what extent the candidate countries have fulfilled their obligations under the Europe Agreements.

It is the Commission's intention to have the first drafts of the opinions completed by the end of 1996, ready for transmission to the Council after the conclusion of the IGC. If the IGC does not conclude before the summer of 1997 there will be an opportunity to update the Commission opinions. Clearly, each applicant wants to be sure that its progress to accession will not be delayed by others. The Commission is firmly of the view that, if some countries have made sufficient progress in preparing for membership, they should not be delayed because others have not reached the same level.

Whilst the associated countries continue with their reforms, so too must the Union adapt its policies to create the conditions for successful entry by new members on an affordable and sustainable basis. In some policy areas, according to the Commission's reports prepared for the Madrid European Council, there will be few problems; in others, such as the CAP or Structural Funds, adjustments will have to be made and transitional periods negotiated. At this stage it is impossible to forecast the financial implications of enlargement because of continuing changes to many EU policies.

In the agricultural sector, for example, the Union has embarked on important reforms to make the CAP more market-orientated, taking account also of international commitments in the Uruguay Round. These reforms, which are already having their effects, will by the year 2000 have resulted in changes which are difficult to predict. Predictions of the development of agriculture in the CEECs over the medium-term are equally uncertain.[11]

IX. THE IGC AND ENLARGEMENT

But the Union is also faced with the challenge of strengthening its own institutions and decision-making procedures to prepare for enlargement. This will be the job of the 1996 Intergovernmental Conference. Essentially the IGC will have to review the operation of the Maastricht Treaty and ensure that the Union has a solid base on which to enlarge. With the prospect of Malta and Cyprus, plus up to ten associated countries from central and eastern Europe joining the Union in the coming years, *the question of institutional reform can no longer be avoided.*

The fundamental question which we need to address is *how to organize a European Union with perhaps 25-plus members on the basis of democracy, transparency and efficiency?* In the Commission's report to the IGC, the necessity of the IGC taking decisions to ensure that an enlarged Union would continue to function effectively was emphasized. The European Parliament has also pointed to the need for major institutional reform whilst Mr Westendorp's Reflection Group came to a similar conclusion. But in the member states, there are very different views on the need for reform. The British government, for example, speaks of the IGC merely undertaking a 5,000 kilometre service whilst in Germany there are influential voices calling for a major overhaul of the engine.[12]

There have been attempts to secure institutional reform in the past but they have never succeeded. As a result of a dispute on institutional matters (the threshold for qualified majority voting) before the EFTA enlargement negotiations were completed, the European Council in 1995 made a direct

---

[11] See *Study on alternative strategies for the development of relations in the field of agriculture between the EU and the associated countries with a view to future accession of these countries,* published by Mr Fischler in December 1995 (CSE (95) 607).

[12] In contrast to the situation before Maastricht, there is now a massive range of documentation concerning the IGC. A large number of these documents, including the positions adopted by the European institutions and the member states, is available on the Europa Server via Internet.

linkage between enlargement and the 1996 IGC when it stated that '*the institutional conditions of ensuring the proper functioning of the Union must be created at the 1996 Intergovernmental Conference, which for that reason must take place before accession negotiations begin with countries of Central and Eastern Europe*'.

In plain language this meant that the institutional question had to be tackled successfully *before* enlargement. This view was underlined by the Commission in its report to the IGC which called for greater recourse to majority voting, simplified legislative procedures and greater transparency.

The IGC already has a heavy agenda but the enlargement issue should concentrate minds on institutional reform. It is clear that each new accession increases the burden of work and the diversity of issues to be handled. This suggests that the IGC will have to pay greater attention to the application of the subsidiarity principle. What should be the balance between decisions taken and tasks attributed at the Union, national, and regional level? How can greater involvement in, and acceptance of, the Union's activities by its citizens be achieved? On the institutional side, attention will need to focus on how to improve the preparation, taking, and implementation of decisions in an enlarged Union which will inevitably involve more complex and diverse considerations.

Perhaps the most sensitive of the institutional issues is the question of changes to the voting system in the Council. The larger states will certainly press strongly for greater attention to the size of population. Another contentious issue will be the range of decisions to be taken by qualified majority vote. Member states are already becoming accustomed to the idea that they may not be on the winning side of every vote but that, on balance, their interests are served by a system which maintains its capacity to act and is not confronted by vetoes. This should give no cause for alarm as history shows that, whatever the formal position, the Union is based on solidarity and has always shown understanding when a member state has a particular difficulty on a major issue.

Other difficult issues include the nature and composition of the six-monthly rotating Presidency/Troika system, the manner in which the Council transacts business (a tour de table with 25 member states, with each speaking for just five minutes, would take over two hours!), and the linguistic regimes and costs of interpretation/translation.

As regards the Commission, there is a wide consensus on the need to reduce the number of Commissioners – but that is the end of the consensus. If rotating Commissioners cannot be agreed, then it may be worthwhile exploring the option of giving the Parliament a greater say in the nomination process. The difficulties surrounding the appointment of Mr Santer have certainly fuelled calls for a more open and democratic system of choosing the Commission President.

As for the Parliament, there does seem to be a consensus emerging to limit its numbers to 700 and to simplify its highly complicated procedures. Although it has gained important new powers under the Maastricht Treaty, it remains far from satisfied with its position *vis-à-vis* the other institutions and it could well seek to use its potential to block further enlargements unless it gains additional powers, particularly in co-decision.

X. CONCLUSION

In conclusion, enlargement is a political imperative for the Union which should promote peace, security, stability and prosperity in Europe. The enlargements which brought Greece, Spain and Portugal into the European Community had as a basic motive the consolidation of democracy and stability in countries which had abandoned totalitarian regimes. For the countries of Central and Eastern Europe, membership of the Union has a similar significance. The efforts required to integrate the applicant countries are well within the capacity of the Union.

If enlargement is to succeed, however, it is essential that it should be well prepared and be accompanied by considerable deepening of the Union. The Union must be able to take decisions quickly, ensure that they are implemented and that they rest on popular support. In effect this means acceptance of a community approach based on the principle of subsidiarity.

The prospect of EU membership continues to offer the best incentive to the Central and East Europeans to persevere with political and economic transformation. The changes which have to be made are often painful, and so far have brought little reward for politicians in office. Without the sustained encouragement of the EU, a number of countries could easily be blown off course.

It is clear, therefore, that there is much work ahead for the associated countries and the Union in preparing for enlargement. But instead of feeling impatient at the time needed to complete this process, we should seize the opportunity offered by the next two or three years to make a real success of the pre-accession strategy. The more that can be achieved in advance, the easier the accession negotiations will be.

14

ECONOMIC ASPECTS OF EU
ENLARGEMENT TO THE EAST

Jim Rollo[1]

I. INTRODUCTION

The purpose of this paper is to explore some of the economic implications of enlargement to the East. The major issue which separates this enlargement from previous enlargements is the question of transition from communism to democracy and the market. In particular, it is the transition to the market that provides the greatest practical test for the countries of the East and contributes to the more than usually opaque processes that are likely to be at work over enlargement. This paper, however, is not about transition, it is about enlargement. Thus while the introductory stages of the paper will make some passing reference to the process of transition[2] and progress on that front, the main focus will be on what is being done and what needs to be done in the countries of the East to make them ready for membership and – the majority of the paper – the implications of membership in both the EU and in the East.

II. THE POTENTIAL MEMBERS, THE CRITERIA FOR MEMBERSHIP AND A TIMETABLE

Before moving on to description and analysis, it is worthwhile reminding ourselves of the countries concerned, the criteria they have to face for membership and the possible timetable. The initial pool for enlargement to

---

[1] Chief Economic Adviser, Foreign and Commonwealth Office, London. This paper represents the personal view of the author. It is not an expression of official British government policy.
[2] It can be argued in this context that the CEEC-10 have implicitly chosen harmonization with the EU as the transition path.

252

the East is made up of ten countries (CEEC-10) who have signed Europe Agreements with the EU. These are Bulgaria, the Czech Republic, Estonia, Hungary, Latvia, Lithuania, Poland, Romania, Slovakia and Slovenia. Within that group, there are sub-groups who may be referred to in the course of this paper. Most obviously the so-called Visegrád-4 of the Czech Republic, Hungary, Poland and Slovakia who were the first to sign Europe Agreements and the CEEC-6 which are the Visegrád-4 plus Bulgaria and Romania since these are the six largest economies and when it comes to the discussion of some of the budgetary effects represent the vast majority of the impact.

The previous paragraph implicitly dealt with one of the criteria for membership, which is to have signed a Europe Agreement with the EU. This in itself implements free industrial trade and a degree of integration into the Single Market. The Copenhagen European Summit of June 1993 set out three main criteria for EU membership. These can be summed up as democracy, the market economy and a stable economic and monetary environment – here interpreted as meeting the Maastricht criteria for EMU. No detailed timetables or tests were set for meeting the democracy or market economy criteria. In 1995, however, the Commission published a White Paper which set out the Single Market legislation that the Central and East Europeans would need to adopt and implement if they were to be fully integrated into the EU. It was not, however, set out as conditions that need to be met before membership, but rather to give the Central and East Europeans a clear vision of what they would need to do before membership and as part of any transition after membership. There is thus an element of uncertainty about how the Copenhagen criteria can be or should be interpreted.

The Central and East Europeans have been pushing since the negotiations for the first of the Europe Agreements for a clear timetable to membership. The EU has resisted giving such a timetable on the grounds that, whatever was said, negotiations take their own time. Nonetheless, at the Madrid European Summit of December 1995 the Heads of State expressed the hope that accession negotiations would begin with at least some of the Central and East Europeans at the same time as those with Cyprus and Malta, six months after the end of the IGC. As a result of this, all of the CEEC-10 have been sent questionnaires by the Commission to collect the information necessary to draw up an opinion on the readiness of each State to open membership negotiations and to become full members of the EU. These questionnaires are due to be returned as this paper is being completed, at the end of July 1996. Commission opinions will follow shortly after the end of the IGC. The timetable for the IGC is uncertain as this paper is being written, but results seem unlikely before the middle of 1997, which puts off the opening of negotiations to the end of the Luxembourg Presidency in the second half of 1997 or the beginning of the British Presidency in 1998. Some in Central and Eastern Europe still speak of membership by the year 2000, but based on historical precedent, that seems unlikely. Some point in the first half of the first decade of the next century seems more probable.

Table 1 The market and wealth in Central and Eastern Europe

	Private Sector Value added as % of GDP 1993	GDP at PPP as % of Greece 1993
Bulgaria	45	39
Czechoslovakia	70	79
Estonia	65	36
Hungary	60	55
Latvia	60	29
Lithuania	55	34
Poland	60	43
Romania	40	34
Slovakia	60	54
Sovenia	45	86

Source: *EBRD* 1996

III. TRANSITION

How far is transition relevant? The Copenhagen market economy criterion makes it very important. How progress of the transition to the market economy is measured is therefore important. Unfortunately there is no easy answer to that (EBRD 1996, World Bank 1996). As Table 1 shows, the private sector is now in excess of half of the economy in the Visegrád-4 and in the Baltics. It has not yet reached that level in Bulgaria, Romania or Slovenia. Even in the countries where the private sector is tending towards two-thirds of the economy, there are ambiguities. Agriculture was always largely in the private sector in Poland and that may give an inflated view of how rapidly Poland is privatizing. Other aspects than simply the nature of ownership may also be important. For example, by July 1996 the Czech Republic, Hungary and Poland had all qualified for membership of the OECD. Most important within that, was the fact that they qualified for the capital market codes, which are a minimum guarantee of freedom to invest and capital market transparency in OECD countries. That is by itself an important indicator of transition. Looked at from the other end, many countries joined the EU or the EC with levels of public sector involvement in the economy close to those in the most advanced transition countries now.

Another consideration often mentioned, though it is not strictly related to whether or not the economy is a market economy, is the level of income per head. Table 1 also shows GDP per head at purchasing power parities in 1993 as a percentage of the Greek level. This shows Slovenia and the Czech Republic as being within striking distance of the Greek level; Hungary, Slovakia and – at a stretch – Poland at around half the Greek level; and the rest around a third of the Greek level. These numbers will change. Currently, Poland is

Table 2 Trade integration with the EU

	Share of Exports 1994
Bulgaria	48
Czechoslovakia	59
Estonia	49
Hungary	61
Latvia	39
Lithuania	30
Poland	69
Romania	48
Slovakia	48
Slovenia	66

Source: EBRD 1996

growing around 6 or 7 per cent a year. That rate of growth could potentially be continued for some considerable time to come (see Rollo and Stern, 1992). It could also be repeated elsewhere in Eastern Europe if restructuring of the economy goes ahead, if trade is open, and if macro-economic policy is prudent. Growth in the European Union is likely to be low by these standards, even among low income members, such as Portugal or Greece which in recent years have not been able to grow more than 3 or 4 per cent. At a growth rate differential of 4 per cent per annum which is possible, if optimistic, (since Greece ought to grow faster than 3 per cent, but has actually only grown at slightly more than 1 per cent per annum in the 1990s so far) Poland could catch up in 20 years and be enjoying an income per head comparable to the UK today. On the other hand, relative income is not by itself a criterion for membership. If it was, none of the Iberian group or Greece or Ireland would have qualified for membership in the 1970s and 1980s. Equally, modern work points to compatibility of economic systems and degree of trade integration as more relevant criteria.

On these last two criteria, Eastern Europeans may do better. A healthy not wealthy economy may be the correct economic criterion on compatibility which brings us back to the transition issue. On trade integration, the picture is better still. The CEEC-10 trade has reorientated extremely quickly from being dependent on the old CMEA countries to being integrated with the European Union. Table 2, which relates to 1994, gives the share of EU destinations in total exports. The Baltics apart, most countries are around 50 per cent or above. For the Visegrád-4, the EU share of exports is of the order of 60 per cent plus. These are high figures. Work in the early years of transition suggested that trade shares with the EU would tend towards 60 per cent or more as transition advanced and GDP increased (Hamilton and Winters, 1992). That was implicitly a medium-term judgment and expected to happen in ten or more years. Instead, it took barely two years for it to happen.

In the early years of transition, it was possible to dismiss this as distress-selling as markets in the East collapsed. As time has gone on, however, these high trade shares, particularly in the Visegrád-4 have been sustained and it looks as if the process of trade integration with the EU is firmly embedded.

Another way of thinking about the integration issue is to pick up on the question of regulatory integration. As noted above, all of the CEEC-10 are faced with the White Paper list of EU directives. They are to a greater or lesser extent legislating them. All have parliamentary committees confronting this issue. Simple measures of numbers of directives, however, are not by themselves enough. There is also the question of implementation, which is difficult to monitor (See Fingleton et al., 1996, for a very thorough discussion of competition issues, including implementation, on which they are rather complimentary.). Effective competition policy has an important role in reassuring EU-15 that the transition States are playing the game. It is also worth noting that the banking system shows signs of being shaky to different degrees in all of the transition countries. On the other hand, there are also good signs. As already noted, Poland, Hungary and the Czech Republic are OECD members. The Visegrád-4, Slovenia and Romania are members of the World Trade Organization which gives some guarantees about the rules which should apply in trade and remedies where they are not applied.

Overall, this is a messy picture with progress consistent within countries, but not across them. This last point is hardly surprising, but worth noting, since it may bear on judgments made in the Commission opinions and during negotiations for membership. It is also worth remembering in this context that in essence the transition countries all have to change their regulatory structures away from communism. They are all doing so in the direction of the EU regulatory model. This may put them in a somewhat easier situation than, for example, Greece, Spain and Portugal on entry, in a sense that they will not have to make significant changes to an existing regulatory system. While it is important not to exaggerate, this means that they may be closer to the EFTA countries in this dimension who all had to adopt the Single Market under the European Economic Area regulations ahead of membership.

IV. A FRAMEWORK FOR CONSIDERING THE ECONOMIC EFFECTS OF ENLARGEMENT OF THE EU

This section draws heavily on Baldwin, 1994. It uses traditional and more modern integration theory to point out the types of effects that might be expected from Eastern enlargement and to look at the impacts on consumers, producers, trade investment and policies at the EU level.

Before turning to more theoretical aspects it is perhaps worth reminding ourselves of the size of the entities involved here. In 1995, the populations of the EU-15 and the CEEC-10 were 370 and 106 million respectively. While at market exchange rates, the EU-15's gross domestic product was valued at $7.6

trillion, the CEEC-10's was valued at $0.25 trillion. So while populations are not hugely out of scale, income is. This reflects both the fall in output in the early years of transition, but also the heavily undervalued nature of the market exchange rate. At purchasing power parities, the Eastern Europeans would be around half a trillion dollars of GDP. The important point to draw from this is that in economic terms, if not political terms, the EU is orders of magnitude more important to the CEEC-10 than is true in reverse direction.

It is also worth reminding ourselves of what membership would mean for the CEEC-10. On the economic side, it would mean giving up a free trade area and joining the EU Customs Union. It would mean integrating into a Single Market completely with implications for regulation, for competition policy, for freedom of movement of capital, freedom of movement of people as well as freedom of movement of goods and services. It would mean signing up for certain regulatory standards on the environment, on social policies. It would mean becoming members of the single currency, though whether immediately on membership of the EU or later is unclear. It would mean signing up for contributions to the EU budget, to membership of the Common Agricultural Policy, to the structural policies in some form, to research policies, and to contributions to aid policies to the developing world.

A. Trade creation versus trade diversion

The traditional way of looking at economic integration is to compare the amount of trade created with the amount of trade diverted. Trade creation takes place when in a preferential trading area the lowest cost producer in the world can take advantage of the free trade zone to expand output and replace high cost domestic producers previously protected by tariffs. Trade diversion takes place when formation of a preferential trading area excludes the low cost producer from outside the market to the advantage of a higher cost producer inside the market.

The first point to make is that under the Europe Agreements, the CEEC-10 are already signed up to a free trade area, i.e. one which all the members have their own independently determined external tariff, but agree to apply zero tariffs to other members. This applies to industrial trade and is on a so-called 'hub-and-spoke' basis, i.e. a series of bilateral arrangements between each country and the EU.

There are, however, remaining barriers. All free trade areas require rules of origin to prevent trade deflection (where imports from outside the area come in through the country with the lowest external tariff), there are anti-dumping provisions and safeguard clauses in the Europe Agreement (sometimes referred to as contingent protection provisions), and agriculture is almost wholly excluded from the trade arrangements. And there are barriers to trade among the CEEC-10 which would disappear on membership. Putting these barriers on one side for the moment and reminding ourselves of the rapid growth in the EU share of CEEC-10 exports over the last five years, it is an assumption that much of the trade creation and/or diversion will already have taken place. The rapid growth of trade and the relatively low tariffs at least initially on the Visegrád-4 side and on the EU side both argue that each side has become a low cost producer on each other's markets, while not being in a position to displace third countries where they are competitive since tariffs are relatively low, or at least were so in the early years of the transition.

On the CEEC-10 side they are such a small proportion of total EU imports – between 1 and 2 per cent – that it is improbable except for some small sectors that they could have diverted trade as a result of the Europe Agreements. Assuming no trade diversion is more problematic on the side of the EU on the CEEC-10 markets. Nonetheless, European firms have significant advantages, notably closeness to market over third country firms and, as long as protection in the CEEC-10 against third countries remains relatively low, then the dangers of diversion from the Europe Agreements is relatively low. Developments in recent years on the latter issue have not been good, however. CEEC-10 tariffs have tended to rise and in some sectors, for example motor vehicles, they are high or are accompanied by quotas. Sometimes these increases in protection have been at the behest of foreign investors from both the EU and outside. And there are in place temporary import surcharges in the Visegrád-4 justified on macro-economic grounds. In any case, the East Europeans have been liberalizing against the EU at a slower rate than the EU has been liberalizing against them which also argues that trade diversion losses in Eastern Europe are not likely to have been high, so far.

What would change on membership is that the Free Trade Area would become a Customs Union. This would have some advantages. First, it would remove the need for rules of origin which are a form of administrative protection and probably reduce investment from third countries (Rollo, 1993). Secondly, it would harmonize tariffs on the EU level which, agriculture apart, are on average lower than the CEEC-10 level, and which by itself should lead to trade creation. Thirdly, in conjunction with membership of the Single Market and implementation of EU competition policy rules, full membership would lead to the disappearance of contingent protection, which would remove potential if not actual trade barriers between the EU and the CEEC-10. It would, however, give the benefit of anti-dumping duties against firms in third countries to CEEC-10 producers. Nonetheless, anti-dumping duties are firm specific and not country specific, hence the impact on potential trade diversion is indeterminate. The temporary nature of anti-dumping duties also makes their long-run effects hard to map.

That is not say there are not dangers of trade diversion. Over the life of the EU, the only policy which has unambiguously generated trade diversion, is the Common Agricultural Policy. This has raised domestic production at the expense of imports throughout the EU. CEEC-10 membership under existing CAP rules would almost certainly raise output and exports to both the EU-15, but also to the rest of the world. This is an issue to which I will return later. The second area where the dynamics of membership may be important is textiles and perhaps one or two other areas where membership of Central Eastern Europe could become the lowest cost producers inside the EU (the other areas that are possible are steel and bulk chemicals, see Rollo and Smith, 1993). In this case it is possible that once they become members of the EU, the CEEC-10 will argue for and obtain higher external protection than would otherwise prevail, thus diverting trade from third countries to themselves. Progress on liberalizing the multi-fibre arrangement and other multilateral liberalizing processes will have an important bearing on these potential sectoral trade diversion problems.

B. Investment

One of the major areas where modern experience and theorizing has brought forth new thinking about integration is investment. Throughout the post-war period capital markets have been slowly liberalizing. Until the end of the 1970s, very few countries had completely liberalized capital flows. Since then barriers have fallen. At the same time, the fall in trade barriers and greater acceptance of the benefits that of multinational firms bring, had led to an explosion in direct investment in emerging markets. As a rule of thumb, since the beginning of the 1980s trade has expanded twice as fast as output at a global level, while direct investment has expanded at twice the rate of trade. These investment flows have generated not just global integration, but also a degree of regional integration, particularly in Asia. At the beginning of the transition period, it was widely held that the transition would be driven by liberal trade flows and foreign direct investment. To an extent the first is true (Polish growth is driven, for example, largely by exports over the last three years) but not, unfortunately, the latter.

The reasons for this are, with the benefits of hindsight, perhaps not so difficult to find. Foreign investors had a number of uncertainties to face. Property rights were uncertain for some time, even in the most rapidly reforming economies. Time was also required to assess the nature and stability of democratic institutions and whether or not the economic environment was going to be stable: there was little benefit, for example, in investing under conditions of hyper-inflation. Where the intention was to build an export platform into the EU the nature of the trade concessions and the difficulties which contingent protection and rules of origin may have offered was also a disincentive. And even where the domestic market was the objective, the political uncertainty, the problems with property rights and the small size of the market as well as the collapse in real income in the early 1990s were all disincentives.

C. The benefits of integration

Theoretical analysis, notably the work of Krugman and Venables on economic geography, suggests that integration should bring investment inflows.

First integration reduces the cost of trade, second it increases competition in the enlarged market which then allows capital to exploit the relatively low cost of human capital in Eastern Europe (high human capital endowment, low real wages). This demonstrates one way in which exports and investment drive growth rates up. There is also empirical evidence that economic integration increases inward investment. Before 1985, Spain was receiving inward investment at a rate of about $\frac{1}{2}$ per cent of GDP per annum. After joining the EU this increased to around $1\frac{1}{2}$ per cent of GDP per annum in the period up to 1990. This was at least partly driven by expectations of economic expansion on the back of integration. A similar boost to cross-border investment took place in the late 1980s within the then EU-12 as a result of expectations driven by the Single Market process. This even led to investment from the EFTA countries into the EU-12 and was a significant factor in the formation of first the European Economic Area and subsequently the pressure for EFTA membership of the EU. These arguments are rehearsed at length in Richard Baldwin's book (Baldwin, 1994) and I will not take them further here.

D. Growth

The combination of higher output as a result of both the trade liberalization plus increased inward investment raises the question of the impact on growth. This is relatively uncharted territory. Most economists are comfortable with suggesting that trade liberalization and the investment it induces will lead to a once and for all boost to output, but are distinctly uncomfortable when asked if it will contribute to growth. Once more, Baldwin has some thinking to offer on this (Baldwin, 1990). In the context of the Single Market, he started with the Cechini Report estimates of $1\frac{1}{2}$–4 per cent increase in GDP and then adduced dynamic effects driven by rationalization of capacity; by increased competition and overall more competitive firms. He applies some of this analysis in Baldwin 1994 and comes to the conclusion that integration should increase growth rates in both the East and, to a lesser extent, in the West.

V. POLITICAL ECONOMY – WHO WINS, WHO LOSES?

The immediate answer to this question is that it is too early to tell because we do not know how EU policies are going to change. Nonetheless it is worth having a first look at the issue, not least because it may give us some hints about how EU policy might have to change in the face of enlargement. It is also worth looking at the issue of winners and losers in the short and longer term.

A. Who wins?

In the short term, CEEC export industries, notably those in the sensitive sectors (agriculture, steel, chemicals, textiles (Rollo and Smith, 1993, Neven,

1995)) and labour-intensive manufacturing are more likely to gain as increased access to EU markets allows them to increase market share. Also in the short term, EU exporters will gain as CEEC-10 protection, particularly for high value added consumer goods and services, is reduced. The outcome of that is that consumers from both the EU and the CEEC-10 should benefit from lower prices as competition increases on both markets. The one potential and important exclusion from this is agriculture. Unless the CAP is reformed, consumer and farmgate prices will not fall in the EU, but they will rise in Central and Eastern Europe. Finally, Central and Eastern European taxpayers could benefit from increased fiscal flows from the EU-15. These could both reduce tax burdens (depending on whether they are additional or not), but also as a result of the secondary effects raise real incomes (a point to which I will return).

In the longer term, the same groups will benefit, but I would also expect higher value added export industries to begin to develop in Central and Eastern Europe and at a faster rate than they would have done without EU membership (see the section above on investment).

B. Who loses?

In the short term, it is possible that CEEC-10 producers of high value added goods, of traded services, and in the finance industry could suffer from increased competitive pressures. Also, as noted above, CAP prices would reduce consumers' benefits from enlargement. In the EU, low skilled labour in agriculture and manufacturing as well as the taxpayers who may have to pay for higher agricultural bills and more expensive structural funds. Over the longer term, I am tempted to say that no one loses after adjustment since economies reoptimize. However, this is a variant on the jibe attributed to J. M. Keynes that in the long term we are all dead.

C. Dynamic political economy

This section is about the areas of policy that will cause problems in both the EU and the CEEC-10 and will require, or at least may lead to, policy adjustments. On the EU side the potential taxpayer costs of unreformed CAP and structural funds generate one set of problems. Leaving aside the implications of increased competition in declining industries (the sensitive products again) the other issue which may lead to significant problems, at least at a political level if not at an economic level, is migration. On the side of the CEEC-10, different problems will be generated by unreformed EU policies. First, as we will see, the levels of financial transfers that might be generated by unreformed policies could cause macro-economic absorption problems. Secondly, adapting to EU competition and state aids policies, might cause difficulties with domestic pressure groups which might arise at a sectoral level (the CEEC-10 have their own sensitive products). Thirdly,

Table 3 Estimates of budgetary costs of CEEC accession to the CAP

Study	Cost of V4 (BECU)	o/w direct payments (%)	Cost of CEEC-6 BECU	o/w direct payments (%)	% GDP at market prices	Comment
Brenton and Gros (1992)	4–31		5–42		2.3–19.6	Dated. Based on pre-McSharry CAP.
Anderson & Tyers (1993)	37				21.4	Based on sophisticated model of agricultural output. But data and relationships open to question.
Tyers (1993)	22–27				12.7–15.5	As above. But with some relationships adapted to be more plausible.
UK Government (1994)	15	6 (42)	23	10 (43)	9.7	Assumes CEECs reach same levels of technical efficiency as those currently achieved in similar parts of the EU.
Australian Bureau of Resource Economics (1994)	12.3	4.4 (35.7)			7.1	Based on model based simulations of agricultural recovery in CEECs.
Tangerman (1994)	13.3	4.3 (32.3)	19.3		9.0	Work still in progress on final model. Projected recovery of output fits facts.
Mahé (1994)			12.2–16.1	4–7.3 (32.7–45.3)	5.7–7.5	Output recovery roughly same level as Tangerman. Range given by different accession dates: 2000 for lower, 2005 for higher.
EC Commission[a] (1995)			8.9	6.6 (74.2)		Based on comprehensive review of individual supply changes. Assumes accession 2000 and no further CAP reform. Some consider crop projections low.

[a] NB for CEEC-10

Note: Results depend on differences in timing of accession; rate of recovery of output; connection of direct payments to production.

competitiveness of the CEEC-10 industries might be threatened by immediate and full application of environmental regulation and social protocol requirements which are not sustainable at current levels of productivity and income. Finally, EMU may cause problems, though perhaps not of the sort most commonly expected.

VI. FINANCIAL COSTS TO THE EU OF APPLYING EXISTING POLICIES

A. The CAP

Table 3 summarizes the main studies of applying the current CAP to the CEEC-10. They all start from an underlying assumption that prices will rise significantly as a result of application of the CAP and that compensation payments will be made available to the CEEC-10 (even though the latter were designed to compensate EU-12 farmers for cuts and prices under the 1992 reform of the CAP). These studies are undertaken from differing sets of assumptions about underlying conditions in the CEEC and using more or less sophisticated approaches to modelling the impact of CAP prices and subsidies on production. Table 3 starts with the oldest study and goes to the most recent estimates of CAP costs. It gives details of both the Visegrád-4 and the CEEC-6 (with the implicit assumption that the Baltics plus Slovenia will be relatively low cost mainly as a result of their size). It also shows, where available, the extent to which the costs are driven by compensation payments and where relevant what the budgetary transfers to the CEECs concerned would represent as a proportion of GDP. This last bears on the macro-economic absorption question.

The table can be summarized as suggesting that if there is little or no production response, then the budgetary costs are likely to be of the order of 8 billion ECU with a low estimate of 4 billion ECU (the low estimate from Brenton and Gros and the higher estimates from the Commission). If there is a positive production response, the budgetary costs rise to between 12 billion ECU and 40 billion ECU with a clustering around 20–25 billion ECU in the more sophisticated work by Mahé, the British Government and, above all, Tangerman for the CEEC-6. The other sophisticated modelling carried out by the Australian Bureau of Economics looked only at the Visegrád-4 and came up with the number of about 12 billion ECU, which is broadly comparable with Tangerman for the Visegrád-4. The highest estimates come from a complex model by Tyers and Anderson and estimates based on a range of output assumptions, but not rigorously model based, by the Dutch Finance Ministry. The Tyers and Anderson work had considerable publicity when it was used by Baldwin (Baldwin, 1994), but subsequent examination suggests that while the modelling is high quality, the data and the policy simulations were not of equivalent quality. On the basis of reputation and quality of understanding of how the CAP works, Tangerman's figure of the order of 20 billion ECU is plausible if there is a significant supply response in Eastern Europe. Of this, some 40 per cent seems likely to be generated by direct payments (British Government and Mahé both came out in this region). The Commission suggests that almost three-quarters of the costs would be direct payments, but only by assuming low supply response. CAP transfers could represent almost 10 per cent of 1994 GDP at market prices.

B. The structural funds

Structural funds here means the regional funds and the cohesion funds. We will be talking about these at country level, but for the regional funds in particular, they are of course based on the existence of a national regional policy. Some existing member states, e.g. Ireland, are treated as a single region for this purpose, but this is not the norm. As a result, it is possible that extrapolating the impact of the existing expenditure patterns from the EU-15 to potential recipients in Central and Eastern Europe may not give entirely accurate results. But this is largely the method that has been followed. Starting from receipts per head in the so-called Cohesion four countries – meaning Spain, Portugal, Greece and Ireland – and applying them grossed up by population in Central and Eastern Europe. This approach is based on the fact that GDP per head at PPP in Eastern Europe is well below the levels of even the Cohesion 4 (see Table 1) plus the lack for the moment of the detailed information on the underlying circumstances in the CEEC-10 that would allow a more precise simulation. Table 4 reports a series of estimates mainly by official sources which try to put numbers on costs using this basic methodology. The ranges usually depend on which subset of receipts per head (e.g. the average, the poorest, etc.) within the Cohesion-4 are used and which year's numbers are used. They take no account of whether as a result of EU membership some countries would graduate from the structural and cohesion funds as the average income per head in the EU falls. The figures in Table 4 thus represent both gross and net estimates of the impact. These

Table 4 Structural funds
Estimates of Structural and Cohesion Funds payments to CEECs

	V4 receipts (BECU)	CEEC-6 receipts (BECU)	% GDP
UK Government	21	31	16
Baldwin 1994		26	13

Note: All estimates rely on same basic methodology of assuming an allocation per head of structural and cohesion Funds to the CEECs upon membership; ranges determined by assumptions about whether the CEECs receive the Greek average receipts per head or the Cohesion-4 receipts per head.

numbers are by any measure large, and point to something approaching a doubling of the structural funds. More interestingly they represent somewhere approaching 10–15 per cent of the recipient countries GDP averaged over CEEC-10 as a group.

C. Absorption problems in the CEEC–10

Before moving on to possible reactions to these numbers in the EU-15, it is worth reflecting on their implications for CEEC-10. The transfers are large in absolute terms, but they represent about two-thirds of 1 per cent of EU-15 GDP. For the CEEC-10, however, as Table 5 shows, the numbers could be substantially greater. These are based on British Government estimates of CAP transfers and structural funds allocated on a country basis among the CEEC-6. As can be seen from this, transfers among the Visegrád-4 vary from 17–24 per cent and in Bulgaria and Romania from 29 per cent to a staggering 56 per cent of GNP. This compares with a transfer of 7.6 per cent of GDP to Greece – 4.8 per cent structural funds and 2.8 per cent CAP. These numbers have very significant implications if they were ever to come to pass. Even 17 per cent of GNP transferred year in and year out to Hungary would have an immediate and significant effect on the exchange rate which would appreciate. It would also impact on the fiscal side, partly because the structural funds in particular may require national contributions before they can be triggered, which could well increase public expenditure. At the same time inflows of these magnitudes would allow very significant balance of payments deficits to be run and reduce the pressure on governments to run prudent

Table 5 CEEC-6: the absorption problem
Impact of Possible Community Transfers to Central and Eastern Europe

	Structural Funds[a]	CAP transfers[a]	Total	% GDP[b]
Czech Republic	3398	2100	5498	18
Hungary	3339	2200	5539	17
Poland	12555	9600	22155	22
Slovakia	1749	700	2449	24
Bulgaria	2929	1700	4629	29
Romania	7482	6200	13682	56

Note: Table 5 illustrates the scale of transfers which would be made to the CEECs from the main Community programmes. This contrasts with a level of 7.6% (4.8% structural funds; 2.8% CAP) for Greece, the largest recipient of EU funds in the current Union.

[a] UK Government estimates
[b] At market exchange rates

fiscal policies. Even the Maastricht criteria would not be sufficient to rein in the potentially inflationary effects of these levels of inward transfers.

These numbers are clearly untenable. So even if the EU-15 feels unable to afford transfers of this magnitude, the CEEC-10 can less afford to receive them. This is the background against which potential for change in EU policies should be examined.

VII. THE POLICY OPTIONS FOR THE EU AHEAD OF ENLARGEMENT

As noted above, the enlargement negotiations are likely to begin around the end of 1997 or the beginning of 1998. They will take place against a background of exceptional potential for policy change within the EU-15. 1999 represents a year of challenge for the EU-15.

The Edinburgh guidelines on the EU budget which both determined the overall envelope on the budget of 1.27 per cent of EU GNP and the agricultural guideline within that are both up for negotiation. This will take place against the background of fiscal retrenchment as EU-15 countries work to stay within the Maastricht fiscal criteria. It will also take place against the background where two of the net contributors, Germany and the Netherlands, have begun a high profile campaign for a reduction in their budgetary contributions and where the United Kingdom will continue to work extremely hard to reduce the size of the EU budget and to defend its budget rebate.

The structural funds themselves come up for review in 1998. At this point, a number of regions within the EU-15 might cease to qualify for so-called objective 1 regional aid, notably Ireland (which passed UK GDP per head at PPP exchange rates in 1946 according to OECD), but also individual regions in Spain, the United Kingdom, Italy and Germany. Such changes will not take place without a serious and difficult negotiation.

Finally, the agricultural negotiations under the Uruguay Round which concluded with the Blair House Agreement in 1993 are due to be reopened in 1999.

Against that background, EU enlargement is simply another factor in the reform equation. The WTO negotiations will affect both the EU-15 and those of the CEEC-10 which are parties to the Uruguay Round Agreement, notably Poland, Hungary, the Czech Republic, Slovakia and Romania. Already, it is becoming clear that adding up the agreements of the EU-15 and just the applicants in the Visegrád-4 on export subsidies and volumes of support make it unlikely that an enlarged Union would be able to live within these aggregate commitments (Tangerman, Buckwell, et al.). The next section will therefore look at agriculture and structural funds and ask what the options are against this background for absorbing Central and Eastern European applicants into the EU at affordable cost to the EU-15 and without imposing huge absorption problems on the CEE applicants.

A. Agriculture

Pressures from the rest of the world looking for CAP support price cuts, pressures internally, particularly from consumers also looking for lower prices, but also from Treasuries looking for lower budget costs and from the CEECs who – although their farmers might like higher prices – will have to think about the impact of high CAP prices on their consumers (who are on average much poorer than EU-15 consumers). There are two broad approaches to this dilemma. One is a more market-orientated approach and the other is some variant on the status quo.

A more market-orientated approach would take the EU in the direction of world prices for agricultural products – ideally all the way to world prices. This would deal with the agricultural trade problem in the WTO, but it would not deal with a perceived agricultural income problem within the EU, enlarged or not. To deal with this would require income-related subsidies paid to specified farmers (presumably meeting some income criterion) and not tied to the production of any specific commodity. This is close to the economist's ideal. It allows economic efficiency through world prices; it reduces, not to say eliminates, trade tensions and it gives government support only to those who need it against specified criteria. So why the problem? First of all there is a political economy problem inasmuch as farmers do not wish to be considered social security recipients (NFU, 1994). Second, there is a potential cost problem. As noted above, existing compensation payments brought in as part of the McSharry reforms in 1992 already represent a significant proportion of the budget and could, if applied to Central and Eastern Europe, represent at least 40 per cent of the costs. This expenditure was generated where only a few commodities had their prices reduced and then not all the way to world levels. The other difficulty with the compensation payments under McSharry, is that they are not production neutral: they contain an element of incentive to produce.

If the costs of this reform to the budget – and remember that the budget will already be under pressure from those wishing to cut their contributions and from the other elements of the enlargement costs – then there are a limited number of ways forward on the market-orientated approach. One would be to make the compensation degressive, that is time limited and declining. This would suit Finance Ministries, but may not be saleable to the agricultural pressure groups. The other alternative would be – within a strict application of the state aids rules – to allow nationally financed compensation payments.

Either of these approaches would run into difficulties. First, all such reforms are not one-off. Even if it was agreed in the first place that compensation payments should be degressive, there is no guarantee that this part of the deal would not be reopened, particularly if agriculture in the Union had one or two bad years. Secondly, common financing has totemic qualities in the Union with respect to existing common policies. Any move to

267

renationalize, rational though it might be, would be portrayed by some as a move backwards in European integration and hence difficult to deliver politically. These difficulties suggest that while market-orientated reform will play an important part in any approach to the agricultural problem, it may not deal with all of the issues.

Variations on the status quo may, therefore, come into play, for example through use of supply controls. By an extension of production quotas to the East and a tightening of quotas in the existing EU-15; or the extension of set aside within the existing EU-15 as well as to the CEEC-10 (but this would require compensation for output lost); some countries may hope to contain both the costs of agricultural support within the budget envelope and also reduce potential exports so as to meet the existing or new WTO negotiated limits on the volume and value of EU export subsidies. This, combined with the non-payment of McSharry compensation to Central and Eastern European members, could potentially contain the costs of enlargement (but note the cost of extended set aside and that supply controls would add new economic disturbance to the CEEC's agriculture). There are difficulties however. It may be politically impossible to set quotas low enough or set aside high enough to meet the WTO constraints. Equally, it is difficult to see how under the Treaty, the new members could be excluded from compensation payments, even though they never enjoyed the high prices on which the compensation is based. Once more, there is no obvious feasible single answer.

This is not a new experience in reforming the CAP. Almost every attempt at reform since the first under Mansholt in 1968 has resulted in some mix of new measures and intensification of existing measures. Thus under McSharry, while price cuts and compensation was an entirely new approach, continued dependence on milk quotas, herd limits, set aside plus a non-reform of the sugar regime was a continuation of the status quo. It seems possible, if hardly desirable, that any reform of the CAP (under the pressures outlined above and by around the end of this century) will contain lower prices certainly, but possibly also a continuation of quotas in the dairy sector (due for review in 1999 in any case) and of set aside in the arable sector. Compensation will perhaps be at lower levels than now and more clearly delinked from production to meet WTO requirements on export subsidies and total volume of support. Whether compensation will be extended to new members may depend on the nature of the scheme, but if it is, then there may be an element of degressivity or of national financing to make it palatable to Finance Ministries in the countries which are net contributors to the budget.

B. Options for the structural funds

Given the size and numbers above, some thinking has gone into how integrating the Eastern applicants into the structural funds could be made affordable to the EU-15. Two main approaches have emerged: one based on graduating existing recipients out of structural funds, the other based on limits on overall receipts. The first is in many ways the most rational. It keeps the structural funds roughly in their current form with their current purpose of dealing with the low income parts of the Union.

As noted above, it is possible that at the review of the structural funds in 1998/99 some countries will find they are graduated out in all or in part of receipts under the so-called objective 1 regions – those with income per head below 75 per cent of the Union average – even before enlargement. Ireland had a GDP per head of 72 per cent of the EU average in 1990 in PPP terms. This had risen to 82 per cent by 1996 and by 1996 had surpassed UK average GDP per head according to OECD (1994), p. 202. Similar graduation issues could effect some Spanish regions, notably Catalunya and some Italian regions. More radically, some have suggested excluding current net contributors to the regional and cohesion funds from receipt, meaning the UK, Germany, France, Bennelux and the Scandinavians. With these sorts of exclusions it is possible that the Central and East Europeans could be absorbed into the structural funds without a huge increase in the overall envelope.

The problem, however, is getting the turkeys to vote for Christmas. Spain, Greece, Portugal and Ireland together come close to forming a blocking minority. In addition there is the fact that Germany would be very reluctant to give up regional aid for the Eastern Länder and that, similarly, for other net recipients the gross receipts from the regional funds play an important political role both internally and with respect to attitudes towards the EU. There is likely to be a major internal debate over what solution could produce a qualified majority for Social and Cohesion Funds reform. It may, therefore, be difficult to put together a qualified majority for reform.

A variant on graduation would be not to do it at once, but to have a defined process of graduation which tapered payments to the existing recipients downwards, while at the same time allowing a gradual increase in payments to the Central and East Europeans. This still has to confront the turkeys and Christmas problem, but might be easier to negotiate. It runs into another problem, however, which is that the applicants, if they continue to grow, will receive less money in the early years of membership when they are poorer and more later when they are richer, which runs counter to the purpose of the scheme. On the other hand this approach does have the advantage that it reduces the absorption problems referred to above.

The alternative approach would be to leave all the existing policies in place, but to put an upper limit on net receipts from the structural funds – and perhaps other sources of Union financing – so as to deal with the absorption problem. I have suggested elsewhere (Rollo, 1995) a figure of 5 per cent of GDP. This is entirely arbitrary, but is more than the existing highest level of receipts in the EU-15 which is 4 per cent of GDP to Greece. The Commission has suggested something similar, as part of an overall scheme to maintain structural fund spending within the current envelope of 0.46 per cent of Community GDP when combined with some graduation of existing recipients (Hughes & Grabbe, 1996).

The main justification for such upper limits is the absorption problems referred to above. The numbers, however, would be significant even at 5 per cent of GDP. This would represent in 1994 GDP terms a total of around 10 billion ECU which would be ten times the current PHARE spending. And there would be additional receipts from Common Agricultural Policy sources even, I surmise, if the CAP were reformed radically. So the macroeconomic difficulties are only reduced, not removed.

This approach also runs into the same difficulty in logic that the tapering approach does: as these economies grow they will get more money from the regional funds rather than less. Despite these drawbacks, however, I cannot see how it would make sense for member states to receive transfers at levels which would complicate macro-economic policy in the way that unconstrained transfers from the structural funds would.

VIII. PROBLEMS IN THE REAL ECONOMY

As noted in passing above, it will be difficult for the applicant member states to apply the requirements of the social protocol of the Maastricht Treaty or the degree of environmental regulation that is now embedded in the *acquis communautaire* immediately and in full. They are at a lower level of economic development, they have a lower quality capital stock, they have less good public sector infrastructure. All of which would point to the situation where the Social Protocol and environmental standards are legislated for but not implemented in any meaningful way. That would only bring the EU into disrepute and could spread to other parts of the *acquis* which are relevant and enforceable in the current circumstances of the applicants. The impact of the application of such social and environmental regulations (IFO Munich estimate up to 5 per cent of GDP p.a. needs to be invested for fifteen years to meet environmental standards (EBRD, 1996, p. 80)) will be to restrict the competitiveness of industries and the new applicants, reduce their profitability, their ability to export and in the long run the growth rate of the countries concerned. Such a slow down would reduce their rate of approach to EU economic and social norms (see Smith et al., 1996). This seems a prime area where long transition periods granted to the East Europeans would make sense. This would be complex because sectoral interests within the EU would – no doubt in conjunction with environmental campaigners and trade unions – argue that trade was unfair and hence should be restricted if it did not meet these norms. Down that route lies a break in the Single Market.

At the same time, for political rather than economic reasons, some of the same groups, notably in the EU-15 labour movement, may find it difficult to accept free movement of labour from the new member states. Real wages are currently low in Central Europe relative to Germany in particular and the opening of borders must be presumed to lead to increased migration. In economic terms, this would be entirely to the good. It would reduce real wages, particularly in relatively low skilled activities and increase the competitiveness of Western European firms leading in turn to an increase in demand and output. Those whoever who have to compete with this lower price labour will hardly welcome the prospect. This is a political problem for governments of the EU-15. Those in the applicant States will see no advantage in being excluded from Western labour markets. In the world of realpolitik there may be room for some sort of trade-off between freedom of movement of labour on the one hand and Social Chapter and environmental standards on the other.

IX. CENTRAL AND EAST EUROPEAN APPLICANTS AND EMU

As noted above, the Copenhagen criteria might be taken to imply the need for the Central and East Europeans to be ready for EMU membership when they joined the EU. This raises the particular issue of fixed exchange rates and the countries in transition. Exchange rates in Eastern Europe are below their long-term levels. The difference between market exchange rates and purchasing power parity exchange rates (market rates on average half of PPP rates (EBRD, 1996, p. 10)) is one measure of that. In any case, it was expected, as indeed happened, that as the transition process got underway, market exchange rates would fall relative to the artificial exchange rates in place under the old CMEA regime (Rollo and Stern, 1992). This, combined with the need for the traded goods sector in Eastern Europe to become competitive on world markets by retooling and reorientating their output, also leads to the expectation of undervalued exchange rates.

Over time, therefore, one would expect the real exchange rate in Eastern Europe to appreciate relative to the rest of the world. This can happen in a number of ways. The most straightforward is through nominal appreciation accompanied by low inflation. The alternative is through fixed nominal exchange rates and relatively high domestic inflation. In many countries that trade-off is hedged with an attempt to use the exchange rate as a nominal anchor for the economy to keep inflation down, but with occasional nominal appreciations. In other countries (Poland, Hungary and Russia are obvious examples at the moment) there is an attempt to force the exchange rate down against the background of high domestic inflation so as to sustain the competitiveness of exports. This last strategy may be sustainable in the short term, but not in the long, not least in circumstances of inward capital flows, as has been the case in Hungary and, to a degree, in Poland in recent years.

The real question is what would happen if the applicants moved to irrevocably fixed exchange rates against their main trading partners. The first point is that the CEEC-10 will be extremely competitive over the longer term against the rest of the EU, which should give rise to export-led growth. That however in turn will lead to capital inflows which will also in turn lead to local inflationary pressures, mainly through rising real wages if demand is not damped otherwise. The main way of doing that would be to tighten fiscal policy so that these countries run fiscal surpluses rather than deficits.

The conclusion, therefore, that one might draw from this is that there would be no harm to the real economy from membership of EMU, indeed the opposite, since the applicants could lock themselves in at very advantageous exchange rates for the long term. The dangers lie on the fiscal side where the Maastricht criteria on budget deficits and government debt are likely to be too loose rather than too strong. Even the Waigel stability pact suggesting an upper limit of 3 per cent on the budget deficit and an average budget deficit of 1 per cent of GDP would be too loose. These countries, if they are successful in pursuing export led growth, will require tighter fiscal policy than that. This is as much a danger before membership as after, if they are treated as a target not as a ceiling. Already the Polish authorities, for example, point out that their budget deficit meets the Maastricht criteria. However, even if combined with capital inflows and a relatively buoyant balance of payments suggests that they should be aiming for budget surplus. The Maastricht criteria may be leading the CEECs to be complacent. That is bad enough now when they have control over the exchange rate and could change policy. It would be more difficult within EMU where exchange rate policy is out of their hands.

X. THE EASTERN ENLARGEMENT AND THE REST OF THE WORLD

Before concluding, it is worth reflecting on the implications of enlargement for the rest of the world. This mainly has its relevance in the sphere of commercial relations. Let me first begin with what I see as the positive aspects of this for the rest of the world.

First the Central and Eastern European countries will become part of the Customs Union which has important consequences for the rest of the world. Notably – and to repeat points made above – tariffs will be lower on average and bound; there will be an end to rules of origin and to EU anti-dumping and other contingent protection against Central and Eastern Europe both of which will be good for investment. Outside trade policy, it will extend the Single Market to Central and Eastern Europe. This will have two effects. First, it will extend the *erga omnes* provisions of the Single Market to the Central and East Europeans. The impact of this will be to give a single passport for services and on standards for third countries across a much wider market. Secondly, it will improve the investment climate because it will embed property rights and the regulatory structure in a credible way.

On the downside are two main issues. First is the problem of dealing with an EU of up to 27 members in the WTO (including, perhaps, Malta and Cyprus). The difficulties here mainly come in the context of the internal negotiations required within the EU before it can come to a multilateral negotiations in the WTO. This was a difficult problem in a Union of twelve during the Uruguay Round and the increased numbers and the wider range of interests to be taken into account are likely to make it harder still in the future. That said, it may end up being no more difficult than in a large country such as the US where the interaction between administration and Congress and the industrial lobbies is at least as complex as that within the EU, as difficulties in 1996 on the WTO Telecoms negotiation demonstrated.

The second potential downside is the possibility of increased sectoral protectionism generated within the Central and East Europeans. The example to look at here might be that of Portugal who, when outside the EU, was a proponent of liberalization of EC textiles regimes, but once it became a member, became a defender of the multi-fibre arrangement in particular. This is an expression of the dangers of trade diversion outlined above.

Finally and more speculatively, a Union of 25-plus with its own internal agenda which goes beyond trade and international economic linkages, may find it difficult to summon the energy or the bureaucratic resources to deal properly with the rest of the world. In short, a more inward-looking EU.

XI. CONCLUSIONS

This paper has attempted to survey a number of economic issues which are likely to arise in the context of EU enlargement to the East. To that extent, it is not meant as a balance sheet of costs and benefits (but on which see Baldwin et al, 1997). Nonetheless, some points do emerge and might be briefly summarized as follows:

- Enlarging the EU to the East will be good for: consumers on both sides; producers of agricultural and other sensitive products and labour-intensive manufactures in the CEEC-10; and exporters of high value capital goods, consumer goods and traded services in the EU-15. It may also be good for taxpayers in the CEEC-10 (depending on the level of transfers and how far they substitute for existing spending). It will be bad for producers in protected sectors in the CEEC-10; for producers of low value added manufactures and products benefiting from high protection in the EU-15. It will also add to taxpayers' bills in the EU-15 and if the CAP is not significantly reformed to consumer costs in the CEEC-10.
- It will increase trade in both directions and should make a significant difference to the inflow of investment to the East. The two together should contribute to sustaining and perhaps increasing high rates of growth in Eastern Europe with benefits for Western Europe from the dynamism induced. There are risks of trade diversion, but outside agriculture they are small.

- The application of unreformed European policies, particularly in agriculture and for the structural funds to Eastern Europe, would generate large budget costs, possibly of the order of 50 billion ECU. Such numbers are untenable in the current fiscal context of the EU-15. They would represent 25 per cent of 1994 CEEC-10 GDP and generate very significant problems of macro-economic management to the extent that they would cause more harm than good.
- The opportunities for agricultural reform are increasing as we approach 1999. Budgetary pressures within the EU-15, the need to renegotiate the Uruguay Round agreements on agriculture beginning in 1999, and enlargement all come together to put pressure on the CAP. There are pressures both for more market-orientated agricultural policy – ideally world prices and income subsidies delinked from production – and also for continued use of supply controls. It is too early to tell the outcome of these pressures.
- On structural funds there is to be a review in 1998 which, combined with the review of EU budget financing in 1999, may of itself bring reform. In any case, some regions could graduate from objective 1 status, which may release some funds. Another possibility is to put upper limits on receipts to deal with the macro-economic absorption problems noted above. Some combination of graduation and limits may be needed to make the policy both affordable and sensible in application.
- Other parts of the *acquis communautaire* could also cause problems to both the EU-15 and the applicants. For the EU-15, labour mobility whatever its economic benefits – and they are real – may cause political problems. For the new members, application of the social protocol and the immediate and full application of the environmental standards embodied in the *acquis* could significantly affect the competitiveness of their firms, and hence their export performance and their growth potential.
- Membership of EMU could well help the Eastern applicants by locking their exchange rates at long-term undervalued levels against EU-15 partners. The Maastricht fiscal criteria, however, risk being too lax for the new members and may tempt them to fiscal complacency.
- Enlargement would bring benefits for the rest of the world, mainly lower tariff barriers and probably also non-tariff barriers, extension of Single Market to a wider area, all of which could add to increased investment opportunities. On the downside, an EU of 25 or more could be more difficult to negotiate with and more inward-looking.

REFERENCES

Andersen, Kym and Rod Tyers, 1993, *EC Enlargement and East European Agriculture*, Working Paper 792 (CEPR, London).

Australian Bureau of Agricultural & Resource Economics (ABARE), 1994, *Directions of change in EU Agricultural Policies*, presented at Royal Institute of International Affairs round table on Future Directions for EU agricultural policy, London.

Baldwin, R., 1989, 'Growth Effects of 1992', *Economic Policy*, 9.

Baldwin, R., 1994, *Towards an Integrated Europe*, CEPR.

Baldwin, R., J. Francois, and R. Portes, 1997. *The Costs and Benefits of EU Enlargement to the East, Economic Policy*, April.

Brenton, P. and D. Gros, 1992, *The Budgetary Implications of EU Enlargement*, CEPS Working Paper 78 Brussels.

Buckwell, A. et al. (1994), *Feasibility of an Agricultural Strategy to prepare the countries of Central and Eastern Europe for EU accession. Report to the European Commission (DG1)*.

European Bank for Reconstruction and Development: *Transition Report 1996*.

European Commission, 1995a, Directorate General for Agriculture, *Agricultural Situation and Outlook in the Central and Eastern European Countries. Summary Report*, Brussels.

European Commission, 1995b, *European Economy*.

Fingleton, John, Eleanor Fox, Damien Nevin & Paul Seabright, 1996, *Competition Policy & the Transformation of Central Europe*, Centre for Economic Policy Research, London.

Hamilton, C. and L.A. Winters, 1992, 'Opening up International Trade with Eastern Europe', *Economic Policy*, 14.

Hughes, Kirsty & Heather Grabbe, 1996, *EU Enlargement & the Structural Funds*, mimeo, RIIA, London.

Krugman, P. and A. Venables (1989), 'Integration and Competitiveness of Peripheral Industry' *in* Bliss and Braga de Macedo (eds), *Unity with Diversity in the European Community*, CUP for CEPR, 1990.

Mahé L.-P., 1994, *L'agriculture et élargissement de l'Union européenne aux pays d'Europe centrale et orientale: transition en vue de l'intégration ou intégration pour la transition*, Report to DG I of the European Commission.

Neven, D., 1995, 'Trade Liberalization with Eastern Nations: Some Distribution Issues', *European Economic Review*, 39.

NFU, 1994, *Real Choices for the CAP*, National Farmers Union, London.

OECD (1997) *Main Economic Indicators*, April.

Rollo, J. and J. Stern, 1992, 'Growth and Trade Prospects for Central and Eastern Europe', *World Economy*, Sept.

Rollo, J., 1993, *Economic Transition and European Integration*, RIIA Mimeo.

Rollo, J. and A. Smith, 1993, 'The Political Economy of Eastern European Trade with the European Community: Why so Sensitive?', *Economic Policy*, 16.

Rollo, J., 1995, 'EU Enlargement and the World Trade System', *European Economic review*, 39.

Smith, A. et al., *The EU and CEE: Pre-Accession Strategies*, SEI Working Paper 15, Sussex European Institute, 1996.

Tangerman, S. and T.E. Josling (1994), *Pre-accession agricultural strategies for Central Europe and the European Union. Report to the European Commission (DG1)*.

Tyers, R., 1994, *Economic Reforms in Europe and the Former Soviet Union: Implications for International Food Markets* (IFPRI, Washington).

UK Government (1994). As presented by Atkinson N. and J. Slater at Agricultural Economics Society Conference 1995.

World Bank, *World Development Report 1996*.

15

TOWARDS A SINGLE PERSPECTIVE.
ECONOMICS AND POLITICS OF
EASTERN ENLARGEMENT

Jacek Saryusz-Wolski[1]

I. INTRODUCTION

The successful enlargement of the European Union to include the Eastern and Central Europe (hereinafter CEEC – Central and Eastern European Countries) is the key condition for the reunification of Europe. The term reunification involves the economic as well as the political and security structures of Western and Eastern Europe. Therefore, it is important to work out a consistent conceptual framework which would place political and economic factors within a single perspective. At present, one may distinguish two ways of linking Eastern enlargement to the political and economic context. The first approach regards politics – broadly understood – as the main engine behind Eastern enlargement. According to this view, the CEEC should be accepted into the EU because of strategic, political and cultural considerations. The economy, on the other hand, is seen as a principal stumbling block in the future negotiations due to the presumed magnitude of the financial costs for the Union.[2] Contrary to this position, the second approach, while recognizing political benefits of enlargement, argues that the economics itself provides essential arguments in favour of enlargement. Both contentions are grounded in the analyses of the economic aspects of enlargement. Therefore, the first purpose of this article will be to review the existing research on cost estimations and to discuss the origin of this discrepancy. Subsequently, I shall suggest a research area on which to focus in order to provide us with a more complete view of the economics of enlargement. Finally, I would like

---

[1] Vice-Rector of the College of Europe in Warsaw.
[2] This point of view has been summarized by Baldwin: 'If EU politics is the engine behind an Eastern enlargement, economics is the brake', R. Baldwin, *Towards an Integrated Europe*, CEPR 1994, 156.

to propose a new framework which would encompass both the economic and political side of enlargement.

II. WHY ECONOMICS IS SO IMPORTANT IN THE PROCESS OF ENLARGEMENT

The first reason why economics is so important in the process of enlargement is the afore-mentioned discord in the Western approach to political and economic rationalization of this process. The issue of Eastern enlargement has been on the agenda since 1991 and it is therefore somewhat surprising that on the West European side there is still no clear consensus around it. From our point of view such a situation is a worrying one, because it means that Western decision-makers are not quite sure how to present the enlargement to their electorates. This may result in slowing down the whole process. Some politicians choose to speak about the enlargement in terms of Western responsibility for the Yalta Agreement which, against the will of its inhabitants, left Eastern Europe under the rule of the Soviet Union for the next 45 years. Whereas one may argue that such responsibility indeed exists, the Bosnian crisis demonstrated that moral considerations provide a rather feeble basis for political actions. The second line of reasoning seems to offer more solid grounds in this respect since it refers to the policy and security issues: it is argued that enlargement is indispensable for the creation of stable political systems in Eastern Europe. The disadvantage of this approach is that currently the probability of political turmoil and instability (with consequence for domestic defence outlays) appears low, even without the prospect of the immediate membership of the CEEC in the EU. Moreover, most of the profits have been cashed already; five years after the fall of Berlin Wall the 'peace dividend' which alleviated public defence budgets (due to the increase in Western security stemming from the collapse of the Warsaw Pact) is taken for granted.

What the two positions have in common is the conviction that the enlargement would entail enormous financial costs to Western Europe. These costs are due to the fact that the CEEC are supposed to be incapable of meeting fully the obligations of membership and are thus perceived as a price to be paid for a clear conscience, political stability and military security. Whereas in the first period following changes in the post communist countries the West declared that it was prepared to meet this price, it is clear now that this is no longer the case. Hans van den Broek put it in a nutshell when he stated recently that: 'No candidate for membership of the European Union can assume that enlargement will go ahead anyway for broadly political reasons'.[3] The origins of this change in attitude are obvious: the Maastricht criteria restricting budgetary expenditure, high unemployment, the crisis of social

---

[3] Van den Broek's address at the EU–Slovakia Joint Parliamentary Committee on June 3, *European Report* No. 2137, 5 June 1996.

security systems and low rates of economic growth. Since the economic and political setting of the European Union does not seem likely to change radically in the coming years, the economic dimension of the enlargement will gain even more importance as we approach the beginning of the negotiations. This would lead to the situation in which, as noted by one of the Western politicians, an appeal to solidarity, to the European ideal, and to the institutional links with the countries of Central and Eastern Europe might not be sufficient to sway public opinion.[4] Put another way, a successful enlargement will not take place until Western politicians and public opinion are convinced that enlargement will not entail negative economic consequences and huge budgetary costs.

III. HOW MUCH THE ENLARGEMENT IS GOING TO COST

Western research on the budgetary costs of the enlargement went through two phases:

In the initial phase, cost estimations were based on *ad hoc* models, which took for granted that the structure and, consequently, response of the CEEC economies to the new stimuli provided by the enlargement, would be analogous to that of developed Western economies. Perhaps the most striking example of this approach might be found in the analyses on the extension of the CAP to Poland. Typically, the calculation of CAP costs for Poland accepted an 'equal production equal consumption' assumption, which implied that Polish agriculture could attain Western productivity levels in five to ten years.[5] Agrarian output was thus considered as a linear function of agrarian prices; as a result, the increase in the prices following Poland's accession to CAP would entail a steep rise in production and virtually bankrupt the EU budget. Needless to say, such an approach overlooked completely the wealth of structural – economic and social – factors which make such an increase entirely unrealistic.

A similar approach may be found in the analysis of the costs of extending the EU's regional policy to the CEECs. Here the methodological point of departure was most often a regression line based on variables derived from the EU member states' economies.[6] Another way of arriving at huge budgetary

---

[4] D.-J. van den Berg, 'Opening Address by the Secretary General of the Ministry of Foreign Affairs of the Netherlands', *Report of the Conference Enlargement of the European Union with Central European Countries; Challenges and Constraints*, The Hague, 17–18 March 1995, 2.

[5] See, for example, *Implications of EC expansion for European agricultural policies, trade and welfare*, CEPR Discussion Paper, June 1993 (829); *Impact of Enlargement to the East on the Common Agricultural Policy*, Agra-European Outlook Conference, 22 February 1995, London; *Report of UK Ministry of Agriculture, Fisheries and Food*, London, 1995.

[6] F. Breuss, *Costs and Benefits of EU's Eastern European Enlargement*, WIFO Working Papers, 1995 (78); R. Baldwin, et al., *Is Bigger Better? The Economics of EC Enlargement*, Monitoring European Integration 3, CEPR, London, 1992.

costs was to assume that CEECs would receive per capita financial transfers equal to those received by Greece or other cohesion countries. Such issues as absorption and management capacities or the ability of CEEC economies to co-finance potential investment projects were left out.

No wonder, then, that the overall picture presented to the Western public was rather gloomy – massive budgetary costs combined with the flood of cheap agricultural imports from the CEEC. This way of conceiving enlargement shifted the focus of public attention to the budgetary aspects and from the very beginning the integration of Eastern Europe was associated with high financial costs for the EU. Moreover, all this happened in the key phase of setting the agenda for the EU strategy in the 1990s, when the problem of the enlargement was presented to the public for the first time. As a result, the initial public support faded away and the whole issue began to be viewed as one-sided sacrifice by the EU member states. This opinion has been shaping the 'public mood' in the enlargement debate up until know. In my view, the current, increasingly sceptical approach of Western public opinion towards the enlargement (as shown by opinion polls) is a result of the findings provided by this phase of research, even though studies published more recently have thoroughly discredited the initial calculations.

The second phase in the Western research on the enlargement overcame some of the initial methodological fallacies. The basic change was due to the inclusion into the analysis of structural factors inherited by CEEC economies from the communist period. Thus, more recent studies became more realistic: enlargement costs were substantially reduced, forecast agrarian output trends were trimmed down. An example of this new approach has recently been provided by the Commission's White Paper on CEEC agriculture, which recognized most of the obstacles limiting the productive potential of Polish agriculture.[7] It has been acknowledged that Polish agriculture has proven slow to react, both to negative and positive price shocks. Thus, it will most likely imitate the pattern of Portugal and Spain, where the supply response was less than expected.[8] Another element modifying the view on the costs of CAP was the analysis of trends in the agricultural trade between the EU and the CEEC. The myth of a flood of agricultural products supplied into the EU by cheaper producers from Poland and other Central European countries showed up for what it was: a myth. Those who were forecasting massive agrarian imports from the CEEC and, consequently, large agrarian trade deficits on the EU side, had to confront their research with actual changes in the agrarian trade flows following the Europe Agreements. In the

---

[7] 'Poland', in: European Commission, *Agricultural Situation and Prospects in the Central and Eastern European Countries*, June 1995; See also European Commission, *Study on alternative strategies for the development of relations in the field of agriculture between the EU and the associated countries with a view to future accession of these countries*, December 1995.

[8] A. Kwieciński, 'EU Agricultural Policy; Some Comments from a Polish Perspective', in: *Report of the Conference Enlargement of the European Union with Central European Countries; Challenges and Constraints*, The Hague, 17–18 March 1995, 38.

last five years all the CEECs, with an exception of Hungary and Bulgaria, and CEECs as a whole, recorded increasing deficit in the agrarian trade with the Union. Poland, which in 1991 had a trade surplus of 847 million dollars, in 1994 had an 88 million dollar deficit.[9] What is interesting, this deficit is mostly due to the decrease in Polish exports to the EU, despite the presumed asymmetry stipulated by Europe Agreement. The negative impact of the Union's agrarian policies is also felt on other markets where Polish exporters cannot compete with subsidized exports of member states. Although all these facts were well known to the EU – on this basis the Commission proposed recently to continue to increase tariff quotas by 10 per cent annually – the Union decided to reduce the pace of the liberalization of the agrarian market, suspending the concessions approved by the Copenhagen Summit. From 1996 onwards, tariff quotas for most of the CEEC agrarian imports will increase by 5 per cent annually, instead of 10 per cent, while several products have been exempted from the reduction in custom duties. It is difficult to conceive that such a move is taken on the basis of trade analysis – as we have seen trade figures do not offer any grounds for such behaviour. I would rather argue that the real reason was the pressure from interest groups and public opinion in member states influenced by the aforementioned negative public image of the enlargement.

The analysis of the costs of extending Structural Funds to CEEC underwent a change similar to that concerning the costs of CAP. Although the official position of the Commission still refers to the figures based on Greece's receipts, it acknowledges that financial transfers of this magnitude to CEEC would meet the barrier of absorption and co-finance.[10] Therefore, the real figures should be based not on per capita receipts but on the percentage of GDP of the beneficiaries; the numbers circulating in the Commission vary from 1.5 per cent (current transfers to eastern Länder of Germany) to five per cent (transfers to Greece in 1999).

The magnitude of the reduction in projected costs may be best seen if we compare some estimations produced in the first phase of research with those found in the most recent studies. Baldwin's book – perhaps the most influential and representative study published in the first phase – estimated overall costs for the Visegrad group at 58.1 billion ECU or a 74 per cent increase in the EU budget.[11] Recent proposals by the Commission suggest that the enlargement will be possible without any overwhelming financial lines for the years 2000–2005.[12] According to the Commission the costs of CAP – estimated by Baldwin at 37.6 billion ECU – should not exceed 9 billion ECU, that is no more than 10 per cent of the entire EU budget.

---

[9] Source: *Eurostat.*
[10] European Commission, *The Impact of the Enlargement on the Structural Policy,* 1995.
[11] R. Baldwin, op. cit., 174.
[12] 'Brussels sees EU expansion eastward without budget rise', *Financial Times,* 26 June 1996; Unterrichtung durch Frau Dr M. Wulf-Matthies über *Die Refom der Strukturpolitik insbesondere im Hinblick auf die Erweiterung,* Session of Bundestag, 19.06.1996.

IV. THE OVERALL PICTURE – BUDGETARY COSTS AND ECONOMIC INTEGRATION

Nevertheless, while it is true that this new approach provides a more realistic basis for the negotiations, it is also true that the main focus still remains on the cost side. From the point of view of Western public opinion, this does not change the overall situation much, the only difference being that the costs might be lower. This attitude is still being fuelled by some politicians who, when it is politically convenient, return to Baldwin's numbers, even though now it is perfectly clear that he overestimated the costs of the enlargement by a huge margin. A similar attitude is prevailing in the academic world. Most of the ongoing research on the enlargement makes no real attempt to invest-igate overall economic consequences implied by the integration process. The benefits are usually referred to in general, qualitative terms while the costs have a solid, quantitative form expressed in billions of ECU. Curiously enough, academics are ready to provide the exact numbers with respect to CAP and structural aid, that is two union policies whose shape at the moment of the enlargement is still unknown. They are less enthusiastic, however, when it comes to the estimation of those effects of the integration which are well known to the economic theory and which are much more certain than the future budgetary costs regarding agriculture and regional aid. This discrep-ancy is present in the analysis of the economic effects to date of the applica-tion of Europe Agreements, as well as in the calculation of potential gains stemming from the full integration of the CEEC economies into the EU. The few analyses carried out so far which at least made an attempt to take into account not only the budgetary but also the economic effects of integration, clearly demonstrated that the enlargement entails economic gains for both the EU and the CEEC. It has been estimated that in the last five years, 2.2 per cent increase of real GDP (or 50,000 jobs) in Austria could be attributed to the increase in trade with the CEEC.[13] This is a confirmation of the fact that, as indicated by the large balance-of-trade deficit of the CEECs, the Western community is profiting to a much greater extent from the new open markets. This tendency is likely to continue in the medium and long term – an analysis carried out for Denmark showed that in the medium term, higher budget contributions would be more than offset by the increase in productivity of at least 0.75–1 per cent.[14] Calculations taking into account all the member states predict that in the long term the increase in growth rate would be substantially higher than the rise of budget contributions.[15]

---

[13] Quoted after F. Breuss, *Cost and Benefits of EU's Eastern European Enlargement*, WIFO Working Papers, 1995 (78), p. 4; See also Interview with Erhard Busek, in *Die Zeit*, 6 June 1996.

[14] *Economic Perspectives of Enlargement of the European Union with the Central and Eastern Euro-pean Countries*, Ministry of Economy, Denmark, 1996.

[15] See, for example, Observatoire Français des Conjonctures Economiques, *Rapport d'Information fait au nom de la délégation du Sénat pour l'Union européenne, sur le conséquences économiques et budgétaires de l'élargissement de l'Union européenne aux pays associes d'Europe centrale et orientale (PAECO)*, Sénat, No. 228, 1996. This report estimates budgetary costs of enlargement at 0.2% GDP of member states while the increase in growth rate is estimated at 1.5% GDP.

In fact, the very basic truth behind these observations is that economic growth of closely intertwined economies has benevolent effects for both sides. The major win-win opportunities are: 1. huge infrastructure markets in the CEEC; 2. increase in trade volume benefiting both sides; 3. better exploitation of comparative advantage increasing the EU's competitiveness against Asian competitors; and 4. much needed growth opportunities offered to the EU economies as a result of integration with CEEC. To the best of my knowledge, up until now there has been no evidence of any negative effects of integration at the national, sectoral or regional level.[16]

Lower labour costs in CEECs are often perceived as a threat to the labour markets in the EU. Interestingly, though, such opinions are rarely voiced by EU entrepreneurs. In a recent interview, Wolfgang Roth, a Vice-President of the European Investment Bank, argued that any approach restricting market liberalization would seriously damage the competitiveness of the EU producers and decrease their share in the world markets. The only result of such a policy would be a shift of investment from CEECs to the Asian countries.[17] On a similar theme, David De Pury, the Co-Chairman of ABB, one of the largest investors on the Polish market, emphasizes that the EU must realize that it needs Central and Eastern Europe to regain its global competitiveness, just as much of Japan's future lies in the expanding Asia Pacific.[18] This is true even for sensitive sectors. For instance, in textiles, the weaker EU producers may benefit from the outsourcing of textiles production to CEEC and regain competitiveness vis-à-vis the Far East.

This view on the economic consequences of the enlargement is not unknown to Western politicians. However, the argument that the enlargement is going to benefit the EU in 'the medium and long term' is not very helpful for the politicians who face elections in the perspective of four years. This concern that the EU is losing sight of the strategic benefits of the enlargement was recently voiced by Laszlo Kovács, the Hungarian foreign minister, who pointed out that 'the benefits of security and stability will only appear in the long run, while budgetary commitments will be felt in the short term'.[19] This is a 'democracy trap' encountered by all those who try to pursue a path of economic reform which brings results in the more distant future. Moreover, one cannot exclude the possibility that some politicians seeking votes might find it tempting to resort once again to the already discredited estimates of the enlargement costs. Yet, sooner or later, Western

---

[16] See R. Portes and R. Faini, *European Union Trade with Eastern Europe: Adjustment and Opportunities*, CEPR 1995. The conclusions contained in this volume show that liberalizing trade, even in sensitive sectors, will not bring any damage to EU producers.

[17] 'We are not a transformation bank', in: *Gazeta Bankowa*, 4 August 1996.

[18] Interview with David de Pury, Co-Chairman of ABB Group, in *The Wall Street Journal Europe*, 3 February 1996, 2. See also E. Vaes, *EU Enlargement to C&E Europe. ABB Views and Concerns*, May 1996.

[19] 'East Europeans Fear Slippage in Timetable for EU Expansion', in: *Herald Tribune*, 1 August 1996; also intervention by Minister Kovács at the Third Ghent Colloquium on the Relations between the EU and Central and Eastern Europe, 6 March 1996.

political elites will have to convince their voters about the necessity of the enlargement. It is essential, therefore, to start working on the positive view of enlargement now, without further delay. The presentation of the results of a fair, holistic approach to the economic and political consequences of the enlargement should constitute a central element of this strategy.

V. SINGULAR APPROACH – ECONOMICS AND POLITICS MERGED

The economics can tell us only one side of the enlargement story. However important, it cannot provide us with a complete picture of what may happen after enlargement, both to the CEEC and the member states of the Union. Therefore, we have to call upon the politics, because political decisions – though supported by an economic analysis – are made on the basis of values and convictions.

When the programme of economic reform was started in Poland in 1989, we did not know what its precise result would be. Of course, our expectations were based on some successful examples of well-functioning market economies, but – we are all now conscious of that – there was no model of transformation of the socio-economic and political system from the communist regime to the liberal democracy founded on free market economy. Nevertheless the reform was launched because we could not imagine choosing any other way of solving our country's problems. We did it in the name of 'normality' for the country, we did not do it for the sake of 'approaching' the European Union. This is not supposed to mean that we did not desire Union membership – yes, we thought about it from the very beginning. Yet, our reforms came out of the determination to put our country in order, while our intention to join the Union was a natural consequence of the path we had chosen: liberal democracy based on the principle of free market economy.

Just as there was no example for the path to follow when coming back from communism, there is no precedent for the future Eastern enlargement of the Union. This venture will be qualitatively and quantitatively different from all previous enlargements of the European Communities both in terms of the number of candidate countries and of the diversity of social and economic conditions involved.

This is why we have to make a political choice. We have to base our approach towards enlargement also on political values, on the common historical and civilization links between the countries of all Europe struggling to avoid any recurrence of war between them. This effort is present in the very fundamentals of European integration just as much as in the claims frequently raised by the Central and Eastern Europeans that there is a vacuum in the heart of Europe, which has preferably to be filled by the Western institutions – NATO and the EU – as quickly as possible.

Politics always overlaps with economics. Together they influence people's economic behaviour. When we speak about security in the region we have in mind not only the strategic security and the efforts to avoid the war, mentioned in the previous paragraph. We also mean 'soft security' of our region. The economic side of the future enlargement can be seen in the context of 'soft security' as thousands of individual decisions to invest in our countries and trade with them, to travel there, to build lasting private links with their friends in the CEEC. This fundamental effect of the future enlargement cannot be estimated in sheer numbers, but this is what we call – inversely – the costs of 'half-Europe', the costs of non-development. Politics on its own is not capable of creating wealth and well-being for the citizens of the polity, nevertheless the very vocation of politics is to create possibilities for the polity.

We can observe the merger between politics and economics in daily activities of the European Union. However these are expressed in economic terms, the so-called convergence criteria of the Economic and Monetary Union put forward in the Maastricht Treaty on European Union are of a political nature. They correspond to our call for 'healthy, not wealthy' approach towards enlargement: we prefer our candidacy to be considered in terms of macro-economic criteria, but not – for example – in terms of GDP per capita. We welcomed thus the criteria presented by the Copenhagen European Council.[20] They manifest the political nature of the contemporary stage of European integration where economics sometimes forms an obstacle to be overcome, if often tool to achieve the aims, and primarily a means to make integration happen.

VI. 'THE POLITICAL IMPERATIVE'

The latest expression of European political will can be found in the Reflection Group report for the Madrid European Council. This report, itself a product of the meetings of member states and European Parliament representatives in the second half of 1995, constitutes an interesting example of political commitment as it calls future Eastern enlargement a 'political imperative'.[21] This formulation, as opposed to many detailed issues reviewed by the Reflection Group, seems to derive from an overall consensus. Yet it is subject to the equally necessity conditions of preparing enlargement well. In fact, it must be done well enough for the Union to be able to cope with this process, as called for by the Copenhagen European Council.

---

[20] They are formulated as follows: 'Membership requires that the candidate countries have achieved stability of institutions guaranteeing democracy, the rule of law, human rights and respect for and protection of minorities, the existence of a functioning market economy as well as the capacity to cope with competitive pressure and market forces within the Union. Membership presupposes the candidate's ability to take on the obligations of membership including adherence to the aims of political, economic and monetary union.', *Bull. EC*, 6-1993, 13.

[21] 'A Strategy for Europe', the first part of the IGC Reflection Group's Report, Reuters, REU1729 4 OVR 1071 (ECR) F0501057, 5 December 1995.

Therefore, we should note here that the very issue of enlargement largely depends of the success of the 1996 Intergovernmental Conference. However, the preparations for this, as well as its initial proceedings, do not present much hope of starting the enlargement quickly. Given the deep differences of opinion among the member states on fundamental issues concerning the future shape of the Union, one may reasonably wonder about the solidity of the commitment to enlargement.

It would be hard to formulate any viable diagnosis of this peculiar state of European affairs, but we can clearly see possible consequences of it, both for the EU and its Eastern enlargement and for the CEECs themselves. Perhaps the most important repercussion would be the undermining of the very objective of enlargement, clearly perceived by the Reflection Group as the 'best option for the stability of the continent and for the economic advancement not just of the applicant countries but for this Europe of ours as a whole'.[22]

So why not grasp this 'best option'? As was observed earlier, there has been a lot of misunderstanding about enlargement based on miscalculations of its costs. However, we do not only need proper calculations, but also proper European integration perspectives. Regardless of inherent differences dividing the member states today, there has always been – since the very beginning of the integration process – a clear perspective of peace and security, coupled with growing prosperity. This has not changed. What has changed is that now there seems to be insufficient political will. It is probably due to the lack of a firm, clear and sufficiently convincing formulation of common European perspectives. Such a formulation should be expected from the political elite of Europe and its nations. The European elite of the late 1940s and 1950s stood up to their times. The time of challenge for Europe is there again. It is called 'enlargement and a thorough reform of the Union'. These two elements do not have to be contradictory ones. They can easily be mutually reinforcing. Fortunately, our time of challenge is not called 'war' any more.

VII.   ONE FINAL REMARK

My main conclusion is that budgetary expenditures caused by the enlargement cannot be considered separately from the economic and political effects of integration. Any calculation of costs should also include those gains to the EU which have been accruing in the last five years and which can potentially be much higher in the future. We also need analyses showing the costs of 'half-Europe', the costs of prolonging the process of the CEEC's accession to the EU, the costs of not making full use of the economic potential of integration. In order to be successful, enlargement of the Union must meet with the approval of the citizens of the Union. I do not see any reason why

---

[22] Ibid.

this approval should not be based on a realistic analysis of costs and benefits to the European Union and its member states. What I am arguing for, though, is a fair approach to this issue, an approach which would meet the requirements of completeness and credibility. In this respect, particular responsibility rests on the academic community. The issue of enlargement – which is quite exceptional – gives the academics an opportunity to influence the world of politics. This should not be understood as a call to provide politicians with hastily prepared studies which ignore the socio-economic conditions of the CEEC or which take into account only selected factors.

16

COSTS AND BENEFITS OF CZECH MEMBERSHIP IN THE EU

Kamil Janáček[1]

I. INTRODUCTION

The Czech Republic is determined to strive for full EU membership. As the date of membership negotiations approaches, attempts to assess the costs and benefits of EU membership have started. The present paper tries to sum up some preliminary results of these discussions.

II. ECONOMIC LEVEL AND CATCH-UP

Full membership will undoubtedly speed up the process of catch-up with the advanced EU members – as association is already doing. It is clear that the more links there are with the leader (in case of Czech Republic, the EU), the faster the convergence of GDP and consumption per head in the follower country can be achieved.

In recent years the Czech economy has already been growing faster than the EU average in 1994, 1995, and 1996. The catch-up process has already started and narrowed the gap between EU and the Czech Republic (see Table 1). Last but not least, association increases the credibility of the Czech economy and facilitates the inflow of foreign capital needed for restructuring.

Of course, the predominance of EU countries in the international economic links of the Czech Republic can also bring some risks. A recession or slowdown in the EU may hamper Czech growth and the catch-up process. For the small Czech economy, a high degree of dependence on one territory may be a potential source of vulnerability. This is being felt at present, when recession in Germany hampers Czech exports and industrial growth (Germany having a 35 per cent share in Czech exports).

[1] Chief Economist, Komerční Banka, Prague.

Table 1

	1994	*1996*	*2000*
GDP per head at PPP (as % of EU average)	49	59	65

Source: UN Comparative Project, New York – Geneva, 1995.

Table 2 Average level of import tariffs in 1994 (in %)

Czech Republic	4
Poland	10
Hungary	12

Source: WTO Statistical Yearbook 1995, Geneva, 1995.

III. COMPETITIVE ENVIRONMENT

The shift from Comecon markets (in 1989 Comecon countries accounted for 67 per cent of Czech external trade, the EU only 25 per cent) to EU markets (59 per cent at the end of June 1996) has proven the adaptability of Czech exporters to the EU single market. At the same time, the opportunity to export into the EU has accelerated the adaptation, which can be seen as a clear benefit for the Czech economy. Full membership will further improve the competitive environment for Czech producers.

This trend is fully in accordance with the philosophy of the Czech transition programme, which is to liberalize the economy as much as is feasible. For example, in the Czech economy, liberalization of external economic links has reached the highest level among all Visegrád countries (see Table 2).

The Czech Republic also uses fewer non-tariff instruments than some other associated countries. As a result, the asymmetry granted by the EU is less pronounced in the Czech case as compared to other associated countries.

On the other side, competition from the EU can undermine the position of numerous Czech companies, and lead to their collapse. The alteration in the trade balance with the EU from surplus to deficit between 1993 and 1996 could indicate a possibility of such a development at least in some industries.

IV. EU TRADE POLICY

The above-mentioned benefits and risks are closely connected with further trends in EU trade policy. The 1993 Copenhagen Summit has accelerated the abolition of tariff barriers in relation to associated countries.[2] The same

---

[2] See Council and Commission Decisions of 20 December 1993 on the conclusion of Additional Protocols with all countries with whom Europe Agreements have been signed, *OJ*, 1994, L 25/1.

Table 3 Quota utilization in 1994, textiles and clothing (in %)

Poland	42
Hungary	30
Czech Republic	61
Slovakia	34

Source: Commission Services, Brussels, 1995.

is true of the Essen Summit, which stressed the harmonization of legislation concerning competition as a condition for integration of the Visegrád countries into the EU.[3]

Some risks can be seen in the use of anti-dumping measures, regardless of procedures agreed in the association treaty – e.g. in attempts to use the concepts of social or environmental dumping, if classical dumping cannot be proved. A clear example is the attempt by steel companies from Germany, Italy and France to stop Czech and Polish exports by initiating anti-dumping procedures in August 1996. It is highly probable that this attempt will fail – as several previous ones did. In no case so far, has social or ecological dumping been proved. Such attempts are detrimental both for Central European exporters, and for EU consumers.[4]

As to the widely-discussed problem of quotas, we repeatedly hear of the necessity of a step-by-step approach, and of regulation for the so-called sensitive items. Otherwise, it is argued by EU representatives, accession of CEECs would cause large losses of jobs and output – especially in steel, textiles, agriculture and chemistry. Would the costs of the entry of four Central European countries really be so high?

Reality shows that in the so-called sensitive items, direct quotas are underutilized. This implies that the danger for EU producers (from Visegrád countries' exporters) is much lower than generally declared (see Table 3). The important issue in fact is competitiveness in a broader sense – while quotas are, and will be, detrimental for both sides.

Integration of additional countries into the EU, even if their economic level is lower, will bring beneficial effects to both parties. On the one hand, the market will grow wider, and competition stronger. This will bring a positive welfare effect for consumers in all EU countries. Increased competition, of course, can lead to loss of some jobs in a few sensitive industries. At the same time it would lead to growth in high-tech industries (including new job opportunities), where EU countries have a substantial competitive advantage. This can already be observed at present: EU countries form a basis for the technological restructuring of Central European economies. Data on trade and payments balance between EU and the four Central European countries give a clear evidence of this fact.

---

[3] On the competition provisions in the Europe Agreements, see *Van den Bossche*, above, p. 84.
[4] For deeper analysis, see P.N. Giraud, *L'Inégalité du Monde*, Gallimard, Paris, 1996.

Table 4 Key Figures for EMU, Czech Republic

	inflation rate	public deficit	public debt	exch.rate stability	long-term interest rates
CR 1995	9.1	0.0	18.2	+1.4 (DM) −4.7 (DM)	11.4
CR 1996 ref. value	8.8	0.1	15.5	−	11.9
EU 1995	3.8	3.0	60.0	+/−15.0	9.3

Source: Ministry of Finance of the Czech Republic, Czech National Bank, 1995.

V. MAASTRICHT CRITERIA

The Czech economy, though not bound by the Maastricht Criteria, orientates its monetary and fiscal policy toward their fulfilment. This happens because there is no long-term contradiction between the Maastricht Criteria and the goals of transformation of the Czech economy. Thus the Criteria are useful in promoting economic reforms and growth, which again will improve the chances for earlier EU membership. The present situation is shown in Table 4. The criteria have a clear 'disciplining' effect for Czech policy-makers. This is even more important now, having in mind the outcome of parliamentary elections in spring 1996.

In spite of relative success, inflation remains an open problem. Fast economic growth and accelerating capital inflows make it difficult to bring inflation down faster (and to lower the interest rates, as well as the interest rate differential).

There are some dilemmas that we shall have to solve in our exchange rate policy as well. Starting from 1991, the Czech Crown (CZK) had a stable exchange rate for five years and two months. The stability was achieved by a system that could be called 'adjustable peg without adjustments' – actually, it amounted to a fixed rate, with only a ±0.5 per cent fluctuation band, beyond which the central bank intervened. The stable rate eventually led to large inflows of foreign capital which undermined the central bank's monetary targets.

On 28 February 1996, the fluctuation band was widened to ±7.5 per cent. The aim was to increase the autonomy of monetary policy, and limit the inflow of speculative capital. From a broader perspective, the wider band can also be seen as a step toward verification of the exchange rate by market forces.

The question now is: will the band really re-establish the autonomy of the Czech National bank in targeting the money supply? Can the new exchange rate policy be used to bring inflation down substantially, before the CZK will

Table 5 Share of agriculture in total employment, 1994, in %

Czech Republic	5
Poland	26
Hungary	10
Italy	6
France	5
Germany	4

Source: Review of Agricultural Policies – Czech Republic, OECD, Paris 1995; Agricultural Policies, Markets and Trade in Transition Economies: Monitoring and Evaluation, OECD, Paris, 1996.

Table 6 Average size of an agricultural farm, 1994, in hectares

Czech Republic	65
France	33
Germany	25
Portugal	5
EU Average	20

Source: Review of Agricultural Policies – Czech Republic, OECD, Paris 1995; Agricultural Policies, Markets and Trade in Transition Economies: Monitoring and Evaluation, OECD, Paris, 1996.

have to be fixed again within some narrower band on our entering the EU? And, what are the dangers of such a 'dirty floating'? Is it true that the crisis of 1992 proved that it is the worst of policies, combining the weaknesses of both fixed rates and a full floating? Or was the 1992 crisis actually caused by discrepancies in economic fundamentals – which were only revealed but not caused by the capital flows and speculation?

VI. AGRICULTURAL POLICY

The Czech Republic has a comparative advantage compared to Poland, Hungary, or Slovakia: transformation has made Czech agriculture more competitive, and better prepared for EU membership. Some data are shown in Tables 5 and 6.

Another advantage of the Czech agriculture is its ability to function with a relatively low level of production subsidies. This is a result of the policy of cutting subsidies, continued since 1990 (see Table 7).

This situation also brings some risks: on full membership, Czech farmers will be exposed to competition from highly subsidized EU farmers. If the Common Agricultural Policy is not changed, we could moreover be forced to re-subsidize Czech agriculture.

Table 7 Production subsidies (% share of subsidies per 100 production units, in national currencies)

EU Average	50
OECD Average	43
Czech Republic	26

Source: Review of Agricultural Policies – Czech Republic, OECD, Paris 1995; Agricultural Policies, Markets and Trade in Transition Economies: Monitoring and Evaluation, OECD, Paris, 1996.

VII. SOCIAL SYSTEM

The Czech Republic has up to now avoided the pitfalls of the Welfare State. The share of public expenditure in GDP went down from 60 per cent in 1990 to 44 per cent in 1996 (now it is ten percentage points lower than in France, and six points lower than in Germany).

Yet the Czech social safety net, education system, etc., are considered to be the best among the Visegrád countries. There is a trend to combine public and private sources in some areas of social welfare (supplementary pension systems, gradual raising of the retirement age, etc.).

As in most European countries, in the Czech Republic the ageing of the population brings risks for the balance of social system budgets. The same applies to the growing costs of health care. Our full membership will hence require some additional steps in reforming the social care system.

VIII. LEGISLATION

The Czech Republic is accelerating the adaptation of legislation and other standards, so as to finish the main part of convergence in this field before the full membership negotiations start. The larger part of this goal has to be tackled at governmental and parliamentary level. However, the private sector also takes an active part, adapting to EU technical norms and standards for producers, EU bank rules and directives, etc. Introduction of EU-compatible legislation is seen as an important competitiveness factor by Czech companies and banks.

A no less important task will be the ability to apply correctly EU legislation ('acquis communautaire') by the national legal system. So far, there are few capable and skilled experts on EU legislation and on its application, especially in the Government and public service; and the universities do not have enough capacity to educate all the new experts needed.

If the Central European economies are allowed to join by the year 2000, they will have to absorb an estimated 20,000 pages of the EU's *acquis*, namely the content, principles and political objectives of the Treaties, including those of the Maastricht Treaty, legislation adopted pursuant to the Treaties and the case law of the Court of Justice, statements and resolutions adopted within the Community framework, international Agreements and Agreements concluded among themselves by the member states relating to Community Activities. The acceptance of these rights and obligations by a new member may give rise to technical adjustments, and exceptionally to temporary derogations and transitional arrangements to be defined during the accession negotiations – but this process can in no way undermine the Community rules.

The Europe Agreements noted that the success of Central European countries in absorbing the *acquis communautaire*, in particular as to competition and state subsidies, would be a determining factor in the timing of each associate's accession to the EU. Thus, a cornerstone in the transition from association to accession is the drawing-up of the key elements of the *acquis communautaire* into a clear route-map or timetable.

On the other hand, there is a need for the candidates to obtain from the EU a clearer vision on the future development of EU legislation – in the light of preparing the third stage of EMU, or of elaborating Common Agricultural Policy reforms. The *acquis communautaire*, based on the present state of EU legislation, is not a clear guide in such 'flexible' fields. Instead of an *acquis communautaire statique* offered by the White Paper adopted by the Cannes Council of June 1995, an *acquis évolutif* would be a better guide.

REFERENCES

G. Denton, 'Eastern Enlargement and the Future of the European Union', in *Report of the Conference Enlargement of the European Union with Central European Countries; Challenges and Constraints*, Netherlands Institute of International Relations, The Hague, 17–18 March 1995.

R. Faini and R. Portes, *European Union Trade with Eastern Europe: Adjustment And Opportunities*, CEPR, London 1994.

S. Janáčková and K. Janáček, *European Monetary Union – A View from Outside*, paper prepared for the College of Europe and TEPSA Conference 'The Future of the European Constitution', Bruges, 23–24 June 1995.

EUROPEAN COMMISSION, *The Czech Republic and its Integration with the European Union, Country Study*, Brussels, 1995.

The Preparation of the Changeover to the Single European Currency, Interim Report by the Expert Group on the changeover to the single currency submitted to the European Commission, January 1995.

J. Van Ginderachter, *The Economic and Monetary Union*, Discussion paper prepared for the College of Europe and TEPSA Conference 'The Future of the European Constitution', Bruges, 23–24 June 1995.

B

The Intergovernmental Conference and the Common Foreign and Security Policy

17

RELATIONS EU–CEECS AND THE INTERGOVERNMENTAL CONFERENCE

Erik Derycke[1]

I. INTRODUCTION

When the great European project was started during the 1950s, the founding countries were determined to lay the basis of an ever stronger alliance between the peoples of Europe. They decided, by acting in common, to guarantee social and economic progress, thus lifting the barriers by which they had been divided. This was the right decision: the process of European integration, joined by more and more West European countries, played a decisive role in creating peace, prosperity and welfare in this part of the continent. However, due to the Cold War, a number of countries were excluded from this process. The countries of Central and Eastern Europe, equally badly affected by two World Wars, were not given the opportunity to take part in building the structures through which the member states moved towards peace and prosperity. In the post-Yalta era, communist regimes were imposed under Soviet dominance at a time when Western Europe clearly opted for democracy. For 40 years, the Cold War imposed political and military barriers. The collapse of the Berlin Wall and the spectacular changes which have occurred since 1989 though, have offered promising prospects to these countries.

Attracted by the successful formula of the European Union, they now hope to join our safe haven of peace and prosperity as soon as possible.

It is in our best interest to fulfil these aspirations. The disappearance of the existence of two power blocs which kept each other in balance has caused a void, which can quickly lead to serious instability. Forty years of Soviet rule have largely blocked political evolution and dialogue in Central and Eastern Europe. Nationality problems and minority questions are still on the agenda in today's political debate.

[1] Minister of Foreign Affairs, Belgium.

Moreover, it will still take years before the damage caused by 40 years of planned economy is wiped out.

If the Union member states lock themselves into a Europe of rich nations, there will be a divided Europe once again, and even more dangerously. It is obvious that the 'money wall' would not hold for very long. Political instability in Central and Eastern Europe, which would be caused by keeping our doors closed, would force us quickly to install – this time on our initiative – a new Iron Curtain . . .

The Union is aware of this. In 1993, the Copenhagen European Council decided in principle to open, in time, the doors of the Union to twelve new-comers, among which ten countries of Central and Eastern Europe. The political and strategic reasons for their membership are now part of a broad political consensus. Linking these states to the structures which have care-fully been built up since the Second World War, creates a unique opportunity for offering better security, stability and prosperity on our continent.

Therefore, the question is not whether enlargement will take place, but merely *when* and *how* it will take place.

The Madrid European Council of December 1995 set a starting date. After completing the Intergovernmental Conference (IGC), and in the light of both its results and the advice and the opinions of the Commission, the Council will take the necessary steps to start discussions on membership without delay. The Council aims at having the initial phase of those nego-tiations coincide with the start of the Cyprus negotiations. (Malta had also intended to open negotiations for membership, but at the time of publication of this text they have decided against this.) A first round could normally start six months after the end of the IGC. This is a deliberately chosen moment: a successful IGC offers the best guarantee for positive enlargement of the Union, as the 'Westendorp Reflection Group' emphasized in its final report.

Although the original purpose of the IGC is to examine the effectiveness of mechanisms and institutions of the current Union, as laid down in the Maastricht Treaty, nothing can prevent the IGC from adding the dimension of enlargement to the debate. This amibitious objective will have to be care-fully prepared. It will not be simple. The future member states substantially differ from the 1992 Twelve, as well as from the most recent three new-comers. Practically all the future member states are on average poorer, and they therefore will become net receivers. The lack of a suitable legal and administrative framework, the limited influence of trade unions and the lack of sufficient social protection give rise to the kind of abuse inevitable under any kind of uninhibited capitalism.

Before offering these countries their legitimate place within our Euro-pean house, we will have to make sure that our house has been thoroughly reinforced, and that its rules have been adapted to take a larger number of members into account. In that respect, it is essential that European institu-tions can continue to work effectively and that the added value which the

Union offers, when compared to the merely intergovernmental level, remains guaranteed. This implies not only preserving but also reinforcing solidarity between member states, whereby a general balance between their rights and obligations must continue to exist. Deepening the Union is therefore a *conditio sine qua non* for enlargement.

Using a few basic data, I would like to show the link between a number of Belgian proposals for deepening the European Union and an enlargement that would prove successful. Widening and deepening are no opposite poles, on the contrary – and this is the essence of my argument – they are complementary and inextricably linked with each other. The more we deepen the Union, the more we make it suitable for enlargement.

II. THE SOCIO-ECONOMIC, DEMOGRAPHIC AND POLITICAL DIMENSION

From the European Union's perspective, the economic weight of enlargement should not be overestimated. It adds less than 5 per cent to the GDP of the Fifteen. The common GDP of the ten candidate member states approximately equals the Belgian GDP. However, there are obvious economic benefits for the Union such as the incorporation of a market with a high growth potential and an increase in the Union's competitiveness *vis-à-vis* other growing world economies.

Over 100 million additional consumers will give a boost to the European economy. Present EU member states already now benefit from high growth in their exports to the candidate countries. The Commission has estimated that, due to advanced integration, trade between the ten countries of Central and Eastern Europe on the one hand and the current EU member states on the other hand, could reach a level which is three to five times as high as the 1989 level. From an industrial point of view, the candidate member states provide 'new blood', with a country like Hungary attracting significant foreign investment from the European Union.

However, the biggest problems will appear inside the candidate countries themselves. In most of them, the agricultural, industrial and service sectors will remain involved in a painful restructuring process for a long time. Instant membership, without any accompanying measures, would expose their private sector to the extreme competition of the EU internal market. The risk of an accumulation of company closures and a very high unemployment rate is only too real. It is up to countries concerned to consider the positive and negative effects of an early entry. It is not unlikely that a number of them, out of enlightened self-interest, decide that full accession needs to be delayed or spread over a longer period.

For the moment, let us assume that most of the applying countries will go for it and become full Union member states. The economic and social gap between new and old members would be enormous. The present average

GDP per capita amounts to approximately 30 per cent of the EU average. The Commission calculated that, in order to reach 50 per cent of the EU average by 2001 (which corresponds with the relative level of Portugal at the time of its accession), the applying countries need to grow approximately 11 per cent more rapidly than the Union, which is clearly an unrealistic target.

Therefore, the principle of solidarity, which is so typical of the European construction, will need to be fully implemented. It is a principle that definitely attracts future members. In exchange for handing in a portion of their sovereignty, they count on receiving both political and economic advantages offered by cooperating within a unified market.

On the basis of extrapolations of current macro-economic figures, it has been argued that European policy will become extremely expensive. For the four Visegrád countries alone, direct transfers via Community funding have been estimated at 60 billion ECU per year. This would mean almost doubling the contributions of each member state. Other direct consequences for the Fifteen would be that Spain would become a net payer and that a region like Hainault (Belgium) would no longer be listed under 'Objective 1' of the European Regional Fund. In the light of this, voices have already been raised thoroughly to adapt the European policy instruments within the framework of the IGC, and more in particular in the area of structural funds and Common Agricultural Policy. In view of these preoccupations, the Madrid European Council asked the Commission to submit – simultaneously with the publication of its opinions on individual candidate countries – a 'composite paper'. This study on the horizontal aspects of future enlargement must offer, *inter alia*, a calculated evaluation of the cost picture. It must be clear at the outset that such a calculation will have to take into account a great number of uncertainties: which countries will join and at what date? A simultaneous accession of all ten appears most improbable. Even if we knew how the enlargement process will evolve, economic and macro-financial developments remain highly uncertain. The Commission will present the composite paper only after the IGC has been completed, as it will also need to take into account the new institutional context.

Without wishing to minimize these problems, it must be emphasized that our own history should not be forgotten in this debate. The stabilization of Western Europe after the Second World War, which brought peace and prosperity, also required an enormous effort at its inception. Everything started with the Marshall plan. The boldest figures submitted by some people in relation to the cost of enlargement suggest that the Community budget would more than double, thus amounting to between 150 and 200 billion ECU. Assuming that the amount were equal to 3 per cent of the GDP of the current Fifteen and that half of this amount were spent on helping Central and Eastern Europe, this effort would be comparable to what the Americans contributed to the Marshall plan. During five years (from 1948 to 1952), the US spent about 1.4 per cent of their GDP on the reconstruction of Western Europe. Another comparison: 3 per cent of the GDP equals half of the money transfers made by the Federal Republic of Germany to East Germany. Finally, the cost of the alternative for preserving peace on our continent, i.e. defence expenses, must be kept in mind. As this cost would at least be of a similar order, investing in the economic development of our Eastern neighbours will be, in time, more secure and cost-effective.

Much will depend on the way in which enlargement is brought about. Transition periods which are flexible in duration and, for a number of sectors, transition periods linked to criteria similar to those established for EMU are to be preferred. Starting from a non-discriminatory treatment of all the applicant countries gathering at the start, enlargement could be realized by coupling it with both a time factor and gradual transition based on objective criteria. In that respect, it should be kept in mind that the candidate countries themselves will have to make a permanent effort to fulfil membership conditions as laid down by the Copenhagen European Council in June 1993. Their institutions will have to permanently guarantee democracy, the rule of law, respect of human rights and protection of minorities. Furthermore, they will need to have an efficiently run market economy capable of facing competition within the Union. Finally, they need to demonstrate their ability to implement the *acquis communautaire* and assume the obligations of the European membership.

In the meantime, the Union is negotiating a new Treaty in the IGC in order to bring about deepening and to create viable institutions for enlarging the European Union. The candidate countries thus aim at a moving target, preparing themselves for as yet unknown policy-making mechanisms and possibly new Community policy fields.

While enlargement may seem relatively insignificant in terms of economic weight – as mentioned earlier – it does have great importance from a demographic point of view, as the population of the Union will increase by more than 25 per cent! This large group of future Union citizens, over 100 million people, currently produce together a mere 5 per cent of the Community's wealth. There are huge internal differences, and some Baltic States, Romania and Bulgaria definitely still have a long way to go. The shift towards a free market economy requires a huge effort. Poland for instance, which introduced changes rather early on, only reached in 1995 the production level of the year preceding the start of the transition process. Moreover, national income is now less equally distributed. For the average person, general conditions of living have not necessarily improved.

Generally, the Central and East European authorities have taken care not to neglect their social welfare systems too much. However, as restructuring moves on, pressure on social budgets increases and these countries will be faced with painful choices. Full entry into the internal market could suddenly speed up this process. It is obvious that the accession of new member states without adequate social security systems can cause serious distortions within the internal market. This might lead to a social crisis which could in turn destabilize the enlarged Union. Therefore, the opportunity offered by the

IGC must be seized in order to prevent such a situation and to create mechanisms for completing the internal market. While macro-economic convergence in accordance with EMU criteria is a useful goal, it does not provide sufficiently strong conditions for guaranteeing permanent prosperity and welfare for the citizens of Europe. Having solved the monetary question, further elaboration of a number of accompanying policies of the internal market, namely social policy, fiscal policy and environmental regulations is still needed. These policies have to be approved by majority decisions. Countries with inadequate social security systems may not be inclined to agree on basic standards in this field, as differences in terms of labour cost and social regulations can be a factor in attracting investors. If unanimity voting in the field of social and fiscal policy is maintained, a form of competitive deterioration of social standards and downward pressure on taxation will become inevitable.

With a view to maintaining social peace and stability within an enlarged Union, it is essential that the internal market should be completed using a common social base. This implies the following: including the Social Protocol in the Union Treaty; confirming the results of social dialogue at the institutional level; harmonizing social definitions upwards; elaborating convergency criteria for social welfare; adding social and environmental clauses to the common commercial policy; and defining and implementing universal services.

Without the necessary accompanying measures at the social level, the extreme competition within the internal market could destroy the Union. Moreover, the elaboration of a common base at the social, fiscal and environmental level is vital for people who, like me, want to consolidate the 'Rheinland model'. I mean a society in which both the right of individual initiative and solidarity, both individual freedom and collective social provisions can coexist.

III. THE INSTITUTIONAL DIMENSION

In political terms, the enlargement towards the East means a 'landslide', whereby the number of member states, including Cyprus and Malta, jumps from 15 to 27. This almost doubling of the number of member states leads me to the conclusion that an intergovernmental approach will be less effective than ever. The lack of clear-cut responsibilities and the implementation – still too frequently – of the unanimity rule lead to an increased risk of immobility.

Unanimity has proved to be paralysing, particularly in the area of foreign and security policy. The slow pace at which the Union acted at the beginning of the Yugoslav drama sadly illustrates this. Moreover, unanimity voting has stimulated the phenomenon of setting up contact groups. If the decision-making mechanism remains unchanged after enlargement, there will be a higher risk that the real decisions are taken in the corridors by the large countries via some contact group and outside the grip of the European Union structures.

What will have to be aimed at during the IGC – certainly in the light of enlargement – is the creation of a more determined Europe, which takes decisions in an effective, democratic and transparent way, without upsetting the institutional balance. In order to preserve the effectiveness of decision-making, we need to opt unconditionally for the so-called 'Community method', which must be further elaborated within the First Pillar and extended to the two remaining pillars whenever possible. In practice, this means that the central role played by the Commission as an initiator and protector of Community interests, needs to be confirmed and extended.

This process also involves introducing more decision-taking by qualified majority voting in the Council. I do realize that the generalized use of this method, when combined with an increase in the number of small countries, will obviously require some level of correction. This is entirely related to the relative weight of the various 'large states'.

It becomes even more probable that the larger member states will insist during the IGC that the demographic factor be increased, allowing for decisions taken by qualified majority to be also politically 'relevant' for their populations. Taking into account the concerns of the larger member states, several options have already been suggested. There are those who want to increase the voting weight of the larger countries, while others want to introduce a double majority whereby each qualified majority undergoes – automatically or not – an additional 'demographic check'. This would consist in examining whether the decision taken is supported by a majority of the European population.

However, within the Council, the dividing line is rarely drawn between smaller and larger member states, but rather between protectionists and free traders, between Northern and Southern member states or between net payers and net receivers. This explains why some voices are raised in favour of changing the voting weight, whereby economic and financial factors would be taken into account in addition to demographic factors.

In this discussion, I would finally like to say that the current decision-taking structures allow for a subtle balance to be struck between the various institutions. In order both to maintain this balance and to protect the legitimate interests of smaller member states, the composition of the Commission should permanently meet the criteria of representation, recognition and proximity *vis-à-vis* the peoples of all member states whenever the voting formula is changed.

With regard to the composition of the European Parliament – which already has 626 members – the question of establishing a ceiling can be raised. We believe that degressive proportionality in combination with a guaranteed minimum number of seats for the smaller member states should be recommended. This brings us to the democratic character of decision-making. More democracy means above all extending the competences of the European Parliament, which needs to have greater control over decision-making by the Council. The consultation procedures need to be simplified and their number reduced, while the procedure of co-decision must occupy a more central place.

In order to ensure the implementation of Community decisions in a Union of 27 member states with different legal 'cultures' and diverging legal systems, the role of the European Court of Justice needs to be preserved as a guarantee for independent and uniform implementation of European legislation. In this respect, the question can be raised whether, assuming that there will be 30 judges, such a number would not put too much pressure on a coherent vision of law, and thus endanger a vital element. Therefore, the IGC will need to strike a balance between the requirement of sufficient representation of the various national legal systems on the one hand and securing the collegiate character of this institution on the other hand. Where competences are concerned, judicial powers should be extended as much as possible towards the new areas of cooperation within the Treaty. This is particularly the case for the areas of Justice and Home Affairs.

With the prospect of a considerable increase in the number of Union member states, the IGC will not only need to lift institutional barriers. In a variety of policy areas, the Union will have to prepare itself for fulfilling the high expectations of the newcomers. I have already demonstrated what this implies for the so-called First Pillar. It should not be forgotten, though, that countries of Central and Eastern Europe are not only attracted by the level of social and economic prosperity within the Union, but also by the level of internal and external security it provides.

With regard to internal security, a lot still needs to be done – even within the present Union of fifteen. Enlargement towards countries where social disruption following the collapse of communism has led to a serious increase in the level of organized crime, requires substantial progress in the field of Third Pillar cooperation. We must prevent at all cost a situation whereby our populations might reject enlargement, because the lack of mechanisms for fighting crime within the Union would make a larger Union a less safe place to live, to work and to raise children.

With regard to external policy, the Union will only be able to transform the numerical increase of its members into an increased influence on the international scene if the IGC also introduces the necessary reforms in the Second Pillar. The prospect of common defence is part of this. The institutional 'rapprochement' between WEU and EU with a view to fully integrating the WEU in the EU, seems to be the most appropriate way to forge an individual European identity in the area of security and defence policy. The IGC will have to set this process in motion. However, in order to secure at the same time the operational character of this process, it should not be separated from the Transatlantic solidarity offered by the NATO Alliance. Taking into account the susceptibilities of a number of current Union member states, and in the light of Union enlargement towards Russia's close neighbours, great caution and flexibility are needed. It therefore seems likely that the various processes of enlargement of the Union, the WEU and NATO, though inextricably linked, will have to proceed at their own pace and according to their own criteria.

IV. CONCLUSION

Considering the great disparity between member states in an enlarged Union, the IGC will need to find solutions to preserve the necessary dynamics of the integration process. Institutionalized differentiation may be considered as a solution of last resort. A form of differentiation has always existed one way or another, though it has been given a new dimension by EMU. Certain areas are well suited to a differentiated approach. Our main concern though must be not to obstruct the functioning of the internal market and to preserve the Community institutional system. A poorly functioning Schengen Treaty is a perfect example of the limits inherent in an intergovernmental approach.

It is no coincidence that the Copenhagen European Council introduced the Union's capacity for including new members while at the same time preserving the 'élan' of European integration as a condition for allowing Central and East European countries to join. It definitely does not serve the interests of adhering countries to become a member of a weakened Community, which, due to lack of determination and policy instruments, was incapable of creating the necessary incentives for a genuine 'rapprochement' of its members. A diluted Union cannot bring about the envisaged integration of Central and East European countries in a democratic Europe, and European solidarity would collapse. It is our historic mission to prevent this from happening.

18

THE EUROPEAN COMMISSION'S APPROACH TOWARDS THE IGC

Günter Burghardt[1]

I. INTRODUCTION

The preparation for and carrying out of enlargement of the European Union to the East and South is one of the major challenges facing the EU. At the 1995 Madrid European Council, the Heads of State and Government listed a number of key issues which the Union would have to resolve in the coming years. In addition to enlargement, the 'Agenda for Europe', with a view to being implemented by the turn of the century, includes:

- the launching and successful conclusion of the forthcoming Inter-governmental Conference with a view to further deepening the process of unification as the necessary condition for preparing the enlargement process;
- the introduction of a single currency (the Euro) in line with the time-table and conditions on Economic and Monetary Union already established in the Maastricht Treaty;
- determining the budget and financial arrangements for the period after 31 December 1999, including reform of the major spending policies (Structural Funds and Common Agricultural Policy);
- establishing a new European security architecture, whilst drawing the lessons from the ex-Yugoslavia drama;
- strengthening the transatlantic partnership, whilst simultaneously reinforcing relations with neighbouring countries of the EU, particularly Russia, Ukraine, Turkey and those in the Mediterranean littoral.[2]

---

[1] Director-General, DGIA, European Commission. The opinion expressed in this article is that of the author and does not necessarily reflect that of the institution he works for.
[2] For Text, see *Bull. EU*, 12-1995, 9.

Given the immensity of these tasks facing the EU, it is vital that the member states approach the IGC with a concept of *strengthening the Union*. In other words, a substantial deepening is a prerequisite for a successful widening. This was indeed the principal message of the Commission report to the IGC which was aptly entitled '*Reinforcing Political Union and Preparing for Enlargement*'.[3]

Before examining a number of issues related to the IGC and reforms of the CFSP it may be useful to say a few words about enlargement. Never before, indeed, have so many countries wished to join the Union. This is proof of the success and magnetism of the process of European integration. For many years, the novel process of changing the political landscape of Europe through a policy designed to pool parts of national sovereignty and to organize solidarity and interdependence in a Community of nations and peoples, was confined to Western Europe. But with the ending of the Cold War we now have the opportunity to extend this historic experience to cover the whole of Europe. Today, the question is not so much whether the associated countries will join the EU, but rather how to secure a genuine European Union with 20 to 30 members.

It is sometimes said that progress since the 1993 Copenhagen European Council has been too slow, and that the momentum of enlargement has not been maintained. I want to refute that suggestion. Since the Copenhagen Summit, the EU has developed, together with the associated countries, a pre-accession strategy which has been substantiated at the European Councils at Essen (1994) and Cannes (1995). Thus, in a record time from the European Council in Copenhagen in June 1993 to the Madrid European Council in December 1995, the Union has defined the parameters of the enlargement process. At Madrid, further progress was made on clarifying the timetable for enlargement.

The answers of the associated countries to the series of questionnaires by the Commission, which the latter has now received, will be a great help in preparing a detailed assessment of the situation in each individual country. Naturally, I cannot prejudge what conclusions the Commission will reach in its Opinions. What I can say is that we will treat all applicants equally and evaluate their degree of preparation for membership, taking account of the political and economic criteria set out at the Copenhagen European Council. This requires not only an assessment of the situation and progress which each applicant has made at the time of the Opinion, but also a judgment of the progress which it can be expected to make in the future in preparing to take on all the obligations of membership. These obligations are important and numerous, for they concern the whole of the Union's policies and regulations: the *acquis communautaire*.

Most of the applicants have already made considerable progress, but much remains to be done if accession is to be successfully achieved. It must be

---

[3] COM(96) 90 final, 28 February 1996.

recalled that the speed of the last enlargement negotiations was largely due to the exceptionally good preparation which the EFTA countries had already made. For example, before the accession negotiations even commenced, through the EEA they had already taken on the obligations of the Internal Market and a number of other accompanying policies.

II. THE IGC

The IGC must build on the experience of the past 40 years of operating a Community approach to decision-making which has served the external as well as the internal interests of the Union well. The present structures are a successful mix of the Community and intergovernmental methods. Europe is composed of nation states with common institutions, but the aim must be to continue to break down barriers in all fields and unite the peoples of Europe, an aim which all member states subscribed to in both the Rome and Maastricht treaties. To create a Europe based merely on a partnership of nations would be to risk returning to the instability of the League of Nations period. In fact, the well-known recipe of cooperation among governments was already opposed to the then European Economic Community in the 1950s, when the UK led the EFTA grouping. It did not take the UK long to recognize that real influence could only be gained by full membership of the EC and that the Community method of decision-making was far more efficient than the inter-governmental approach.

In February 1996, the Commission published its report for the IGC called 'Reinforcing Political Union and Preparing for Enlargement'.[4] This report includes proposals to make the Union more open and relevant to its citizens; the indispensable institutional reforms; and, finally, a list of what needs to be done to reinforce and increase the visibility of the Union's external policies.

III. A PEOPLE'S EUROPE

The Commission stated that the European model of society – which is built on a collection of common values (democracy, open economy, solidarity, cohesion) amongst which feature the access of citizens to services of general benefit or public services – must be confirmed and made more explicit.

Human rights

The priorities are:

- to secure Union accession to the European Convention on Human Rights or alternatively make direct reference in the Treaty to the rights protected by the Convention;

[4] See previous note.

- to make provision in the Treaty for a ban on discrimination of any kind, notably in relation to equal opportunities for women and men, going beyond the current equal-pay provisions, and to outlaw racism and xenophobia.

A Union based on the rule of law

The EU should agree:

- to give the Commission the means to enforce Community law, in particular in relation to the Internal Market;
- to strengthen the role of the Court of Justice, particularly as regards compliance with its judgments;
- to establish the legal basis for combating fraud against the Union's financial interests.

The social dimension

Ensuring a common base of social rights for all Union citizens chiefly means:

- integrating the Social Protocol into the Treaty;
- spelling out certain provisions for cooperation between member states on matters such as combating poverty and exclusion;
- involving more closely those sections of civil society that can develop initiatives and new forms of solidarity.

Employment

Employment is a matter of common interest. Specific provisions on employment must be written into the Treaty to:

- establish the conditions for a common strategy for employment;
- stimulate cooperation between all interested parties;
- consolidate arrangements for multilateral surveillance of member states' multiannual programmes;
- take account of employment in all Community policies.

Sustainable development

The Treaty should be strengthened with provisions for:

- the citizen's right to a healthy environment and duty to preserve it;
- integration of care for the environment into other Community policies.

Establishing an area of freedom and security

The shortcomings of Title VI of the EU Treaty (cooperation in the fields of justice and home affairs) should be remedied. This will require the following objectives to be set:

- the establishment of common rules on the entry, residence and status of nationals from non-member countries in the Union;
- the effective mutual recognition of judgments by national courts;
- the adoption of measures to combat all forms of crime and fraud;
- stimulation of effective cooperation between public administrations of the member states.

IV. DECISION-MAKING AND INSTITUTIONAL REFORMS

As regards the institutional changes for an enlarged Europe, the Commission proposed:

- replacement of unanimity by qualified majority voting as a general rule;
- closer involvement of the European Parliament;
- extension of the Commission's power of initiative in all the fields concerned;
- providing the Union with more effective legal instruments than the common position, joint action or international agreements;
- decisions to be subject to review by the Court of Justice;
- simplification of the Council's present working structures;
- transfer of justice and home affairs to the Community framework, with the exception of judicial cooperation in criminal matters and police cooperation;
- incorporation of the content of the Schengen Agreement in the Treaty.

Making the Union more open and democratic

In this key area, the Commission proposed:

- to push forward the application of the subsidiarity principle;
- closer involvement of national parliaments in Union business by giving them timely access to all the information they need;
- to simplify and consolidate the Treaties as far as possible.

Simplifying and democratizing Union decision-making

Responding to widespread public confusion about the operation of the treaties, the Commission proposed:

- limiting the types of decision-making procedure to only three: decisions adopted on Parliament's opinion, those adopted with its assent, and the codecision procedure involving Parliament and the Council;
- simplification of the budgetary procedure arrangements and consolidation of all that has been achieved with the interinstitutional agreements;
- simplification of the codecision procedure, notably by setting time limits for first readings, by dropping the announcement of the intention to reject a proposal at the second reading stage, and by dropping the third reading;

- all acts of a legislative nature to be subject to the codecision procedure and the cooperation procedure to be abandoned;
- 'constitutional' matters (Treaty amendments, own resources) to be subject to Parliament's assent; this procedure should not, however, be applicable to legislative decisions or to Community action programmes;
- clarification of the scope of the assent procedure as regards international agreements;
- review and simplification of procedures for implementing measures.

The Commission also suggested:

- that majority voting become the general rule;
- the possibility of 'super qualified' majority voting in particularly sensitive fields;
- the possibility of amending Treaty provisions, other than those of a 'constitutional' nature, by a procedure that imposes fewer constraints than at present.

The European Parliament

The Commission was in tune with the Parliament's own views when it proposed:

- acceptance of Parliament's own proposal that membership be limited to 700;
- establishment of an electoral procedure which ensures that members are as representative as possible.

The Council

As regards the Council, the Commission proposed:

- examination of ways of extending the scope of the presidency's powers of action and the order of rotation of the six-monthly terms of office;
- maintenance of the existing balance either by adapting the weighting of votes or introducing a new system which makes reference both to a majority of the member states and a majority of the Union's population;
- no raising of the normal threshold for a qualified majority which has been set at around 71 per cent since the inception of the Community.

The Commission

Concerning its own powers and authority, the Commission proposed:

- guarantees for its right of initiative, its executive powers and its function as guardian of the Treaties;
- designation of its President by the European Council and approval by the European Parliament. The President must play an important role in the choice of Commission Members, to assure collegiality. Members

of the Commission must be designated by way of common agreement between the President of the Commission and the respective governments of the member states;
– reduction in the number of Members to one per member state. The Commission is conscious of the fact that its composition and its structure will have to be reviewed above a certain number of member states. The IGC must foresee a suitable procedure for this.

The Court of Justice

Turning to the Court, the Commission proposed:

– a solution to the problems, identified by the Court, posed by the number of judges after enlargement;
– to extend the duration of the mandate for the members of the Court and provide that this mandate is not renewable (the position suggested by the Court).

Organizing flexibility

The Commission firmly rejected any idea of a 'Europe à la carte', but the European Union must allow for forms of closer cooperation or integration between some of its members with due respect for the following principles:

– compatibility with the objectives of the Union;
– consistency with the institutional framework of the Union;
– opportunity for other States to join at any time if they are willing and able;
– safeguarding of the single market and the policies accompanying it.

The general thrust of the Commission's report was thus the need to make the Union more open and relevant to its citizens, and to reform the Union in order to ensure that it continues to function efficiently after enlargement.

V.   REINFORCING AND MAKING MORE VISIBLE THE UNION'S EXTERNAL POLICIES

In creating the Common Foreign and Security Policy (CFSP) at Maastricht, member states called on the EU 'to assert its identity on the international scene'. Sadly, as we have seen in the tragic example of former Yugoslavia, the EU has been unable to meet the greatest challenge to European security since the end of the Cold War.

The reform of CFSP is high on the agenda of the IGC and it is important to recognize that there is some consensus, as well as there being differences of opinion, as to how the EU's performance in external relations may be improved. There is widespread agreement, for example, that the EU should increase its coherence in dealing with the outside world. But it is highly unlikely that the EU will be able to increase its coherence, or be able to speak with one voice, if economic, diplomatic and security policies continue to be conducted following three different procedures.

When observers assess the Union's external relations, they usually point to the successful Community approach towards Russia, Ukraine, Central and Eastern Europe, the Mediterranean countries, and even to areas far from the Union such as South Africa or the Mercosur group in South America. The reason for the success of these policies is that they are Community external policies – not policies carried out under a CFSP hat. Today's diplomacy is increasingly based on economics, trade, finance, the transfer of technical knowhow, etc. and this can clearly be organized best on a Community basis.

But even here, despite the obvious advantages of negotiating as a single body, as seen in the Uruguay Round, some member states are reluctant to update Community competence to reflect changes in the world economy and to ensure that the Community continues to speak with one voice in international negotiations.

As regards the CFSP, it is essential that member states demonstrate the political will to work together in this sensitive field. CFSP starts in the capitals of the member states, not in Brussels. Despite the sensitive nature of CFSP, it is manifestly clear that member states operating together can exert far more influence than if they go it alone.

Reforms are necessary at all stages in CFSP: conception, decision-making and external representation. One area of consensus is the need to establish a joint planning and analysis unit. In the Commission's view, this unit should be composed of experts from the member states and the Commission, possibly with a contribution from the WEU. Its analyses would be useful for the Presidency and the Commission when drawing up proposals based on a definition of common interests. The formulation of foreign policy would also be facilitated by the incorporation of a permanent Political Committee into the Council's existing machinery for preparing decisions in Brussels.

With regard to decision-making in CFSP, particularly in an enlarged EU, there is a very strong case for qualified majority voting, except for decisions involving military matters.

There already exists a structure for EU representation to the outside world, a structure which has proved its value even in dealings with major partners such as the US and Russia. This is the tandem of the Presidency-Commission which enjoys both the legitimacy and the competence to represent the EU to outside partners. During the IGC it will be important to consider measures for reinforcing this tandem.

What is not necessary is a new structure, such as the creation, in addition to the two actors of the tandem, of a Mr or Ms CFSP, who would not only lack legitimacy but be a recipe for confusion. The proposal for such a new structure is really an excuse for those who do not wish to see any substantial progress in CFSP and hence put presentation before content.

313

But the example of ex-Yugoslavia also reveals the importance of a coherent set of foreign policy aims which must be backed up by a credible military component. The chances of the EU developing its own security and defence identity (ESDI) are considerably greater than they were five years ago, during the Maastricht negotiations. Firstly, the need to reduce public expenditure and the costs of going it alone in the defence field are becoming prohibitively high for any one State. Secondly, there has been a complete change in US policy, with the Clinton administration as wholehearted supporters of greater European efforts in the security field. Thirdly, the change in French policy towards a reformed NATO has opened the perspective of a greater convergence in European attitudes towards security structures.

NATO will remain responsible for territorial defence for the foreseeable future. But a European pillar, based on the Western European Union (WEU), should be strengthened to enable the Europeans to carry out crisis management, peacekeeping and humanitarian tasks when the US does not wish to become involved. There would seem to be no reason why the EU should not take on political responsibility for these tasks. Thus, organizing a European military capacity 'separable but not separate' within the framework of a reformed North Atlantic Alliance and making policy-making inside a strengthened EU (encompassing WEU) is the only efficient long-term solution. The incongruence of EU/WEU/NATO memberships will have to be taken into account through specific decision-making procedures (akin to those agreed for EMU) in the EU Council of Ministers.

In addition, in its recent Communication to the Council, the Commission emphasized the economic and security arguments in favour of an internal market for the armaments industry. The security and defence of the Union are dependent on the existence of a solid and competitive industrial base. This requires better integration of the armaments industry into the general Treaty rules, greater solidarity and cooperation including the establishment of an armaments agency, and a consistent approach to foreign trade. There is a rapidly growing awareness in the European armaments industry that if they do not integrate further, there will not be much left of the industry in face of world competition.

VI. CONCLUSION

The European Union is today at a crossroads. It has numerous creditable achievements to its name: the pillar of West European recovery after the calamity of the Second World War, providing the framework for the historic Franco-German reconciliation, creating the world's largest civil power, with a good record of development aid and assistance to its neighbours to the East and South. Expectations about the place and role the Union should, and will, have to play in tomorrow's world are high. President Santer correctly pointed out at the Davos Conference, in 1995, that the EU is far from pulling its economic weight in the world. Just as Germany used to be described as an economic giant and a political dwarf, so might one describe the Union today.

The above reforms would go some way towards preparing the Union to play a more coherent and credible role in world affairs. But as Santer's predecessor, Jacques Delors, commented after Maastricht 'are the member states prepared to demonstrate the political will and provide the necessary resources to match their ambitions?' The answer to this question – through the IGC and the next enlargement process – will be decisive for the future direction of European politics. On the one hand there is the opportunity to establish a united and stable Europe, 'whole and free', having collectively drawn the lessons of two World Wars; on the other hand, there is a danger of reverting to the 'European Concert', based on outdated and in the last resort inherently instable classic forms of cooperation amongst a network of numerous nation states, with the ultimate risk of succumbing to well-known temptations of shifting alliances, the balance of power and 'go-it-alone' politics.

19

THE INTEGRATION OF CENTRAL AND EASTERN EUROPE INTO THE COMMON FOREIGN AND SECURITY POLICY OF THE EUROPEAN FIFTEEN

Pál Dunay, Tamás Kende and Tamás Szücs[1]

I. THE EVOLUTION OF A COMMON FOREIGN AND SECURITY POLICY WITHIN THE EUROPEAN COMMUNITY

The Common Foreign and Security Policy of the European Union constituting the second pillar of the architecture created at Maastricht in 1991 is the result of a continuous evolution within the West European[2] integration process. Throughout the past four decades there has been a general consensus both in political and academic circles that the imbalance between the economic and political-military capabilities of Western Europe is untenable. After various failed attempts of the fifties and the sixties the Hague Summit of 1969 paved the way for a relatively efficient, yet low-key initiative, which discovered its legal basis only after its consecration by Title III of the Single European Act.[3] However, the Hague initiative, resulting in the establishment of the European Political Cooperation (hereunder: EPC), did not lead to a real and effective common foreign policy, but rather to a coordination of the foreign policies of the member states. Despite all its weaknesses, from the early 1980s, EPC has become the number one multilateral foreign policy decision-making mechanism of the European Community. Under the impact of the Gulf War and the considerable pressure of the events unfolding in Central and Eastern Europe at the end of the decade, it could have been expected that the 1991 IGC would have come up with comprehensive proposals aimed

---

[1] Pál Dunay and Tamás Kende are Associate Professors of International Law at the ELTE Law school, Budapest and members of the Budapest bar; Tamás Szücs is a policy analyst in Brussels. The views expressed here are strictly personal and do not necessarily reflect that of their institutions.

[2] Throughout this contribution we use the term Western Europe in the political sense, enshrining the whole or a part of Europe not dominated by the former Soviet Union.

[3] *International Legal Materials*, 1986, 510–19.

at the significant improvement of foreign policy cooperation. The creation of EPC's successor, a Common Foreign and Security Policy (hereafter: CFSP) in the Maastricht Treaty (hereafter: Treaty on European Union-TEU) did, however, not change fundamentally the substance of the process. Therefore, although the name has changed, CFSP is still not a common foreign policy, but a modestly enhanced version of its predecessor. It has practically remained[4] an intergovernmental process[5] based on a voluntary submission of issues that raise a common concern of the member states,[6] ensuring consensual decision-making.

A. An overview of EPC–CFSP activities

If one looks at the developments of the past two and a half decades it would be hard to deny that a gradual approximation of foreign policies has taken place. This cooperation has been particularly successful in three fields: the UN, the CSCE/OSCE and between the diplomatic missions delegated to third countries.[7] It has become a rule that member states get together prior to the UN General Assembly (hereafter: UNGA) meetings, and as a consequence Western Europe has been acting as a voting block in the General Assembly. This is less obvious in the Security Council where two permanent and one or two non-permanent members are also member states of the EU.[8] The member states were less successful in influencing the voting pattern of Britain and France in the Security Council because of the resistance of these two nations. In the CSCE[9] – renamed OSCE in December 1994 in Budapest[10] – the powers of the EPC–CFSP have been undisputed and the coordination of the policies of the member states has been exceptionally efficient.[11]

---

[4] An element of perceptible change is that the EPC–CFSP intergovernmental mechanism slowly becomes less intergovernmental and less and less separated from the external policy of the Union. On the effects of the TEU on the common foreign policy, see Buchanan (1993), 42–67; Edwards (1985), 84 et seq.

[5] The role of the European Commission is very modest as it still has no right of initiative. Yet the Commission is starting to play a more important role in foreign policy-making as well. EPC–CFSP economic sanctions, reprisals or economic embargoes against third countries have almost always been put into effect by the Commission on the basis of Art. 113 EC Treaty, see Fink-Hooijer (1994), 175.

[6] Hurd (1981), 383–93; Bot (1984), 149; Pijpers (1984), 135.

[7] Hill (1983), 135–46; Anderson, in Rummel (1992), 151–64; Edwards, in Rummel (1992), 165–90.

[8] An additional member of the Security Council is elected from the group of the Central and Eastern European Countries excluding the Russian Federation but including Malta and Cyprus. It remains to be seen whether the accession of some of these countries will reposition these nations to Western Europe.

[9] Conference on Security and Co-operation in Europe: Final Act, *International Legal Materials*, Vol. 14, No. 5, September 1975, 1285–325.

[10] Organization for Security and Co-operation in Europe: Budapest Summit Declaration on Genuine Partnership in a New Era, *International Legal Materials*, Vol. 34, No. 3, May 1995, 767–807.

[11] Pijpers (1984), 135.

Cooperation between diplomatic missions[12] has been running smoothly in peacetime, but the balance is not nearly as solid during a period of crisis.[13] Western Europe has been unable to coordinate its reaction[14] in a number of crises, or was even unable to react at all.[15] Besides the well-known case of Yugoslavia,[16] the examples are numerous: the Tienanmen Square massacre of 1989 had prompted only limited economic, but extensive political sanctions from the then Twelve, while the same countries did not take a position with regard to the American military intervention in Panama. Throughout the 1990s – German unification, war in Kuwait and Iraq, disintegration of the Soviet Union, crisis in Somalia, embargo against Libya, blockade against Haiti, fall of the apartheid in South-Africa, Arab–Israeli dialogue, and last, but not least the political rebirth of Central and Eastern Europe – the balance of EPC–CFSP is far from impressive. The principle of coordinated foreign policies was given up whenever matters of an especially sensitive nature came into play.

B. The structure and devices of CFSP

Under the TEU the European Council sits at the apex of the pillar structure of the Union overseeing the work of the three pillars, including, of course, the functioning of the CFSP. The role of heads of state and governments in the second pillar is to issue general guidelines on matters of common foreign policy. The Council of Foreign Ministers (General Affairs Council) determines – on the basis of preset guidelines – the issues where a joint action shall be necessary and reconsiders its joint actions if new circumstances so require. Besides joint actions, common positions seek to promote the cooperation between the member states.[17] The Presidency represents the Council on matters of foreign policy in cooperation with the Troika[18] and it may call

[12] Bot (1984), 149.

[13] An often mentioned success story is the Falklands war between the UK and Argentina – where one of the member states was directly implicated – and where it was possible to introduce, in the form of a joint action, an economic embargo against Argentina even if some member states had interests that would have mandated them to take a less committed position.

[14] The American bombing of Tripoli in 1986 led to a serious international crisis. Sir Geoffrey Howe, the then British Minister of Foreign Affairs, had attended the emergency meeting of the Ten dealing with Libyan terrorism, withholding the information from the others that American warplanes had departed earlier from British airports and were heading for Tripoli for a punitive mission against the headquarters of Kadhafi.

[15] The crises during which EPC has most seriously underperformed expectations are the Arab–Israeli war of 1973 and the ensuing energy crisis, the Greek coup and the Turkish invasion of Cyprus in 1974 and the Portuguese carnation revolution of 1975, see Hill (1992), 140. No common positions were arrived at and no joint action were taken with regard to the Soviet invasion of Afghanistan in 1979, the taking of American hostages in Teheran in 1980, the Polish military coup of 1980, the Israeli invasion of Lebanon in 1982, the grounding of the South-Korean KAL 007 passenger aircraft by the Soviets, etc., see Nuttall (1992), Chapter 5.

[16] Edwards, in Rummel (1992), 165–90; Hill, in Rummel (1992), 139–50.

[17] Although in principle joint actions concern long-term practical cooperation while common positions are concerned with the coordination of ad hoc diplomatic démarches, in practice the two are indistinguishable, Report on the operation of the Treaty on European Union, Sec (95) 731 final, 67.

[18] Nuttall, in Monar (1993), 137; Fink-Hooijer (1994), 186.

for emergency meetings on urgent matters. In the national foreign ministries the Political Directors are responsible for cooperation when preparing and executing Council decisions in the Political Committee. The basic personnel of this cooperation consists of European correspondents in the national foreign ministries, and the European Correspondent Unit in the Council of the EU. These officials (normally at counsellor level) participate in various working parties, draft position papers, operate the day to day communication between member states through both meetings in person and via the COREU[19] system. They are also in charge of preparing the regular meetings of political directors.

II. THE RAPPROCHEMENT OF CENTRAL AND EASTERN EUROPE

A. An *ad hoc* alignment and the creation of the regulatory regime

As early as 1990 – thus prior to the signature of the Europe Agreements – the governments of the CEECs[20] started to make significant efforts to align their foreign policies with those of Western Europe on an *ad hoc* basis. The rediscovery of the 'European destiny' needed to be substantiated by the CEECs. This could easily be done through the CEECs governments' policies on remote crises, which at the same time also intended to prove their independence from Soviet hegemony. Though much of these policies followed the new political philosophies of the democratically elected governments, it seems that at least some of them stemmed more from the will to demonstrate political solidarity than from genuine political concern or economic interests.[21]

The first wave of Europe Agreements was signed with the then three Visegrád countries on 16 December 1991. Because of the long ratification process, the treaties entered into force more than two years later, and it was only an interim agreement enshrining the commercial aspects of these agreements that entered into force in March 1992. The political dialogue, however, already started by a meeting at the level of political directors on 2 April 1992 in Lisbon while the first meeting of the dialogue on highest level was held on 28 October 1992 in Birmingham.[22] A more institutionalized form of cooperation – beyond an *ad hoc* approximation of positions – was only established after the Copenhagen Summit of June 1993, when a decision to formulate a structured relationship between member states and the associated countries was taken. Partly as a result of the Hurd–Andreatta initiative in December 1993, and partly due to a natural evolution process this cooperation

---

[19] The COREU is the internal confidential communication system of the foreign services of the member states.

[20] In this contribution the expression 'CEECs' refers to the Visegrád states, the Baltic states, Bulgaria, Romania and Slovenia.

[21] This is why the so-called Visegrád countries felt compelled to participate – even with a limited, usually non-combat force – in the Allied effort against Iraq, see Gabányi (1992).

[22] Orgoványi (1995), 202–4.

was further extended by resolutions of the General Affairs Council on 7 March 1994 and guidelines accepted by the political directors on 25 October 1994.[23] It has reached its current format through various initiatives launched primarily by the German Presidency and later on with the revised guidelines of the political dialogue accepted by the political directors on 19 October 1995.

B. Proliferation of associated states

Although the cooperation of the EU and the associated states started with only the six countries which had signed Europe Agreements at the time, it has been continuously evolving, and by now it extends to twelve states, of which two are not CEECs. The inclusion of the Baltic States after signing Europe Agreements, and later also the inclusion of Malta, Cyprus and Slovenia[24] have automatically altered the character of the dialogue, though the changes seem to be rather of an informal and practical nature. The participation of twelve states in the dialogue inevitably results in time constraints, a decrease of intensity of the dialogue, and the strengthening of the 'group treatment' approach from the EU side. The Commission initially argued for a group treatment by referring to the fact that the Europe Agreements were not yet in force. Later also the lack of resources and staff was invoked as a reason why the political dialogue should be conducted in a multilateral framework. The Commission also argued that the CEECs' ability to cooperate is a yardstick for their preparedness for integration.[25]

The tendency to group all associated countries together whenever it seems possible is, of course, at first sight, a very logical and practical solution on the part of the EU. Under closer consideration, though, this approach immediately reveals its paradoxical nature. Due to the gradual enlargement of the original group of six associated countries, the multilateral dialogue has become more and more diluted. The various interests of the individual states may be very divergent. It is easy to observe a reversed proportionality in this process: the more countries achieve associated status, the less justified group treatment should become. One does not have to search for long to find evidence for this. Formulating a common position by Cyprus and the Baltic states on

[23] This information is largely based on a number of interviews conducted in the ministries of foreign affairs. The guidelines themselves were not made public.

[24] Malta and Cyprus participated in the structured dialogue since September 1995, but Malta suspended its participation in November 1996. In principle the EU intends to maintain a dialogue with these countries which is similar to that of the CEECs. However, there are some major differences: Malta and Cyprus do not participate at the special session of the General Affairs Council together with CEECs; Certain meetings between them and the EU at the level of ministers take place in their capital instead of Brussels (the first such meeting was held in October 1995 in Malta); The number of working groups in which Malta and Cyprus participate is different, and these groups are not necessarily the same as those of the CEECs. Slovenia, for its part can participate in the political dialogue since June 1996, as its association agreement was signed on 10 June 1996.

[25] In 1991–92, the Visegrád countries acted together on several occasions, see: the Memorandum of the Visegrád countries 'Strengthening integration with the EC and the perspectives of accession', October 1992, quoted in Orgoványi (1995), 205–6.

nuclear non-proliferation issues, or by Malta and the Czech Republic concerning the fight against drugs, is obviously not of equal relevance for the countries in question. This fact naturally influences their approach and behaviour.

Notwithstanding the foregoing, the tendency only to emphasize the common characteristics of all associated countries – which undeniably exist – seems so far to prevail, disregarding not just the wishes of some of the CEECs (notably the Czech Republic, Poland and Hungary repeatedly expressed their need for a bilateral, individual treatment), but also the realities which could make this cooperation effective.

C. The legal basis

The Europe Agreements with the CEECs only provide a broad framework for cooperation in the field of foreign and security policy.[26] For example Article 1(1) of the Europe Agreement concluded with Hungary sets out as the objective of the association to provide an appropriate framework for a political dialogue allowing the development of close political relations. The regular political dialogue under Article 2(1) Europe Agreement, amongst other things:

- assists the associated country in its full reintegration into the community of democratic nations;
- involves better understanding and an increasing convergence of positions on international issues;
- enables each party to consider the position and interests of the other party in their respective decision-making process;
- contributes to the rapprochement of the parties' positions on security issues and enhances security and stability in the whole of Europe.

Articles 3–5 of the Agreement name the ministerial, political directorial and parliamentary levels as the channels for communication between the EU and the associated country. According to Article 4 cooperation takes place at all diplomatic levels but primarily in the UNGA and the CSCE. The other form of cooperation especially set out in this article is through regular information provided to the associated country on the activities of CFSP. The Parliamentary Association Committee is also named as a channel for political dialogue.[27]

---

[26] The association agreements with Malta (*OJ* 1971 L 61/1) and Cyprus (*OJ* 1973 L 133/1) entered into force in the seventies. The association agreements with Hungary (*OJ* 1993 L 347/1), with Poland (*OJ* 1993 L 348/1) entered into force 1 February 1994. The agreements with the Czech Republic (*OJ* 1994 L 360/2), Slovak Republic (*OJ* 1994 L 359/2), with Romania (*OJ* 1994 L 357/2), with Bulgaria (*OJ* 1994 L 358/2) entered into force on 1 February 1995. The association agreements of Slovenia, Lithuania, Latvia and Estonia are awaiting ratification at the time of writing. The various CEEC association agreements contain similar provisions on the political dialogue in this respect. For reasons of simplicity we limit ourselves to the assocation agreement with Hungary.

[27] *OJ* 1993 L 347/3–4.

III. MODALITIES OF THE NEW RELATIONSHIP

The structured relationship creates an intermediate position between that of third countries and that of the member states.[28] The status achieved by the associated states, therefore, is unique, as previous (and current) EC–third country relations differ from it in various respects.

The two major partners in this regard are the USA and Russia[29] both of which succeeded in establishing a political dialogue with the European Union. In fact within the CFSP framework the US–EU political dialogue served as the basic model for the political dialogue both with the associates and Russia, although due to the different nature of these relationships one can find several distinctive characteristics. The US–EU political dialogue[30] is rooted in the Transatlantic Declaration of 1991[31] – confirmed in 1995[32] – and strictly speaking has no proper legal basis. It is not the only, or not even the most essential form of cooperation between the two sides, but rather one element – gaining more and more importance – in the very rich texture of various other forms of cooperation. Its structure is largely the same as the one comprising the associated states with summits, meetings of foreign ministers, political directors and working groups. Since the Berlin Summit[33] 'Shadow European Correspondents' have also been formally appointed, but in practice this level has less importance. After a relatively short period of time of 'getting accustomed to each other' characterized by a rather formalistic exchange of views it has become a substantive and effective dialogue with thirteen to fifteen working groups attended by high level experts from both sides. The groups are selected and the agendas are set jointly with the support of the various directorates of the General Secretariat of the Council in a pragmatic, down-to earth manner.

It should be emphasized that regular bilateral arrangements have been continuously in the foreground only with the US and Russia.[34] For the rest of

---

[28] The relationship of the EU with the members of the CIS, Albania and the former Yugoslav republics – exept Slovenia – i.e. 'Eastern Europe' outside the CEECs, is much less intense than the structured relationship (Van Ham (1994), 45–9 and 56–7) and it aims primarily at conflict prevention (Munuera (1994), 25–100; Van Ham (1994), 25–9, 45–52).

[29] The Russian–EU dialogue has a very similar structure to that of the CEEC–EU, but there are some important differences: the level of European Correspondents does not exist; the number of working groups in which Russia participates is considerably lower (5–6); it was only under the Spanish Presidency that the dialogue took a structured format with preset dates for the meetings of the working groups.

[30] It is worth noting that paradoxically North America (i.e. the US and Canada) is the only region which has no desk or directorate within the CFSP Unit of the General Secretariat of the Council. This is mainly due to the exceptional political weight of US–EU relations. It would be difficult to find a proper arrangement to deal with such an enhanced responsibility. Moreover, the unique and complex world-wide web of interests of these two entities results in a very intensive and multi-layered dialogue that requires direct contacts. On US–EU relations, see Lord Carrington, 1–12; Murray, 213–20.

[31] Déclaration conjointe sur les relations entre la Communauté européenne et les Etats Unis, 23 November 1990. Documents d'actualité internationale, No. 2, 15 janvier 1991, 39–40.

[32] Sommet euro-américain: Plan d'action transatlantique, Madrid, 3 décembre 1995. Documents d'actualité internationale, No. 3, 1 février 1996, 109–12.

[33] Summary of Conclusions of the Berlin Meeting of the Council, *International Legal Materials*, Vol. 30, No. 5, September 1991, 1349–56.

[34] Recently China, Japan and Ukraine have acquired a somewhat similar position.

the world – thus with the CEECs, or for that matter, with the Mediterranean[35] – the EU prefers to pursue a basically multilateral dialogue.

Not surprisingly, as has been indicated above, the reactions of CEECs to this approach vary according to their level of development. Those who feel they are in a more advanced position strongly resist the EU's attempts to treat these countries as a group, while the rest tend to be generally in favour of non-differentiation. The reasons for their different attitudes seem perfectly clear, just as much as those of the European Union. Countries considering themselves as 'les avant-gardes' rightly fear that if all twelve states are constantly kept together, then the 'slowest one in the caravan sets the pace' of integration and their relative advantages gradually diminish. Of course, a joint approach is in the interest of the others, who would like to be seen as already being at the same level of development, claiming that there are only minor differences, and striving not to be excluded from the next round of enlargement. It remains to be seen which one of these strategies will finally be accepted by the EU when it comes to taking real, long-term decisions, such as opening accession negotiations with the applicants.

A. Forms of cooperation

The CEECs are associated to the Second Pillar via the following mechanism:

A regular meetings between:	B contacts between:	C regular information provided to:	D co-ordination between:
– Leaders of the EU and CEECs	– the European correspondents and the Associated European correspondents	– the heads of the Brussels missions of the CEECs	– representations of the EU members and the associated countries at international fora and in third countries
– Ministers of Foreign Affairs	– officials at the permanent representations of the EU member states to Brussels and the CEECs' CFSP contact points		
– Political Directors – Working groups			

---

[35] In this respect see Euro-Mediterranean Conference held on 27–28 November 1995 in Barcelona, bringing together the fifteen EU members and twelve non-EU Mediterranean states.

a. Regular meetings

1. Summit meetings between the heads of state and governments of the Fifteen and of the CEECs

The resolution of the Ministers of Foreign Affairs on 7 March 1994 and the Corfu European Council decided that members of the European Council together with the President of the Commission should meet with each of their Central and Eastern European counterparts at least once a year. In practice, however, the associated countries have since then been invited and it seems that this pattern will continue in the future. Although in the autumn of 1994 a dispute occurred over whether the CEECs should be invited to all European Councils to the Essen European Summit[36] by the Cannes Summit[37] the invitations had already been sent well before the event. There was practically no discussion on the associated countries' participation at the Madrid, Florence and Dublin Summits. However, due to the envisaged closure of the ISC in Amsterdam, the CEECs were invited to a special briefing ten days after the summit.

The content of this participation is, of course, of a much more general nature than pure foreign policy cooperation. It involves the structured dialogue between the two sides in its entirety, so there is scope for most issues of primary interest to be discussed. Although in principle the heads of state and governments of the fifteen member states and their counterparts from the CEECs have a unique opportunity to exchange their views at these meetings, in reality the time left for discussions is limited and rarely allows either side to go beyond formalities, even if there were intentions to do so. The reason why these meetings are nevertheless still considered as having a special importance besides their structural significance is, that they give the associated countries an unequalled opportunity to present their ideas at the highest level[38] simultaneously with the member states.

2. Regular ministerial, political director and European correspondent level meetings

These meetings themselves have a piecemeal structure. By and large the same topics are discussed at the three levels, with the correspondents at the bottom, and the ministers at the top, and the whole exercise points to the summit meetings at the end of each Presidency.

---

[36] There was a divergence of interpretation due to the fact that it was not clear whether the reference to 'one year' in the Corfu decision referred to calendar years or to a period of twelve months counted from July 1994, see *Magyar Hírlap* 26 November 1994, 2: 'Németország zavarban van'. As a result of the fact that, since December 1994, the CEECs have been invited to all summits, this discussion has lost much of its significance.

[37] SN 211/95-Part A 10.

[38] In this respect the so-called 'Essen Memorandum' presented by Hungary in December 1994 at the Summit of the German Presidency should be recalled. This was the first formal presentation of one of the associated states' positions on the basic issues of its integration policy in such a format at an EU Summit and was well received by the member states, see Memorandum der ungarischen Regierung zur Integration der assoziierten mittel- und osteuropäischen Staaten in die Europäische Union, vorgelegt von Ministerpräsident Gyula Horn zur Tagung des Europäischen Rates am 10. Dezember 1994 in Essen, *Internationale Politik* (1995), 117–19.

It has been agreed that the General Affairs Council shall invite the Ministers of Foreign Affairs of the associated countries in conjunction with one of its sessions.[39] The agenda of these special meetings is decided by the Presidency with a view to discuss foreign policy matters of common interest. In practice a consultation procedure also exists with the associated countries, and as a result, occasionally, the Presidency takes on some of their informal proposals. The experience so far has shown a gradual development from a formal and limited, though still useful, exchange of ideas towards a substantive dialogue at ministerial level. The topics usually reflect the primary interest of the EU, but since in general these are also in the foreground of that of the associated states, the meetings can provide a proper forum to demonstrate the unique links, and the correlating opinions of the two sides.

Prior to each European Council meeting during each Presidency the Political Committee arranges at least one meeting with the Political Directors (or with their equivalents) from the national foreign ministries of the associated states. One of the objectives of these meetings is the preparation of the meetings of foreign ministers, who, in turn prepare the summits of heads of state and governments. The agenda normally – though not always – is already a draft agenda for the foreign ministers, therefore these meetings can serve as a kind of coordination forum with the associated partners before the finalization of their programme. However, they are dialogue meetings in their own right, handling specific substantive issues as well.

The meetings of European Correspondents (ECos) and Associated European Correspondents (AECos) form an integral part of a special relationship which is also based on the rules of the structured dialogue. The main long-term objective of this relationship is gradually to involve AECos in the everyday practice of the Union's foreign policy mechanism through the establishment of regular links with their EU partners, the ECos. It was in the Summer of 1994 that the Ministries of Foreign Affairs of the CEECs nominated a number of diplomats to take up the newly created position of AECos. According to the arrangements of the political dialogue, ECos and AECos meet twice a year during each Presidency, theoretically once at its beginning and once in preparation for the Ministerial and Political Director level meetings of the fifteen plus twelve.[40] They discuss the subject matter of the political dialogue, the agenda and keynote addresses of the meetings to come.

3.   Meetings of the working groups
It has also been agreed in principle that within the framework of the structured dialogue the national experts of the ministries of associated countries can cooperate with a number of EU working groups. In practice this means that there is one special session of any given working group during each

---

[39] See Minutes of the Council of Ministers meeting on 7 March 1994.
[40] At the moment of writing this text, Malta – as a result of the victory of the labour party at the elections held in October 1996 – decided to suspend its participation in the structured dialogue.

presidency where the associated countries are invited to participate. At these occasions it is usually not the delegates of the fifteen member states, but only those of the Troika, accompanied by officials from the General Secretariat of the Council alongside with the European Commission that represent the EU. In exceptional cases some of these meetings[41] are held in the larger, 15+12 format, but despite reiterated claims of the associated states, the European Union seems to be reluctant to establish this larger framework as the general norm. Since the Troika format has been applied to the similar meetings with the US, and prior to their accession with the EFTA countries as well, the EU's reference to work pressure and time constraints as the two major purely technical, non-political factors preventing the extension of this format seems justified. Considering the fact that the EFTA countries gained access to the proper working groups themselves only after their signature of the accession treaties, it is unrealistic to expect that the current set-up would be significantly altered in the short or medium term.

Of 25 Council working groups, the associated states currently have access to 10–13 depending on the invitation of the Presidency in office.[42] This is a substantial increase compared to the first such period during the Belgian Presidency when they were only invited to six CFSP working groups, but it still does not fulfil the expectations and reiterated demands of the associated states, who would like to participate in more groups, and of their own choice.

As for the substance of the special sessions of these joint working groups, it depends to a large extent on the specific qualities of the experts both on the side of the EU and the associated states. If the Presidency is well prepared, the agenda carefully drawn up and distributed in time, the meeting can turn out to become a meaningful dialogue indeed. This is, however, a rather idealistic scenario, that due to various reasons only rarely occurs. It seems clear that once an internal consensus after an often painful process in any given issue has been reached, the EU is not particularly interested in engaging in another probably time-consuming and perhaps sensitive exercise, unless it has some particular interest to involve the associated countries. As a result – especially at the early stages of the cooperation – most sessions consisted merely of presenting monologues on both sides without actually reacting to the other's position. However, this practice seems to be changing. This is partly due to the more and more active role played by the associated countries and partly due to the fact that, as time goes by, both sides see more and more scope for real cooperation, especially in the politically less controversial areas where the original position of most associated countries usually coincides with that of the EU. In this respect it is interesting to see the similarities and differences of the voting patterns of the associated countries and EU members in the UN (below, pp. 330–31).

---

[41] The working groups on the OSCE, and on security are normally held in the 15+12 format.
[42] The number and the exact configuration of these groups varies. There were eight groups during the Greek, twelve during the German, French and Spanish presidencies, and thirteen in the case of the Italian. Some groups have been continuously present throughout the last three presidencies.

b.   CFSP contact points

The General Affairs Council on 7 March 1994 called for the nomination of CFSP contact points at the Brussels missions of the CEECs in order to establish and maintain regular contacts with the permanent representations of the member states, the Commission and the Council Secretariat. In the periods between the correspondent level meetings, the cooperation between the contact points and the Council Secretariat is to ensure fast and reliable communication between the EU and the CEECs. Its modalities are decided by the participants themselves. Normally contacts are made through faxes, various meetings in person, or in any given case through the provision of information on an *ad hoc* basis by the Council Secretariat about the work of the various Council working groups.

The institution of contact points was originally established because the EU was unwilling to permit direct access for the associated countries to either the decision-making or to the internal information exchange system, the COREU.[43] Currently, contact points at the missions of the associated states in practice act more or less in the same capacity as CFSP counsellors at the permanent representations of the member states. They accompany the national experts (or substitute them if they cannot participate) at the working group meetings, handle daily foreign policy affairs and assist both in the preparation and conduct of the meetings of correspondents, political directors and foreign ministers.

c.   Coordination at international fora and regular contacts in third countries

The EU and the associated CEE countries are expected to cooperate at international fora taking into consideration the particular nature of the forum.

From the viewpoint of CFSP-CEEC cooperation there are four types of issues.

The first type is a faraway crisis situation with remote political and hardly any economic interest for CEECs or other matters of major general interest to the world community but of no direct and immediate concern to the CEECs. No doubt, the massacres of Kigali and Bujumbura and the problem of North-Korean nuclear armaments fall into this category. On these matters, the sheer voting power of these countries in the UN General Assembly and at international conferences[44] makes the CEECs precious partners. Since their alignment in these cases does not result in any immediate economic burden, CEEC-governments are more than ready to offer their votes expecting obviously a due reciprocation later on.

---

[43] In the beginning of 1996 a special e-mail contact was established between the CFSP Secretariat and the CEEC permanent missions. This e-mail contact is limited because it does not link the CEEC foreign ministries with the EU foreign ministries.

[44] Such as the one on the extension of the Nuclear Proliferation Treaty, see text in *International Legal Materials*, Vol. XXXIV No. 4, July 1995, 959–74.

The second type is a remote crisis where the CEECs have important economic interests. This was the case with regard to the embargo against Libya, the partial – primarily American – embargo against Iran, and some of the diplomatic and legal measures against China and Indonesia.

This sensibility has been taken into account by the EU in the examined period and the loyalty of the CEECs was not put to a test on controversial issues,[45] although, when, for example, the EU offered the possibility of adherence to a measure condemning China regarding the restrictions on the freedom of movement of diplomatic personnel, the measure received mixed reactions from the CEECs. Poland, Hungary and Bulgaria[46] for example were wary about condemning China.[47] This was, however, not only due to the perceived national interest. As the restrictions had been in place for almost five decades, Bulgaria, Hungary and Poland may not have seen a particular opportunity in April 1995 to change the Chinese system. Thus, the European declaration to which they were invited to adhere was not only against their immediate interests but may have seemed completely futile to them. The opinions of the Czech, Slovak and Romanian governments were different.[48]

The third type is a crisis in the immediate neighbourhood of the CEECs, particularly in the Russian Federation or in the territory of the former Yugoslavia. In these crises on the brink of the CEEC-region the commitment of the CEECs to follow the policies set out in Brussels has been less strong.

On matters related to the Soviet coup or the Soviet threats to the Baltic nations, the CEECs reacted much more quickly and much more strongly, and their political positions and initiatives have been at times more forceful then those of the Twelve.[49] In the Yugoslav crisis, the policies followed by the CEECs were clearly designed along the lines of self-interest and political traditions, but the commitments made to the EU, NATO and the WEU have also shaped these rather restrained policies. Hungary, by permitting the flight of the AWACS planes over Hungarian territory and alongside with Romania

---

[45] See Table 3 underscoring this point.

[46] The Czech Republic, Slovakia and Romania did not find it difficult to adhere to this démarche.

[47] Based on interviews in the Ministry of Foreign Affairs in Budapest.

[48] Based on interviews with the Ministry of Foreign Affairs in Budapest and Slovak diplomats.

[49] On the reaction of NATO, see 'The situation in the Soviet Union: Statement issued by the North Atlantic Council meeting in ministerial session at NATO headquarters, Brussels, on 21 August 1991', *NATO Review*, Vol. 39, No. 4 (1991), 9. Some analysts have argued that the Council in its formulation: 'Noting the enhanced concern of Central and Eastern European states we reiterate our conviction that our own security is inseparably linked to that of all other states in Europe, particularly to that of the emerging democracies' has taken a particularly forceful position, weakened only by the statement '. . . all other states in Europe . . .' introduced on a French initiative. The fact that concerns were extended to every European country, including the Soviet Union, caused speculations whether the Atlantic Alliance was to become an organization of collective security rather than collective defence. The Visegrád countries have coordinated their reaction, see the Statement by the Government of the Hungarian Republic on 21 August 1991 (Press Release Ministry of Foreign Affairs 13/1991). See on the reaction of the Nordic countries Mouritzen (1995), 156–76. He points out that while Finnish reaction was appeasing whoever may come out victorious from the coup, the Swedish and primarily the Danish reaction was much more openly and actively against the extreme-left coup.

and Bulgaria permitting WEU warships to patrol the border-waters,[50] has manifested readiness for a substantial limitation of its sovereignty in exchange for a limited security commitment and a longer term political reciprocation from the EU. It is also true that in the case of all three nations an alignment with Western-European policies – to the extent they existed – have also prevented these countries from being drawn into the Yugoslav military and diplomatic struggle. On the other hand on Bosnia there was on certain occasions a marked difference between the positions taken by the various CEECs: Hungary followed the US and not the Franco-German lead[51] unlike the other associated countries who abstained at most of these votes.

The fourth type of crisis is between two nations in the region or it is inside a single CEEC. On these issues one of the main features also characterizing the EPC–CFSP cooperation becomes important: the CFSP itself as well as its cooperation with the CEECs is primarily a foreign policy-making mechanism, which is not concerned with either domestic problems or interstate problems between the member states.[52]

The creation of the structured relationship did not turn domestic or interstate problems in the region of the CEECs into a 'no go' area for CFSP. The EU has actively intervened in the domestic political matters of the associated countries through the CFSP mechanisms.[53] At the same time, as was already observed previously, the rules of the political dialogue do not allow the participation of the CEECs when a CFSP action is directed towards one of these coutries. This means that the main thrust of the dialogue is a coordination of the foreign policies of the two sides in areas outside their own territories.

It is worth analysing the CFSP–CEEC cooperation in more detail. Table 1 suggests that through the almost full realignment of their foreign policies CEECs have become a small, but reliable voting partner.

Although voting coincidence[54] has significantly increased between the EC/EU and US since 1989, the increase has been far more dramatic in the case of the CEECs and to some extent the EEG countries. In 1994 all examined CEECs surpassed the EU average in voting coincidence with the US and in fact they have come close – in terms of the percentages – to the ratios of the UK–US special relationship. Although on the basis of the data available it is not possible to define precisely the voting coincidence between the examined CEECs and the EU countries, it would appear fair to say that coincidence is higher than 90 per cent.

---

[50] Gabanyi (1994), 114.

[51] See votes on A/RES/47/21 and A/RES/49/10.

[52] For example, the problem in Northern Ireland and the Basque conflicts do not fall within the ambit of the EPC or the CFSP. Regelsberger (1985), 42 uses for these 'no go areas' the term 'domaines réservés' and also mentions Gibraltar as a source of intra-community dispute.

[53] See e.g. the EU démarche regarding the circumstances of the change of government in Slovakia and the state of democracy or the EU démarche concerning the real estate legislation in Slovenia (démarche 6 March 1995) mentioned again in the Conclusions of the Presidency, Cannes Summit SN 211/95-Part A, 10, para. 2.

[54] Regelsberger (1985), 38 also measured voting coincidence between EC member states from 1978 to 1984. The data in that crisis period suggested declining coincidence.

Table 1 Percentage of voting coincidence* with the US in the UN General Assembly plenary (1989–1994)

Nation	1989	1990	1991	1992	1993	1994
Hungary	15.4	42.2	56.8	61.4	71.0	79.6
Czech Rep.**	9.4	46.3	63.0	61.9	70.0	78.8
Poland	10.4	48.7	61.7	58.0	68.4	78.4
Slovakia	**	**	**	**	70.5	79.5
EEG***	n.a.	n.a.	n.a.	49.6	59.8	72.2
Belgium	66.7	67.2	70.0	63.8	72.5	77.7
Luxembourg	66.7	67.9	68.0	63.8	74.4	77.7
Netherlands	68.1	67.2	70.0	63.8	74.4	81.4
Germany	70.5	69.0	71.3	63.8	74.4	77.8
France	69.0	76.7	70.5	63.8	71.0	75.8
Denmark	48.1	50.0	61.2	56.4	67.5	75.0
Spain	46.4	45.1	52.0	51.0	59.5	68.3
Portugal	66.2	61.8	59.5	58.7	69.1	75.0
Italy	64.3	65.5	66.0	63.8	73.7	79.2
Ireland	42.5	41.0	53.2	54.5	65.8	70.5
Greece	32.9	41.7	48.9	50.0	58.5	71.4
UK	77.8	81.8	79.6	73.5	80.0	84.3
EC/EU	59.9	61.2	64.2	60.8	70.0	76.3

* Not including consensus votes.
** Czech and Slovak Federal Republic until 31 December 1992.
*** EEG stands for Eastern European Group. In the UN terminology this comprises all European former socialist countries except the former USSR.

Source: *Voting practices in the United Nations 1992*, Report to Congress Submitted Pursuant to Public Law, US Department of State, 1993, 101–67; *Voting practices in the United Nations 1994*, Report to Congress Submitted Pursuant to Public Law, US Department of State, 1995, 101–67.

It is clear from Table 1 that there have been wide differences in the voting pattern of the EC/EU nations (see for example in 1989 when the figure for the UK is 77.8 per cent while the corresponding figure for Greece is 32.9 and for Ireland is 42.5 per cent). It is also interesting to examine whether the alignment of the CEECs is with the positions of the EU as a group or with that of a particular country. Table 2 shows how in 1994 seven selected countries voted on issues and issue categories put to a vote in the General Assembly of the United Nations. On these issues Hungary voted identically with Germany[55] and Poland nine times out of ten, with France and the Czech Republic eight times out of ten, with the US and Russia respectively six and four times out of ten. It was on a resolution on the situation

---

[55] On these issues the UK and Italy voted identically with Germany.

Table 2 Votes of selected countries on certain important issues in 1994

Topic	Hungary	Czech Rep.	Poland	Germany	France	US	Russia
1	A	A	A	A	Y	N	Y
2	Y	A	A	A	A	Y	A
3	Y	Y	Y	Y	Y	Y	A
4	A	A	A	A	A	N	A
5	Y	A	Y	Y	Y	N	A
6	Y	Y	Y	Y	Y	N	A
7	Y	Y	Y	Y	Y	Y	Y
8	Y	Y	Y	Y	Y	Y	Y
9	Y	Y	A	Y	Y	Y	Y
10	Y	Y	Y	Y	Y	Y	Y
11	90.5%	86.4%	90.5%	86.4%	88.5%	100%	72%
12	100%	100%	100%	100%	91.7%	100%	66.7%
13	50%	53.3%	46.7%	50%	42.1%	100%	72.7%
14	100% (1992)	100% (1994)	–	–	100%	100%	98.7%

1: US embargo of Cuba (A/Res/49/9); 2: Situation in Bosnia and Herzegovina (A/Res/49/10); 3: Situation in Croatia (A/Res/49/43); 4: Israeli Nuclear Armament (A/Res/49/78); 5: Israeli Settlements (A/Res/49/132); 6: Palestinian Self-Determination (A/Res/49/149): 7: Human Right in parts of the FRY (A/Res/49/196); 8: Human Rights in Cuba (A/Res/49/200); 9: Human Rights in Iran (A/Res/49/202); 10: Human Rights in Iraq (A/Res/49/203); Issue categories*: 11: Arms control; 12: Human Rights; 13: Middle East; 14: Security Council Votes (in a year)

Explanation to the table:
Issue categories are types of votes regrouped either functionally or regionally. A: abstained; Y: yes; N: no; %: percentage of voting together (coincidence) with the US. There were 32 votes on arms control, 12 on human rights and 24 on the Middle East in 1994.

Source: *Voting practices in the United Nations 1992*, Report to Congress Submitted Pursuant to Public Law, US Department of State, 1993, 101–67; *Voting practices in the United Nations 1994*, Report to Congress Submitted Pursuant to Public Law, US Department of State, 1995, 101–67.

in Bosnia and Herzegovina, condemning the Bosnian Serb party for its refusal to accept the proposed territoral settlement that the Hungarian vote and German and Polish votes differed because the Hungarian delegate – on that one issue – sided with the US. On other important matters as well as on issues of less importance Germany, Hungary and Poland voted identically.

On the other hand it is striking how big the distance with Russia has become within a short time-frame. In this sense it is also interesting to point out that the Russian position hardly has any impact on the vote of these countries while the US position is not nearly as decisive as is the case within the EU.

When examining the voting pattern of the Hungarian non-permanent Security Council delegation in 1992 and of the Czech delegation of 1994 we find that they both voted identically with the US, the UK and France who in turn also acted together on all matters.[56]

B. Devices of cooperation

The associated countries have access to three foreign policy instruments at present. They may align themselves with EU declarations, may adhere to EU political démarches and may participate in EU joint actions.

In each case the conditions of participation are decided strictly by the EU and the extremely cautiously worded provisions of the guidelines leave ample room for finding reasons not to invite the CEECs at the EU's full discretion. Of course, this impact is ensured not by direct political statements, but by devising very flexible rules. According to the revised 'Guidelines for enhanced political dialogue' accepted on 19 October 1995, 'due to the *time factor* involved . . . it may not always be possible to have the associates participate'. Moreover, 'the EU side reserves the right to derogate from the above guidelines when this is warranted by the *urgency* of the matter or *other overriding concern*'.[57] The guidelines contain a further inbuilt restriction as well, though this may have some justification. The last sentence of Point 1 reads: 'in particular, the above guidelines may be non-applicable when a declaration or a demarche is addressed to one of the associated countries.'[58]

It is also clear, that of the two new foreign policy instruments of the CFSP introduced in the Maastricht Treaty (J.2/3 and J.2/2) the associated states have access only to one, namely that of 'joint actions', while the EU has consistently denied direct participation in 'common positions'.[59] With regard to joint actions, the EU has invited the associated partners only a few times to participate since the beginnings of the cooperation. Therefore, the main devices of foreign policy cooperation between the associated countries and the EU are in fact instruments which were characteristic features of the EPC,

---

[56] Voting practices (1994), 202.

[57] Point 1 of the guidelines, while point 6 reads: The EU and the associates will instruct their representatives 'in international fora to cooperate *whenever possible*' (emphasis added).

[58] See above on the fourth type of crisis.

[59] As a recent development, the CEECs have been offered the option of aligning themselves with certain EU common positions as agreed upon by the member states. As of April 1997 this has happened in relation to East Timor, Myammaz, Afghanistan, the Biological and Toxical Weapons Convention and the arms embargo for ex-Yugoslavia.

and which continue to predominate even after Maastricht,[60] namely: declarations and démarches. Even among these, the vast majority of EU invitations have been issued for declarations, and only in exceptional cases were these countries invited to a démarche, which may sometimes have been of much more importance. A closer look at the details reveals that the continuing intergovernmentalist tendency of foreign policy cooperation is even more obvious in this relationship than in the normal procedures of the member states.

a. Alignment with EU diplomatic declarations

In the revised 1995 guidelines for enhanced political dialogue, the EU undertook to inform the CEECs as early as possible of its intention to take presidential or Troika démarches or to make EU declarations.[61] The initial information provided by the Council Secretariat to the CEEC permanent missions in Brussels usually does not provide all the information about the details of the declaration or démarche to be made but rather limits itself to communicating the general direction of the measure or the mere fact that it is planned to be taken.[62] The associated countries have to inform the Council Secretariat regarding their acceptance of the proposed measure. After the text of the démarche or declaration has been finalized, the Council Secretariat gives a short period of notice – ranging from a few hours to three or four days, but in most cases around 24 hours – for the CEECs to give their consent.

When all associated countries agree with a declaration, the latter simply refers to this fact, while if some of them do not wish to align themselves, the declaration enumerates only those countries which support the measure. Out of the almost 200 declarations made by the EU since the entry into force of the TEU, the CEECs – as Table 3 suggests – had the possibility to adhere to about 30. These declarations mainly concerned matters of a less direct importance to the CEECs, such as democracy and peace in various Third World countries. Also the logic of the invitations is not always clear: for example the CEECs were invited to two declarations concerning the trial of an opposition leader in Nigeria but were not subsequently invited to the declaration condemning his execution. At first sight, this may appear to be rather disturbing for the associated countries: a right is granted to them, but then in practice may only be exercised sporadically and on non-essential issues. Yet, we believe, this would be a hasty conclusion to draw, as by their

---

[60] Background Report on the 1996 IGC, Jean Monnet House, September 1995, 8.

[61] By the end of December 1995, 45 joint actions and 32 common positions were approved according to the statistics provided by the General Secretariat of the Council; according to our calculations these numbers increased to 18 and 174 respectively.

[62] It appears from interviews conducted in the Hungarian Ministry of Foreign Affairs that during the Spanish Presidency in one case at the end of a meeting at the political director level there was simply an oral invitation to join a démarche on Yugoslavia. Without having clearly seen the direction of the démarche only some CEECs decided to join.

Table 3 Declarations adhered to by the CEECs until December 1995[a]

Nations	Democracy in Africa. Number of proposed actions (15)	Democracy and peace in Asia. Number of proposed actions (7)	Democracy in South America. Number of proposed actions (1)	NPT. Number of proposed actions (4)	Joint declarations on matters of CEEC and Europe (3)
Bulgaria	1, 2, 3, 4	11			
Czech Republic	1, 2, 3, 4	10, 11			
Hungary	1, 2, 3, 4	10, 11			
Poland	1, 3, 4	10, 11			
Romania	1, 2, 3, 4	10, 11			
Slovakia	1, 2, 3, 4	10, 11			
Lithuania, Latvia, Estonia	8, 9				
CEECs together	5, 6, 8, 9, 22, 23, 24, 25, 26[b], 29	12, 13, 14, 27, 28	15	16, 17, 18, 19	20, 21, 30

1 = Angola, 2 = Niger, 3 = Gambia, 4 = Nigeria, 5 = Guinea, 6 = Gabon, 7 = Liberia, 8 = Sudan, 9 = Zaire, 10 = Chinese sea, 11 = Burma, 12 = Kazakhstan, 13 = Sri Lanka, 14 = Liberation of Suu Kyi, 15 = Contadora Declaration (Guatemala), 16 = Adhesion of Algeria to the NPT, 17 = Adhesion of Ukraine to the NPT, 18 = Adhesion of Moldova to the NPT, 19 = Adhesion of Argentina to the NPT, 20 = Former Yugoslavia, 21 = Chechnya, 22 = Ethiopia, 23 = Comores, 24 = Burundi, 25 = Nigeria, 26 = Nigeria, 27 = China, 28 = Burma, 29 = Tanzania, 30 = Legislative elections in Russia

[a] Based on statistics of the General Secretariat of the Council of the EU (DG E–CFSP Unit.). By April 1997 the CEECs had joined 40 new declarations out of a further 150 yet the proportions in the main subject areas of the invitations have remained basically unchanged.

[b] The declaration of 9 November 1995 regarding the proceedings against Ken Saro-Wiwa was supported also by Malta, Cyprus and the remaining EFTA countries.

gradual integration into the CFSP mechanism a broader new world has opened up to these countries. They are invited to formulate and to communicate opinions on matters on which otherwise they would probably not have been able to do so. On the other hand, the fact that their opinions are asked almost exclusively on these matters and that even on these matters invitations to adhere are occasional, may suggest that the EU only makes a real effort to invite the CEECs when the presidency is 'enlargement-minded' or when – on non-controversial issues – it can be politically demonstrated that the presidency is conscious of the fact that it may draw on the support of the CEECs.

b. Adherence to démarches and participation in the implementation of joint actions

As mentioned earlier, the dominant tool of the CFSP dialogue with the CEECs has been the invitation to declarations. Invitations to démarches have been relatively rare, and most of these fell within the scope of EU joint actions, instead of being offered on their own right as individual measures. Nonetheless, some démarches in specific, separate issues have also been available to the CEECs. Of these, the most relevant subjects seem to be the missing persons in ex-Yugoslavia and the extension of the UNPROFOR mandate in Croatia. Formally, if all associated countries agree, the doyen of the heads of missions of the associated countries may accompany the EU Troika in its démarche. If not all associated countries agree to the démarche then the Troika declares which of the associated countries align themselves with it.

The EU also offered to inform the CEECs on its proposed joint actions[63] if their participation appears to be 'possible and appropriate'. It has, however, retained the right not to consult with the CEECs if the urgency of the matter or another consideration so requires.[64] In practice, however, compared to the high number of declarations, there have been only a few occasions where invitations to participate in the implementation of EU joint actions have been received.[65]

Summarizing the accessibility to and use of the various foreign policy devices of the EU–Associated countries cooperation, it is clear that the integration process of the associated countries still has a long way to go. It is remarkable that practically since the beginning of this special relationship there have been only a few occasions where the associated countries could use a 'real' CFSP tool. In all other cases the CEEC participation has been limited to the devices of the old EPC mechanism. Of course, the cooperation with these countries cannot precede the internal EU developments which also lag behind the 'ideal Maastricht scenario', both in terms of reliance on the new tools and on qualified majority voting. However, an intensification and extension of the current dialogue would probably not just be warmly welcomed by the associated countries, but it may well give a much needed new impetus for the Union itself.

---

[63] Up to the end of December 1996 45 joint actions were taken.

[64] See the CFSP démarche regarding the change in government in Slovakia, *Magyar Hírlap*, 26 November 1994, 2 'Vegyes fogadtatás'.

[65] These issues until the end of 1995 concerned the European Stability Pact (93/728/CFSP, *OJ* L 339, 31 December 1993; 94/367/CFSP, *OJ* L 165, 1 July 1994), the review conference of the 1980 Vienna Convention in 1995 and the universality of the NPT Treaty. See Note from the EU General Secretariat DG E–CFSP Unit. Direction Geo. II., 12 January 1996.

IV. THE CURRENT REFORM PROPOSALS

A. Suggestions to develop CFSP after 1996

Although it is not the task of this contribution to elaborate the various ideas concerning the reform of CFSP at the 1996 Intergovernmental Conference, it seems worthwhile to look at the possible implications these may have on the associated states in the near future. It is widely accepted that the CFSP has achieved far less significant progress than was expected when it was enshrined in the Maastricht Treaty.[66] Soon after its signature, it was already predicted that, due to the insufficient compromise arrived at as a result of the struggle between the federalist and intergovernmentalist schools, the provisions of Title V would scarcely be adequate to achieve the stated aims of the Treaty.[67] These doubts have been confirmed by the events during the years that have passed since the entry into force of the Maastricht Treaty and it is clear that substantial reforms are needed. Jacques Delors has properly compared the CFSP experience to 'the body of a Jaguar with the engine of a lawn mower inside'.[68]

Theoretically, the main objective is to gain more efficiency, but in the absence of an unambiguous political will this might be impossible to attain by solely relying on legal instruments. The lessons of former Yugoslavia have clearly shown again that, even if the means are there, their usage is very often far from adequate.[69] The conduct of the Balkan crisis has also caused considerable dismay in several smaller member states as well as in the Commission itself. There was a lack of transparency and proper coordination among the fifteen member states. Various sources have voiced, with increasing frequency, the fear that the 'contact group model' might well lead to a revival of the traditional 'big power' attitude, and if it is taken together with the growing diversity of EU members resulting from a new enlargement, the overall impact could potentially weaken the still fragile CFSP mechanism.[70] Although the problems themselves are fairly clear in this context – and there seems to be a general consensus concerning the priority areas for CFSP reform – the proposed solutions differ widely. For example, the Commission and some 'federalist oriented' member states (notably Belgium and Italy) would like to see the abolition of the pillar structure and the gradual extension of the Community method to this field.[71]

On the other hand it is widely known that some governments would rather prefer a return to the purely intergovernmental pre-Maastricht scenario. There

---

[66] See the background reports of the Commission, the Council and the EP on the IGC preparations, as well as the background report of the Jean Monnet House, 8.

[67] Edwards and Nuttall, in *Maastricht and Beyond*, 89.

[68] *Agence Europe*, 13 January 1995, 10.

[69] Lecture given by G. Burghardt at the Asser Institute on 'The TEU – Suggestions for revision' in The Hague on 16 September 1995, 4.

[70] Among others, see ibid., 5 and the speech of Mr. E. Derycke, Foreign Minister of Belgium on 13 October 1995, at the symposium of the P-H. Spaak Foundation (quoted in *Agence Europe*, 14 October 1995, 2/b).

[71] See Burghardt above, and a speech of H. van den Broek in EIPA, Maastricht on 19 October 1995.

is almost general agreement on the need to establish a foreign policy planning cell, but there are contradicting views on its location and functions. The creation of a 'Mr or Mrs CFSP' is also a divisive issue not just among the member states, but also among EU institutions. It is impossible here to go into details, but it seems worth recalling that behind all technical debates the real underlying issue is – as it has always been in this respect – whether national foreign policies should complement common EU actions, or whether it should be precisely the other way around.

The big question for the CEECs is: which of these schools of thought is going to prevail and how will that affect the political dialogue with the European Union? Of course, any reply to this necessarily has to rely on the extensive use of hypothetical statements, but a brief look at some essential options could prove to be useful. An option coming up quite regularly is a scenario in which some (or all) associated countries would be integrated into the CFSP earlier than into other areas.[72] Besides the technicalities involved this would immediately raise the much larger issue of partial accession, which so far has been consistently rejected by most of the countries in question. The reason invoked by the associated countries for rejecting partial accession has an ideological and a practical element. The ideological one is that they all want to join the EU fully in all its aspects. The practical one is that they expect to benefit from economic integration as well. One must not forget either that the members of the Union have already benefited significantly from the association agreements as the CEECs have gradually opened up their markets in the face of considerable quantities of goods produced in the Union. If this resistance is maintained – which seems likely to be the case – most efforts to achieve qualitatively different modalities for more intensive participation by the associated countries may well need a careful, although at the same time politically rewarding, diplomatic exercise on both sides in the future. Another recurring possibility is the gradual merging of the three pillars of the Maastricht Treaty. This would obviously tilt the balance of European integration away from an intergovernmental approach, and the consequences for the CEECs would basically depend on the new structures to be set up. At this moment it would not be appropriate to work out any specific details for these (or other, equally unpredictable) scenarios, but it seems well worth reflecting on them, both in view of the IGC and in conjunction with the next enlargement.

B. How to improve the modalities of the CFSP dialogue?

Notwithstanding the major strategic options outlined above, the issue of further improvements both regarding the forms of cooperation and the devices of foreign policy are constantly on the agenda of foreign policy-makers in the associated states as well as in the EU. There is ample room for enhancing this special relationship also in the currently existing multilateral framework;

---

[72] See H. and W. Wallace, *Flying together in a larger and more diverse European Union*, Netherlands, Scientific Council for Government Policy, The Hague, 1995, 49.

the accumulated effects of these at first sight minor achievements could probably accelerate the process of integration itself.

As a result of the ongoing exchange of information between government officials the main thrust of suggested technical improvements are formulated with the aim of including them in the revision of the guidelines governing the political dialogue. The first revision of these guidelines took place at the meeting of ECos–AECos on 19 October 1995. Although no major changes were introduced, the relatively minor alterations had an ambiguous effect. On the one hand the new text gives more scope for cooperation in third countries, and this was definitely a development warmly welcomed by all associated countries. An extension of Article 5 of the original guidelines makes it possible for CEEC ambassadors to attend EU briefings in third countries on CFSP issues with the objective to contribute to their 'growing visibility'. On the other hand the reaction seems to be somewhat different to another new provision, opening up the possibility of inviting the associated embassies for *ad hoc* briefings on subjects of mutual interest by Foreign Ministries in EU capitals. This can be seen as a further step towards 'group treatment' by some associated countries who argue that it would be politically much more valuable and effective if they were to be informed jointly with their EU partners on topics of common interest in the capitals. Furthermore, the omission of a reference (from Article 5) to establishing direct bilateral E-mail links between Brussels and the capitals of the associated countries seems to assert a political decision demonstrating that the EU is still not ready for such a close engagement, but rather prefers to communicate with the Brussels missions of the CEECs.

It is not surprising that it is the associated side that tends to come forward with bolder, more and more detailed and demanding proposals aimed at enhancing the CFSP dialogue, while the EU has a more careful, somewhat reserved approach in this respect. So far, efforts of the associated countries to approximate the 'US-EU model', i.e. to select the working groups, and to set their agenda jointly have not always been successful. Neither have they been able to achieve a substantial extension of the current framework. In theory, the areas of improvement are fairly clear: an increasing number of invitations for démarches and joint actions, granting direct access to common positions, establishment of a proper follow-up mechanism, opening up most working groups – to mention just a few. However, in the short run it does not seem realistic to expect major changes in this direction. Before the closure of the IGC the Union would probably not take the risk of adding involuntarily one more controversial item to its already congested agenda.

V. INTEGRATION OF CEECS IN THE WESTERN EUROPEAN UNION

Parallel to their relations with the EU, the CEECs also developed relations with the WEU, the 'defence arm' of the former. Unlike NATO the WEU followed the pattern of differentiation established by the EC, focusing its cooperation efforts on states which were associated with the EC.[73] In June 1991, WEU foreign and defence ministers proposed *ad hoc* meetings at ministerial level and links between the embassies of the CEECs and the WEU Secretariat General and between the government of each CEEC and the embassy of the country acting as WEU President. At the meeting in Bonn in November 1991, WEU foreign and defence ministers agreed to enhance the security dialogue, formalizing the differentiation of Central and Eastern Europe from the Soviet Union, by inviting the foreign and defence ministers of Bulgaria, Czechoslovakia, Hungary, Poland and Romania to a special meeting with the WEU Council.[74]

In the beginning of 1992 the WEU Parliamentary Assembly recommended to 'associate the Czech and Slovak Federal Republic, Hungary and Poland with WEU'. The Parliamentary Assembly was willing to differentiate in favour of the countries of the Visegrád group, to initiate a peace-keeping agreement with them and to hold, at least twice a year, a meeting of the enlarged Council incorporating their ministers for foreign affairs and defence. Other potential candidates for EU membership – the Baltic States, Bulgaria and Romania – were only offered the opportunity to consult the WEU at ministerial level at least once a year.[75] But no distinction was made between the two groups of states where the recommendation referred to the need to '[e]stablish in WEU an automatic mechanism for mobilizing politico-military consultation in order to react to serious crises in Central and Eastern Europe'.[76] This reference made clear that the WEU was prepared to become increasingly involved in the security affairs of the region concerned and that it wanted to be consulted, however, without being obliged to participate in the resolution of the possible emerging conflicts.

A few months later at Petersberg[77] the Council of Ministers adopted a declaration inviting those states which had either signed Europe Agreements with the European Community or had started negotiations to that effect to become cooperation partners of the WEU. The offer was addressed to eight countries: the five former non-Soviet Warsaw Treaty member states: Poland, Czechoslovakia, Hungary, Romania and Bulgaria and the three Baltic States: Estonia, Latvia and Lithuania. They were all invited, *inter alia,* to participate at the WEU Council of Ministers once a year. On the one hand, the Council, contrary to the recommendation of the Assembly, was not prepared to differentiate in favour of the members of the so-called Visegrád group. This was somewhat disappointing for the Visegrád countries as they were convinced that they had taken the biggest steps in introducing democracy and market

---

[73] Podraza 1992, 28.
[74] Communiqué, WEU Council of Ministers, Bonn, 18 November 1991, 1–2.
[75] Recommendation 516 on a new security order in Europe, A/WEU (38) PV 2, points 1–3.
[76] Ibid. point 4.
[77] Tagung des Ministerrats der Westeuropäischen Union (WEU) mit den Außen- und Verteidigungsministern Bulgariens, Estlands, Lettlands, Litauens, Polens, Rumäniens, der Tschechoslowakei und Ungarns am 19. Juni 1992 in Bonn, *Europa Archiv* (1992), D 485–6.

economy in Central and Eastern Europe. On the other hand, however, the WEU differentiated in favour of the eight countries *vis-à-vis* the other CEECs. According to a report of the WEU Assembly the reason for this differentiation was not the consideration that the eight countries were more mature for cooperation and later eventually for membership than the others. The Report emphasized that

> it would, in fact, have been possible to invite some of the Soviet Union's successor states, in particular Russia, Ukraine and Belarus, and also those republics that used to form part of Yugoslavia and had been recognised by the Twelve, which would have been logical if priority had been given to organizing security throughout the continent. But such an initiative would have placed WEU in competition with the North Atlantic Cooperation Council (NACC), organised by NATO, and with the CSCE. Therefore, by choosing to discuss security matters with the eight countries invited, WEU decided . . . to set itself in the context of Maastricht and to establish relations with countries which seem, in the more or less long term, likely to join the European Union with which three of them are already associated.[78]

With this reference the WEU emphasized the link with the EU following the adoption of the Maastricht Treaty. Experience has demonstrated that every CEEC which signed an association agreement with the Union could also join the associated partners of the WEU. It also referred to NATO in a negative connotation, namely by avoiding the establishment of a structure parallel to the one set up by the Atlantic Alliance, NACC.

It remains questionable whether the eight and, after the dissolution of Czechoslovakia, the nine, countries can be regarded a group. Even though there may be security reasons for maintaining the unity of the group if the membership criteria of the EU are to apply to membership in the WEU – particularly if membership of the former provides the member state with the option to become a member of the latter – differentiation and individual treatment based *inter alia* on considerations involving the economic performances of the respective states will be unavoidable.

The political framework of dialogue thus established was not regarded as sufficient by the CEECs. In this respect the situation was similar to that of NATO, where the CEECs emphasized dissatisfaction with NACC. They provided neither security guarantees, nor offered membership. At the same time the WEU carried out certain missions, and facilitated the monitoring of the enforcement of economic sanctions imposed on former Yugoslavia.[79] The mission was terminated in November 1995 following the initialling of the Dayton General Framework Agreement for Peace in Bosnia and Herzegovina of 22 November. If one regards this early form of cooperation as part of a process leading to membership, the question essentially becomes one of timing and criteria of accession. This is precisely the area where doubts have most frequently been formulated by the CEECs.

---

[78] Goerens 1992, 18, emphasis added.
[79] See *Meeting of the WEU Forum on Consultation at Ministerial Level*, Rome, 20 May 1993, point 4.

The cooperation established under the Petersberg Declaration between the WEU and the CEECs contains certain shortcomings. Even though only 'selected' partners participated in this framework, some of them also had a certain mistrust towards one another; the cooperation, apart from certain cooperation in the enforcement of sanctions against Yugoslavia, remained exclusively political. Hence the desire to integrate in security institutions extended to the wish to intensify the cooperation and to extend it to the military sphere.

The WEU reacted positively to the request of those nine CEECs which have become cooperation partners. The Kirchberg Declaration of May 1994 offered associated status to them. This was welcomed by the CEECs particularly because the offer promised to open up the structures of the organization instead of creating a separate structure for cooperation, as NATO did both in NACC and Partnership for Peace (PfP). It meant that representatives of these countries can participate at WEU Council meetings, they will be regularly informed by the Council of activities of its working groups, and that they may also be invited to participate in working groups on a case-by-case basis. They may also have a liaison arrangement with the Planning Cell.[80] A document specifying the modalities of participation of the nine CEECs stated that, in principle, half the meetings of the Permanent Council will take place with the participation of associate partners. They will also be provided 'as much information as possible on WEU's activities'.[81] In spite of the comparatively little importance attributed to the WEU the CEECs accepted the invitation. It is expected by the associated countries that the transparency of the WEU and the pragmatic, daily cooperation with CEECs will serve as an effective socialization process resulting finally in membership.

Russia opposed the May 1994 step of the WEU in a lukewarm manner. The speaker of the Russian Ministry of Foreign Affairs, Mikhail Demurin, reacted to the Kirchberg Declaration as follows: 'It is a mistake to bank on cooperation in which there is no place for such a country as Russia. Such a trend, if it picks up steam, is fraught with raising artificial barriers and creating a threat for a new split in Europe.'[82] It may be true that the WEU enlargement is not so strongly opposed by Moscow as that of the Atlantic Alliance but one cannot exclude the possibility that Russian opposition might increase once it becomes clear that some CEECs reach the point of effectively becoming WEU members. In this context Baranovski's observation is worth recalling. According to him 'Russia's attention was so fully focused on the task of preventing Eastern and Central Europe's entry into NATO, that the endeavour of these countries to join the EU and get the status of

---

[80] Western European Union, Kirchberg Declaration, 9 May 1994, part II. The Planning Cell is a small unit that deals with military planning with respect to eventual operations which will be carried under WEU command. Its activity also extends to humanitarian and rescue missions carried out under WEU 'flag'.

[81] Document on the Modalities, WEU Restricted CM (94) 25, points 1.1 and 3.1.

[82] Reuter East European Briefing, 16 May 1994.

associate members of WEU went practically unnoticed for a very long time' and 'the former Warsaw Pact allies will in this way be included in the western security zone and the rowdy campaign over Eastern and Central Europe and NATO, becomes obsolete'.[83]

A specific problem results from the fact that the WEU is in a peculiar position being the European pillar of NATO[84] and at the same time 'an integral part of the development of the European Union'. Therefore, it is not an entirely independent institution. Being a pillar of NATO may create the impression that countries which become members of the WEU also acquire NATO security guarantees. In the past there have been some attempts by CEECs, when disappointment about the slow pace of the development of relations with the Atlantic Alliance was strong, to give priority to developing relations with the WEU. However, in the light of this link between the two organizations, it is unlikely that this organization could decide on its own whether to enlarge or not. Moreover, given the partly identical membership of the three organizations an 'independent' action not coordinated with the others by any of them, including the WEU, is unthinkable. Thus, it is not surprising that it has become the predominant view that membership in the WEU is preconditioned by membership in the EU or NATO or both. The condition of EU membership stems from the Declaration of the member states of the WEU, issued on the occasion of the 46th European Council meeting on 9 and 10 December 1991 in Maastricht at which it adopted the TEU.[85]

It is true that the WEU does not face such intensive pressure from the CEECs as regards enlargement as do NATO and the EU. For this reason it is not so obvious – as in the case of NATO and EU – that the more developed associated states are increasingly dissatisfied at being taken as a group. For the EU, it is not security and defence issues that are dominating considerations when accepting new member states. It is likely that, apart from the internal development process of the EU, the economic performance of the CEECs will be decisive. Hence, there is no reason to put the WEU under pressure to accept more differentiation favouring some countries at the expense of others. The WEU will continue to play a limited role both in European affairs and in the integration of the CEECs in the western centre of gravity. Notwithstanding this, there is some benefit from the comparatively low importance of the WEU in today's Europe. Low profile and pragmatic cooperation activities can be prepared, such as joint planning for certain contingencies,

---

[83] Baranovski 1995.

[84] See 'Declaration of the Heads of State and Government Participating in the Meeting of the North Atlantic Council held at NATO Headquarters, Brussels, 10–11 January 1994,' *Press Communique M-1 (94)3*, para. 5.

[85] I. Declaration of Belgium, Germany, Spain, France, Italy, Luxembourg, the Netherlands, Portugal and the United Kingdom of Great Britain and Northern Ireland, which are members of the Western European Union and also members of the European Union on the Role of the Western European Union and its relations with the European Union and with the Atlantic Alliance, International Legal Materials, Vol. XXXI, No. 2, March 1992, 370–2.

etc. in a framework that could be regarded as provocative by some countries if they were organized by another institution, such as, for example, NATO. It is therefore essential that the preparation of the associated CEECs for an eventual future membership in the WEU be as extensive as possible, embracing both political and military aspects.

VI. CONCLUSIONS

When assessing foreign policy, security and defence cooperation between the EU/WEU and the CEECs it has to be emphasized that these areas are of particular importance, and form an integral part of the region's approximation to the overall European structures. The process is slow and gradual, the experience so far is recent and limited. By and large, however, it does seem to harmonize with other aspects of the associates' integration. These states have no reasonable alternative, but to gain accession to the European Union. Irrespective of the institutionalization of the cooperation, the CEECs have been voting practically together in the international organizations with those in the CFSP mechanism. In crises this has been largely successful because the CEECs have been ready to trade in some of their important interests expecting an enhanced recognition of their conformity with the Western identity.

Still, the political dialogue has been a moderate exercise. Its intensity depends to a considerable degree on the 'good will' of the member state holding the presidency. For the time being, it is usually limited to adherence to certain political declarations of peripheral importance. Participation in joint actions and démarches has been severely restricted, while there has been a strong tendency to treat all CEECs as one single group despite forceful objections from the more advanced CEECs. All these phenomena suggest that, in spite of several encouraging statements, the European Union is still lacking the unanimous political will and the clear, practical vision needed for the next enlargement. The conflicting views on enlargement and security taken together with competing concepts of a more differentiated Europe of several speeds result in a lack of clarity concerning the future role of the CEECs in a new general European framework.

REFERENCES

D. Allen, R. Wessel and W. Wessels, *European Political Cooperation*, London, Butterworths, 1982.

S. Anderson, 'Western Europe and the Gulf War' in Rummel (ed.), 1992, 151–64.

Background Report on the 1996 IGC, Jean Monnet House, September 1995.

Background reports of the Commission the Council and the EP on the IGC preparations for the Reflection Group.

V. Baranovski, 'Russia and European Security', *Eurobalkans* (1995), 4–17.

B.R., BOT.: 'Co-operation between the diplomatic missions of the Ten in third countries and international organisations' *LIEI* (1984), 149.

D. Buchan, *Europe: The strange superpower*, Aldershot, Dartmouth, 1993.

G. Burghardt at the Asser Institute on 'The TEU – Suggestions for revision' in The Hague on 16 September 1995, 4.

G. Edwards and S. Nuttall, 'Common foreign and security policy', in Duff, Pinder and Price (eds), *Maastricht and beyond*, London, Routledge, Federal Trust, 84–103.

G. Edwards, 'European responses to the Yugoslav crises: an interim assessment', in Rummel (ed.), 165–90.

F. Fink-Hooijer, 'The common foreign and security policy of the European Union', *EJIL* (1994), 173–98.

French Defence Policy at a Crossroads, IISS – Strategic Comments, No. 10, 13 December 1995.

A.U. Gabanyi, 'Rumänien in der Golfkrise: Akute Schwierigkeiten, chronische Probleme' *Südosteuropa* 10–12/1992.

A.U. Gabanyi, 'Die Moldaurepublik zwischen Wende und Rückwendung', *Südosteuropa* 3–4/1993.

R. Ginsberg, *Foreign Policy Actions of the European Community, the Politics of Scale*, Adamantine, London, 1989.

C. Goerens, *European Security Policy – Reply to the Thirty-Seventh Annual Report of the Council*. Assembly of Western European Union, Document 1342, 6 November 1992.

W. Hanreider (ed.), *West German Foreign Policy 1949–1979*, Westview, 1980.

C. Hill and W. Wallace, 'Diplomatic trends in the European Community', *International Affairs* (1979), 47.

C. Hill (ed.), *National foreign policies and European political cooperation*, London, 1983.

C. Hill, 'EPC's performance in crises', in Rummel (ed.), 1992, 139–50.

D. Hurd, 'Political Cooperation', *International Affairs* (1981), 383–93.

D. Hurd, 'Developing a Common Foreign and Security policy', *International Affairs* (1994), 421–8.

G. Kolankiewicz, 'Consensus and competition in the Eastern enlargement of the EU', *International Affairs* (1994), 477–97.

Lord Carrington, 'European political co-operation: America should welcome it', *International Affairs* (Winter 1981–1982), No. 1, 1–12.

P. Luif, 'EFTA-Staaten und Europäische Union – Neutralität und GASP im Einklang', in: Regelsberger (ed.), *Die Gasp der EU*, Bonn, Europa Union Verlag, 1993.

J. Monar, 'The foreign affairs system of the Maastricht Treaty: a combined assessment of the CFSP and EC external relations elements', in Monar 1993.

J. Monar, W. Ungerer and W. Wessels (eds), *The Maastricht Treaty on European Union, Legal complexity and political dynamic*, Brussels, European University Press, 1993.

H. Mouritzen, 'Testing weak-power theory: three Nordic reactions to the Soviet coup', in Calsnaes and Smith (eds), *European foreign policy, the EC and changing perspectives in Europe*, New Delhi, SAGE, 1995, 156–76.

G. Munuera, *Preventing armed conflict in Europe: lessons from recent experience*, Chaillot Papers, Institute for Security Studies No. 15/16, 1994.

C.W. Murray, 'View from the United States: Common Foreign and Security Policy as a Counterpiece of US Interest in European Political Union', in Rummel (ed.), 1992, 213–20.

S. Nuttall, *European Political Co-operation*, Oxford, Clarendon, 1992.

S. Nuttall, 'European Political Co-operation and Single European Act' *JCMS* (1986) 203.

S. Nuttall, 'Interaction between European Political Co-operation and the European Community', *YEL* (1987), 211–49.

S. Nuttall, 'The foreign and security policy provisions of the Maastricht Treaty: Their potential for the future', in Monar 1993, 133–8.

A. Orgovány, 'Magyar-EU politikai párbeszéd', in Halm (ed.), *Magyarország úton az Európai Unióba* Budapest, 1995, 197–201.

A. Pardalis, 'European Political Co-operation and the United States', *JCMS* (1987), 271–94.

A. Pijpers, 'European political co-operation and CSCE process', *LIEI* (1984), 135.

A. Pijpers, E. Regelsberger and W. Wessels (eds), *European Political Cooperation in the 1980s – A common foreign policy for Western Europe?* Kluwer, Dordrecht, 1987.

A. Podraza, The Western European Union and Central Europe: A New Relationship. RIIA Discussion Papers 41.

E. Regelsberger, 'From ten to twelve – A new dimension for European Political Cooperation (EPC)', *International Spectator* (1985), 34–44.

J. Roper, 'Defining a common defence policy and common defence', in Martin and Roper (ed.), *Towards a common defence policy*, Paris, The ISS WEU, 7–12.

R. Rummel (ed.), *Toward political union. Planning a common foreign and security policy in the European Community*, Boulder, Westview, 1992.

J. Santer, 'The European Union's security and defence policy', *NATO Review* (1995), 3–9.

Ph. Schoutheete de Tervarent, 'L'Introduction d'une politique extérieure et de sécurité commune: motivations et résultats', in Monar (1993), 129–32.

Ph. Schoutheete de Tervarent, *Coopération Politique Européenne*, Labor, Bruxelles, 1986.

A. Smith and H. Wallace, 'The European Union towards a policy for Europe', *International Affairs* (1994), 429–44.

T. Taylor, 'Maastricht and beyond', *International Affairs* (1994), 1–16.

J. Thinnes, *Germany's foreign policy after unification*, Aspen Institute conference report, 19–21, 1991 March.

H. Tint, *French foreign policy since the Second World War*, Weidenfeld and Nicolson, London, 1972. Voting practices in the United Nations 1992, 1994 (Report to Congress Submitted Pursuant to Public Law, 101–67 (US Department of State, 31 March 1993, 1995).

P. Van Ham, *Ukraine, Russia and European Security: Implications for Western Policy*, Chaillot Papers, Institute for Security Studies No. 13, 1994.

H. Wallace, 'Distributional Politics: Dividing up the Community Cake', in Wallace, Wallace and Webb, *Policy-Making in the European Community*, London, John Wiley and Sons, 1983.

H. and W. Wallace, *Flying together in a larger and more diverse European Union*, Netherlands, Scientific Council for Government Policy, The Hague, 1995.

J. Wyles, 'Political co-operation in the European Community', *European Trends* (1981) Spec. Rep. No. 1.

C

Globalization / Differentiation

20

ENLARGEMENT TO THE CEECS: WHICH DIFFERENTIATION?

Françoise de La Serre and Christian Lequesne[1]

I. INTRODUCTION

By the end of the 1980s, the first steps of the Community Ostpolitik had given the impression that in its policy towards the Central and East European Countries (CEECs) the Community of Twelve would favour a 'differentiated approach' to cooperation, taking into account the particular situation of each State with regard to certain criteria: the respect of agreements signed within the framework of the CSCE (Conference on Security and Cooperation in Europe) and the progress towards pluralist democracy and market economy.

The Trade and Cooperation Agreements signed from September 1988 onwards exerted pressure in the same direction, by organizing – depending on the liberalization of political and economic regimes – a varying combination of commercial clauses and projects of economic cooperation. A similar signal was given when the PHARE programme was set up to help the recovery of the Hungarian and the Polish economies. But the extension of this programme to other benefiting countries, together with the conversion of the Trade and Cooperation Agreements into Association Agreements, gradually wiped out the particularities of the relation between the European Community and each of the CEECs. In June 1993, the European Council of Copenhagen set an important landmark in this process by declaring that 'the associated countries in Central and Eastern Europe that so desire shall become members of the European Union. Accession will take place as soon as an associated country is able to assume the obligations of membership by satisfying the economic and political conditions required'.[2] Moreover, the four states of the Visegrád

---

[1] CERI, Fondation Nationale des Sciences Politiques, Paris. This text is an elaborated version of the first draft published in French in *Revue du Marché Commun et de l'Union Européenne*, 1996, 642–7.
[2] *Bull. EC*, 6-1993, 13.

Group who thought themselves to be placed favourably in this contest did interpret it that way. Not having the same interest in the regional cooperation set up specifically to hasten their accession, they however leaned more towards the policy of 'every man for himself'.

Where are we now, after the European Councils of Essen (December 1994) and Madrid (December 1995) have traced out the way for the enlargement of the European Union with a pre-accession strategy?

II. THE DIFFERENTIATED APPROACH WITHIN THE GLOBAL PROCESS

The first point to be noted is that, with consensus among the member states, the debate on enlargement has ended in a first differentiation which defines the European borders to the East, whereas the Commission in its report to the European Council in Lisbon was indicating, up until June 1992, that it was 'neither possible nor opportune to establish now the frontiers of the European Union, whose contours will be shaped over many years to come'.[3] The European Union being defined more by its political content rather than by its geography or history, the Twelve, and later the Fifteen, decided that the Association Agreements would be the criteria determining its borders. The countries likely to be admitted in the European Union are the associated countries of Central Europe and the Balkans, Slovenia and the three Baltic States. So, in the East, the European Union ends at the borders of the Commonwealth of Independent States (CIS). In the south-east, it currently excludes the states emerging from the former Yugoslav federation – with the exception of Slovenia – as well as Albania, although the association and then the subsequent membership of these states ultimately seems to present in principle fewer problems than the accession of Russia or Ukraine.

It was this 'family picture' of the associated members promised future membership which was presented by the 1995 Madrid European Council. It was accompanied with details emphasizing equality of treatment for the applicants. It expressed the wish that 'the initial phase of negotiations will coincide with the start of negotiations with Cyprus and Malta'[4] (some six months after the IGC). It also invited the Commission actively to prepare its Opinions on the applications. However, this equality of treatment, guaranteed by the uniformity of procedure dissimulates the probability of a differentiated treatment of the applicants. Although it is not explicit, a case-by-case approach is more than likely to occur. On the one hand the declarations of the Madrid European Council continue to stress the respect for the criteria defined at the 1993 Copenhagen European Council, and it is up to the Commission to assess whether they are fulfilled: stability of institutions guaranteeing democracy, the rule of law, human rights, respect for and protection

[3] *Bull. EC*, Suppl. 3/92, 11.
[4] *Bull. EU*, 12-1995, 18.

of minorities, the existence of a functioning market economy as well as the capacity to cope with competitive pressure and market forces within the Union. On the other hand, the interim report on the 'effects on the policies of the European Union of enlargement to the associated countries of central and eastern Europe' presented by the Commission to the European Council of Madrid insists on the fact that 'each application must be considered on its merits' and that 'if some applicant countries have made sufficient progress in preparing for membership, they should not be delayed because others have not reached the same level'.[5] The CEECs themselves play upon the competition induced by this case-by-case method to push forward their applications.

The same message is to be found in the Information note about enlargement, published by the Commission on 30 July 1996.[6] It is indicated that 'each applicant country will be considered on its own merits, in a scrupulously objective way' as regards the decision to begin the negotiations as well as the substance of these very negotiations. The disparity of situations on both political and economic grounds justifies this 'differentiated' approach, as the applicant countries do not equally fulfil the conditions laid down by the Copenhagen European Council. Whether it concerns the protection of minorities, the division of powers principle (notably the judiciary's ability to enforce respect for constitutional principles) or a civil society characterized by freedom of the press and of association, major differences exist between the States. Democracy has not reached the same level everywhere. As regards security, some countries also present problems in so far as the volatile relations they maintain with their neighbours – notably due to the presence of minorities – cannot be 'imported' in the European Union.

The list of economic indicators also shows the disparity between countries in their effort to set up a market economy and the restructuring this implies. Even though the statistical data available in the CEECs does not always allow the comparison of otherwise comparable factors, the differences between the Visegrád countries (although they are considered relatively homogeneous) are apparent.[7] This need to appreciate the specific merits of each candidate is likely to revive the debate about the criteria used for the appraisal of the degree of readiness for membership. In 1993, the French government had proposed to draw up some ten criteria to narrow down the general criteria of Copenhagen. More recently a study by the CEPS[8] has advocated a similar approach by suggesting the use of three groups of criteria: the results of the growth during the previous decade; the transition indicators of the EBRD;

---

[5] *Interim report from the Commission to the European Council on the effects on the policies of the European Union of enlargement to the associated countries of central and eastern Europe* (06.12.1995), CSE (95) 605, 5.

[6] *Europe Documents*, No. 2000, 9 August 1996.

[7] For a detailed comparative analysis, see 'Degré d'avancement dans la transition vers une économie de marché des "4 de Visegrád"', in Centre Franco-Autrichien, *Les pays d'Europe centrale et orientale*, Colloque de Bratislava, 4–5 mai 1995, 106.

[8] Centre for European Policy Studies, *Preparing for membership. The Eastward and Southern enlargement of the European Union*, Brussels, January 1996.

and a 'basket' of economic indicators. In view of this data it seems probable that each of the applicants will follow a 'differentiated' path to membership. But the question is, according to what modalities and with what particularities, compared to the established model of the previous enlargements?

III. CLASSIC OPTIONS FOR ENLARGEMENT

Different studies have traced out several paths for the modalities of enlargement to the CEECs. In fact two major options exist. Should the new enlargement be organized around the method which has prevailed so far and which is based on the acceptance – although spread out in time – of the Union's *acquis*? Conversely, should it stretch to a differentiated application of common policies to the candidates, favouring exemption (possibly permanent) as much as transition?

The first option would consist in taking up the pattern of previous enlargements. The membership would imply the acceptance, with no opting out, of the four elements constituting the Community *acquis*: the content, the principles and political objectives of the ECSC, EC and EURATOM treaties, the secondary legislation adopted for the implementation of these treaties, as well as the case law of the European Court of Justice; the declarations and the resolutions adopted within the Community framework; the international agreements signed between the EC and third States as well as the bilateral agreements between the Member States relating to the activities of the Communities. That would also imply the complete acceptance of the two intergovernmental pillars of the Maastricht Treaty. The evolution of the concept of the transition period from one enlargement to the other would allow the applicants to negotiate a gradual and prolonged acceptance (20–30 years) of the *acquis*. That classic scenario coupled with a flexible approach is what the applicants are putting forward in their plea. Apparently, the Commission was following that line when it declared: 'it is not possible at this stage to prejudge the nature or length of transitional arrangements, which would be the object of accession negotiations'.[9] The consequence of this scenario would be the development of the existing differentiated integration pattern in the EC-15, which may be qualified as 'multi-speed Europe': the member states accepting the common aims and objectives but introducing different speeds to allow the varying capabilities to adjust to the political will. The Maastricht Treaty has reinforced this differentiated approach by adding to the concept of transition periods that of the convergence criteria for passing into the third phase of the EMU (Article 109 J).

Although this approach seems orthodox, it raises some questions. Firstly, the European Union will have a lot of difficulty in setting up as a principle,

[9] *Interim report from the Commission to the European Council on the effects on the policies of the European Union of enlargement to the associated countries of central and eastern Europe* (06.12.1995), CSE (95) 605, 10.

right from the beginning of the negotiations, the acceptance of the *acquis* and the absolute nature of the treaty by all the candidates, when it has already conceded important exemptions to Denmark and the United Kingdom. On the other hand, the borderline between 'transition' and 'exemption' cannot be established clearly, in so far as certain technical solutions may modify the basic rules of the Community, particularly in the field of the internal market. An excessive delay in the application of the social policy or the environmental policy would for example, distort the rules of competition. Secondly, the European Union can hardly make the applicants bear the main adjustment costs accompanied with promises of subsequent compensation, as was the case in the past with the creation of a Regional Fund for the United Kingdom, and the creation of the policy of economic and social cohesion in the wake of the Mediterranean enlargement. On the one hand, this strategy seems to have attained its limits: the application by the new member states of 'budget gulping' policies such as the common agricultural policy or the policy of social and economic cohesion would entail costs on the current members of the Union, which will be judged prohibitive by the net contributors to the Community budget. It is highly unlikely that the renegotiation in 1999 of the new financial perspectives of the Union will end with a substantial increase in the Community budget and, *a fortiori*, release the resources necessary to allow the new members full access to the CAP and the structural funds. The German finance minister pointed out in September 1996 that the compensatory mechanism conceded by the European Council of Fontainebleau (1984) to the United Kingdom to correct its net contribution to the budget remained valid for any member state in the same position (Germany contributed 30 per cent of the Community budget in 1996 while it ranks sixth among the member states in terms of GDP).[10]

Without entering into the details of the varying and controversial cost estimations of the eastward enlargement, it could mean an increase of the Community budget from 50 to 100 per cent.[11] It is thus an urgent matter to reform some of the policies, first and particularly the common agricultural policy and the policy of social and economic cohesion. However, the room for manoeuvring is rather small between the temptation to 'sanctify' the *acquis* and the risk of reducing the Union to a free trade area. The differences of opinion among the current member states about what has to be kept and what has to be eliminated in these policies will henceforth make the future negotiations extremely complex. Consequently, it is not certain that the 1999

---

[10] *Financial Times*, 9 September 1996. The final communiqué of the European Council of Fontainebleau generalized the principle of the 'fair return' by specifying that any member state bearing an excessive charge in relation to its relative prosperity could ask for a corrective measure.

[11] On this subject, see R. Baldwin, *Towards an Integrated Europe*, Centre for Economic Policy Research, London, 1994. See also a more recent study carried out by OFCE upon the request of the French Senate's Delegation for the European Union. Report of Senator D. Badre, *Les conséquences économiques et budgétaires de l'élargissement à l'Est*, No. 228, Paris 1995–96.

budgetary package will end, as has been the Community tradition, with a positive sum gain for all the participants.[12]

Finally, in the institutional field, the traditional method has already shown its limits with the entry of the three EFTA countries. The minimal (or purely arithmetical) adaptations to which this gave rise affected the efficiency of the decision-making system. Since a repeat of these arithmetical adaptations is excluded, much depends on the ability of the IGC to adopt the reforms to facilitate decision-making within the Council (notably with the introduction of more qualified majority voting). The IGC will also have to ensure that the balance between the 'big' and the 'small' member states (the latter being more numerous amongst the applicants for membership) is not disturbed in favour of the latter and at the expense of the former, which represent two-thirds of the population of the Union as well as being the main net contributors to the Community budget. From this point of view, the admission of the CEECs presents a specific difficulty. During the previous enlargements the new member states always participated in the policy amendments for which they had transitional arrangements. But will the newcomers not be tempted to use their veto power to prevent reforms contrary to their interests (for example those concerning structural funds)?

IV. 'PARTIAL MEMBERSHIP'?

The difficulties mentioned above and the perspective of an increasing heterogeneity in the enlarged Union have led to the exploration of a second path, and to the proposal of formulas of 'partial' or 'affiliate membership'. This approach, allowing the coexistence of different levels of integration, is evidently related to the concept of flexibility introduced by the Maastricht Treaty on the one hand, and the ongoing debate within the Union about a differentiated integration on the other.

Thinking in this direction was first started off in 1991 by Mr Frans Andriessen,[13] then Vice-President of the Commission, and later developed by Mr Hurd and Mr Andreatta, Ministers for Foreign Affairs of the United Kingdom and Italy respectively. Taking into consideration the pillar structure of the Maastricht Treaty, they proposed to give the applicants full membership of the Union, while limiting their participation to the Second and the Third Pillars (CFSP, Justice and Home Affairs) until they were ready to join the Community pillar.[14] It is interesting that this idea was taken up recently by Rudolf Seiters, the CDU spokesman for foreign affairs. Taking into account the time required for the adaptations of the applicants so

---

[12] C. Preston, 'Obstacles to Enlargement: the classical Community method and the prospects for a wider Europe', *Journal of Common Market Studies* (1995), 457.
[13] Speech on 19 April 1991 to the 69th plenary assembly of Eurochambers.
[14] *Agence Europe*, 22 December 1993.

that they become fit to participate fully in the Community pillar, Mr Seiters suggested starting with a limited accession to the Second and the Third Pillar.[15]

These proposals concerning areas of intergovernmental cooperation were followed by a reflection on the possibility and the modalities of a differentiated membership of the Community pillar. This inspired the work of R. Baldwin[16] and it also reflected the preoccupations expressed by some of the applicants.[17] Challenging the method used in previous enlargements, and identifying the obstacles – costs of the CAP and of the structural policies, decision-making process, migratory pressures – Baldwin recommends an intermediate phase prior to membership. It would consist of two stages. First, an interlocking system of association agreements aiming to promote a pan-European Free Trade Area for industrial products. Second, a participation in the internal market resembling the formula of the European Economic Area, but without the free movement of persons.

Since then, the possibility of a partial and differentiated participation in the Community policies has evolved further. In this scenario, applicants are considered members of the European Union but their participation is limited to the internal market, to the CFSP and to the cooperation in matters of Justice and Home Affairs. However, it excludes participation in the CAP market policy or in the economic and cohesion policy.

To a certain extent the pre-accession strategy set up by the 1994 Essen European Council draws on all these proposals. In fact, it adds to the instruments consisting of the Europe Agreements and the PHARE programme, a preparation for the single market sketched out in the Commission White Paper and in the 'structured dialogue' concerning the Second and the Third Pillars as well as some regulatory policies (energy, environment, science and technology, etc.). What are the opportunities of having such a strategy after the enlargement?

The formula of partial accession of the CEECs to common policies raises a number of serious problems. First, it undermines the interdependence of some policies, which is a characteristic of the Community system and which has led to the constitution of *de facto* competence blocks.[18] Secondly, it calls into question the package-deal method which makes it possible to base the elaboration of compromises between the member states on the granting of mutual concessions, which proceed from the linkage between the different policies. Finally, the institutional translation of such a pattern is not easy. Two options are possible. Either one chooses the generalization of the

---

[15] *Financial Times*, 21 May 1996.

[16] op. cit., pp. 207–24.

[17] On the exemptions wished by the candidates themselves, see specially the declarations of the Hungarian Secretary of State, M.E. Juhasz, in Pisani–Ferry, *L'Europe à géométrie variable. Une analyse économique*, Paris, CEPII, 1995, 9.

[18] For a legal analysis see J.-L. Dewost, *Des espaces restreints d'intervention sont-ils compatibles avec l'ordre juridique européen*, Colloquium of the European Movement, Paris, 26 June 1996. For an economic approach see Pisani–Ferry, op. cit., 12–17.

mechanisms which ensure the implementation of the Social Protocol without the United Kingdom (London does not participate in the voting within the Council), accompanied by protracted wrangling and theological quarrels about the role of the European Parliament. Or one opts for the possibility that all the member states participate in the decision-making. However, is it possible to conceive that countries which do not participate in a common policy take part in its formulation? Is it possible to imagine that something which already poses problems within the framework of a transition period could also be envisaged in the context of exemptions?

Obviously the introduction of a 'variable geometry' approach for the accession of the CEECs is strongly influenced – and also biased – by the ongoing debate in the current Union. This debate highlights two trends which reflect opposing views about the European construction. In this context, therefore, the positions with regard to enlargement reveal and serve as a pretext for other strategies.

A first version of the flexible approach was presented in September 1994 in Leiden, with the speech given by John Major, and is largely the inspiration behind the memorandum *A Partnership of Nations* which the United Kingdom elaborated in March 1996 for the IGC. It urges for a 'flexible' Europe within which the common commitment of all the member states would be the internal market. For other policies, variable groupings of member states could be constituted. It would be some sort of generalization of the situation with regard to the Social Protocol – from which the United Kingdom was exempted – to cover all policy fields. This integration 'à la carte' is presented as a solution allowing the rapid integration of the CEECs, because the newcomers would have the possibility of adhering only to the policies of their choice. While it safeguards the *acquis* of the internal market, it also leads to the disappearance of common policies based on a redistribution principle. It undermines the unity of the institutional system and favours the logic of intergovernmental cooperation.

The other idea – with some variations – favoured by the majority of member states envisages the introduction of some flexibility not as a means to water down the present integration, but as a lever with which to further this integration. This approach is based on the observation that it is impossible for all the member states of the enlarged Union to progress at the same pace. It is also based on the hypothesis that a group of fast track countries would exert a force attracting all those who are temporarily left behind. The debate, launched by the Schaüble–Lamers proposals of September 1994 on the establishemnt of a core community around the participants of the EMU, further evolved around the notion of 'enhanced cooperation' and the possible variants of this concept. From the Chirac–Kohl letter of December 1995 onwards, it has been on the agenda of the IGC. France and Germany are in fact suggesting a general clause allowing the States which have the desire and ability to develop among themselves enhanced cooperation to do so within the single institutional framework of the Union.

Whatever the precise modalities of introducing such a clause in the treaty may be, is it likely to facilitate the enlargement negotiations and possible formulas of differentiated accession? Nothing is less sure. This clause is in fact meant for promoting enhanced instances of solidarity and not for defining modalities of 'refused' solidarity. It does not fit well with the simplifying solutions which suggest excluding some countries from the policies which form part of the *acquis*.[19] All the more so since the Community pillar is at the heart of the negotiations for accession. The introduction of enhanced cooperation would then suppose that the problems raised by enlargement negotiations have already been solved.

In the present state of the debate – and assuming one does not adopt the British point of view – 'variable geometry' does not seem to be a panacea likely to solve all the enlargement problems. We are thus brought back to the starting point, having noted the limits of the Community method and the limits of the method of differentiated integration. Given the difficulties raised by the enlargement to the CEECs, the Community will probably adopt the 'variable geometry' approach without calling it as such. It will achieve this by stretching to the utmost the Community method and by making the borderline between 'transition' and 'exemption' vague. Perhaps then, as some studies suggest, it will have to proceed to 'un examen clinique de l'architecture communautaire en vue de définir des niveaux pertinents d'intégration'.[20] In the short run, two tests will be decisive. The first concerns the attitude which the IGC will adopt as to the introduction of an 'avant-garde clause' in the Treaty. The second, and undoubtedly the more significant one, will be the implementation or not of the Single Currency in 1999.

---

[19] See Dewost, op. cit., previous note.
[20] Pisani–Ferry, op. cit., 3 and 13–17.

21

THE GLOBALIZATION OF THE EASTERN
ENLARGEMENT OF THE EUROPEAN UNION:
SYMPTOMS AND CONSEQUENCES

Péter Balázs[1]

All the Central and East European countries (CEECs) associated with the EC have similar motives in their endeavours to join the European Union. Since the beginning of fundamental political and economic changes in the late 1980s, the EC/EU has also given more and more uniform answers to their requests. A new global approach has taken shape, embracing at least ten of the so-called transition economies.[2] The main question raised in this contribution is whether the global handling of the associated CEECs and, on a larger scale, of the ex-CMEA and other countries of the Central and East European region undergoing transformation, is the adequate treatment and the most convenient approach in view of the political and economic problems to be solved by integration methods.

The first part of the paper deals with the motives of the CEECs wishing to join the EU. In the second part, the gradual 'globalization' of relations between the EU and its eastern neighbours will be demonstrated. The closing section attempts to highlight some of the *contradictions* resulting from globalizing the integration of the CEECs.

I. INTEGRATION MOTIVES OF THE CEECS

A. Four different time horizons

In their integration endeavours, the Central and East European would-be members of the EU are led by a mixture of political and economic motives.

[1] Associate Professor of the Budapest School of Economics; Ambassador of Hungary to Germany.
[2] The 1994 December Essen Summit selected those Central and East European States which could be accepted as future members of the EU. The same countries have concluded 'Europe Agreements' with the EC. The associated CEECs are: Poland, the Czech Republic, Slovakia, Hungary, Romania, Bulgaria, Slovenia, Estonia, Lithuania and Latvia.

The integration objectives of the *avant garde* – Poland, Hungary and the Czech part of dissolved Czechoslovakia – constitute the model which is then followed by other countries of the region.[3] The actual composition of the 'integration objective package' varies from country to country. Its character depends on political, economic and cultural specificities and also on the distance between the avant garde and the 'follow-up countries'.

This paper takes as an example one of the model-forming cases, the Hungarian experience. In Hungary, the following immediate, short, medium and long-term objectives can be distinguished in connection with the motives of reintegrating the country with the West.

a. The 'irreversibility' objective

In the early 1990s in Hungary, the immediate motive had a strong political character and served the objective of rendering the political changes irreversible. The same motive could be detected even earlier, behind the efforts of the reformist wing of the Hungarian 'one-party' political leadership. These efforts viewed the acceleration of internal changes as leading ultimately to systemic transformation. In fact, since the early 1980s, Hungary has made particular efforts to 'normalize' her relations with the EC. By that time, these efforts were in contradiction with the explicit Soviet ban (mostly in form of CMEA decisions) on the conclusion of any bilateral agreement within the scope of Community competence and covering the general scope of relations.[4]

Also in 1988, during the negotiations of the first 'normal' Trade and Cooperation Agreement, immediate political motives prevailed. Hungary was the first to sign this type of agreement with the EC, thus confirming her incontestable first place in transition.[5] The hasty conclusion of the agreement was connected with the aim of Hungary to confirm her newly reestablished 'European' identity. In fact, by that time Hungary attached more importance to the date of signature of the Trade and Cooperation Agreement than to its economic content.

In 1991, when the three Visegrád countries negotiated the first series of association agreements with the EC, the situation was rather similar. Competition among them for a 'first place' in the region increased further the importance of the political element, to the detriment of economic results. The demonstrative political fact of concluding the Association Agreement with the EC (in parallel with the signature of the Maastricht Treaty) was, by then, more important then economic support for transition.

---

[3] The 'model role' finds its origins in the parallel start of transformation and, as a first result, the simultaneous signature of the first documents establishing closer relations with Western based organizations in 1991–92, e.g. the 'Partners in Transition' cooperation programme with the OECD, 'Europe Agreements' with the EC, etc. The early distinction of the first three 'transforming countries' has some relevance as to future segmentation of the group of the CEECs, too.

[4] The maximum of the *de facto* recognition of the EC was the conclusion of sectoral agreements. Hungary concluded the first agreement of this kind on steel products in 1978.

[5] On 26 September 1988, see *OJ* L 327, 30 November 1988.

b. The 'stabilization' objective

Short-term integration objectives have concerned the *stabilization of the economy* in the special conditions of transition. In fact, the sudden fall in economic growth, the loss of huge and protected CMEA markets, previously unknown and rapidly growing unemployment and increased inflation had shifted the emphasis from internal political motives, i.e. the above-mentioned 'irreversibility objective', to the field of the economy. This set of short-term objectives combines two elements: a dominant internal economic content on the one hand, and a strong external orientation towards the West in both political and economic terms, on the other. The aggravation of the economic situation in the country was expressed by an increasing demand for preferential market access for exports and for foreign economic aid and assistance, as well as by a thirst for foreign direct capital investment. These requests were addressed, in the first place, to the already biggest trade and economic partner, the EC.

However, the definition and the expression of short-term economic objectives did not surface in Hungary before the early conclusion of the Hungary–EC Association Agreement. Two main reasons played a role in the relatively late identification of economic interests on the Hungarian side. The first was the slow development of the economic features of transition as compared with the rapidity of its political side. The second was the slow pace of formation of new, market-based interest groups in the country (e.g. chambers of trade and industry, employers' unions etc.) as well as the time needed to find the structures and channels for these to express their wishes. As a result of these two main factors, during the negotiations of the Association Agreement with the EC in 1991 the Hungarian Government was not under internal political pressure of an economic origin. Consequently, external political considerations prevailed which were still connected with the 'irreversibility objective' of the preceding stage. This sequencing was the result of the given political and economic context in Hungary in the early 1990s. The first critical voices concerning the poor economic content of the Europe Agreement gathered momentum during the lengthy ratification process (in the EC member states) in 1992–93. A few months later, after the 1994 parliamentary elections, the new Hungarian Government was forced to acknowledge the gap between the urgent character of economic stabilization tasks on the one hand, and the limits of Western economic help on the other.[6]

c. The 'transformation' objective

Medium-term objectives came to the forefront in parallel with the disillusionment concerning Western economic support for transition. This type of

---

[6] A package of tough and immediate economic measures was taken by the government on 12 March 1995, bearing the name of the Minister of Finance (the 'Bokros Package'), combining the objectives of rapid improvement of the balance of payments with that of systemic changes in social welfare structures financed from the state budget.

integration motive focuses on accelerating and achieving systemic trans-formation. However, in the leading CEECs, the deepening of relations with the EC was not an absolute precondition for the establishment of a market economy. Even adaptation to EC norms was already underway without any special assistance from the Community. For example, in Hungary the first pro-gramme of legal harmonization with the *acquis communautaire,* with special regard to the internal market, even preceded the publication of the EU's White Paper on this issue by seven years.[7] In 1995, the Hungarian Government also launched a 'modernization' programme on its own initiative. Due to some terminological confusion and overlapping of various motives, this programme mainly covers medium-term integration goals connected with systemic trans-formation objectives, which are seen as external political support and sources of technical assistance for ongoing changes.

d. The 'modernization' objective

The *long-term motives* of the CEECs behind their efforts to join Western-based organizations for economic integration, are rooted in the late moderniza-tion of their societies. In this context, 'modernization' is a synonym for delayed 'westernization', embracing industrialization and the construction of a civil society. On the Eastern periphery of the industrialized centre of Europe, this historical process led by the political elite has been interrupted several times – mostly by foreign interventions.[8] In 1989, new perspectives opened up for the completion of 'modernization'.

One important characteristic of the retarded modernization process in Central Eastern Europe is the impact of the last 40 years of Soviet influence. In fact, the CEECs belonging to the Western (Catholic–Protestant) culture were set back by the forced Soviet-type development of both the economy and society. Ideological intervention in the late 1940s and early 1950s into the already disturbed process of closing up caused deep wounds (e.g. forced industrialization, collectivization of agriculture, elimination of practically all types of private initiative, deprivation of people from national and religious identity, etc.), which can hardly be cured. At the same time, Soviet modern-ization had some incontestable positive results in the CEECs (e.g. the abolition of aristocratic privileges as a precondition for democratization, equal rights for women, universal schooling and health care, widespread cultural educa-tion, etc.). For all these reasons, in the 1990s the inherited deformation of societies in Central and Eastern Europe has to be taken into consideration

---

[7] A programme of harmonizing Hungarian law with the legislation of the Single Market was adopted by the Hungarian Government in September 1988, a few days before the signature of the Trade and Cooperation Agreement.

[8] For example, in Hungary, in 1849 the Habsburg emperor and the Russian tsar intervened in order to defeat jointly the independence war, aiming at the acceleration of national moderniza-tion. In 1919 the 'Entente' powers crushed the Soviet-type revolution in Hungary with the same objective. In 1949, the Soviet Union transformed post-war democratization into a monolithic system and maintained it with force against the 1956 national upheaval, until its own collapse by the end of the 1980s.

and dealt with very carefully. Any further attempt at 'modernization' could provoke new shocks, especially in relation to the possible effects of forced integration.

B. National preferences

In the above short overview, four different time horizons relating to integration motives and, accordingly, four different tasks have been indicated. The two goals, namely the immediate motivation and the long-term objectives, are of a predominantly political nature. Of course, both the urgent task of ensuring the irreversibility of political changes as well as the long-term goal of modernization have important economic sides too, but the motives and the results are decidedly political in content. The two other goals, short-term stabilization and medium-term systemic transformation, bear a strong economic character. At the same time, their political impact is not negligible.

In contrast to the theoretical distinction between various objectives connected with different time horizons, empirical facts reveal a mixture of the motives enumerated above in the actual government programmes and actions of the CEECs. The exact composition of the above objectives varies from country to country. Even in the case of one given State, the emphasis also shifts with time from one dominant objective to another. In 1996, at the start of the Intergovernmental Conference of the EU, the situation may be characterized by dividing the CEECs into the following three broad categories.

a. The 'avant garde'

Some associated countries have definitely passed the political 'point of no return', that is to say, the initial phase of transition during which political regression on the basis of the survival or the rebirth of important elements of the 'old regime' was still possible.[9] Impatience and political pressure urging EU accession are motivated by the wish to regain (West) European status, which was interrupted by Soviet occupation. The 'irreversibility factor' is still present in a vague, diffuse form. NATO membership is considered as a guarantee against external dangers of political regression.

In these countries, integration motives are based mainly on medium and long-term considerations. Short-term economic stabilization is well underway even without additional support from the developed world. Systemic changes are not connected with external help either but constitute an organic part of internal evolution. European integration is seen basically as a confirmation of the results achieved and an accelerating factor to help the completion of transformation. Integration is supposed to promote long-term modernization, in other words, the late and retarded 'westernization' of these countries. Poland, the Czech Republic, Hungary and Slovenia can be classified into this category.

---

[9] Such key elements are, for example, totalitarian control of the mass media, strong nationalism, slow privatization and the dominance of state ownership, etc.

b. The 'follow-up' countries

A second category among the CEECs covers the rest of the 'Associated Ten'. They are at an earlier stage of political transformation. These countries are guided mainly by immediate and short-term motives. For them, EU integration would mean a strong support in avoiding political regression. However, for the same reasons, internal political forces are divided as to the utility and timeliness of EU accession. As economic transformation is also at an earlier phase, external aid is needed in order to help stabilization. Technical assistance is also welcome to guide systemic transformation (e.g. in the form of the EU's White Paper on legal harmonization, etc.). Political integration objectives for the foreseeable future are mainly connected with the promotion of transition. Long-term modernization goals are rarely stressed. As to their relations to the EU, these countries try not to fall back but to maintain a relatively close 'follow-up' position in relation to the above *avant garde*.

c. Non-associated CEECs

Non-associated CEECs are the ex-Yugoslav States, with the exception of Slovenia, and the CIS countries. They have a different international legal position. They do not aspire to EU membership. At the same time, they share with the associated countries the foreign aid funds of the EU. Consequently, the success and speed of their transition have an indirect 'globalizing' effect on the economic support the EU can grant to the associated and non-associated CEECs in total.

II. GLOBAL REACTIONS OF THE EUROPEAN UNION

A. The symptoms

What answers has the European Union given to the CEECs' expectations and requests? If one analyses the EU's reactions to the development of political and economic transition in Central and Eastern Europe, with a special emphasis on the associated countries, the following three main conclusions can be drawn. First, the answers have been late and cautious; secondly, they have taken on a more and more global character; and third, an autonomous legal approach can be observed. Let us explain these statements.

a. Delayed answers

Since the very start of the process of 'normalizing' relations, the EC/EU reacted with a clear tardiness to the political and economic needs and demands of the CEECs (Table 1 summarizes the Hungarian experience: it lists Hungary's requests on the one hand, and the reactions of the EC/EU on the other, as of the beginning of the political changes).

Table 1 Political and economic transformation and the development of relations with the EC: The case of Hungary[a]

Year	Hungary	EC/EU
−1988	*Political factors* – Warsaw Pact and CMEA membership – Soviet Army presence *Economic factors* – reformed planned economy – state controlled foreign trade – CMEA trade preferences – lack of convertibility *Requests to the EC* – non-discriminatory trade (1973) – economic cooperation (1982) – effective economic advantages (1982)	*Political reaction* – discriminative treatment ('state trading' regime) *Economic reaction* – specific quantitative restrictions on imports – selective safeguard clause (in GATT) – COCOM export limitations
1988–1989	*Political factors* – 'Perestroika' in the Soviet Union – international recognition of the EC *Economic factors* – speeding up of economic reforms (privatization, foreign direct investments, etc.) *Requests to the EC* – tariff preferences – seizable economic advantages	*Political reaction* – *de facto* recognition of the CMEA – 'normalization' of bilateral relations with the individual CMEA Member States – Trade and Cooperation Agreement *Economic reaction* – *de jure* non-discriminatory treatment (*de facto* from 1995) – starting economic cooperation
1989–1990	*Political factors* – systemic changes – proclamation of the Republic of Hungary – dissolution of the Warsaw Pact and CMEA *Economic factors* – liberalization of the monopoly of foreign trade – liberalization of import licensing	*Political reaction* – selection of Poland and Hungary – support to political transformation *Economic reaction* – *de facto* non-discriminatory treatment (as from 1990) – GSP treatment – PHARE Programme

Table 1 (*Cont'd*)

Year	Hungary	EC/EU
	Requests to the EC – preferential treatment – important economic aid	
1990–1991	*Political factors* – pluralistic parliamentary elections – retreat of the Soviet Army – 'Visegrád' declaration of cooperation *Economic factors* – Compensation Law – acceleration of privatization – extension of market economy *Requests to the EC* – perspective of EC membership – preferences for agriculture – free movement of labour – financial protocol	*Political reaction* – conclusion of 'Europe Agreement' *Economic reaction* – free trade in industrial goods – closer economic cooperation
1991–1992	*Political factors* – irreversibility of political changes in Russia (August 1991 coup in Moscow) *Economic factors* – EC gains dominant market share – permanent deficit in EC trade *Requests to the EC* (unchanged)	*Political reaction* – refusal of commitment on EC membership – limits of the content of association *Economic reaction* – limitations on market access conditions – refusal of any concession on labour – refusal of a financial protocol
1992–1993	*Political factors* – systemic changes are stabilized – enlargement of CEFTA and CEI[b] *Economic factors* – difficulties in stabilizing and transforming the economy	*Political reaction* – enlargement of the circle of associated CEECs – unilateral promise of future EC membership – proposing the 'structured dialogue'

Table 1 *(Cont'd)*

Year	Hungary	EC/EU
	Requests to the EC – convergence programme – more economic support – fixing a timetable for accession	*Economic reaction* – slight improvement of market access conditions
1994–1995	*Political factors* – NATO Partnership for Peace – requesting full EU membership – parliamentary elections confirming the stability of pluralist democracy	*Political reaction* – further extension and definition of the circle of associated CEECs – starting negotiations 'after the IGC' (jointly with other associated CEECs)
	Economic factors – acceleration of privatization – growing foreign direct investment – difficulties in stabilizing and transforming the economy	*Economic reaction* – 'White Paper' on legal harmonization
	Requests to the EC – starting entry negotiations – intensifying cooperation – preparation of accession	

[a] A correct understanding of the short references in Table 1 presupposes a detailed knowledge of systemic changes in Hungary and of the history of bilateral relations between this country and the EC/EU. The limits of this paper do not permit explanation of all these important events. This Table was annexed to an article 'A periferizáció határai' (The Limits of 'Peripherization') in *Európa Fórum*, Budapest, 4/1995.

[b] CEFTA: Central European Free Trade Agreement; CEI: Central European Initiative.

In comparing the demands of a growing number of CEECs with the answers from the EC/EU, a *regular time gap* between the two can be observed. (Table 2 presents the decreasing and once more increasing time gap between Hungary's requests and accomplishment of these on the part of the EC/EU). One could immediately refer to the necessarily slow decision-making process of the EU. In fact, a sophisticated and multifunctional, 12 to 15 member organization could hardly be expected to give rapid reactions to unexpected and unprecedented new situations. However, in the special case of the EC/EU–CEECs relationship, the time gap between requests and their accomplishment has been bigger than that merely due to the dead-weight of the

Table 2 Reaction time of the EC/EU to requests of Hungary

Request	asked	granted	'reaction time' years
Accomplished			
Non-discriminatory trade	1973	1988 (1995)	15+7
		1989 (1990)	16+1
Economic cooperation	1982	1989	7
	1988	1991	3
Effective economic advantages	1982	1991	9
	1988	1991	3
Tariff preferences	1988	1989 (1990)	1+1
Free trade	1989	1991	2
Possibility of EC membership	1991	1993	2
Convergence programme	1992	1995	3
Open			
Important economic aid	1989	?	(7)
Financial protocol	1991	?	(5)
Preferences for agriculture	1991	?	(5)
Free movement of labour	1991	?	(5)
More economic support	1992	?	(4)
Timetable for accession	1993	?	(3)
Fixing the date of negotiations	1994	?	(2)

Note: For the open items reaction time indicates the number of years from the presentation of requests until 1996.

interest-forming process of integration. For this reason, it may be admitted that the flow of retarded reactions has most probably been *conscious* on the part of the EC/EU.

Let us take two important examples. In 1991, during the negotiations about the Europe Agreements, the three Visegrád countries attached a special importance to their future EC membership. The expression of the political will of both parties concerning EC accession would have lent strong support to the 'irreversibility' of political changes.[10] However, the EC gave its first positive answer to this request only in 1993, in the final statements of the Copenhagen meeting of the European Council. Another example is the submission by Hungary and Poland of their application for a full EC membership in April 1994. Both countries asked immediately about the possible date of starting negotiations. The answer came in December 1995, at the Madrid meeting of the European Council, in a rather nebulous formulation expressing 'the hope' of the EU that 'the preliminary stage [!] of negotiations will coincide with the start of negotiations with Cyprus and Malta', namely six months after the end of the IGC. This means only a rather vague possibility

---

[10] See above in section IAa, p. 359.

Table 3 Gradual extension of the treatment of the CEECs

Year	Action of the EC/EU	Number of partners	CEECs concerned
1988	'normalization' of relations	1	the 'Soviet bloc' (all European CMEA Member States)
1989	PHARE programme	2	Poland and Hungary
1991	conclusion of 'Europe Agreements'	3	the 'Visegrád' countries (adding Czechoslovakia)
1994	structured dialogue	6	the 'associated six' (adding Romania and Bulgaria)[a]
1994– 1995	'entry negotiations may start after the IGC'	10	the 'associated ten' (adding the Baltics and Slovenia)

[a] The federal State of Czechoslovakia was split into two independent States: the Czech Republic and Slovakia on 1 January 1993.

of starting some action in connection with the future negotiations with all the associated CEECs simultaneously (other examples are presented in Table 1).

b. Gradual 'globalization'

One of the main reasons for the tardiness and anxiety of the EC, described above, is the gradual 'globalization' of the treatment of the CEECs. In fact, the subsequent steps, leading from the initial 'normalization' of relations up to the pre-accession strategy (as it stands in the year of the IGC), covered more and more countries of the Central and East European region (see Table 3). Starting from a uniform treatment of the 'Eastern bloc', the EU is tending again towards a similar homogenization subdivided into two new 'blocs', i.e. the associated and the non-associated CEECs.

The gradual extension of the uniform treatment of the associated CEECs also has a second dimension. Initially, each of the subsequent steps taken by the EC concerned a given number of countries. At the beginning, this number was rather limited, but the circle of countries participating in each action has – so far – been further enlarged each time.[11] Obviously, this double enlargement of the circle of the associated CEECs did not permit the EC to deepen its relationship with those countries that have been at the forefront of establishing closer connections with the Community. Of course, some deepening

---

[11] For example, the PHARE Programme received its name from the two beneficiary countries of 1989–90, namely Poland and Hungary; in 1996 the PHARE Programme embraced all the associated CEECs and Albania. The number of countries concluding a Europe Agreement with the EC was enlarged, step-by-step, from three to ten, etc.

of relations took place as new elements were added, again and again, to the pre-accession strategy of the EC/EU. But these new elements concerned in each case a growing number of countries (as is demonstrated in Table 3). Consequently, the content of the pre-accession strategy was tailored to a larger and larger group.

From the viewpoint of those transforming States who were in the lead, this kind of 'expanding evolution' resulted in a gradual watering down – a 'banalization'[12] – of their relationship with the EC/EU. As a matter of fact, this 'homogenization process' has led to a slowing down in the forging of new relations between the EU and the leading transforming countries on the one hand, and a speeding up with those States lagging behind in the transformation process, on the other. The 'globalization' of the pre-accession strategy represents the EU's expectations and ability to help as they concern a 'good average transforming country'.

c. Autonomous legal approach

A striking characteristic of the EU's strategy towards the CEECs in general is the predominantly autonomous legal form of its actions. In this respect the following illustrations can be mentioned:

- *The PHARE Programme* came into the world as unilateral support for the beginnings of political and economic transformation. Later on, the Europe Agreements referred to this Programme in its original, unilateral (autonomous) form, without any sign of a bilateral legal consolidation (the EC refused to transform it into a bilateral financial protocol).
- *The possibility of full EU membership* was unilaterally proclaimed by the European Council at the 1993 Copenhagen Summit. The readiness of the Union to accept the new European democracies as members – depending on certain conditions – was not translated into bilateral legal commitments (the EC did not accept the idea of attaching this readiness to the Europe Agreements, in the form of an additional protocol).
- *The structured dialogue* was based on the 'Hurd–Andreatta initiative' and was offered to the associated countries in 1994, as a unilateral gesture by the EU. In fact, the regular meetings of a growing number of ministers (starting with 12+6 and growing to 15+12) would badly need some contractual (in this case, multilateral) 'structure', in particular jointly set objectives and some kind of rules of procedure (in practice, the structured dialogue replaced the bilateral meetings foreseen by the Association Agreements).
- *The circle of possible future EU member states* was defined by the Essen Summit in December 1994, quite independently of bilateral legal instruments. The wishes and the legal steps taken by the CEECs were also neglected – in a positive way for several of them – and the EU did

---

[12] This expression is used by Prof. M. Maresceau, see the introduction to this volume, p. 5.

not pay any special attention to whether or not they had introduced a request concerning membership.[13] At that time, only Hungary and Poland had asked for EU membership and, what is more, Association Agreements had not even been concluded with all the countries in question (not with the Baltic States and Slovenia).

- *The White Paper* approved at the Cannes Summit in June 1995 has also proved to be a unilateral message, a kind of 'integration homework for transition economies'. Apart from its obvious usefulness, this document is absolutely silent as to the consequences of the associated countries' completing these legal harmonization tasks. This means that the EU has not made any commitment on its part for the case where a country accomplishes the whole programme of the White Paper (the EU has not promised an earlier start for entry negotiations, etc.).

- Finally, and characteristically, it should be noted that the only contractual element of the pre-accession strategy, namely the Europe Agreement, has also been supplemented with improved market access conditions in an autonomous way, in accordance with the decision of the 1993 Copenhagen European Council. The modified quotas and timetables were decided and published by the EU unilaterally, and were only later formalized in bilateral protocols.[14]

Consequently, the unilateral legal approach of the EC/EU reflects an extremely cautious attitude towards the CEECs and towards the whole process of preparing the eastern enlargement of the EU.

B. The 'crawling strategy'

a. The elements

The above characteristics indicate a *deliberate strategy* on behalf of the European Union concerning its eastern enlargement. Of course, interest-formation and decision-making on the part of a twelve or fifteen member organization cannot be very quick. But in the special case of the pre-accession steps of the EC/EU towards the CEECs, a retardation of reactions can be observed. This is a clear sign of a highly cautious approach to the unprecedented phenomenon of political and economic transition. This attitude and the actions taken can be described as a 'crawling strategy' composed of the following main elements:

---

[13] This approach means that the EU has acted independently from the national interest-formation and political decision-making of those CEECs which, by the time of the Essen Summit, had not requested EU membership.

[14] See, for example Additional Protocol to the Interim Agreement on trade and trade-related matters between the European Economic Community and the European Coal and Steel Community, of the one part, and the Republic of Hungary, of the other part, and to the Europe Agreement between the European Communities and their member states, of the one part, and the Republic of Hungary, of the other part, *OJ* 1994, L 25/7.

- The EC/EU has so far avoided proposing any complete programme to the associated CEECs as to the whole process and timetable of their accession.
- The EC/EU has avoided legal commitments and has built up its pre-accession strategy of unilateral (autonomous) gestures and declarations.
- The EC/EU has given partial and late answers to the requests by the CEECs for more economic aid and support for their painful transition process.
- And, finally, the EC/EU has *not* so far paid any special attention to country specificities, but has put the emphasis of the pre-accession strategy on a more and more global approach to a region composed of at least ten CEECs.

The result of all this is primarily an 'enlargement' of the pre-accession process rather than its 'deepening'. In other words, the consequence of the global approach of the EU to its eastern enlargement is a 'crawling strategy': it does not shed light on the whole process, but only indicates the next few steps. In this strategic concept, the EU's expression of its willingness does not exceed a time horizon of two-to-three years, and leaves long-term objectives in nebulous uncertainty.

b. The motives

The reasons behind this behaviour are manifold. Five possible main motives of the EU can be distinguished:

- On the eve of the eastern enlargement, the internal interest-formation of the EU has become more complex than ever before. This complexity is the result of parallel developments of the functions and the actors.[15] Any decision-making in the Union is necessarily more complex and slower than before.
- The EU is not yet prepared to face all the challenges of an unprecedented new enlargement as it has not yet fully digested the procedural and institutional consequences of its last enlargements. A fundamental revision of the internal functioning of the organization is on the agenda of the 1996 IGC. As long as internal disputes are not settled, member states try to avoid taking on any firm commitment that might disturb their 'balance sheets' with the EU.
- The eastern enlargement represents a qualitatively new engagement in the extension of the EU's sphere of activity. It goes beyond the cultural, security and economic system borders simultaneously.[16] At the same time, the unprecedented number of candidate countries – combined

---

[15] The Treaty of Rome was signed by six countries, the Single European Act by ten, the Treaty on European Union by twelve and the IGC involves fifteen member states. In addition, the next enlargement would involve twelve other countries.

[16] See more in detail in P. Balázs, *Strategies for the Eastern enlargement of the European Union*, CORE Working Paper 15/1995, Copenhagen.

Table 4 Bilateral 'balance sheets' between the EU member states and the joining countries

Year of negotiations	Number of		Number of bilateral 'balance sheets'			
	EC/EU members	joining countries	total	integration	negotiation	peripheral
1970–1973	6	3	36	15	18	3
1976–1981	9	1	45	36	9	0
1978–1986	10	2	66	45	20	1
1993–1994	12	3	105	66	36	3
1998–	15	12	351	105	180	66

Notes: 'total': the overal number of bilateral relations between old and new member states

'integration': bilateral relations inside the EC/EU between its member states

'negotiation': bilateral relations between EC/EU member states and joining countries

'peripheral': bilateral relations between new members

with the above-mentioned internal complexity of the organization – multiplies the number of 'balance sheets' a member state is keeping with all the other participants of the integration bargaining process, including possible new members (see below in point III.B. and Table 4).

- The East European transition process contains a high risk factor as to the outcome of political and economic transformation. The final results are hardly predictable. Surprises are possible even in the short run. Of course, unexpected changes in the political or economic evolution of the Central and East European 'transition countries' can also be positive. But the EU still prepares itself for 'worst case scenarios' and tries to avoid any commitment that would be binding on it in an unforeseeable situation.

- An internal conflict between two motives, political and economic, makes it even more complicated for the EU to take a position. The political motive of the West, in general, is the stabilization of the whole East European area, covering as many CEECs as possible. This consideration favours the maximum extension of a global approach to the region. From the angle of its economic interests, the EU would prefer as segmented an approach as possible, in order to minimize risks and costs. This contradiction is also reflected by the fact that the EC/EU has been reacting to the *political* events of the transition process, but using mainly *economic* tools in expressing its approval and intentions to help.[17]

---

[17] See the example of the Hungary–EC/EU relations in Table 1.

372

III. CONSEQUENCES AND DILEMMAS

A. Regional treatment *v* differentiation

The first result of the 'crawling strategy' is a growing inconsistency in the EU's handling of the eastern enlargement. The main feature is a contradiction between a more and more global (collective) pre-accession programme and the promise of individual negotiations. Each of the subsequent steps of the 'crawling strategy' have so far been 'globalizing', collective actions. At the same time, the 'crawling peg' of integration perspectives has been set further and further. As has already been pointed out, this time horizon has never been longer than 'two to three years from now' as far as concrete programmes and promises are concerned. Long-term perspectives have still remained uncertain. On the eve of the IGC, the 'associated ten' were told to start entry negotiations after the Conference and simultaneously, but there have been allegations of different dates for concluding the entry talks. Some voices have even mentioned the possibility of different results of the negotiations, i.e. not necessarily full membership for all the associated countries. All this suggests that differentiation would take place sometimes during the negotiation process.

The associated CEECs are divided as to these ambiguous perspectives. The leading countries have serious reservations against any form of 'bloc treatment'. The longer the 'globalizing' approach takes, the greater their concerns are of a 'second class' membership instead of full integration.[18] In fact, they fear a slowing-down of the integration process if 'the slowest ship determines the speed of the convoy'. At the same time, the 'follow-up' countries prefer, for obvious reasons, collective development of the enlargement process. Their best chance is not to be separated from the 'avant garde'. They fear that in case of a real differentiation and individual entry negotiations only three or four of the best performing transition countries would join the EU, and all the others would stay on the level of some kind of (external or internal) association.

On the basis of the above experience, and having in mind the complexity of transforming and enlarging the EU simultaneously, there is some chance of a continued 'crawling strategy'. This approach would maintain the global treatment of the associated CEECs even further, instead of favouring a fundamental differentiation among them. This strategy contains *serious risks*, both for the EU and the CEECs. The main risk factors are the following:

B. Enlargement negotiations *v* trans-regional bargaining

The internal and external interest-formation of the EU, as a multifunctional organization with a high number of member states, is a sophisticated, multi-dimensional bargaining and negotiating process. The next enlargement would

---

[18] The road leading to the globalizing 'crawling strategy' has been paved with 'second best' solutions, e.g. 'Partners in Transition' with the OECD, 'Partnership for Peace' with NATO, 'European association' with the EC, observer status in international organizations like CEN, CENELEC, etc.

not only add twelve new member states but has already extended the sphere of negotiations (Table 4 presents the growing number of actors and bilateral 'balance sheets' in connection with each wave of enlargement negotiations). It may be seen that the coming eastern enlargement would more than triple the total number of such 'balance sheets'. Within this number, the 'negotiation' type relationships between old member states and countries joining the EU would grow five times bigger than during the last (EFTA) enlargement. The biggest boom is to be expected outside the direct sphere of enlargement negotiations, particularly among the candidate countries themselves. The increase of 'peripheral' bilateral 'balance sheets' would jump to 20 times as many as at any previous enlargement. In fact, this is a new dimension of the enlargement process, due to the growing number of the EU member states and more particularly to the suddenly increasing number of candidate countries. Simultaneous membership for the CEECs would offer a smoother solution to possible bilateral tensions, with a special regard to relations between neighbouring countries. This problem would merit closer analysis, taking into account the possibility and the probability of non-simultaneous full membership of all the associated CEECs.

In addition to this complexity of the next enlargement, two regions on the EU's periphery are also closely concerned by its eastern extension: the Mediterranean area and those CEECs not joining the EU during the next eastern enlargement wave. In both cases, the States of a contiguous neighbouring region are connected to the EU by close economic links but, at least for the foreseeable future, they will be excluded from the benefits of EU membership. A global eastern enlargement would increase the need for coordinating the distribution of wealth in the Euro-Mediterranean-Asian macro region. This macro region embraces, around a supposed 27–30 member EU, an equal number of third States, composed of about twelve South and East Mediterranean and about seventeen South and East European countries.[19]

C.   Political risks *v* economic risks

A global and simultaneous eastern enlargement of the EU is supposed to minimize political risks in avoiding the creation of new dividing lines. But the global approach would cumulate and maximize the economic costs and risks of the next enlargement of the EU. Consequently, it would help to preserve the old dividing line: the inherited East–West gap. All in all, it could result in a slowing down of the whole process of transition. The main contradiction is that the EU, by trying to escape political instability risks in the associated CEECs, preserves the main source of instability, namely economic backwardness on a large, regional scale.

---

[19] The first sign of the need to coordinate the eastern enlargement with other interested components of the above-mentioned macro region was the growing pressure on the EU from its traditional Mediterranean partners for more aid and cooperation.

The global treatment of the transforming countries has proved to be slow and far too cautious. The 'delayed reactions' of the EU have offered little help to the solution of the most important problems of political and economic transformation. A global and necessarily stalling enlargement process would further retard the completion of the transformation and catching-up process of the eastern periphery of the EU. The West European integration organization would do better, also for its own sake, in offering to its eastern neighbourhood a quick opening of a segmented and differentiated enlargement process. In view of the urgency of certain tasks and the necessary adaptation, a reversed order of the 'Maastricht pillars' seems to be the right sequencing:[20]

- Cooperation in justice and home affairs is a burning problem between the EU and its eastern (and also southern) neighbours. A rapid 'enlargement' of some key elements of such cooperation should precede its controversial 'deepening' among the 'EU-15'.
- The EU itself constitutes a 'soft security organization'. In contrast with the past, when NATO members joined the EC, the enlargement of the EU has already stepped beyond the hard security borders of the bipolar system. Further perfection and deepening of the CFSP and strengthening of the WEU (with a new name?) could involve the associated CEECs soon.
- Economic integration is the slowest process of all the three 'pillars'. Its completion will need a long transition period. For this reason, the institutional start should not be delayed until the 'happy end' of the IGC. It could already begin, for instance, with a joint 'reflection group' following the example of the preparation of the IGC. The EU could also consider transforming autonomous legal actions into bilateral commitments as a preparatory phase to full membership, etc.

Of course, any new approach would need more courageous political thinking, a new look at old rules and habits, and the consideration of long-term interests instead of short-term reflexes and the protection of the benefits of past integration bargains. In this case, the 'crawling strategy' could be transformed into immediate action.

---

[20] This idea was first proposed by the author in a CORE Working Paper, see footnote 15.

22

THE NEW INTRA-EUROPEAN RELATIONS AND RUSSIA

Youri Borko[1]

I. TWO PRELIMINARY REMARKS

The title of this contribution may at first sight appear to be somewhat equivocal. In principle, it would seem that the notion 'intra-European' also ought to cover Russia while the title appears to imply that the process of the European integration only covers the European countries to the west of Russia or the CIS. It is now indeed more and more apparent that the relations between the EU and Russia are and will be institutionalized outside the framework of the EU, or at least in a different way from that currently being organized with the other Central and Eastern European countries (CEECs). This difference is a matter of fact, and I take it for granted.

The second remark relates to the content and scope of this paper. Generally speaking, Russia has developed relationships in Europe with four main organizations – the EU, the NATO, the Council of Europe and the OSCE. In the light of the scope of this paper, I am limiting myself to the EU–Russia relationships. As far as the other above-mentioned organizations are concerned, they will be mentioned only where necessary or, perhaps, inevitable. To sum up, a more precise title of my paper could therefore be: 'The European Union of the 1990s and Russia'.

II. THE MAIN TRENDS IN EUROPE IN THE 1990s

Now, six or seven years after dramatic events took place in the Eastern part of Europe, it is possible to draw some conclusions as regards new important shifts and drifts developing in Europe. Three trends have to be mentioned in particular:

[1] Professor, Institute of Europe, Moscow.

A. The process of differentiation of post-communist countries in transition

The CEECs, and the Visegrád group in particular, are moving 'back to Europe'. In other words, they reform the State and their respective societies according to the Western European patterns, and this process tends to develop more or less smoothly. Simultaneously, they have joined the Council of Europe and are going to join the EU and NATO. The second group in Eastern Europe is Russia and its partners within the CIS. As far as Russia is concerned, it is obviously also a country in transition. But it moves to the market economy and democracy in a much more difficult way and at a considerably slower pace, than the CEECs. Unlike them, the Russian case is rather a transition through sharp collisions and, maybe, set-backs. Moreover, even if the country continues to move forward, its new economic and political system will differ significantly from the 'European pattern'. The emerging market economy in Russia is not a 'liberal' one in the sense known in Western Europe. Rather, it will be a kind of mixed economy strongly influenced by the state, which uses various methods of bureaucratic interference in the economic process and which does not limit itself to elaborating and supervising the game for the economic actors. As far as the political system is concerned, it will be a combination of democratic institutions with authoritarian practices of state administration, probably with a predominance of the State over civil society. Moreover, in spite of the serious defeat of the communists and the so-called 'national-patriots' in the recent presidential election, a new return to dictatorship (or a kind of dictatorship) cannot be excluded for some years at least. Thus, the uncertain situation in Russia necessarily tends to predetermine the vagueness of its future relations with Europe and necessarily affects its relations with Western Europe and the EU in particular.

B. The integration process of the 'from Brest to Brest' is in motion

This policy is strongly promoted by the EU and NATO in accordance with their strategies of eastward enlargement. However, this process is not an easy one; it faces difficulties and oscillates between acceleration and delays. This is sufficiently demonstrated in the various contributions elsewhere in this book.

C. The process of rebuilding an all-European system of security and cooperation is developing more slowly

This slowness is connected, to a great extent, with the specific features of the internal situation in Russia. The more difficult the country's advancement along the way of transition is, and the more uncertain the perspective of consolidation of political democracy becomes, the greater the asymmetry between integration and consolidation under auspices of the Western alliances, on the one hand, and the advancement to a 'new Europe' of unity, democracy and peace, as proclaimed by the CSCE Summit in Paris, on the other. Unfortunately, the increase in this asymmetry is counter-productive for both Russia and Europe. After all, it can result in the reappearance of a 'hard' dividing line between them, resulting in a loss for the stability and security of Europe as a whole. Undoubtedly, the crucial question is whether Russia continues its course of reforms, and how quickly it moves forward. But many things depend on the West, its perceptions of Russia and its policy towards that country. I cannot examine here in detail the evolution in Russia's and the West's mutual perception of these relationships, but they seem to have worsened as compared to the period when the USSR under Gorbachev initiated its policy of reform or the period immediately after the crash of the communist coup in August 1991.

Meanwhile, at present, there are also some signs of a trend towards more balanced perceptions and approaches. They were conceptualized, for example, in the report 'Engaging Russia' written by Robert Blackwill, Rodric Braithwaite and Akihiko Tanaka for the Trilateral Commission. Taking into account both the names of authors and the role of the organization they addressed it to, one can conclude that the publication of this book is symptomatic. The core of their position is formulated in the following way: the title of the paper is in the contrast

> with what we see as the inadequate and intermittent commitment of much Trilateral policy towards Russia and the other countries of the former Soviet Union since 1991.... There are different views among the authors about the likelihood of fundamental success for Russian reform over the long term, and about continued progress in the 3–5 years immediately ahead. There are differences about some of the policy prescriptions. But we believe that the positive trends in Russia are sufficiently strong to justify the strategy of engagement that we propose, and we share the judgement that the broad aim of Trilateral policies should be to reinforce these positive trends, while hedging against major reverses.[2]

Some recent steps made by Western countries can be considered as agreeing with this approach. I bear in mind not only the cooperation between the NATO and Russia in Bosnia and the intensive political contacts with a view to searching for a more flexible correlation between NATO enlargement and the NATO–Russia cooperation. Some other actions can be mentioned as well: the confirmation of the EU strategy for future partnership with Russia by the 1995 Madrid European Council, and, last but not least, Russia's accession to the Council of Europe.

---

[2] R. Blackwill, R. Braithwaite and A. Tanaka, *Engaging Russia. A Report to The Trilateral Commission*, published by The Trilateral Commission, New York, Paris and Tokyo, 1995, 137.

These and other steps of the West are met positively by both the Russian authorities and a great part of public opinion. Nevertheless, the problem of interconnection between the enlargement of the Western alliances and Russian–European relations remains valid.

III.   RUSSIA AND THE EU AFTER MAASTRICHT

Taking account of various arguments – such as the negative 'image' of the NATO and the specific field of its activity, the limited competences and resources of the Council of Europe – some Russian experts and politicians suggest that the EU could play a much more active and positive role as a partner of Russia within the framework of the European system of co-operation. The 'deepening-and-widening' policy of the Union is met by Russian public opinion quietly, or even with indifference. For a start, people are overburdened by a number of domestic preoccupations such as wages, prices, the Chechen war, crime, etc. As far as the EU is concerned, there is an additional source of indifference: in particular, there is the evident imbalance between the excessive attention of politicians and mass media to NATO enlargement, on the one hand, and the evident deficit of information and knowledge as regards the EU.

Meanwhile, Russian experts and politicians hold different opinions. Negative views towards the EU stem either from traditional anti-Western ideology or from an analysis in terms of 'gains-losses'. The second group of opponents believes that the EU enlargement will be unfavourable for Russia. In their opinion, at least from a political point of view, the enlargement will result in the marginalization of Russia and isolation as a result of the new barrier between it (or the CIS as a whole) and the rest of Europe. Another argument relates to economic consequences, which it is claimed are also unfavourable because of the worsening terms of the Russian trade with European countries as compared with the CEECs once they have joined the EU.

None of these arguments can be ignored, but they do not seem to be undisputable. The first counter-argument is connected with considerations about the future development of European integration itself, what shape the EU will take after the IGC, etc. This is not a point which will be addressed here in detail. Let me just enumerate some of the issues. The past progress of the integration process seems to be a strong basis for new success. Clearly, the establishment of EMU together with an almost simultaneous doubling of the number of member states is the most ambitious programme since the 1950s. No doubt the EU will face many obstacles. The difficulties are mainly of an internal nature. The EU will have to find the right balance between 'deepening' and 'widening', to coordinate the three-speed advancement to the common goal (two groups of the 'old' member states, with different perceptions or willingness to participate in economic and monetary union, and the group of 10–12 potential new members), to solve the very complicated financial problems of enlargement, to reform the institutional structures and everyday activities of the EU. Many things depend on the results of the ongoing Intergovernmental Conference. In any case, it now seems clear that the pace of advancement to the new goals will be slower than was expected two or three years ago. However, some other factors also have to be taken into account: the ambivalent influence of the situation in post-communist countries, and some negative phenomena in Western Europe, including evident symptoms of reviving nationalism, the decline in any moral incentive for labour, the growing opposition against 'Eurobureaucratization'. Taking all these elements together, it seems that the post-Maastricht period of European integration will be more complicated than the pre-Maastricht one. Be that as it may, the EU has accumulated the richest experience and potential of integration dynamics, which will be used for the gradual, 'step-by-step' advancement to its further goals, including enlargement.

The crucial question now is whether Russia is more interested in strengthening or, on the contrary, in weakening the EU. To me it would appear that Russia is not interested in the failure of European integration, which is one of the cornerstones of stability in Europe. From the strategic point of view, Russia is interested in strengthening this stability, mainly for two reasons. First, Europe is and will be in the foreseeable future a single stable region near the Western border of Russia and the CIS, as opposed to real or potential instability along its southern and east-southern borders. Secondly, the EU is by far our greatest trade and economic partner, and certainly much more important than other world regions, even including the CIS. In 1995 the share of the EU in Russian external trade was 35 per cent, while the share of the CIS diminished to 23 per cent.[3] Even if recently the EU share has a tendency to decrease somewhat, due to Russia's efforts to diversify its external trade, the EU will nevertheless remain Russia's most important economic partner.

As far as 'marginalization', 'isolation' or 'worsening terms of trade' are concerned, the consequences of 'deepening and widening' of the European integration will largely depend on Russia itself. If its reforms fail, barriers between it and the rest of Europe will reappear, no matter how many countries join the EU. So, the main pre-condition to prevent the above-mentioned negative trends is the gradual advancement of Russia to a market economy and democracy.

Another pre-condition for stable relations is the institutionalization and development of cooperation between Russia and the EU (of course, the same is applicable to the NATO and the Council of Europe). No doubt, Russia is interested in a balanced interconnection between the EU's enlargement and the development of Russia–EU relations. The political and legal framework of these relations is worked out in the Partnership and Cooperation Agreement (PCA) signed in June 1994.[4] The Interim Agreement on trade

---

[3] Calculated on the base of 'Russia: Foreign Economic Relations. Trends and prospects', Quarterly Review (VNIKI, Moscow), 1996, N 1, 67.

[4] For text: COM(94) 257 final.

signed in July 1995,[5] which came into force in February 1996, can be perceived as showing the readiness of the Parties to accelerate the implementation of the PCA and to soften the asymmetries mentioned earlier.

This brings me to the objectives and contents of the Partnership and Cooperation Agreement. But before analysing them briefly, some preliminary remarks as regards the impact for Russia of the future CEECs' accession to the Union may be in place. It is well known that in the initial post-cold war phase political and economic relations between Russia and the CEECs have been far from idyllic. Leaving aside political matters, the trade pattern of the former COMECON countries changed in a radical way. From 1993 to 1995 the ratio of the CEECs trade with the EU and with Russia was six or seven to one. After the reorientation of the CEECs' trade towards Western Europe, the share of the CEECs in Russian external trade was 11–12 per cent, that is less than a third of the share of the EU.[6] In the long-term perspective, economic cooperation between Russia and the CEECs will be of minor importance as compared to their respective economic links with Western Europe. Nevertheless, this cooperation could create additional opportunities and offer a large potential as well as a better division of labour in Europe. In some respects this cooperation could even be more promising than that offered through the existing frameworks between the CEECs and EU or Russia and EU. For the CEECs, trade with Western Europe and trade with Russia are complementary. As was already the case before the changes, these countries are interested in Russian oil, gas and raw materials in exchange for their industrial goods and agricultural products. Moreover, in some respects the Russian market is still more accessible for the CEECs than that of the EU. Russia, in turn, is interested in the diversification of its external trade in order to export semi-manufactured and finished manufactured goods. In addition, the development of transport communications sector with Western Europe is of significant importance for Russia.

The mutual interest of the CEECs and Russia in restoring their trade is becoming more apparent, particularly because of the sharp growth of the negative trade balances of the CEECs with the EU. It was in 1995 when, for the first time since the 1980s, the volume of CEECs' trade with Russia increased by 33 per cent as compared with 1994, and the share of the CEECs in the Russian external trade increased to 13.3 per cent.[7] But while the prospects for economic cooperation seem favourable, they will remain rather modest as a result of the slowness of the Russian economic recovery, the redistribution of Russian oil and gas exports in favour of Western Europe at the expense of the CEECs, and the growing competition on the markets of both Russia and the CEECs.

Besides trade exchange, intensification of economic links can also be achieved by industrial cooperation, of which the partners have considerable and

[5] For text: *OJ* 1995, L 247/1.
[6] See note 3.
[7] *Bulletin of External Commercial Information*, 1996, 3 August, N 89, 1.

positive experience. In fact, the restoration of direct links between enterprises has begun. There are also various opportunities for extending exchange of services in transport, banking, information. On the whole, a gradual increase in reciprocal trade and the widening of forms of economic cooperation can be expected. It is likely that even this modest progress could play the role of a multiplier as regards political relations between these countries and Russia, if it is not impeded by other political factors.

It is difficult as yet to evaluate what impact EU membership would have on economic cooperation between the CEECs and Russia. At first sight it does not seem to be considerable. From the political point of view, both the Russian upper strata and public opinion have *de facto* recognized that it is inevitable and acceptable if combined with Russia's participation in the European system of security and its gradual integration into a European economic area. As regards economic aspects, it is necessary to take into account that with the Interim Agreement EC–Russia currently in force and the postponed timetable of the CEECs' accession to the EU, differences in terms of trade, the average of the customs tariffs etc., are rather insignificant.

The third, and final, question relates to possible or even inevitable negative consequences which could arise from EU enlargement if the process of deepening and widening the European integration is not combined with establishing the institutional framework and developing the all-embracing cooperation between the EU and Russia. This brings us to an evaluation of the Partnership and Cooperation Agreement Russia–EC.

IV. THE PARTNERSHIP AND COOPERATION AGREEMENT (PCA)

The PCA was signed at Corfu in June 1994 after more than two years of negotiations, including exploratory talks, eight official rounds, two reconsiderations of the negotiating directives, and a lot of informal meetings. These joint efforts resulted in the broadest and most comprehensive agreement concluded so far between Russia and any Western country or organization.

The PCA covers a wide range of future political, commercial, economic and cultural cooperation between the Parties. A detailed analysis of the PCA would require too much space for this book. Here, I will limit myself to a short enumeration of the most important aspects of this agreement.

1. Unlike the Europe Agreements, the PCA neither aims at establishing an association between Russia and the EU, nor to prepare for future EU membership of Russia. Meanwhile, the agreement aims at achieving a new quality of relations, called 'partnership'. Though this notion is not defined, the Preamble and General Principles of the PCA fix some criteria which constitute the very basis of the partnership, namely: 'strengthening the political and economic freedoms', 'respect for democratic principles and human rights as defined in particular in the Helsinki Final Act and the Charter of

Paris for a new Europe' and 'the commitment of the Parties to promote international peace and security as well as the peaceful settlement of disputes'. A violation of these democratic principles may be considered as an infringement of the obligations under the Agreement and lead to 'appropriate measures' taken by one of the Parties (Article 107 PCA).

2. Another important feature of the PCA is that it includes a number of provisions relating to the interconnection between 'the continuation and accomplishment of Russia's political and economic reforms' and the EU–Russia relationship itself. The PCA is the first bilateral agreement in which Western countries consider Russia 'as a country with an economy in transition'. The Parties proclaimed, for the first time as well, their intention 'to provide an appropriate framework for the gradual integration between Russia and a wider area of cooperation in Europe' (Article 1). It was also decided that the partners shall examine in 1998 'whether circumstances allow the beginning of negotiations on the establishment of a free trade area' (Article 3). These clauses are of great importance for Russia. The latter is not considered to be a potential member of the EU for two reasons: it does not fit in the very conception of European integration, nor is membership compatible with Russian national priorities given its geopolitical position. Nevertheless, Russia looks for ways for future integration into the European economic area, and the idea of establishing a free trade area corresponds to this aim.

3. The PCA provides an appropriate mechanism for political dialogue between partners, including meetings at presidential level twice a year, regular meetings at ministerial level within the framework of the Cooperation Council, etc. The political dialogue should contribute to the strengthening of links, to an increasing convergence of positions on international matters of mutual concern and to cooperation as regards the implementation and the observance of the principles of democracy and human rights.

4. The commercial chapter of the PCA provides for market access on the basis of a mutual most favoured nation (MFN) treatment in tariff matters. With the PCA in force, Russia will apply various articles of the GATT/WTO in its trade relations with the EU, even before its accession to this multilateral organization. As was already mentioned before, the Interim Agreement on trade and trade-related matters already entered into force in February 1996.

The PCA regulates all aspects of commercial relations: the problem of discrimination, quantitative restrictions, anti-dumping or countervailing measures, safeguards, tariff protection, special treatment for textiles, steel products and nuclear materials, etc. Two points can be mentioned in this context. In accordance with Article 5, the MFN treatment granted by Russia under the PCA shall not be applied during a five-year transitional period in relation to advantages granted by Russia to other countries of the former USSR. This period may be extended by mutual consent of the Parties. The second point concerns the asymmetrical obligations of the Parties as regards quantitative restrictions. While in principle goods originating in Russia shall be imported free of such restrictions to the EU, Russia has a right to impose new restrictions, if they relate to sectors which are undergoing restructuring, or are facing serious difficulties of a social character, or facing the elimination or a drastic reduction of the total market share held by Russian companies or nationals, or where newly emerging industries have to be protected (Article 53(2.3) and Annexes 2 and 9).

5. The PCA includes a great number of provisions with regard to business and investment, labour conditions, the establishment and operation of companies, cross border supply of services, payments and capital, intellectual property, as well as some general provisions concerning joint EU/Russian companies, movement of persons, provisions regarding taxes, etc. They foresee in many cases either MFN or national treatment. In some cases (banking and insurance, the establishment and operation of companies in particular) exceptions from MFN or national treatment are envisaged during a transitional period and with a view of evolution towards national treatment (Articles 29 and 33).

6. The PCA stresses the importance of fostering economic cooperation in a very broad range of areas, including industrial cooperation, investment promotion and protection, cooperation in science and technology, agriculture, energy, the nuclear sector, space, environment, transport, postal services and telecommunications, consumer protection, small and medium-size businesses, education and training, regional development, statistics, tourism, etc.

7. Special attention is paid to cultural cooperation, with the aim of reinforcing the existing links between peoples and encouraging the mutual knowledge of the Parties' respective languages and cultures, while promoting mutual access to cultural values. This field of cooperation is of the highest importance in view of the very long period of isolation and 'the iron curtain' between Russia and Europe.

8. Last but not least, according to Title XI of the Agreement institutions have to be set up, including a Cooperation Council, a Cooperation Committee and a Parliamentary Cooperation Committee, for monitoring the implementation of the PCA and for working out new recommendations for further cooperation, settling disputes as regards the application or interpretation of the PCA, as well as for exchanging views on a broad range of matters of interest to the Parties.

To conclude, the PCA could be a solid basis for a long-term and stable cooperation between Russia and the EU. This does not mean, however, that the Agreement corresponds fully to Russia's interests and needs. As a matter of fact, Russia was the weaker bargaining partner in the course of negotiations and it insisted both on the extension of the spectrum to be covered by the PCA, as well as on more favourable terms for itself.

The Russian delegation focused on two items of great political importance, namely treating the country as an economy in transition and inserting in the PCA the idea of Russia's future inclusion in the global European economic area. These conceptual approaches were finally accepted by the EU,

384

but at present both of them have lost much of their political impact. There is no question about the transitional character of the Russian economy, and it is very doubtful whether the idea of a free trade area between Russia and the EU could be carried out during the next ten years.

On the other hand, some preferences, which were granted by the Union to facilitate the process of economic reforms in Russia, appeared to be minimal. Brussels rejected the Russian proposal to abolish anti-dumping procedures used by the European Community against Russian imports in the EU. At the same time it became clear that, probably, the most vulnerable point of the PCA was that Russia was given too short a period for taking unilateral measures with a view to protecting particular sectors of economy which are in the process of restructuring and/or suffer from severe competition from imported goods. It seems that the complexity and duration of the first stage of Russia's transition to a market economy was underestimated, and the five-year period fixed for implementation of such measures too short. An additional argument in support of this view is that Russia is much less experienced than the EU in implementing these measures, and there are many doubts as to whether they will be used in the most efficient way. However, in spite of all these reservations and critical comments, the Russian Parliament ratified the Agreement almost unanimously in November 1996. It was, undoubtedly a very important step both from a political and an economic point of view. On the whole, one may say that the PCA could contribute to widening the area and methods of cooperation; also the well-known proverb 'the sooner, the better' seems to the point here.

V. PROSPECTS FOR IMPLEMENTATION OF THE PCA

It is expected that the ratification process may be completed in 1997. Of course, if new events similar to the Chechen war occur, this would cause delay. What are the further prospects for implementation if the PCA comes into force? At first sight, they seem to be modest, mainly as a result of the vague perspectives of the economic and political development of Russia during the first decade to come. In the first years of its implementation, Russia will face a newborn market economy and this is not the most conducive factor for smooth relations with advanced Western economies.

As far as trade and competition is concerned, the following remarks must be made. At present, trade between Russia and EU member countries is asymmetric in two senses. From 1994 to 1995 Russia's share in the total trade of the EU was only about 3 per cent, while the EU's share (including three new member states) in total Russian external trade (with the exception of the CIS) was nearly 35 per cent. The pattern of trade by product is also very asymmetric. Russia exports mainly oil, raw materials and semi-manufactured goods. West European countries export mainly machines, transport equipment and manufactured goods.

In the long term, the potential for trade exchange between Russia and Western Europe is very significant. But the approaches of the partners do not coincide. Russia is interested in changing the pattern of trade to make it closer to that between developed countries, in other words to base it more on industrial specialization and the exchange of manufactured goods. Western Europe at present and for the immediate future is more interested in the existing pattern of trade, although in the long run the restructuring of imports from Russia is the only way to ensure a stable growth of exports to Russia.

Another problem concerning mutual trade is competition. Oil is the only category of goods where competition between Russia and West European countries is not significant. Where other kinds of goods are concerned, the problem of competition does exist. This was one of the most difficult topics during the PCA negotiations. At the last minute, severe disagreement with regard to the Russian export of nuclear materials even put the signature of the Agreement in danger.

The PCA changed both the character of the problems under consideration and the list of 'hard' questions. As mentioned before Russia, is no longer considered to be a 'State-trading country', and the trade policy measures applying to this group of countries have been abolished by the EU, except as regards anti-dumping. The EU has no tariff protection for oil, raw materials, minerals and some other goods, which constitute more than the half of Russian exports in terms of value. Since January 1993, Russia has also been included in the Generalized Scheme of Preferences.

In spite of these favourable changes, which removed many former sources of disputes between Russia and the EU, the problem of competition is still a subject of disagreement and may lead to further discussions within the PCA framework. However, the scale and extent of Russian competition on the EU markets should not be exaggerated. This applies to manufactured goods in particular. In 1994 Russia only occupied the 27th place as an exporter of machines and transport equipment to the EU (about 0.3 per cent of the total EU import of these goods), and the 16th place as an exporter of other manufactured goods (about 2.2 per cent correspondingly).[8]

Trade disputes in the future are not to be excluded and could in the first place concern a very limited group of 'vulnerable' goods, semi-manufactured and manufactured goods. This could be the case if a sudden increase in Russian exports were to threaten the balance on the global market of one particular kind of product, as happened, for example, with aluminium. Some other goods can also be named: fissiles, steel, fertilizers, etc. But as a competitor in Europe, in general, Russia will be far behind the USA, Japan and some other countries due both to a low competitiveness on external markets and a far from saturated internal market.

[8] Calculated on the base of: Eurostat. External Trade, 1995, N 8–9, 25, 27.

A much more complicated situation might arise as regards competition on the Russian market. The PCA allows Russia some possibilities to protect its economy in transition. The sales crisis in most branches of Russian manufacturing industry and agriculture has given rise to demands from the producers for protectionist tariffs on imports and has led to the Government's decisions to increase customs duties on many imported goods, including foodstuffs. At present the average tariff is raised to 14–15 per cent, and the pressure of national enterprises for a new increase continues.

For many years to come, the Russian authorities will be engaged in searching for a 'middle of the road approach' between protectionism and integration in the world economy. In the immediate future, the trend towards protectionism is very likely to prevail. The problem of competition on the Russian market will therefore possibly be a source of tension and may be a topic of sharp disagreement between partners, in particular when at some stage all exceptions in favour of Russia are abolished.

Energy is one of the most important areas of cooperation. In spite of the very concerned attitude of government and public opinion, the export of oil and gas will be the main item in Russia's exports to Western Europe for the next 10–15 years at least. About half of Russia's hard currency earnings come from energy exports. Russia provides about 10 per cent of Western Europe's oil imports and more than 30 per cent of its gas imports.[9] It is likely that the Russian share in EU oil imports will fall because of the severe crisis in the national oil industry. Nevertheless, it will be an important reason for diversification of the EU oil supply. Opportunities in the gas industry are much wider, on account of Russia's enormous natural reserves. If the 'Yamal–Germany' pipeline project (through Belarus and Poland) is carried out, Russian exports of gas to European countries could almost be doubled.

As for priorities, West European consumers are interested first of all in the full liberalization of Russian oil exports and in security of supply. Russia is interested in large-scale investment, in order to renew both equipment and technologies and to overcome the oil industry crisis. The interests of the partners do not coincide, but they are interconnected. They therefore need to be balanced on the basis of compromise.

Another topic of dialogue is the European Energy Charter, signed in 1991. It aims at an efficient utilization of both natural energy resources, especially in Russia, and of Western technology and investments. Russia was one of its initiators, but abstained until the very last moment from signing the Energy Charter Implementing Treaty, which provides a legal framework for East–West energy investment, cooperation and trade. The compromise finaly found by the EU and Russia, was *inter alia* to allow Russia a period of three years to adapt and complete its legislation in accordance with the

---

[9] Eurostat. External Trade, 1995, N 8–9, 50–52; Moscow News, 1995, 28 August–11 September 4, N 35, 27.

Charter and the Treaty. Russia finally signed this Treaty in December 1994, together with 47 other states.

Investment is also an important factor in EU–Russia relations. The economic reasons and stimulus for Western investment in Russia are well known. Russia considers them a *conditio sine qua non* for the modernization and reconstruction of its national economy, industry in particular, in the light of its domestic needs and the requirements of external trade. Western investors are interested in the vast new markets and in the expected large returns.

The potential scale and benefits of this field of cooperation make it a major political priority for both Russia and Western Europe. But the approaches of the two sides are not identical. For the Russian Government it is a matter of high political priority and the real proof of the Western countries' readiness to help Russia in its process of transition. The Western countries, however, tend to perceive the problem of investment mainly as an economic and institutional issue. In other words, it is a problem of balance between incentives and risks, adequate legislation, etc. As a result of this, the situation as regards Western investment in Russia is far from satisfactory. Different sources of information give contradictory data, but according to recent estimates the total amount of foreign investment was $7,855 million by the beginning of 1996.[10] Russia is lagging behind many Asian and Latin American countries. Up to now the main donors to Russia have been the international institutions: IMF, World Bank and EBRD. Their cooperation with the Russian authorities is evidence of the support rendered by the G-7 and other Western countries to promote economic reform in Russia. However, the activities of these institutions are limited mainly to objectives of a 'pre-investment' nature: to assist financial and economic stability, to promote the formation of a sound economic infrastructure and to create a more favourable climate for foreign direct investment in production. The last is a task for the Western private sector, but business still prefers to maintain a 'wait and see' approach, in particular West European companies, which are now behind American investors – the latter being prepared to take more risks. The sources for this state of affairs are well known: they include political instability, unsatisfactory legislation as regards foreign investment, inconsistent economic policy by the government, a high level of criminality, etc.

The internal political and psychological climate in the country as regards Western investment is also deteriorating because of intensive 'national-patriotic' propaganda, which interprets foreign direct investment in terms of 'the West enslaving Russia'. As far as the Russian Government is concerned, it aims at promoting foreign investment in the national industry. Between 1994 and 1996 new legislative acts and administrative decisions were passed to stimulate foreign investment, including the granting of customs advantages to foreign exporters of goods if they make a direct investment, property

---

[10] Russia: Foreign Economic Relations. Trends and Prospects. – 'Quarterly Review' (VNIKI, Moscow), 1996, N 1, 28.

guarantees and freedom to transfer profits. These measures favoured the growth of foreign investment, which increased to $2.8 billion in 1995, i.e. 2.7 times as much as in 1994,[11] and further increase is expected in the immediate future. At the same time, the Government feels a growing pressure from Russian business circles who are afraid of competition from the Western investors, in particular in the key-branches of the national economy. All this makes it difficult to predict how investment will evolve in the years to come.

The PCA lists also about 30 fields for economic cooperation. It is neither possible nor necessary to consider them one by one, but several of them should be mentioned because of their importance. Top priorities are: (a) R&D cooperation; (b) space; and (c) the safety of nuclear stations and control over nuclear materials. Besides their economic significance, the first is a very sensitive one for Russian public opinion, which is afraid of the 'brain drain' effect of opening borders to the West. Space is another field of great importance in both scientific research and commercial competition. Russia has joined the 'club' of competitors, and the search for compromises in this area is inevitable. The issue of nuclear safety is of course also of special sensitivity after Chernobyl.

In fact, in many areas cooperation is developing. Emerging problems have various origins, including the shortage of financial resources, inadequate knowledge and experience of Western and Russian specialists participating in the joint projects, the lack of or inadequate Russian legislation and, last but not least, the notorious Russian bureaucracy. Taking all this into account, the progress in each of these areas will be, most probably, modest. But the total amount of modest achievements could produce a multiplier effect with regard to cooperation as a whole.

A final word about political partnership. This will be the most sensitive and vulnerable area of cooperation in the framework of the PCA. Three elements can be mentioned to explain this. First, as a rule, serious controversies on economic matters covered by the Agreement will need political decisions. They will be the subject of lively discussions in the Cooperation Council or the Cooperation Committee. Secondly, the positions and approaches of the Parties as regards the situation in Europe and other regions of the World will in many cases not necessarily coincide. Of course, a lot of international problems relate to competences of other international organizations. But the political dialogue at top level cannot but include an exchange of views on a broad range of domestic and international matters. The third reason seems to be the most important one. It concerns the problem of democratization, human rights and ethnic conflicts in Russia, as well as ethnic conflicts and civil wars in the other CIS countries. In March 1995, the EU already temporarily 'froze' the signing of the Interim Agreement on trade and the ratification process of the PCA. It is not excluded that a future event of a similar kind undermining democratization and violating human rights in Russia could put an end to the PCA itself.

[11] Ibid.

VI. CONCLUSION

It is possible that some of the opinions and prognoses discussed may create a rather pessimistic impression, but a good degree of caution is needed.

The recent presidential election in June–July 1996 contributed to a more positive estimation of chances for the development of cooperation between Russia and the Union. Three features of this election seem to be important: a very high level of voters' participation (65–70 per cent), a convincing victory by Boris Yeltsin (54 per cent as against 41 per cent) and the very quiet attitude of defeated parties and their voters. Therefore, one is inclined to conclude that the great majority of the population accepts and supports democratic rules for choosing and replacing persons in power, and that it prefers a peaceful development of the country on the basis of the Constitution in the framework of the newborn economic and political system. Last but not least, the national-patriotic and anti-western slogans used by the opposition did not play any noticeable role during the pre-electoral campaign. All these features will necessarily contribute to a more transparent domestic and foreign policy of Russia, including its relations with the EU and the West as whole. However, there should be no illusions, because of both the scale of internal economic, social and political problems which post-communist Russia has to deal with, and the scale of the gap between Russian and Western economies. But if it is true that the potential PCA implementation over the next ten years will remain modest, it is also true that the accumulation of experience of partnership and cooperation between Russia and Europe will increase. There is no other alternative than to develop the 'step by step' strategy along the lines defined by the Agreement. On the base of this experience, relations may further be deepened and improved.

INDEX

391